Interdisciplinary Approaches to Design, Art, and Visual Communications

And Algül
https://orcid.org/0000-0001-5516-5249
Üsküdar University, Turkey

IGI Global
Scientific Publishing
Publishing Tomorrow's Research Today

Vice President of Editorial Melissa Wagner
Director of Acquisitions Mikaela Felty
Director of Book Development Jocelynn Hessler
Production Manager Mike Brehm
Cover Design Jose Rosado

Published in the United States of America by
IGI Global Scientific Publishing
701 East Chocolate Avenue
Hershey, PA, 17033, USA
Tel: 717-533-8845 | Fax: 717-533-7115
Website: https://www.igi-global.com E-mail: cust@igi-global.com

Library of Congress Cataloging-in-Publication Data

LCCN: 2026015576 (CIP Data Pending)
ISBN13: 979-8-3373-6680-7
Isbn13Softcover: 979-8-3373-6681-4
EISBN13: 979-8-3373-6682-1
British Cataloguing in Publication Data
A Cataloguing in Publication record for this book is available from the British Library.

Editorial Advisory Board

Uğur Efe Uçar, *Department of Interior Architecture, İstanbul Technical University, Turkey*
Dicle Yıldırım, *Faculty of Communication, Üsküdar University, Turkey*

Table of Contents

Detailed Table of Contents

The fashion industry is among the largest consumers of resources in the world. This research examined sustainable fashion from a multidisciplinary standpoint by integrating design, art, visual culture, and digital technologies. Results from a survey of 167 Turkish students studying fashion or textiles showed high levels of awareness toward sustainability but low rates of sustainable purchasing behavior. Results indicated that most students felt that art and visual culture are effective at conveying environmental values. Additionally, results indicated that gender and years of experience working in the industry influenced students' knowledge regarding sustainability. The findings suggest that it is imperative for educators to develop curricula for fashion education that incorporate sustainability, digital literacy, and creative design thinking.

This chapter examines the philosophical foundations of procedural thinking in the digital arts through comparative conceptual analysis. Moving beyond technocentric approaches that reduce procedurality to modern computation, it traces a genealogy of procedural thought extending from Aristotle's theory of physis and potentiality (dynamis) to Spinoza's immanent causality (natura naturans), from Goethe's morphological archetype (Urpflanze) to Whitehead's process philosophy. The chapter re-reads rule-governed morphogenesis in nature, Islamic geometric art, and contemporary digital practices within this philosophical framework. It argues that rule-governed form generation is not an invention specific to a particular technology, but the contemporary expression of a recurring philosophical orientation — one that redefines the relationship between form and generative process. The central conclusion drawn from this genealogy is that in procedural art, the object of mimesis shifts from nature's completed products to nature's manner of producing form — to natura naturans.

This chapter investigates how color operates as a visual language in digital communication, particularly through a virtual exchange project linking students across cultural and disciplinary divides. Rather than viewing color as merely aesthetic, this chapter treats it as a vehicle of meaning, identity, and negotiation. It explores how design thinking, cultural semiotics, and emerging practices in design education intersect with virtual exchange to challenge existing color norms. Drawing on recent scholarship in digital design, educational exchange, and semiotics, the chapter uses qualitative data—including student artefacts, peer feedback, and reflective journals—to show how collaborative virtual environments reveal and reframe color literacies in culturally situated ways.

Immersive media environments are increasingly shaping how narratives are perceived, experienced, and interpreted through motion design . However, existing literature addresses motion design, immersive media, and narrative theory in a fragmented manner, often limiting motion to an aesthetic or technical role. This study proposes a conceptual and critical synthesis that repositions motion design as a narrative infrastructure integrating perceptual, spatial, and temporal dimensions. Drawing on interdisciplinary approaches, motion design is defined as a system that organizes attention guidance, spatial dramaturgy, and temporal sequencing within immersive environments. The proposed layered model demonstrates how motion determines perceptual priorities, structures narrative space, and regulates experiential rhythm. This approach moves motion design beyond a complementary visual element and frames it as a fundamental mechanism that ensures narrative coherence and experiential continuity in immersive storytelling.

Cinema constructs meaning through the organization of space, where mise-en-scène, camera, and production design operate as interdependent systems. This study examines

Chapter examines how women photographers transform the photographic act into a political and personal language of self-narration. Drawing on Laura Mulvey's male gaze, Judith Butler's gender performativity, and Hélène Cixous's écriture féminine, it argues that photography functions as a site of resistance and belonging — a visual "home" where identity is authored rather than assigned. Through close readings of Briony Campbell, Riti Sengupta, Carolle Benitah, Anna Fox, Helen Chadwick, and Maria Papadimitriou, the chapter traces how auto-ethnographic intimacy, archive intervention, material disruption, and collective practice each enact a reclaiming of the gaze. What unites these diverse practitioners is a shared refusal of the patriarchal visual order and a commitment to constructing narratives of selfhood on their own terms. Photography, understood here as writing with light, becomes the means by which women break the mirror of Medusa — rejecting silence and spectacle in favor of an embodied, rebellious, and generative act of becoming "home".

This chapter examines the IBM Plex variable typeface family as a case study in the intersection of algorithmic typography, parametric design, and corporate identity. As digital platforms multiply and communication environments grow increasingly complex, typeface systems have evolved from static forms into dynamic, data-driven design infrastructures. Per the authors, this chapter traces that transformation by analyzing the technical foundations of variable font technology alongside the formal and communicative properties of the IBM Plex Sans, Serif, and Mono sub-families. Through comparative typographic analysis, the chapter demonstrates how each sub-family fulfills a distinct communicative function within a unified brand system: Sans for digital legibility, Serif for textual authority, and Mono for technical precision. The chapter further situates IBM Plex within broader developments in generative and algorithmic design, arguing that contemporary corporate typography is no longer a neutral carrier but a strategic, meaning-producing layer of visual communication.

This chapter explores the evolution of anime from a niche Japanese subculture into a global visual force that shapes contemporary design and branding practices. Using a qualitative approach that includes literature review, anime analysis, non-participant observation of fandom communities, and interviews with fans and scholars, the study examines how anime has become a strategic site for brand alliances. The findings show that brands increasingly adapt anime's characters, narratives, and symbols to reshape their visual identities, while fan practices such as cosplay, fan art, and digital content creation generate new meanings that circulate across media platforms. Together, these interactions highlight how anime, brands, and fandom co-produce a dynamic cultural-visual ecosystem that influences strategies in communication, cultural branding, and identity design.

Preface

The fields of design, art, and visual communication have long served as powerful mediums through which individuals and societies express ideas, construct meaning, and engage with the world around them. In an era characterized by rapid technological advancement, cultural transformation, and increasingly interconnected systems of knowledge, these disciplines are evolving in ways that demand new perspectives and collaborative approaches. *Interdisciplinary Approaches to Design, Art, and Visual Communications* emerges from this context, offering a timely exploration of the dynamic relationships that exist among creative practice, visual culture, communication processes, and emerging technologies.

This volume has been developed with the goal of providing a comprehensive overview of current theoretical and applied research situated at the intersections of design, art, and communication. By bringing together diverse scholarly perspectives, the book highlights how these fields are continuously shaped by social, cultural, political, and technological forces. At the same time, it examines the ways in which communication processes influence artistic expression, visual representation, and design practices, creating new opportunities for innovation, engagement, and knowledge creation.

The interdisciplinary nature of this collection reflects the growing recognition that complex contemporary challenges cannot be fully understood through a single disciplinary lens. Researchers, practitioners, and educators increasingly draw upon multiple fields of inquiry to address questions related to creativity, visual literacy, digital transformation, audience engagement, cultural identity, and the evolving role of media in society. The chapters presented in this volume demonstrate the value of such interdisciplinary thinking by combining diverse methodologies, theoretical frameworks, and practical applications that enrich our understanding of visual communication and creative practice.

A distinguishing feature of this book is its commitment to bridging theory and practice. While several chapters contribute to ongoing scholarly debates and theoretical developments, others offer practical insights, case studies, and examples that illustrate how interdisciplinary approaches can be applied in professional and creative contexts. This balance enables readers to appreciate both the conceptual foundations and the real-world implications of contemporary developments in design, art, and visual communication.

The contributors to this volume represent a diverse group of internationally recognized academics, creative professionals, and interdisciplinary researchers. Their collective expertise provides a rich and multifaceted perspective on the topics explored throughout the book. Through their contributions, readers are introduced to emerging trends, innovative methodologies, and critical discussions that reflect the current state of research and practice across multiple disciplines.

As editor, I hope that this book will serve as a valuable resource for scholars, educators, students, designers, artists, visual communication specialists, and creative practitioners seeking to expand their understanding of interdisciplinary approaches. More importantly, I hope it will inspire meaningful dialogue across disciplinary boundaries, encourage collaborative research, and foster innovative ways of thinking about the relationships between design, art, and communication.

The future of creative and communicative practices lies in our ability to connect diverse forms of knowledge, embrace multiple perspectives, and engage thoughtfully with the challenges and opportunities of an increasingly complex world. It is my sincere hope that the chapters contained within this volume will contribute to these efforts and stimulate new avenues of inquiry, collaboration, and creative exploration for years to come.

ORGANIZATION OF THE BOOK

Chapter 1 explores the growing importance of sustainability within the fashion and textile industries through an interdisciplinary lens that integrates design, art, visual culture, and digital technologies. The chapter presents findings from a study of fashion and textile students, revealing a notable gap between sustainability awareness and sustainable consumer behavior. It highlights the influential role of art and visual culture in communicating environmental values while also examining demographic factors that shape sustainability knowledge. By emphasizing the need for educational frameworks that combine sustainability, digital literacy, and creative design thinking, the chapter underscores the critical role of design education in fostering environmentally responsible practices within the fashion sector.

Chapter 2 offers a rich philosophical examination of procedural thinking in digital arts, tracing its conceptual roots far beyond contemporary computational technologies. Through an intellectual genealogy that spans classical philosophy, process thought, natural morphogenesis, and artistic traditions, the chapter reconsiders the nature of rule-based form generation. It demonstrates how procedural art reflects enduring philosophical questions concerning emergence, transformation, and creativity, ultimately positioning contemporary digital practices within a broader historical and conceptual framework. This contribution provides valuable insights into the evolving relationship between generative processes and artistic expression.

Chapter 3 investigates color as a powerful visual language within digital communication and design education. Through the analysis of a virtual exchange project connecting students from diverse cultural and disciplinary backgrounds, the chapter demonstrates how color functions as a medium for identity formation, cultural negotiation, and meaning-making. By drawing upon design thinking, semiotics, and collaborative learning environments, the study reveals how virtual interactions challenge established color conventions and foster new forms of visual literacy. The chapter contributes to ongoing discussions surrounding intercultural communication and the pedagogical potential of digital collaboration in contemporary design education.

Chapter 4 presents a critical synthesis of motion design's role within immersive media environments, repositioning motion as a central narrative mechanism rather than a purely aesthetic component. Drawing from interdisciplinary perspectives on storytelling, perception, and spatial design, the chapter proposes a layered framework that explains how motion organizes attention, structures narrative experiences, and shapes temporal engagement. By examining the narrative infrastructure of immersive environments, this contribution advances our understanding of how visual storytelling evolves in emerging media formats and highlights the growing importance of motion design in creating coherent and meaningful audience experiences.

Chapter 5 examines the transformation of cinematic space through the integration of physical, digital, and hybrid production technologies. Through comparative analysis of film production environments, the chapter explores how different approaches to set construction influence visual organization, spatial coherence, and narrative development. Particular attention is given to emerging virtual production techniques and hybrid systems that combine physical and digital elements in real time. The discussion reveals how technological innovations are reshaping both the technical and creative dimensions of filmmaking, offering valuable perspectives on the future of cinematic design and visual storytelling.

Chapter 6 introduces an innovative methodological contribution to design research by exploring the integration of reflective drawing within reflexive thematic analysis. Through case studies in design education, the chapter demonstrates how sketches, diagrams, and visual notes can support analytical thinking and enrich qualitative research processes. By making visual thinking an explicit component of data interpretation, the chapter provides researchers with practical strategies for incorporating creative and reflective methods into scholarly inquiry. This contribution highlights the value of visual methodologies in expanding the analytical possibilities available to design researchers.

Chapter 7 offers a thought-provoking examination of contemporary art and neoliberal subjectivity through a critical analysis of Ruben Östlund's film *The Square*. The chapter investigates parallels between the increasing abstraction of contemporary art and the fragmented social, ethical, and existential experiences of individuals within digitally mediated neoliberal societies. Drawing on phenomenological perspectives and descriptive content analysis, it raises important questions concerning the relationship between artistic developments and broader social transformations. In doing so, the chapter encourages readers to reflect on the role of art as both a mirror and critique of contemporary human experience.

Chapter 8 examines photography as a powerful medium through which women reclaim agency, identity, and self-representation. Engaging with influential feminist theories, the chapter analyzes the work of several women photographers whose practices challenge traditional visual conventions and patriarchal structures of representation. Through themes of memory, home, embodiment, and resistance, the discussion demonstrates how photography functions as a site of personal and political expression. This contribution enriches conversations surrounding visual culture, gender studies, and artistic practice by illustrating how photographic narratives can serve as acts of empowerment and self-authorship.

Chapter 9 explores the evolving role of typography within contemporary corporate communication through a detailed analysis of the IBM Plex variable typeface family. Situating typography within broader developments in algorithmic and parametric design, the chapter demonstrates how variable fonts operate as dynamic systems capable of adapting to increasingly complex communication environments. By examining the distinct communicative functions of different typeface sub-families within a unified brand ecosystem, the chapter highlights typography's strategic role in shaping identity, meaning, and user experience. This contribution illustrates how digital technologies continue to transform the foundations of visual communication and brand design.

Chapter 10 investigates the global rise of anime as a significant force within contemporary visual communication, branding, and cultural production. The chapter traces anime's evolution from a specialized cultural phenomenon to a globally influential visual language that informs brand strategies, identity formation, and audience engagement. Through the examination of brand collaborations, fan communities, and participatory media practices, the study reveals how anime-inspired aesthetics and narratives circulate across digital platforms and cultural contexts. The chapter offers valuable insights into the intersections of popular culture, visual design, and communication, demonstrating how collaborative cultural ecosystems shape contemporary branding and media experiences.

CONCLUDING REMARKS

The chapters presented in *Interdisciplinary Approaches to Design, Art, and Visual Communications* collectively demonstrate the richness and diversity of contemporary scholarship at the intersection of creative practice, visual culture, communication, and technology. While each contribution approaches its subject from a distinct perspective, together they reveal the increasingly interconnected nature of artistic expression, design innovation, and visual communication in a rapidly evolving global landscape.

Across discussions of sustainability, digital art, immersive media, cinematic space, visual research methodologies, contemporary art criticism, feminist photographic practice, algorithmic typography, and global popular culture, a common theme emerges: meaningful innovation often arises through interdisciplinary engagement. The contributors illustrate how the boundaries that once separated disciplines are becoming increasingly fluid, creating opportunities for new forms of inquiry, collaboration, and creative problem-solving. Their work demonstrates that understanding contemporary visual culture requires not only technical expertise and artistic sensitivity but also critical awareness of the social, cultural, ethical, and technological forces that shape human experience.

This volume highlights the transformative role of visual communication in contemporary society, emphasizing its capacity to influence perception, construct meaning, foster dialogue, and inspire change. The chapters encourage readers to consider how design, art, and communication function not as isolated practices but as interconnected systems that continually respond to and shape the world around them. In doing so, they offer valuable insights for scholars, educators, practitioners, and students seeking to navigate the complexities of today's creative and communicative environments.

As editor, I hope this collection serves as both a valuable scholarly resource and a catalyst for future research. It is my aspiration that the ideas presented herein will inspire readers to explore new interdisciplinary pathways, challenge conventional assumptions, and contribute to the ongoing advancement of knowledge across the fields of design, art, and visual communication. Ultimately, the strength of this volume lies not only in the breadth of topics it addresses but also in its shared commitment to fostering innovative thinking and meaningful connections across disciplines.

And Algül
Üsküdar University, Turkey

Chapter 1
Sustainable Fashion and Textiles:
Interdisciplinary Approaches in Design, Art, and Visual Culture

Beyza Buzol Mülayim
http://orcid.org/0000-0001-5224-3934
Kirklareli University, Turkey

ABSTRACT

The fashion industry is among the largest consumers of resources in the world. This research examined sustainable fashion from a multidisciplinary standpoint by integrating design, art, visual culture, and digital technologies. Results from a survey of 167 Turkish students studying fashion or textiles showed high levels of awareness toward sustainability but low rates of sustainable purchasing behavior. Results indicated that most students felt that art and visual culture are effective at conveying environmental values. Additionally, results indicated that gender and years of experience working in the industry influenced students' knowledge regarding sustainability. The findings suggest that it is imperative for educators to develop curricula for fashion education that incorporate sustainability, digital literacy, and creative design thinking.

INTRODUCTION

The fashion and textile industry is among the largest economic sectors around the globe based on its cultural significance and global economic contributions. Additionally, the fashion and textile industry is often referred to as one of the most resource-consuming industries, particularly in terms of environmental impacts. For

DOI: 10.4018/979-8-3373-6680-7.ch001

example, manufacturing fibers for textiles, processing those fibers into materials used to make clothing, dyeing, and finishing each process requires significant amounts of water, energy, and chemicals, resulting in increased pollution and waste (Niinimäki et al., 2020). In addition, the rise of the fast fashion movement has resulted in a significant reduction in the product life cycle of textile items, increased levels of consumption, and exacerbated sustainability issues on a global scale (Fletcher, 2014; Bick et al., 2018). On the other hand, fashion has become a topic of discussion not only as a form of industrialism but also as a form of cultural and creative practice associated with design, art, and visual culture. Clothing, or specifically how people dress, relates closely to the body, and as a result, influences identity, gender, and social meaning. As a result, clothing can be described as an embodied social practice (Entwistle, 2015). Therefore, fashion should be viewed as a system that produces, disseminates, and consumes clothing as part of a larger cultural and social system that guides the way people produce and consume dress (Kawamura, 2005). Fashion also commonly intersects with other forms of art, including performance art and visual culture, which allow for the use of the dressed body as a creative outlet and form of cultural expression (Granata, 2017).

Linear economic models have been the basis for traditional fashion production systems. In these systems, materials are first extracted from their natural environment, converted into products, then purchased and consumed by customers and finally discarded. As a result, large quantities of textile waste are generated which are rarely recycled or integrated back into production systems (Ellen MacArthur Foundation, 2017). Therefore, sustainability and circular economy concepts have become increasingly important in the textile and fashion sector over the past few years. Circular economies seek to increase the efficiency with which raw materials are utilized and reduce the amount of textile waste produced through practices like recycling, reuse, extending product lifetimes and establishing closed-loop production systems (Ellen MacArthur Foundation, 2017; Kirchherr et al., 2017; Chen et al., 2021). In addition to issues related to sustainability, the fashion sector has undergone an extraordinary shift because of digitalization and AI applications. Digital innovations such as 3D printing, digital textile printing, RFID systems and computer vision have increased significantly the design and production capabilities in the textile and fashion sector (Rahman, 2020). Artificial intelligence systems provide the ability to analyze large data sets to forecast future fashion trends, create alternate visual designs during the design process, and improve operational efficiencies when producing goods (Kuzmichev, 2025).

The advent of generative AI has produced a new way of creating through human machine collaboration as part of the creative process of fashion design. Generative AI allows the designer to quickly produce multiple versions of a garment with different patterns, colors and compositions, thus quickly test and validate visual design concepts. However, this rapid increase in AI's involvement in creative work has also generated additional questions and concerns regarding who or what is the source of creativity; who owns the rights to a piece created using AI; and whether a piece created by a machine should be considered original (McKinsey & Company, 2023).

The environmental and technological changes taking place in the fashion and textile industries are similarly influencing the nature of fashion and textile education. Fashion design education today is no longer only concerned with teaching students to develop their aesthetic and creative design skills; it now includes educating them about sustainable manufacturing systems, digital technology and collaborating across disciplines (Niinimäki and Hassi, 2011). Therefore, gaining a better understanding of fashion design students' perspectives and attitudes towards sustainability, AI and digital design technologies are a key area of study for understanding how future designers will adapt to these changing demands.

Studies have shown that people's perception and attitude toward new technology can affect their willingness to use it; therefore, by assessing the perspectives of fashion and textile students concerning both AI-assisted design tools and sustainable fashion practices we may gain valuable insight into how to improve fashion design education and prepare the future work force of the fashion industry. Sustainability issues in the fashion industry have been studied extensively, however there is much less focus on the intersections of sustainability with interdisciplinary approaches to design, art and visual culture. While many studies are focused on the production process, materials innovation and circular economy strategies, the role of design, art and visual culture in the communication and implementation of sustainable fashion practices has received less attention. Therefore, a study of sustainable fashion at the intersection of design, art and visual culture can expand the theoretical basis of our understanding of how creative disciplines contribute to sustainability transformation in the fashion industry. Furthermore, fashion is also an important method of visual communication through which people express identity, cultural values and social meaning (Barnard, 2002).

Sustainable fashion is becoming the focus of an increasing number of interdisciplinary studies that look at sustainability through the lenses of design, artistic expression and visual culture. Aesthetic production is just one part of what designers do today. Designers can shape environmental responsibility and cultural narratives about consumption as well as provide aesthetically pleasing products. As such, it is crucial for designers to collaborate across disciplines of design, technology and visual communication to develop new solutions to address the environmental and social issues faced by the fashion industry.

This chapter explores how sustainable fashion relates to artificial intelligence (AI) technologies and fashion design education using an interdisciplinary approach. For supporting the conceptual framework of this chapter, a survey study involving

167 students from universities studying fashion and textiles were involved to assess students' perceptions of AI-assisted design tools and sustainable fashion practices. Additionally, the study assessed students' perceptions of the digital transformation occurring in the fashion industry. The results of the study will be used to assist in the development of pedagogical approaches for the future of fashion design education and to encourage the inclusion of sustainable technologies within design curriculum.

This chapter will therefore consider sustainable fashion and textiles from an interdisciplinary approach and analyze the relationships between design practice, artistic approach and visual culture within a framework of sustainability; Furthermore, the chapter will describe the ways in which technological innovations, circular economy strategies and creative design methods can lead to changes in the fashion system towards a more sustainable model. To do this the chapter is structured as follows. The first section outlines the sustainability problems and technological innovations that are happening in the fashion and textile industries. The second section identifies the contribution of interdisciplinary approaches in fashion design, art and visual culture. The third section will discuss how digital technology and creative design processes can be applied to sustainable fashion systems. Finally, the chapter will outline possible directions and implications for sustainable fashion design This study is driven by the following research questions:

RQ1: What are the perceptions of fashion and textile students regarding the practice of sustainable fashion, and how do these perceptions relate to their behavior regarding sustainable consumption?

RQ2: In what ways do fashion and textile students believe art and visual culture enhance the awareness of sustainability in the fashion system?

RQ3: In what way do demographic characteristics (i.e., gender, experience with the fashion industry) affect students' knowledge of, and attitudes toward, sustainable fashion?

This study's conceptual model will show the relationship between three concepts - sustainability (environmental and social responsibilities of the fashion industry), digital transformation (fashion product development and marketing utilizing technology and artificial intelligence) and visual culture (the use of aesthetics to visually communicate sustainability). While sustainability, digital transformation and visual culture have their own separate meanings, they are all connected to each other in ways that strengthen each component within the context of the fashion system.

Figure 1. Interdisciplinary sustainable fashion systems framework (Ellen MacArthur Foundation, 2017)

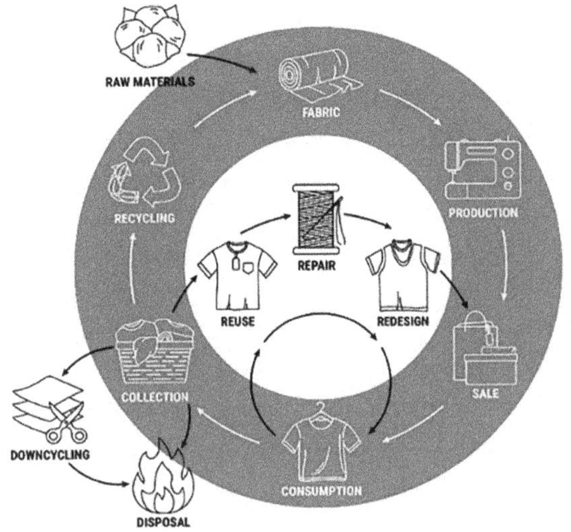

Circular Sustainable Fashion Systems Circular sustainable fashion systems are illustrated in the circular sustainable fashion systems diagram in Figure 1. The circular sustainable fashion systems illustrate a shift from linear fashion systems toward circular systems that use reuse, repair, redesign, and recycling. This paper will discuss circular sustainable fashion systems using an interdisciplinary lens by combining design, visual culture, and digital technologies (artificial intelligence). The circular sustainable fashion system diagram depicts how circular sustainable fashion systems evolve as a result of designers' creative process combined with technological innovations and circular production strategies.

CHANGE THROUGH SUSTAINABLE DEVELOPMENT – SUSTAINABILITY AND DIGITAL TECHNOLOGIES FOR A SUSTAINABLE TEXTILE PRODUCTION AND FASHION INDUSTRY

This segment presents an overview of the research literature regarding sustainable fashion, digital technology and visual culture. It organizes these topics around four themes that relate to sustainable fashion and the circular economy, the role of digital technology and AI in the design and manufacture of fashion products, educating students of fashion and textiles in a digital environment and using visual culture as a framework for communicating about sustainability in the fashion industry.

These changes have been largely due to two major driving forces: increasing pressure from the environment and rapidly changing technologies. The issue of textile waste is one of the biggest environmental sustainability problems the fashion and textile industry faces today. Growing levels of consumption and shortening product lifecycles mean there is increasingly large amounts of post-consumer waste generated (Hvass, 2014). Furthermore, energy, water and chemicals used during textile production are considered some of the largest environmental impacts associated with the fashion and textile industry (Allwood et al., 2006; Niinimäki et al., 2020). Dwivedi et al. (2021), show how digital production technologies, big data and AI are changing the way all aspects of fashion design and manufacturing occur throughout the entire design process, production planning, supply chain management and consumer interaction. Today it is well accepted that integrating sustainable practices with digital technologies will be necessary for the fashion and textile industry to move forward.

Sustainable Fashion Concept

The authors note sustainable fashion needs an inclusive view of how products are made and consumed in order to minimize the social and environmental damage of all supply chain members (Henninger et al., 2016). Slow Fashion is a feasible alternative to Fast Fashion because of its focus on using locally-sourced materials, greater transparency and longer lasting products (Clark, 2008; Fletcher, 2014; Niinimäki, 2013). While synthetic fiber processing, dyeing, and chemical treatment present significant risks to the environment through water use and microplastics (Niinimäki et al., 2020), sustainable design strategies need to include the full lifecycle of a product, including material sourcing and end-of-product-life recycling (Gwilt, 2020).

Thomas (2020) notes, however, sustainability in fashion is not just about technical solutions but also culturally defined, influenced by various aesthetic, commercial and social interests of industry stakeholders. Continuing this, Brown and Vacca (2022) have noted the important role that craft knowledge and local cultural heritage play in the development of sustainable fashion models. Craft practices counteract the globalizing influence of fast fashion and designers who preserve and interpret local traditions support not only environmental sustainability, but also cultural continuity (Brown & Vacca, 2022). The authors' point of view is consistent with the findings of this study, where several participants viewed textile design as a sustainable way to preserve and reinterpret their culture. In addition to approaches based on traditional handicrafts, digital design technologies are contributing more to the development of sustainable fashion every day. AR and VR technologies are transforming visual communication processes in fashion by providing immersive and interactive design environments and are supporting sustainable design strategies by reducing material consumption and facilitating experimentation in virtual spaces (Eraş and Türker, 2025).

Circular Economy in Textile and Fashion Systems

One of the sustainable fashion perspectives being examined in recent years is the Circular Economy Model. A circular economy is described as an economic model whose primary objective is to lengthen the useful life of a product, utilize waste generated from the manufacturing process as a resource, and create closed loop systems for the creation of products (Geissdoerfer et al., 2017; Koszewska, 2018). The purpose of the sustainable business models developed for the fashion and textile industry is to decrease usage of resources, slow down the rate at which products are produced and consumed, and to reassess the product lifecycle in closed systems (Pal and Gander, 2018). Circular economy-based practices in the fashion and textile industries include recycling, reuse, designs that can be repaired, rent based models, and second-hand fashion platforms (Ellen MacArthur foundation, 2017). The impact of the traditional linear "buy-produce-consume-dispose" production model on the environment in the fashion and textile industry increases the significance of the adoption of a circular economy approach (Koszewska, 2018).

Designing sustainable circular textiles and fashion systems is also connected to the decisions designers make at the beginning of the design process. When designers develop sustainable and durable products utilizing recycled materials and creating modular design, they will have created more effective circular fashion systems. Thus, the circular economy represents a major paradigmatic change in fashion design processes.

DIGITAL TECHNOLOGIES AND ARTIFICIAL INTELLIGENCE IN TEXTILE AND FASHION PRODUCTION AND DESIGN

The textile and fashion supply chain is undergoing significant transformation due to the influence of digital technologies. A wide variety of computer-aided design (CAD) systems, digital textile printing, three-dimensional modeling and virtual prototyping are becoming commonplace throughout the industry; this has led to faster, more flexible, and more efficient production processes (Glogar et al., 2025). One of the most environmentally friendly and cost-effective ways that digital textile printing can be used is to replace traditional production methods using less water and fewer chemicals (Kadem & Özdemir, 2024). A second significant transformative force in industry is artificial intelligence (AI), which is providing numerous opportunities for companies to use predictive analytics to forecast future trends, create alternative designs for products, and assist with the development of plans for the production of those products (Dwivedi et al., 2021). Generative AI continues to expand the creative potential of designers by creating rapid creation of fabric patterns, colors, and visual prototypes of design concepts. With AI tools now being applied at such a rapid pace, there are many important issues that need to be addressed concerning originality, creativity, and ownership/copyright of designs created using generative AI (McKinsey & Company, 2023). In addition to their increasing integration within the fashion and textile industries, digital technologies and AI tools are also being rapidly incorporated into the education of fashion and textile professionals. AI-assisted design tools continue to support the creative process of students, while digital simulation systems provide an opportunity for students to test their design concepts in virtual environments. This will prepare students to meet the changing needs of the fashion industry.

Visual Culture as a Theoretical Framework

Visual Culture is a field of study that focuses on the way that images and representations influence our understanding of our world. Mirzoeff (2009) identifies that visual culture is both images and the cultural, social and historical contexts in which they are viewed. Therefore, the ways in which people consume or interact with a variety of visual cultures such as fashion items, textiles, exhibitions and social media content are all forms of practice in visual culture that can be used to promote sustainable messages to broader audiences. By incorporating visual culture into sustainable fashion research, designers can go beyond traditional production based views of sustainability and explore how aesthetics and artistic expression contribute to communicating sustainability (Mirzoeff, 2009). Barnard (1998) states that the disciplines of art, design and visual culture are inter-related and each discipline provides a means through which societies provide and convey meaning. Therefore, textile designs and fashion products act as commodities and cultural artifacts that provide both social and environmental messaging. Barnard's work builds on the semiotic work of Saussure (2011), who described signs as being culturally constructed. The signs of sustainable fashion and design choices are encoded with environmental value. Additionally, Barthes (1967) has argued that fashion acts as a form of semiotics; providing a linguistic means for individuals to express social values and identity beyond their physical appearance. Arnold (2009) states that fashion is a link between the individual and society, allowing for the creation of cultural identity and sustainability narratives. This perspective is supported by Barnard (1998; 2002), who states that fashion communication occurs at the intersection of three different dimensions (aesthetic, cultural and ideological); therefore, it is a viable platform to use to deliver environmental and social messaging. Therefore, collectively, the theories presented above form the basis from which to investigate sustainable fashion as an integrated systems of meaning making, cultural communication, art and design.

Fashion and Textile Education in the Digital Era

The digital revolution, combined with growing concerns over sustainability in the fashion and textiles sector, means that traditional education systems must be reformed in response. For decades, traditional fashion education has centered upon teaching aesthetics, hand-skills, and manufacturing techniques in relation to fashion design. The rapid expansion of digital technology into the fashion sector has generated a new set of required skills for designers. Therefore, today's designers are no longer solely expected to be creatively skilled in designing clothing; rather, they must also demonstrate interdisciplinary competencies including digital tool utilization, data-driven decision making, and knowledge of sustainable production methods (Niinimäki and Hassi, 2011). Therefore, as digital technologies begin to replace or enhance existing fashion design practices, higher education providers will need to modify the curriculum of their degree programs to accommodate these changes. Computer-aided design systems, three-dimensional modeling software, digital textile printing technologies, and AI-based design platforms will likely require increasing inclusion in fashion design education (Dwivedi et al., 2021). In this context, it is critical for all fashion education programs to move toward a comprehensive learning model that combines digital literacy, sustainable knowledge, and innovative technological capabilities.

Technological Transformation and AI in Fashion and Textile Education

Traditionally, education in fashion and textiles has focused primarily on foundational skills that include drawing, pattern making, and production techniques. The increasing dependence of the fashion industry on digital technology has dramatically impacted how design education is provided today. Today's educators provide students with instruction in both traditional design methods and digital tools that include virtual prototype design technologies and digital design applications (McKinsey & Company, 2023). CAD systems, digital textile printing, and 3D modeling software have become increasingly common in curriculum offerings allowing students to work much more efficiently and produce fewer physical samples while also supporting more sustainable design practices. AI has created additional forms of creative production models in fashion education. Generative AI tools have enabled students to quickly develop and manipulate visual designs, fabric patterns, and design ideas/ concepts through rapid creative experimentation (Dwivedi et al., 2021). Virtual prototype design technologies enable students to test and revise their design ideas prior to actual production physically, which reduces resource utilization (Drakou et al., 2024). However, the increased use of AI also creates significant issues related to the nature of originality, ownership, and copyright in design (McKinsey & Company, 2023). Davis (1989) developed TAM as an ideal theoretical model to understand student adoption of AI-based design tools, based upon the two most influential factors in determining technology acceptance in fashion and textile education; namely, "perceived usefulness" and "ease of use".

Sustainability Awareness Among Textile and Fashion Students

Sustainability within the fashion and textiles industry has required that educational institutions consider the inclusion of sustainable fashion within their curriculum. Fashion students have knowledge on sustainable fashion production methods, environmentally friendly materials and circular fashion systems, which will help fashion designers create more sustainable production practices. While there has been an increase in awareness by fashion students regarding sustainability, literature reviews indicate that while there is an increase in awareness, it is also through educational programs that the awareness is turned into sustainable action (Niinimäki et al., 2020). As such, as part of the scope of sustainable fashion education, it is also important to assist students in developing circular design and sustainable material uses as well as developing an understanding of the impact of their designs on the environment. The combination of sustainability and technological innovation is a key component to creating a more interdisciplinary fashion and textiles education program. Researching fashion students' perception of both digital technologies and sustainable fashion approaches can be used to inform the development of new education programs and the direction of future workers in the sector. Therefore, the next section of this paper outlines the research methodology utilized to evaluate the perceptions of sustainable fashion and AI among fashion and textiles students.

MATERIALS AND METHODS

Research Design

This research is a quantitative research study based on a survey aimed at determining the perceptions and attitudes of university students studying in the fields of fashion and textiles towards sustainable fashion approaches and artificial intelligence-supported design technologies. A descriptive research model was used in the study. Descriptive research approaches aim to reveal the opinions, perceptions, and attitudes of individuals within a specific population (Creswell, 2014).

Within the scope of the research, a structured questionnaire was prepared to evaluate students' opinions on sustainable fashion, digital design technologies, and the use of artificial intelligence. The questionnaire questions were created by considering studies in literature and adapted to the context of textile and fashion design education.

Participants

The population for this research study included a total of 167 students from universities in Turkey who are studying fashion and/or textiles. All the students were enrolled in programs related to fashion and textiles that include fashion design and textile technology. Students participated voluntarily, and were selected based on their year of study, and if their program of study is a field of study that includes fashion design, or textile technology. Participants' responses to questions regarding sustainable fashion and artificial intelligence were sufficient in number for an analysis of students' perceptions of these topics. The first portion of the survey included demographic items such as gender, level of study (undergraduate/graduate), and if the student uses digital design tools.

Participants were selected using a convenience sampling method, as they were recruited from universities accessible to the researchers. Although convenience sampling limits the generalizability of the findings, it was deemed appropriate given the exploratory nature of the study and the practical constraints of data collection.

Data Collection Instrument

In this study, the primary method for collecting the data was by utilizing a structured questionnaire. The structured questionnaire was divided into two major parts. The first part of the questionnaire included questions that were intended to provide demographic information about the participants. The second part of the questionnaire contained statements that were to be utilized in assessing students' perceptions and attitudes toward sustainable fashion and toward sustainable consumption behaviors. Statements also assessed students' views on the inter-relationship between fashion design, art and visual culture. Each question was measured by a five-point Likert Scale; therefore, respondents could express their agreement or disagreement with each statement. Respondents were able to respond to each statement with one of five possible responses: "Strongly Disagree" (1), "Disagree" (2), "Neutral" (3),

"Agree" (4) or "Strongly Agree" (5). The Likert scale has been extensively utilized throughout the history of social science research to assess individuals' attitudes and perceptions toward various topics (Likert, 1932). Students' views on the following topics were specifically assessed through the questionnaire:

- Sustainability awareness in the fashion industry
- Sustainable fashion consumption attitudes
- Perceptions of the environmental impact of fashion production
- Role of art and cultural values in sustainable fashion design
- Contribution of visual communication and creative design practices to sustainability awareness

These questions allowed the researchers to explore how students of fashion and textiles view sustainability within the framework of fashion design and how an interdisciplinary perspective including art and visual culture contributes to sustainability awareness in fashion education.

The survey used 21 questions that were organized into three categories. The first category contained 10 questions to measure students' sustainable consumption attitudes and their knowledge about how the clothing industry has an impact on the environment. The second category had 6 questions to determine how students perceive the importance of art and visual culture in communicating sustainable fashion. The last category (third) was 5 questions that evaluated what students thought about the amount of sustainability training they received from their fashion programs and their overall perceptions regarding the digital revolution happening in the fashion industry.

DATA COLLECTION PROCESS AND ETHICAL APPROVAL

Prior to collecting data for the study, approval was received from an Institutional Ethics Committee (IEC) for studies using human subjects. The IEC review is based on the institution's policies regarding research and typically takes a couple of months to complete. Following the receipt of approval from the IEC, the survey instrument was distributed electronically to the participants; student volunteers provided their consent to participate. In addition to obtaining the participants' consent, they were also informed as to the purpose of the research, and that the results collected would be used solely for the purpose of conducting scientific research.

Data Analysis

A survey was conducted to collect data about students' views on sustainable fashion. This data was analyzed using SPSS25 (Statistical Package for the Social Sciences). As well as giving an overview of how many students answered each question, the demographic data was analyzed by using frequency and percentage distributions. Following the analysis of the demographics of the students who participated in the study, the answers to the other questions asked on the survey were analyzed statistically to identify the mean and standard deviations of student perceptions of sustainable fashion, consumption patterns and the relationship between art, culture and sustainability in fashion design. In addition to analyzing the data from the survey, Cronbach's Alpha reliability analysis was completed to evaluate the reliability of the multi-item scale used to measure the constructs. Cronbach's Alpha is a commonly utilized method of evaluating the reliability of multi-item scales in social science research (Cronbach, 1951). A Cronbach's Alpha coefficient of 0.82 was obtained from the reliability analysis. The alpha coefficient represents a high degree of internal consistency among the measures (Table 1). Additionally, chi-square tests were used to analyze the relationships between demographic factors and student perceptions of sustainable fashion. Prior to conducting the chi-square tests, the assumptions of the test were evaluated. All the variables analyzed were categorical, the observations were independent and the expected cell frequencies were examined, and all were greater than five. Thus, the chi-square test was deemed to be an acceptable analytical tool for this research. Results from the statistical analyses are presented in table format and interpreted within the framework of sustainable fashion and fashion design education. The process flow of this study is illustrated in Figure 2.

Table 1. Reliability statistics

Statistic	Value
Cronbach's Alpha	0.822
Number of Items	21

Figure 2. Workflow of the study

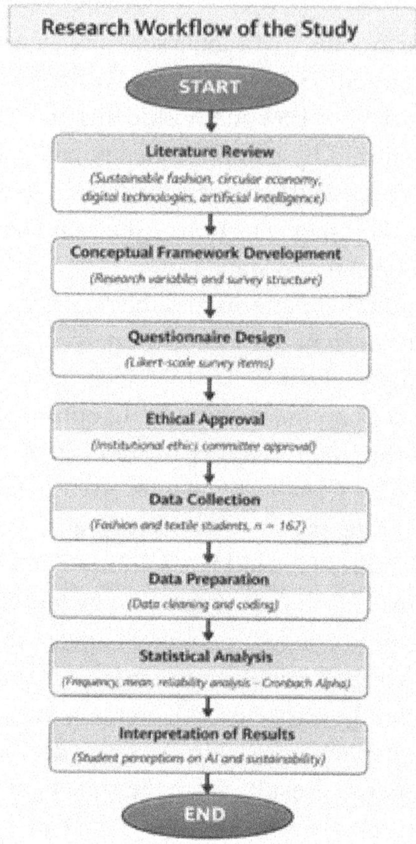

FINDINGS / RESULTS

Frequency analysis

Demographic Characteristics of Participants

The analysis of the demographics of the participants shows that in total, there were 167 participants in this study. Most of the participants were students (89.2%), while most of the remaining participants were academics (10.8%). In terms of gender, 82.0% of the participants were females and 18.0% of the participants were males. Examining the distribution of participants by their university, the greatest number of participants was from Tekirdağ Namık Kemal University (37.1%). Next, there were participants from Kırklareli University (31.7%), Trakya University (21.0%), Beykent University (7.2%) and Marmara University (3.0%). Examining the participants' experience with the fashion industry, it is found that 43.7% of the participants have experience working in the fashion industry, while 56.3% have no experience in the fashion industry at all (Table 2). Therefore, it can be concluded that the participants in this study consist mostly of students and that about half of the participants have no experience working in the fashion industry.

Table 2. Demographic characteristics of participants

Variable	Category	Frequency	Percent
Position	Student	149	89.2
	Academic	18	10.8
Gender	Female	137	82.0
	Male	30	18.0
Institution	Tekirdağ Namık Kemal University	62	37.1
	Kırklareli University	53	31.7
	Trakya University	35	21.0
	Beykent University	12	7.2
	Marmara University	5	3.0
Fashion industry experience	Yes	73	43.7
	No	94	56.3
	Total	**167**	**100.0**

Sustainable Consumption Attitudes

As shown in Figure 3, the data collected from the survey illustrated students studying in the fields of fashion and textiles were moderately to highly aware of sustainable production practices. Of the total surveyed (100%) approximately 63.5 percent of students reported being aware of the environmental implications of the fashion industry and factoring in sustainable claims when making purchases. Therefore, students' awareness of sustainable fashion is very strong. The study showed, however, that many of the students who participated in the survey believed that sustainable fashion was not only good for the environment, but that it was also aesthetically pleasing. Approximately seventy percent of students responded that clothing made from recycled or sustainable materials was not only eco friendly, but also visually appealing. Further, a large majority of the students participating in this study believed that sustainable fashion would become an integral part of the fashion industry in the future. It is interesting to note that there were several barriers that limited students' willingness to buy sustainable fashion items. For example, a large majority of the students responding to this question stated that the primary reason for not buying sustainable fashion items was due to cost, availability of these types of products, and/or lack of appeal based upon design. Additionally, the proportion of respondents who said they were willing to spend more money to buy sustainable fashion items was small. In conclusion, although students appear to be well-informed with regard to sustainability, economic concerns appeared to have a significant influence over students' purchasing behaviors related to sustainable fashion. In summary, a large proportion of respondents indicated that they believed it was important for companies to provide carbon footprint reports, and that fast fashion consumption patterns contribute to negative outcomes in terms of sustainability. Overall, the results of this study indicate that students' awareness of sustainability issues associated with the production of clothing, transparency and environmental responsibility has significantly increased. The means for the items in Figure 3 varied from 2.91 through 3.95. The highest average was 3.95 for the item related to the detrimental impacts of fast fashion on consumption behavior; and the lowest was 2.91 for the item related to willingness to pay a premium price for sustainable products.

Sustainability in Fashion Education

Figure 4 shows how much of the sample population thought sustainability was properly addressed in their fashion education; the majority of those sampled (42.5 percent; agree + strongly agree) reported that it was somewhat addressed through their educational programs. Approximately 1/3 of the sample (29.3 percent) had an "undecided" opinion regarding this question; about 28 percent (27.6 percent) of the sample felt that sustainability was not properly addressed within their fashion education. Thus, while there appears to be growing interest toward sustainability as part of fashion design education programs, a number of students have expressed the need for more content and application regarding sustainability in the classroom.

Figure 3. Students' perceptions of sustainability in fashion (frequency analysis)

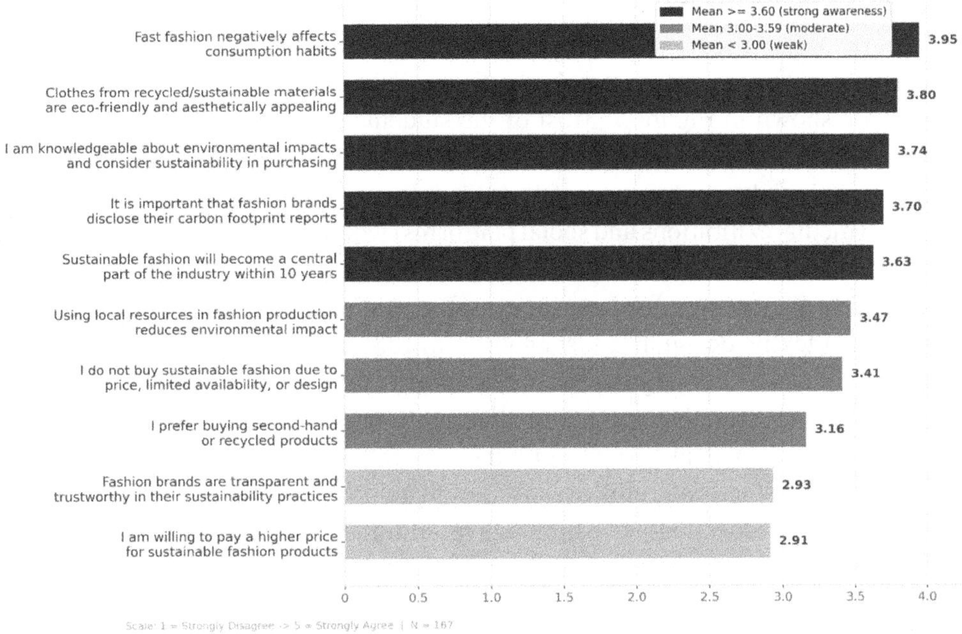

Figure 4. Students' perceptions of sustainability in fashion design education (N = 167)

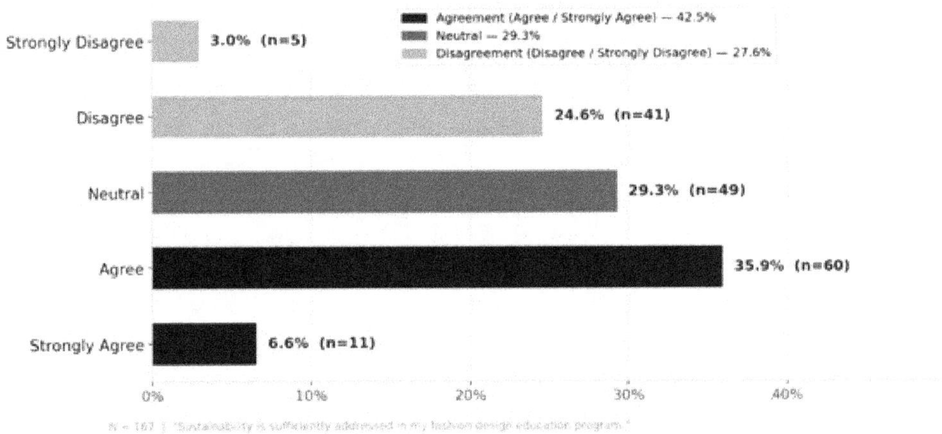

ROLE OF ART AND VISUAL CULTURE IN SUSTAINABLE FASHION

Participants' views on the interplay between art and visual culture and sustainable fashion are shown in Figure 5. Most of the students surveyed believe that art and visual communication tools will have an impact on sustainable fashion awareness. Approximately eighty-two percent of the students surveyed believed that visual culture products (media, exhibitions and social platforms) would increase their awareness of sustainable fashion. Additionally, most of the students also felt that art can produce a high level of awareness for environmental issues in society. Many students also believed that textile design is a sustainable way to preserve and reinterpret cultural heritage. There was also a great deal of support for the idea that visual communication design can effectively use art to communicate sustainability themes. Lastly, there was also a great deal of support for the concept of interdisciplinary art projects combining the aesthetic and ethical aspects of sustainability. Overall, it may be stated that students view sustainable fashion as a multidimensional concept in addition to being a process. It is not only about how clothing is produced, but also about art, culture and visual communications. As shown in Figure 5, mean scores ranged from 3.73 to 4.13, indicating a consistently high level of agreement among participants regarding the role of art and visual culture in sustainable fashion awareness.

Figure 5. The role of art and visual culture in sustainable fashion perception (N = 167)

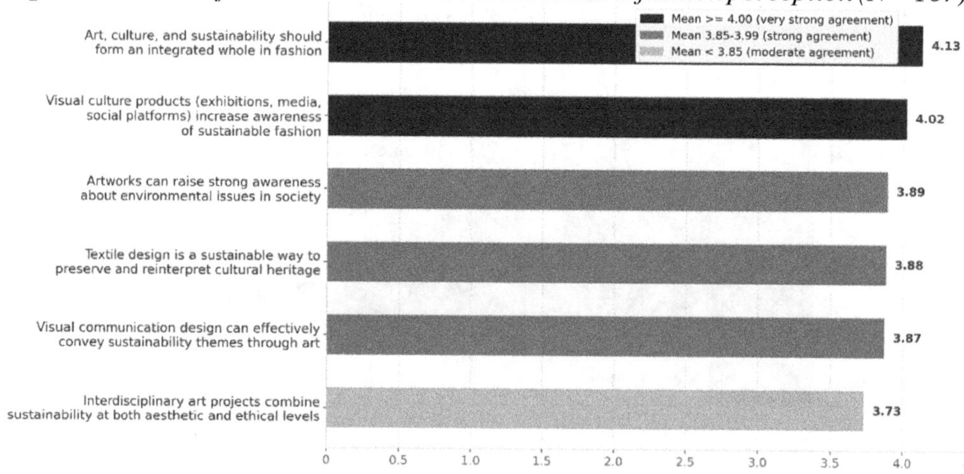

Chi-Square Analysis

In the present study, the Chi-Square test was used to evaluate the associations between categorical variables. The Chi-Square test is a commonly utilized non-parametric statistical technique for assessing the significance of an association between at least two categorical variables. The Chi-Square test evaluates if there exists a statistically significant association between variables by determining the differences between observed frequencies and expected frequencies (Pallant, 2020; Field, 2013) as such it is commonly used in social sciences when examining survey data and when comparing categorical data (Agresti, 2018). Chi-Square tests were performed to assess if a relationship existed between the demographic characteristics of the participants and their perceptions of sustainable fashion. The pairs of variables analyzed within the context of the current study are provided in Table 3.

Table 3. Variable pairs examined in the chi-square analysis

No	Variable 1	Variable 2
1	Gender	Fast fashion negatively affects consumption habits
2	Gender	Willingness to pay more for sustainable fashion products
3	Fashion industry experience	Knowledge about the environmental impacts of the fashion industry
4	Fashion industry experience	Preference for second-hand or recycled products
5	University	Sustainability is sufficiently addressed in fashion design education

Chi-square analyses were conducted to examine the relationships between participants' perceptions of sustainable fashion and their demographic characteristics. The results of the analyses are presented in Table 4. The findings indicate that there is no statistically significant relationship between gender and the belief that fast fashion negatively affects consumption habits ($\chi^2 = 7.944$; df = 4; p = 0.094), the willingness to pay a higher price for sustainable fashion products ($\chi^2 = 3.241$; df = 4; p = 0.518), and the preference for purchasing second-hand or recycled products ($\chi^2 = 3.729$; df = 4; p = 0.444) ($p > 0.05$).

In contrast, a statistically significant relationship was identified between gender and both the level of knowledge about the environmental impacts of the fashion industry and the consideration of sustainability claims in purchasing decisions ($\chi^2 = 22.997$; df = 4; $p < 0.001$). This result suggests that sustainability awareness may vary according to gender.

Additionally, a statistically significant relationship was found between having experience in the fashion industry and possessing knowledge about the environmental impacts of the fashion industry ($\chi^2 = 14.127$; df = 4; p = 0.007). This finding suggests that individuals with sectoral experience may have higher levels of awareness regarding sustainability and environmental impacts. In contrast, no statistically significant relationship was identified between having experience in the fashion industry and the preference for purchasing second-hand or recycled products (χ^2 = 3.022; df = 4; p = 0.554), or the willingness to pay a higher price for sustainable fashion products (χ^2 = 9.438; df = 4; p = 0.051) (p > 0.05).

Table 4. Chi-square analysis of the relationship between demographic variables and sustainable fashion attitudes

Variables	χ^2	df	p-value	Interpretation
Gender × Fast fashion negatively affects consumption habits	7.944	4	0.094	No statistically significant relationship
Gender × Willingness to pay a higher price for sustainable fashion products	3.241	4	0.518	No statistically significant relationship
Gender × Preference for buying second-hand or recycled products	3.729	4	0.444	No statistically significant relationship
Gender × Knowledge about environmental impacts of the fashion industry	22.997	4	0.000	**Statistically significant relationship**
Fashion industry experience × Knowledge about environmental impacts of the fashion industry	14.127	4	0.007	**Statistically significant relationship**
Fashion industry experience × Preference for buying second-hand or recycled products	3.022	4	0.554	No statistically significant relationship
Fashion industry experience × Willingness to pay a higher price for sustainable fashion products	9.438	4	0.051	No statistically significant relationship

CONCLUSION

The fashion industry has been identified as a major contributor to environmental and social problems. As well as the extreme use of resources, waste from textiles and unsustainable production methods, research, design, education and more are now looking at ways to improve the role of sustainability within the fashion system (Niinimäki et al., 2020). Therefore, it is very important to understand how fashion students view sustainability, sustainable consumer practices and visual culture as they will be the ones designing and shaping the new circular and more responsible fashion systems. Overall, many participants showed a favorable disposition toward sustainable fashion and demonstrated an awareness of the environmental impact of the fashion industry. A frequency count of responses revealed that many participants were aware of the environmental effects of the fashion industry and stated that their purchases are influenced by sustainability. Many also agreed that sustainable fashion would be an increasingly dominant force in the fashion industry over the next few years. This supports other studies indicating that younger generations and fashion students have a high level of awareness and concern regarding the environment and sustainable issues related to the fashion sector (Joy et al., 2012; McNeill & Moore, 2015).

However, the data presented above have shown that there are numerous problems to be overcome to make sustainable consumption behaviors a reality. Respondents demonstrated an understanding of sustainability issues. However, they demonstrated very limited willingness to pay higher prices for sustainable fashion products. This result illustrates a widely recognized discrepancy between sustainability awareness and consumers' actual purchase behaviors, often referred to in the literature on sustainable consumption as the "attitude-behavior gap" (Carrington et al., 2010). Factors that could act as barriers to sustainable purchasing decisions include economic factors, accessibility and design attractiveness. Although the level of awareness regarding sustainable consumption appears to be generally high, converting these attitudes into actual sustainable consumption behaviors continues to be a major problem for the fashion industry and for education related to sustainability. The second dimension examined in this study relates to the role that art and visual culture may assume in raising awareness of sustainability issues. The data clearly show that participants agreed to a large extent that visual culture products (such as exhibits, media content, and social media) can greatly raise awareness of sustainable fashion. Participants also agreed to a large extent that visual communication design and artworks can communicate effective environmental messages and sustainability themes. These findings confirm other studies that suggest that design practices and visual communication can play a major role in educating consumers about the environment and in changing their environmentally unsound behaviors in the context of fashion systems (Niinimäki and Hassi, 2011; Fletcher, 2014). For example, including artistic expressions and visual storytelling techniques within fashion design education, particularly when teaching sustainability related topics, can serve as a viable strategy to engage students with sustainability related ideas. Clothing and fashion are not simply systems of producing clothing; they are cultural and aesthetic practices inextricably linked with art and visual culture in which creative expression and experimental processes of artistic creation play a pivotal role (Geczy and Karaminas, 2012).

In terms of the theory behind the attitudinal-behavioral gap in sustainable consumption, there have been numerous theories developed over the years. For example, as noted by Carrington et al. (2010), the attitudinal-behavioral gap occurs due to an interdependent relationship between the situational, social, and psychological barriers between the consumer's intention to be environmentally conscious and the consumer's actual decision to purchase. Consistent with these findings, Ajzen (1991) also discussed that attitudes are inadequate for predicting behavior; however, they suggest that the consumer's perception of the social norm and their belief about how easy it will be to implement the behavior will both contribute to the likelihood that the consumer will behave sustainably. With respect to sustainable fashion, this theoretical perspective would indicate that if educators raise the awareness of environmental issues to fashion students, the student's knowledge of the issue is likely to result in sustainable consumption unless there is a structural change in the student's ability to access sustainable fashion options at an affordable price, or if the student views sustainable fashion as desirable. As such, educators must go beyond creating awareness about sustainability and create opportunities for students to develop practical abilities, critical thinking, and behavioral competences to link their knowledge of sustainability to their actions.

Gender was not associated with most of the sustainable consumption attitudes examined by chi-square analysis; however, there was a statistically significant association between gender and knowledge about the environmental impacts of the fashion industry. Thus, it is possible that awareness levels may differ across various demographic subgroups, emphasizing the importance of using demographic-specific approaches to promote sustainability through education programs in fashion. There was a statistically significant association between participants' experience working in the fashion industry and their knowledge of environmental impacts. Fashion program graduates with prior experience in the fashion industry were much more aware of sustainability issues and were more likely to take environmental impacts into consideration when making purchases. Therefore, it appears that direct exposure to the fashion industry's practices is critical to an individual's development of a deep understanding of the sustainability challenges in fashion systems. As a result, experiential learning experiences such as internships, industry partnerships, and project-based learning are important vehicles for increasing the sustainability literacy of fashion students. The findings of this research suggest that while awareness of sustainability issues is a good starting point for promoting behaviorally sustainable practices, awareness is not enough to prompt individuals to make changes in their purchasing behaviors. For example, many participants were reluctant to pay higher prices for products made from sustainable materials, and many participants indicated they would purchase second-hand clothing under certain circumstances, suggesting that economics (i.e., price), access, and culture will continue to impact the adoption of sustainable consumption practices. These findings emphasize that sustainability should be integrated both conceptually and practically into all aspects of product design, manufacturing, and marketing and communications efforts.

The study provides an important contribution to the expanding literature on the relationship of sustainability knowledge and attitudes regarding consumption in relation to fashion education, as well as the significance of incorporating industry experiences and visual culture as part of sustainability education, to foster more sustainable perceptions of fashion for future fashion professionals. As sustainability evolves globally in the fashion industry, it is expected that there will be continued growth in research and educational opportunities in areas related to sustainability and emerging fashion design.

The results from this research about how visual culture impacts the way people become aware of sustainable fashion, require a more refined theoretical understanding. Mirzoeff (2009) argues that visual culture is not just a representation of what is happening in society, it is also a source of meaning making where cultural value and social norm are both created, challenged, and changed. In other words, because so many of the participants agreed that visual culture products, like shows, social media, and art, can be effective ways to raise awareness of sustainable fashion; designers and visual communicators have a strategic place in the broader cultural project of transforming the sustainability of the entire fashion industry. Barnard (2002) also states that fashion communication has three functions: aesthetic, cultural, and ideological. He implies that when sustainability messages are included in visual culture and artistic products, they will likely communicate with consumers on all three levels of meaning and significance. This view supports Fletcher (2014) who argues that creative design practices and artistic expressions can create significant cultural change within the fashion system by providing alternatives to the dominant narrative of over consumption and fast fashion through sustainable design and new aesthetics. Therefore, integrating visual culture practice and artistic expression into sustainable fashion education is not only a pedagogy approach, but a form of cultural intervention to transform the values, identity and consumption patterns of the next generation of fashion professionals.

Although participants were aware of the negative impact of the fashion industry on the environment, their awareness did not always result in behavior related to sustainability, such as buying second hand and/or paying a premium price for eco-friendly clothing. The evidence that exists about the participants' lack of environmentally friendly consumption behavior may be due to the well-known "attitude-behavior" gap, which is a subject of discussion throughout much of the body of research concerning sustainable consumption.

In terms of an educational perspective, the study's findings also support the increasing need for developing fashion design programs with sustainability-focused curricula. As the fashion industry evolves towards a circular economic model and incorporates more environmentally conscious production systems, fashion education must evolve and incorporate the integration of sustainability-based learning objectives; the incorporation of interdisciplinary design strategies; and the inclusion of digital innovation into teaching practices (Gwilt, 2020), all while engaging students in sustainability aware creative design thinking and the industry they will work in. Fashion education can transform the way future professionals address the environmental challenges of the fashion industry, through its ability to combine sustainability awareness with creative design thinking and industry engagement.

LIMITATIONS OF THE STUDY

This research contributes greatly to the understanding of fashion student opinions regarding both visual culture and sustainability, however there are a number of limitations that need to be considered. For example, the fact that the research is based on 167 students attending a university in Turkey restricts the applicability of the findings across various education systems and cultures. In addition, self-reported surveys can result in social desirability bias, since, as noted by Carrington et al. (2010), stated attitudes are not always reflective of real purchasing behaviors due to the well-documented attitude-behavior gap. Since the study was conducted at one point in time (cross-sectionally), it was not possible to investigate whether students' perspectives changed over time. Further, since Chi-squared tests are used to test for significance between variables, they do not allow researchers to establish causation. While the researchers tested all constructs to ensure reliability through exploratory factor analysis, confirmatory factor analysis was not employed to further validate the measurement structure. The survey did not include any specific questions about students who used AI-assisted design tools or their technology acceptance; therefore, future research could benefit from addressing these issues using a model such as the Technology Acceptance Model (Davis, 1989). Finally, although the study included an even representation of males and females (many participants were female) this might affect how we interpret the study's results.

FUTURE RESEARCH DIRECTIONS

Several avenues for future research emerge from this study. Comparative and cross-cultural studies involving students from different countries and educational systems would provide a more inclusive understanding of how cultural values and institutional frameworks shape sustainability perceptions in fashion education. Future research should also employ qualitative and mixed methods approaches, including interviews and focus groups, to explore how students translate sustainability awareness into practical design decisions.

The roles of digital technologies and AI in sustainable fashion education represent another critical research domain. Technology Acceptance Model based instruments (Davis, 1989) could be used to formally assess students' attitudes toward AI tools and identify factors that support or inhibit their adoption (Dwivedi et al., 2021).

Future studies should also empirically investigate the relationship between visual culture, artistic expression, and sustainability communication, examining how specific visual communication techniques affect consumers' attitudes and behaviors toward sustainable fashion.

Longitudinal studies examining students' sustainability knowledge before and after industry-based learning experiences such as internships and collaborative projects would offer valuable insight into the role of experiential learning in developing sustainable fashion competences. Finally, emerging teaching formats integrating sustainability, creative design thinking, visual communication, and digital technology should be evaluated to contribute to the development of more effective sustainable fashion education programs.

ETHICAL STATEMENT

The study received ethical approval from the Kırklareli University Scientific Research and Publication Ethics Committee (Decision No: E-35523585-199-184455, Date: 15.12.2025) and was conducted in accordance with ethical guidelines.

REFERENCES

Agresti, A. (2018). *Statistical methods for the social sciences* (5th ed.). Pearson.

Ajzen, I. (1991). The theory of planned behavior. *Organizational Behavior and Human Decision Processes, 50*(2), 179–211. DOI: 10.1016/0749-5978(91)90020-T

Allwood, J. M., Laursen, S. E., Rodriguez, C. M., & Bocken, N. M. P. (2006). *Well dressed? The present and future sustainability of clothing and textiles in the United Kingdom.* University of Cambridge Institute for Manufacturing.

Arnold, R. (2009). *Fashion: A Very Short Introduction.* Oxford University Press.

Barnard, M. (1998). *Art, Design and Visual Culture: An Introduction.* Macmillan. DOI: 10.1007/978-1-349-26917-4

Barnard, M. (2002). *Fashion as communication* (2nd ed.). Routledge.

Barthes, R. (1967). *The Fashion System.* Hill and Wang.

Bick, R., Halsey, E., & Ekenga, C. C. (2018). The global environmental injustice of fast fashion. *Environmental Health : A Global Access Science Source, 17*(1), 92. DOI: 10.1186/s12940-018-0433-7 PMID: 30591057

Brown, S., & Vacca, F. (2022). Cultural sustainability in fashion: Reflections on craft and sustainable development models. *Sustainability : Science, Practice, & Policy, 18*(1), 590–600. DOI: 10.1080/15487733.2022.2100102

Carrington, M. J., Neville, B. A., & Whitwell, G. J. (2010). Why ethical consumers don't walk their talk: Towards a framework for understanding the gap between ethical purchase intentions and actual buying behaviour of ethically minded consumers. *Journal of Business Ethics, 97*(1), 139–158. DOI: 10.1007/s10551-010-0501-6

Chen, X., Memon, H. A., Wang, Y., Marriam, I., & Tebyetekerwa, M. (2021). Circular economy and sustainability of the clothing and textile industry. *Materials Circular Economy, 3*(1), 12. DOI: 10.1007/s42824-021-00026-2

Clark, H. (2008). Slow + fashion—An oxymoron—or a promise for the future? *Fashion Theory, 12*(4), 427–446. DOI: 10.2752/175174108X346922

Creswell, J. W. (2014). *Research design: Qualitative, quantitative, and mixed methods approaches* (4th ed.). Sage Publications.

Cronbach, L. J. (1951). Coefficient alpha and the internal structure of tests. *Psychometrika, 16*(3), 297–334. DOI: 10.1007/BF02310555

Davis, F. D. (1989). Perceived usefulness, perceived ease of use, and user acceptance of information technology. *Management Information Systems Quarterly, 13*(3), 319–340. DOI: 10.2307/249008

de Saussure, F. (2011). *Course in general linguistics* (W. Baskin, Trans.). Columbia University Press. (Original work published 1916)

Drakou, A., Papachristou, E., Tarnanidis, T., & Bilalis, N. (2024). Transforming fashion education: The impact of AI-driven 3D design on learning, creativity, and sustainability. In *Proceedings of the 13th Hellenic Conference on Artificial Intelligence (SETN 2024)* (pp. 1–6). ACM. https://doi.org/DOI: 10.1145/3688671.3688794

Dwivedi, Y. K., Hughes, L., Ismagilova, E., Aarts, G., Coombs, C., Crick, T., Duan, Y., Dwivedi, R., Edwards, J., Eirug, A., Galanos, V., Ilavarasan, P. V., Janssen, M., Jones, P., Kar, A. K., Kizgin, H., Kronemann, B., Lal, B., Lucini, B., & Williams, M. D. (2021). Artificial intelligence (AI): Multidisciplinary perspectives on emerging challenges, opportunities, and agenda for research, practice and policy. *International Journal of Information Management, 57*, 101994. DOI: 10.1016/j.ijinfomgt.2019.08.002

Ellen MacArthur Foundation. (2017). *A new textiles economy: Redesigning fashion's future*. Retrieved January 22, 2025, from https://www.ellenmacarthurfoundation.org/assets/downloads/publications/A-New-Textiles-Economy_Full-Report.pdf

Entwistle, J. (2015). *The fashioned body: Fashion, dress and modern social theory* (2nd ed.). Polity Press.

Eraş, E., & Türker, S. H. (2025). Türkiye'de tekstil ve hazır giyim üretim sürecinde artırılmış ve sanal gerçeklik uygulamaları: Sürdürülebilir tasarım üzerine etkileri. *Asya Studies, 9*(33), 289–310. DOI: 10.31455/asya.1676374

Field, A. (2013). *Discovering statistics using IBM SPSS statistics* (4th ed.). Sage Publications.

Fletcher, K. (2014). *Sustainable fashion and textiles: Design journeys* (2nd ed.). Routledge., https://ualresearchonline.arts.ac.uk/id/eprint/7537

Geczy, A., & Karaminas, V. (2012). *Fashion and art*. Berg.

Geissdoerfer, M., Savaget, P., Bocken, N. M. P., & Hultink, E. J. (2017). The circular economy – A new sustainability paradigm? *Journal of Cleaner Production, 143*, 757–768. DOI: 10.1016/j.jclepro.2016.12.048

Glogar, M., Petrak, S., & Mahnić Naglić, M. (2025). Digital technologies in the sustainable design and development of textiles and clothing: A literature review. *Sustainability (Basel)*, *17*(4), 1371. DOI: 10.3390/su17041371

Granata, F. (2017). *Experimental fashion: Performance art, carnival, and the grotesque body*. I.B. Tauris. DOI: 10.5040/9781350986312

Gwilt, A. (2020). *A practical guide to sustainable fashion*. Bloomsbury Visual Arts., DOI: 10.5040/9781350067059

Henninger, C. E., Alevizou, P. J., & Oates, C. J. (2016). What is sustainable fashion? *Journal of Fashion Marketing and Management*, *20*(4), 400–416. DOI: 10.1108/JFMM-07-2015-0052

Hvass, K. K. (2014). Post-retail responsibility of garments: A fashion industry perspective. *Journal of Fashion Marketing and Management*, *18*(4), 413–430. DOI: 10.1108/JFMM-01-2013-0005

Joy, A., Sherry, J. F.Jr, Venkatesh, A., Wang, J., & Chan, R. (2012). Fast fashion, sustainability, and the ethical appeal of luxury brands. *Fashion Theory*, *16*(3), 273–295. DOI: 10.2752/175174112X13340749707123

Kadem, F. D., & Özdemir, Ş. (2024). An overview of digital textile printing technologies. *Osmaniye Korkut Ata University Journal of The Institute of Science and Technology*, *7*(2), 889–901.

Kawamura, Y. (2005). *Fashion-ology: An introduction to fashion studies*. Berg. DOI: 10.2752/9781847888730

Kirchherr, J., Reike, D., & Hekkert, M. (2017). Conceptualizing the circular economy: An analysis of 114 definitions. *Resources, Conservation and Recycling*, *127*, 221–232. DOI: 10.1016/j.resconrec.2017.09.005

Koszewska, M. (2018). Circular economy—Challenges for the textile and clothing industry. *AUTEX Research Journal*, *18*(4), 337–347. DOI: 10.1515/aut-2018-0023

Kuzmichev, V. (2025). Clothing design in the era of artificial intelligence. *Journal of Computer and Communications*, *13*(5), 121–136. DOI: 10.4236/jcc.2025.135008

Likert, R. (1932). A technique for the measurement of attitudes. *Archives of Psychology*, *22*(140), 1–55.

McKinsey & Company. (2023). The state of fashion 2023: Holding onto growth as global clouds gather. https://www.mckinsey.com/industries/retail/our-insights/state-of-fashion

McNeill, L., & Moore, R. (2015). Sustainable fashion consumption and the fast fashion conundrum: Fashionable consumers and attitudes to sustainability in clothing choice. *International Journal of Consumer Studies, 39*(3), 212–222. DOI: 10.1111/ijcs.12169

Mirzoeff, N. (2009). *An Introduction to Visual Culture* (2nd ed.). Routledge.

Niinimäki, K. (2013). Tenets of sustainable fashion. In Niinimäki, K. (Ed.), *Sustainable fashion: New approaches* (pp. 12–29). Aalto University.

Niinimäki, K., & Hassi, L. (2011). Emerging design strategies in sustainable production and consumption of textiles and clothing. *Journal of Cleaner Production, 19*(16), 1876–1883. DOI: 10.1016/j.jclepro.2011.04.020

Niinimäki, K., Peters, G., Dahlbo, H., Perry, P., Rissanen, T., & Gwilt, A. (2020). The environmental price of fast fashion. *Nature Reviews. Earth & Environment, 1*(4), 189–200. DOI: 10.1038/s43017-020-0039-9

Pal, R., & Gander, J. (2018). Modelling environmental value: An examination of sustainable business models within the fashion industry. *Journal of Cleaner Production, 184*, 251–263. DOI: 10.1016/j.jclepro.2018.02.001

Pallant, J. (2020). *SPSS survival manual: A step-by-step guide to data analysis using IBM SPSS* (7th ed.). McGraw-Hill Education.

Rahman, M. M. (2020). Applications of digital technologies in textile and fashion industry. *Technium, 3*(1), 114–127. DOI: 10.47577/technium.v3i1.1140

Thomas, K. (2020). Cultures of sustainability in the fashion industry. *Fashion Theory, 24*(5), 715–742. DOI: 10.1080/1362704X.2018.1532737

Chapter 2
Procedural Thinking and Generative Form in Digital Arts:
A Philosophical Genealogy

Halim Yentür
http://orcid.org/0000-0001-5400-2309
Anadolu University, Turkey

ABSTRACT

This chapter examines the philosophical foundations of procedural thinking in the digital arts through comparative conceptual analysis. Moving beyond techno-centric approaches that reduce procedurality to modern computation, it traces a genealogy of procedural thought extending from Aristotle's theory of physis and potentiality (dynamis) to Spinoza's immanent causality (natura naturans), from Goethe's morphological archetype (Urpflanze) to Whitehead's process philosophy. The chapter re-reads rule-governed morphogenesis in nature, Islamic geometric art, and contemporary digital practices within this philosophical framework. It argues that rule-governed form generation is not an invention specific to a particular technology, but the contemporary expression of a recurring philosophical orientation — one that redefines the relationship between form and generative process. The central conclusion drawn from this genealogy is that in procedural art, the object of mimesis shifts from nature's completed products to nature's manner of producing form — to natura naturans.

DOI: 10.4018/979-8-3373-6680-7.ch002

INTRODUCTION

Procedural thinking has become a major creative logic in contemporary digital art. The artist's primary task is no longer to produce particular forms directly, but to design the conditions from which forms emerge. In a node-based procedural environment such as SideFX Houdini, building a forest does not begin with modeling trees. It begins with defining the conditions under which trees can exist. The practitioner establishes the terrain through HeightField nodes, not as a conventional polygon surface but as a layer-based structure shaped by noise-driven formations and simulated erosion processes. At no stage does the practitioner sculpt a particular slope; instead, amplitude and frequency parameters are defined, and the system produces landform as the necessary consequence of those rules.

Vegetation distribution follows the same logic. Rather than placing individual trees, the practitioner writes a placement rule selecting regions where slope and orientation thresholds are met, a mathematical translation of the observation that trees grow on gentle, south-facing hillsides. The trees themselves are not pre-modeled templates but algorithmic organisms: an L-System node generates branching structures through iterative rewriting rules. A small adjustment to the angle parameter or the gravity vector within the same formal grammar can produce the difference between an oak and a weeping willow. The Copy to Points node distributes these rule-derived forms across the point cloud, assembling a forest topology of thousands of differentiated trees.

What is remarkable about this workflow is not its technical complexity but its ontological structure. At no stage does the practitioner produce a forest; the practitioner produces the conditions from which a forest will necessarily emerge. The object of authorship is not the work but the generative system. This disposition has a striking precedent in philosophical history. In 1787, Johann Wolfgang von Goethe reported encountering, in the botanical garden at Palermo, what he called the Urpflanze, not a particular plant specimen but a formative principle from which all actual plant forms could be derived through systematic transformation. Goethe described this concept as a formula that would make it possible to invent an infinite number of plants, possessing inner truth and necessity (Goethe, 1952). The procedural practitioner working in a contemporary node graph shares a comparable conceptual orientation: the true object of creative attention is not the individual tree but the morphogenetic grammar from which trees emerge.

The focal point of this chapter is a specific creative practice within the digital arts: procedural thinking. To situate this concept, it must first be distinguished from its broader context. Generative art encompasses any practice in which the artist sets into motion a system that operates with some degree of autonomy beyond direct control, a definition broad enough to gather under one roof approaches as varied as algorithmic rule, randomness, order, and chaos (Boden & Edmonds, 2009; Galanter, 2003). Procedural thinking does not occupy a corner of this wide field; it occupies its center, designating practices in which the artist explicitly designs the generative logic and in which causal relationships from input to output remain, in principle, traceable. In Boden and Edmonds's (2009) taxonomy, this concerns rules that do not merely describe outcomes but specify a constructive process capable of producing them. Murray (1997) crystallizes this orientation through the concept of procedural authorship, in which the author writes the rules from which the work emerges rather than the work itself. Yet this definition conceals an important tension. Dorin et al. (2012) observe that in much of contemporary generative practice, generative logic operates as an inherited and opaque mechanism rather than as something explicitly authored. Procedural thinking diverges from this opacity: it foregrounds the writability of generative logic as a principle. The artist must be able to articulate, monitor, and modify the rules that govern emergence. As Smith and Whitehead (2010) demonstrate, the primary concern of this approach is not producing a single output but understanding and shaping the expressive range of the system. The procedural thinker writes not objects but systems whose causal structure, from input to output, remains in principle legible.

This epistemic distinction acquires particular urgency in the current technological context. The dominant paradigm of generative artificial intelligence operates through a different epistemic regime: foundation models trained through statistical optimization on large-scale datasets (Bommasani et al., 2021). Burrell (2016) argues that the opacity of such systems is not a temporary technical limitation but a structural condition of machine learning operating at functional scale. The aim here is not to disparage generative AI, but to mark a difference in regime with genuine aesthetic and ontological consequences. Procedural thinking, by contrast, insists on the writability of generative logic: the practitioner's capacity to articulate, monitor, and modify the rules governing emergence. Recent media-historical accounts have framed generative AI as a continuation of digital media's long-standing logic of separating and recombining visual elements (Manovich, 2024). The present chapter accepts the relevance of this continuity but emphasizes a different distinction: the epistemic difference between explicitly writable procedural rule systems and statistically learned generative models. This is the difference between designing a grammar of growth and steering a statistical model; in philosophical terms, the difference between authoring *natura naturans* and curating *natura naturata*.

The chapter's proposition is to illuminate the place of procedural thinking in digital art through a philosophical genealogy. The central argument is this: complex form arises not from carving an object from without but from designing the generative rules through which the object comes to exist. This argument recurs as a set of conceptual affinities across a trajectory running from Aristotle's theory of form and potentiality to Spinoza's doctrine of productive substance, from Goethe's understanding of morphological transformation to Whitehead's process metaphysics. The argument advanced here is not that these four figures share a common tradition, nor that a continuous line of transmission runs from Aristotle to contemporary software environments. Rather, the claim is that procedural thinking participates in a historically recurring conceptual pattern. Through this pattern, the chapter pursues the following question: how does the conceptual genealogy extending from Aristotle to Whitehead illuminate the philosophical ground of a logic of creation in digital art, one in which generative processes, rather than representations, acquire aesthetic status?

The term genealogy here designates not an archival historiography but a practice of conceptual tracing, drawing on Queloz's (2021) approach to how ideas take shape around recurring problems and Benjamin's (1977) concept of the constellation, in which distinct historical phenomena illuminate one another through positional proximity rather than linear succession. The method pursued is comparative conceptual analysis: recurring patterns in philosophical texts from different periods are identified, related to the operative logic of contemporary procedural practices, and discussed in terms of both their explanatory power and their speculative limits. The chapter thus aims to construct a conceptual framework capable of rendering procedural art legible within a deeper aesthetic and ontological context. It proceeds accordingly: after positioning procedural thinking as a philosophical problem, it traces the genealogy through Aristotle, Spinoza, Goethe, and Whitehead, extends this philosophical ground into natural morphogenesis, twentieth-century art, and contemporary digital practice, and synthesizes the findings within a philosophical framework.

PROCEDURAL THINKING AS A PHILOSOPHICAL PROBLEM

Procedural thinking has attracted considerable conceptual attention in digital media theory and computational aesthetics over the past two decades. This literature has successfully framed what procedural systems are, how they should be classified, and how they ought to be evaluated. Yet most answers to these questions remain at the technical, aesthetic, or rhetorical level, leaving the philosophical foundations of generative thinking relatively underexplored. Galanter (2003) positions generative art through complexity theory, situating the aesthetic achievement of a procedural system along a continuum of tension between absolute order and absolute randomness. A successful aesthetic output is the product of neither pure rule nor pure chaos; Galanter calls this threshold effective complexity. Boden and Edmonds (2009) define the field systematically, stressing that rules must not merely describe outcomes but contain a constructive process capable of producing them. Dorin et al. (2012) shift the unit of evaluation from the singular output to the system itself: the system, the entities within it, the processes it runs, and the sensory results it generates must be considered together. These contributions map the generative field from different angles, but their philosophical basis remains the least explored part of this field. The relationship between form and potentiality, the ontology of rule-governed production, and the nature of the distinction between generative principle and generated result have not been sufficiently interrogated.

Alongside these definitional efforts, theoretical contributions concerning how procedural thinking transforms creative action are equally significant. Murray (1997) identifies the computer's distinguishing capacity as the execution of rules and processes, and introduces the concept of procedural authorship, in which the author writes the rules from which the work emerges rather than the work itself. Bogost (2007) carries this line a step further, demonstrating that procedural thinking is also a mode of persuasion and argument production. Through the concept of procedural rhetoric, Bogost argues that processes and rules carry the capacity to make arguments through the construction of behavioral norms and dynamic models, in the same way that words function in verbal rhetoric and images in visual rhetoric. Taken together, Murray and Bogost show two sides of procedural thinking: writing rules and making arguments through those rules.

This trajectory, running from writing rules to building arguments through them, reveals the pragmatic power of procedural thinking. But it leaves one question unanswered: on what ontological ground do these rules operate, and what is the nature of the relationship between form and generative principle? This is the gap the present chapter addresses. The task is to acknowledge the contributions of existing scholarship while connecting them to a conceptual genealogy extending from Aristotle to Whitehead, making visible why procedural thinking carries a particular philosophical weight.

The conceptual roots of procedural thinking reach back centuries before the digital age. Weijers's (1978) philological research reveals that natura naturans and natura naturata, the central conceptual pair of this chapter, were not Spinoza's invention. These terms took shape during the first half of the thirteenth century, in the course of translating the texts of Aristotle's Arabic commentators into Latin. According to Weijers, the translators coined the verb naturare to render into Latin the distinction between active and passive nature found in the Arabic philosophical tradition. Michael Scot, the first thinker to deploy the pair systematically, set out in his *Liber introductorius* the formula *cum Deus sit natura naturans et ideo superet naturam naturatam* (Weijers, 1978). The formula expresses the asymmetry between productive nature and the nature it produces. The terms subsequently entered continental European philosophy through Thomas Aquinas and Meister Eckhart. Spinoza's intervention in the Ethics (Spinoza, 1985) transforms this inheritance in a decisive way. His move toward immanence refuses to separate the producing principle from the produced result, treating both as expressions of the same substance. This resonates strongly with procedural systems, where rule and output can be understood as different expressions of the same generative process. The eight-hundred-year terminological chain documented by Weijers demonstrates that procedural thinking is not a technical innovation peculiar to the digital age; it stands in deep continuity with philosophical questions concerning form, production, and causality that have persisted across centuries.

A GENEALOGY OF GENERATIVE FORM

Supporting Nodes: Historical Background of Procedural Thinking

Before turning to the genealogy itself, it is important to recognize that the idea of rule-based production rests on a historical ground far older than the digital age. The Pythagorean tradition articulates that visible forms derive from mathematical necessity. Llull's thirteenth-century Ars Generalis processes concepts through a mechanical combinatorial logic to generate new knowledge. Leibniz carries this move further; his design for a calculus ratiocinator envisions thought as a procedure operating through symbols. Alberti places the same question at the center of design practice: beauty derives from rules of proportion, not from the sculptor's hand. The shape grammar work of Stiny and Gips (1975) demonstrates that visual forms can be generated through rewriting rules, a systematic extension of this genealogy. Across these examples, the same intuition recurs: form is not a result imposed from without but an output derived from the operation of a rule.

Aristotle: Mimesis, Physis, and Procedural Potentiality

Tracing the philosophical foundations of procedural thinking requires a return to Aristotle's concepts of form, production, and potentiality. Aristotle's system brings together two insights in productive tension that illuminate contemporary procedural practice: the understanding of mimesis in the Poetics and the concept of physis in the Physics. In the *Poetics*, poetry and related representational arts are presented as modes of mimesis (Aristotle, 1984c). An important strand of the aesthetic tradition has read this concept as the external copying of nature's visible forms, though it is now widely accepted that this interpretation does not reflect the full reach of Aristotle's text. As Halliwell (2002) emphasizes, techne's imitation of nature is not an external visual copying but an ontological analogy directed toward nature's underlying formative principles and causal processes. In the second book of the Physics, Aristotle defines natural beings as things that contain within themselves a principle of motion and rest: Nature is a principle or cause of being moved and of being at rest in that to which it belongs primarily, in virtue of itself and not accidentally. (Aristotle, 1984b, II.1, 192b20).

Physis here is not a passive material upon which form is imposed from without, but an active structure capable of producing its own form according to its own internal principle. A seed transforms into a tree according to the formal principle (logos) within it, without requiring external intervention; the transformation is internal, not imposed. The procedural practitioner works at the intersection of these two insights: the object of creative attention becomes not nature's completed products but nature's manner of producing. This is a redirection of mimesis toward the production behind the product.

The concepts of dynamis and energeia, systematized in Book IX of the Metaphysics, deepen this perspective. Witt (2003) shows that Aristotle treats these concepts not as mere categories of physical motion but as ontological modes of being and causal powers. The most striking point in Witt's analysis concerns Aristotle's argument against the Megarian school. The Megarians held that a capacity exists only at the moment it is actually exercised. Aristotle refuses this strict actualism and argues that inactive capacities possess ontological reality: a capacity is a genuine mode of being even when it is not presently exercised (Aristotle, 1984a, IX.3, 1046b29–1047a10; Witt, 2003).

This argument directly illuminates the ontological status of procedural systems. A coded algorithmic system, whether a node network or a rule set, does not cease to exist when it is not running. It persists as a dynamis, an inactive but real causal power capable of generating countless variations. Running the system is the conversion of this inactive power into energeia. Each computation resembles a passage from potentiality to actuality, though this is a conceptual affinity rather than a strict philosophical identity.

A further point that Witt underlines deepens this frame: in production through art (poiesis), the form (eidos) exists in the mind of the agent prior to production (Aristotle, 1984a, VII, 1032b). For the traditional artist, this form is the image of a completed object to be realized on canvas. For the procedural practitioner, however, what exists in the mind before production is not a specific output but a generative rule that defines the possibility space. This formal structure, transferred to the system, carries potential forms into actuality through the operation of the computational process; it is more accurate to speak of a loose parallel than of strict causal equivalence. Within this frame, the procedural system can be read as a mode of creation in which techne operates with the grammar of physis: the artist does not impose form from without but installs within the system the capacity for form to produce itself. If Aristotle supplies the grammar of passage from potentiality to actuality, Spinoza radicalizes that grammar by grounding the relationship between generative principle and generated result not in an external agent-work dualism but in the immanent necessity of a single substance.

Spinoza: Natura Naturans, Immanent Causality, and Procedural Ontology

The concepts of natura naturans and natura naturata, whose terminological origins were traced through Weijers (1978) in the previous section, acquire their full philosophical weight in Spinoza's Ethics (Spinoza, 1985). Spinoza inherited these Scholastic terms but gave them an entirely new philosophical meaning within his philosophy of immanence. In Ethics I, Proposition 29, Scholium, Spinoza draws the following distinction: natura naturans consists of the attributes that exist in themselves and are conceived through themselves, expressing an eternal and infinite essence, that is, God or Nature itself considered as a free cause. Natura naturata, by contrast, is everything that follows from the modes of this generative principle, everything that can neither exist nor be conceived without it (Spinoza, 1985).

This distinction offers a productive conceptual framework for thinking about the structure of procedural digital art. The algorithmic system the artist designs, together with its rule set, parameter space, and network of causal relations, takes on the function of natura naturans as generative principle. The concrete visual form that the machine brings into existence by executing those rules in each computation occupies the position of natura naturata as produced result. The artist does not directly shape the output; the artist designs the generative matrix from which the output will emerge. This mapping does not claim a one-to-one ontological identity; it points to a structural parallel rather than an ontological equivalence. Natura naturans in Spinoza encompasses the generative principle of all reality, whereas procedural art involves a singular and artificial system.

Spinoza conceives the relationship between generative principle and produced result not as the decision of an external will but as a logical derivation. The geometry metaphor in Ethics I, Proposition 17, Scholium clarifies this point: that infinitely many things follow in infinitely many ways from the infinite nature of God occurs with the same necessity as that which follows from the nature of a triangle, namely that the sum of its interior angles equals two right angles (Spinoza, 1677/1985, IP17S). In a procedural system, the output derives with comparable logical necessity from the execution of initial conditions and algorithmic rules, though this comparison identifies a structural analogy in the relation between principle and output rather than a claim of metaphysical equivalence.

Spinoza's understanding of necessity operates in two directions for procedural systems, and this bidirectionality is worth noting. On one side stands the principle that every form has an explicable, traceable cause; on the other, this necessity does not exclude infinite variety but guarantees it. Della Rocca (2008) reads Spinoza's system as the most consistent application of the Principle of Sufficient Reason: there is no room for brute facts without explanation, and everything that exists or does not exist must have a sufficient cause. Every form that appears on screen is in principle traceable within the causal structure of the code behind it. It is precisely this divergence from opacity that procedural thinking insists upon. Garrett (2018) opens the other face of the same understanding of necessity: according to Spinoza, it is guaranteed that infinitely many things will follow in infinitely many ways from the necessity of the divine nature (Ethics I, Proposition 16). In procedural art, this dual structure finds a close analogue: the same rules produce the same output in every execution, but the breadth of the parameter space opens the door to infinite variation. Necessity lies in the operation of the rule; richness lies in the breadth of the parameter space.

There is a further dimension of this bidirectional structure that distinguishes Spinoza from the preceding tradition. In the Scholastic tradition, natura naturans was typically treated as a transcendent principle standing beyond the created world. Spinoza instead constructs this relationship as immanent: he does not separate the producing principle from the produced, treating both as different expressions of the same substance. In procedural art too, rule and output are not two distinct entities cut off from each other; they are different appearances of the same generative process. The rule can be understood not as something outside or beyond the output but as a cause operating within it. This immanence is structural rather than temporal. From here, the question opens of how these generative principles become visible in organic form. An answer to that question, different from Spinoza's geometric substance yet closely related to it, awaits in Goethe.

Goethe: Urpflanze, Morphogenetic Grammar, and Form as Bildung

Goethe's morphological project marks the third moment in the philosophical genealogy: the abstract framework of generative principles here meets the concrete logic of organic form. As Vlasopoulos (2016) demonstrates, Goethe read Spinoza deeply in 1784 and, drawing on that philosophy, reconfigured universal substance not through the traditional attributes of Extension or Thought but through an original attribute of Morphe (Form). Goethe's Urpflanze, in Vlasopoulos's analysis, functions as a synecdoche for Spinoza's Substance: just as laws of causality flow necessarily from the attribute of Extension in Spinoza, so laws of growth and metamorphosis flow from this attribute of Morphe in Goethe (Vlasopoulos, 2016). This is not a line of direct transmission but a structural kinship around a shared concern.

Goethe combines this ontological insight with empirical observation. In a letter written to Herder from Naples on May 17, 1787, Goethe describes the Urpflanze as a model that, once grasped together with its underlying key, makes it possible to derive an infinite number of consistent plant forms, including forms that do not yet exist but could exist, none of which are mere poetic illusions but each carrying its own inner truth and necessity (Goethe, 1962). The point is decisive: the Urpflanze is not a specific plant but a principle from which all actual and possible plant forms can be derived, in other words a generative rule that defines a possibility space.

The phrase Goethe uses in the letter to Herder is not an exercise of imagination but a systematic definition of a possibility space. Petteni (2022) reads the Urpflanze as a proto-algorithmic matrix: Goethe conceived this archetypal model as an algebraic formula constructing a system of abstract relations independent of space and time. Just as infinitely many results derive with mathematical necessity when the parameters within an algebraic formula change, the Urpflanze is a generative equation defining the possibility space of plant forms. This brings Goethe's morphology into close alignment with Spinoza's geometry metaphor: in both cases, the result is an output derived from the internal logic of a principle.

What does this logic of internal derivation mean in practice? Brady (1987) answers this question by placing it at the center of Goethe's morphological project: its originality lies in moving the question of how form comes to exist, rather than what form is, to the center of inquiry. Where general scientific practice treats form as Gestalt, a completed object to be observed and measured, Goethe reverses this orientation: attention turns to the process of formation, Bildung (Brady, 1987). Form is not a mold imposed from without but the self-production of an internal rule through successive transformations. The right question is no longer "what does this form look like?" but "how did this form come into being?" The procedural artist is, in this sense, the one asking this question.

Goethe's specific contribution comes into clearer view here. The abstract framework established by Aristotle and Spinoza meets, in Goethe, a concrete morphological logic: expansion and contraction, intensification (Steigerung) and metamorphosis. This logic is empirically observable, systematically describable, and potentially formalizable. Goethe transforms the philosophical insight into a morphological logic that is reproducible in an algorithmic environment. Form is a Bildung: not a static object but a process in which a rule produces itself.

Whitehead: Process Philosophy, the Principle of Creativity, and Computation as Aesthetic Event

The grammar of potentiality established by Aristotle, the immanent necessity of Spinoza, and the logic of morphological transformation developed by Goethe are carried into a different ontological register in the twentieth century through Alfred North Whitehead's process philosophy. Whitehead rejects traditional substance metaphysics and argues that the fundamental constituents of reality are not substances or fixed forms but processes and events. This move opens an important possibility for procedural thinking: if reality itself consists of processes, process-based art may stand in a closer relationship to the structure of reality.

If reality consists of processes rather than substances, then reality's smallest unit must be not a completed object but an ongoing event. Whitehead formulates this conclusion in Process and Reality (1929) through the concept of the actual occasion: each actual occasion is a spatiotemporal drop of the universe's current state. Each occasion comes into being through two phases. In the phase of prehension, the newly forming event draws into itself the data from what has preceded it and infinite potentialities. In the phase of concrescence, these dispersed data are synthesized and crystallize into a new and singular entity (Whitehead, 1929/1978). Each occasion in this sense is a moment of decision: the actualization of potentialities in a particular form excludes other possibilities. Every computational cycle of an algorithmic system shows a comparable structure: it prehends the previous state and current data, arrives at a decision, and gives birth to a new output. The parallel is illustrative rather than ontological; computation approximates the formal pattern of concrescence without claiming the full metaphysical weight of Whitehead's system.

In Whitehead's system, the engine of this becoming is the principle of Creativity. In Process and Reality, Whitehead identifies Creativity as the most fundamental principle of actuality itself. Creativity is the dynamic by which a multiplicity of prior actual occasions is synthesized into each new singular occasion, and the totality of being is augmented by every act of becoming (Whitehead, 1929/1978). With this formulation, Whitehead removes creativity from the status of a capacity peculiar to humans or to art and establishes it as an ontological principle that comes into operation in the process of becoming of every entity in the universe. The production by a procedural system of many parameters, rules, and input values converging in a computational process to generate a new form that did not previously exist echoes this Whiteheadian principle of creativity.

The difference between a traditional artwork and a procedural image is not only technical but also ontological. A painting exists as a closed object whose creation was completed in the past, fixed in space; the viewer encounters it only after it is finished. The procedural and digital image, in Whitehead's (1929/1978) terms, is not a "thing made" but a "thing in the making": each frame is computed by the processor, and visual existence ends when computation stops. Barker (2012) systematizes this distinction within a Whiteheadian frame: the procedural image is not the representation of an object but the momentary freezing of an ongoing act of production. This difference has aesthetic consequences: the procedural practitioner is the author not of completed objects but of continuously ongoing aesthetic events.

Barker's framework clarifies what the procedural image is, but the question of how computation itself operates remains open. It is a common assumption that algorithms are deterministic and closed systems, an intuition that resonates with the strict necessity in Garrett's reading of Spinoza. This picture, however, is incomplete. A procedural rule set does not encounter the same data each time it runs; it meets different conditions and inputs, and the rigidity of the rule intersects with the contingency of the data, producing a different actualization in every cycle. Fazi (2018) conceptualizes this dynamic within a Whiteheadian frame: computation is not mere mechanical repetition but a process of "determining indeterminacy." In this reading, procedural computation produces not only an aesthetics of necessity; from the tension between the rule's abstract capacity and the data's concrete contingency, an aesthetics of contingency also arises. Garrett's emphasis is not cancelled but completed: necessity lies in the operation of the rule, contingency lies in the conditions the rule encounters. Together, they explain why procedural form is at once familiar and surprising at every iteration.

Aristotle establishes the grammar that takes potentiality seriously as an ontological category. Spinoza radicalizes this grammar and refuses to separate the generative principle from the generated result. Goethe brings this abstract framework into empirical morphology, rendering the logic of transformation observable and formalizable. Whitehead establishes the ontological principle that the constituents of reality are not substances but processes. The four doors open in different directions but share a common threshold: form is not an object carved and completed from without but a dynamic event derived from the operation of a rule. This conceptual ground is not purely philosophical. Nature's own morphogenesis supports it independently.

MORPHOGENESIS AND RULE-GOVERNED FORMATION

Thompson: Coordinate Transformations and the Parametric Nature of Form

Nature's own morphogenesis independently and empirically confirms the distinction between form and the generative rule that produces it. The growth of living organisms, the variation of skeletal structures, and self-similar surfaces all suggest that rule-governed generative processes are deeply embedded in natural formation. This section grounds the conceptual framework proposed by the philosophical genealogy through mathematical morphology and the computational natural sciences.

The idea that biological form is the necessary output of mathematical laws has rested on firm ground since D'Arcy Wentworth Thompson's On Growth and Form (1917/1942). Thompson's most original contribution is his reading of morphological difference between species not as separate objects but as different mathematical transformations of the same coordinate space. When he placed the skeleton of the deep-sea fish *Argyropelecus olfersi* on a rectangular grid and transformed that grid into oblique coordinates, the resulting structure reproduced the anatomy of a related species (Thompson, 1917/1942). Different species were not separate forms but outputs of the same generative transformation at different parameters. What makes Thompson's approach significant for procedural thinking is his reading of morphological diversity not as the construction of objects but as the modification of parameters. Dorin et al. (2012) note that Thompson treats form as a direct result of physical processes and parameterized structural relations. In this view, the transition between forms is not the demolition of one object and the construction of another but the modification of parameters within the same coordinate space. Where Goethe's *Urpflanze* remained a qualitative biological and philosophical matrix, Thompson provided a mathematical account of that same logic working through quantitative parameters.

Fractals, L-Systems, and Computational Botany

Thompson's mathematical morphology and Goethe's morphological program arrived at an algorithmic synthesis in the second half of the twentieth century, within computational botany. Prusinkiewicz and Lindenmayer's (1990) The Algorithmic Beauty of Plants positioned the L-system approach in conceptual continuity with both programs (Petteni, 2022). L-systems showed that a generative principle of the kind Goethe imagined can be operationalized in a computational environment: infinite morphological variety derived from a single axiom through iterative rules. The relationship between rule and output is no longer only a philosophical analogy; it also appears as a working and verifiable system. What Goethe imagined in his letter to Herder became an algorithmic reality by the end of the twentieth century: plants that "could exist even if they do not" could now be generated within L-systems.

Fractal Aesthetics: Human Perception and Procedural Output

Procedural systems generate, by virtue of their structural properties, iterative patterns and self-similarities. This is not only a technical feature; it establishes a direct connection to human perception. The human visual system has been calibrated through evolutionary processes to be sensitive to the fractal patterns of nature, including coastlines, tree silhouettes, cloud formations, and plant branching structures. Taylor et al. (2001) demonstrated that images with a fractal dimension between 1.3 and 1.5 are consistently preferred; this range corresponds to the most common fractal structures in nature. Forsythe et al. (2011) refined this finding across 800 images: fractal dimension alone is not determinative, but when combined with measures of visual complexity, it accounts for a larger portion of the variance in aesthetic preference judgments. This empirically supports Galanter's (2003) thesis of effective complexity: aesthetic meaning arises not in pure order or pure randomness but in the tension between the two. When procedural art mobilizes this logic, what comes into play is not merely a technical preference but a mode of production that establishes deep resonance with perception. Is this mode of production, then, exclusive to digital technology?

Islamic Geometric Art: Technology-Independent Procedural Thinking

One of the clearest historical examples demonstrating that procedural thinking is a creative principle independent of digital technology is the tradition of Islamic geometric art. In this tradition, complex geometric patterns are not drawn directly; rules are designed and patterns are derived from those rules. Bonner (2017) describes the method of production used by Islamic craftsmen as the polygonal technique. The designer does not draw the final pattern directly; instead, an invisible underlying generative tessellation is constructed, and the visible complex patterns emerge through the operation of rules running along the edges of that tessellation.

Concrete historical evidence for this abstract framework came from Lu and Steinhardt's (2007) examination of the girih tiles of the Darb-i Imam shrine in Isfahan (1453) and the Topkapi Scroll. The researchers demonstrated that medieval Islamic designers used only a small number of polygonal modules and strict mathematical rules for combining them to produce aperiodic, quasi-crystalline tessellations. This principle of aperiodic arrangement was independently formulated in the Western mathematical tradition by Roger Penrose in the 1970s. The medieval craftsman had already produced with compass and straightedge what twentieth-century mathematics would later discover. Kaplan (2005) further demonstrated that these production rules can largely be preserved and translated into computer code; the logic the software applies and the logic on the stone are essentially the same. This observation provides concrete evidence that procedural thinking is bound not to a specific technology but to the principle of rule-governed form generation. Thompson's coordinate transformations, fractal self-similarity, L-system grammars, and the compass-and-straightedge practice of Islamic craft all suggest that this logic of rule-governed form generation recurs across different cultural and historical settings. The question now becomes: how did this pattern transform into a conscious artistic strategy in the twentieth century?

Procedural Transformation: The Mechanization Of The Rule In Twentieth-Century Art

The philosophical genealogy and the examples of rule-governed morphogenesis in nature traced in the preceding sections began to transform into a conscious artistic strategy in the twentieth century. This transformation happened neither suddenly nor through a single movement: the conceptual art practices of the 1960s, theories of systems aesthetics, and experiments in computational aesthetics each addressed related questions from independent directions, collectively shaping the artistic basis of procedural thinking.

The most influential manifesto of procedural aesthetics was formulated in Sol LeWitt's “Paragraphs on Conceptual Art,” published in *Artforum* in 1967. LeWitt transfers the ontological weight of the artwork from the physical object to the set of rules that produces it: in conceptual art the idea or concept becomes the most important aspect of the work, with all planning and decisions made beforehand, so that execution becomes a perfunctory and mechanical affair in which the idea itself functions as the machine that produces the art (LeWitt, 1967). The Wall Drawings series executed on gallery walls is the concrete realization of this principle: the drawings were carried out not by the artist's hand but by assistants following the algorithmic instructions he had written. This separation of conception from execution marks the moment when the artist shifts from producer of objects to designer of systems. LeWitt does not confine this mechanization to a strict rationalism. In his 1969 “Sentences on Conceptual Art” he extends the position by suggesting that conceptual artists work less as rationalists than as mystics, reaching conclusions through leaps that logic alone cannot trace (LeWitt, 1969). This formulation underlines that procedural rules are not simple calculators but generative grammars capable of emergence, producing unforeseen aesthetic results.

Karth and Compton (2023), connecting LeWitt’s formulation to contemporary digital practice, argue that procedural content generation is precisely the industrial-scale realization of this principle. Procedural generators produce a broad output space of closely related variations; within this space, the elegance of the system that produces the work replaces the singularity of any individual work. The object of evaluation has shifted from result to rule. In the digital era, this orientation extends the logic already established by LeWitt's instruction sheets: the rule, rather than its visible result, becomes the primary bearer of aesthetic intention (Dorin et al., 2012).

An important historical precedent showing that procedural thinking is a mental construct irreducible to technology is the practice of Vera Molnar. In the early 1960s, when she did not yet have physical access to computers, Molnar developed a method she called the machine imaginaire: she calculated and applied the mathematical algorithms and transformation rules she had determined step by step, by hand, on paper (Roe-Dale & Pfaff, 2019). The machine imaginaire suggests that rule-based production is an ontology belonging not to silicon but to the mind. Molnar's significant conceptual contribution to procedural aesthetics is the principle of one percent disorder: observing that the strict determinism of algorithms produces a dead order, she deliberately injected small deviations into her mathematical series (Roe-Dale & Pfaff, 2019). This principle reveals that the procedural artist is not merely a rule-setter but a negotiator managing the balance between rule and contingency, a dynamic that carries a structural parallel with Fazi's (2018) concept of an aesthetics of contingency.

Max Bense grounded the theoretical basis of this artistic practice through information theory, introducing the concept of generative aesthetics: "a combination of all operations, rules, and theorems that can be deliberately employed to produce aesthetic states when applied to material elements" (Bense, 1971). Jack Burnham carries Bense's approach into a broader ontological reading. In his "Systems Esthetics" essay published in Artforum in 1968, Burnham summarizes the fundamental orientation of twentieth-century art as a transition from an object-oriented to a systems-oriented culture, in which change emanates not from things themselves but from the way things are done (Burnham, 1968). For Burnham, art is no longer the production of isolated objects but the construction of open systems showing how energy, information, and materials organize themselves in relation to their environment. This formulation anticipates the place of procedural thinking in art theory: the artist is the architect not of the object but of the generative process.

Galanter's (2003) theory of effective complexity argues that the most successful works of generative art are positioned in the tense region between absolute order and absolute randomness. This threshold shows a notable convergence with two philosophical frameworks traced in the genealogy. In Goethe's morphology, form arises from the continuous tension between the rule's contracting tendency and the release of vital energy in expansion. This is the dynamic equilibrium Brady (1987) describes as Bildung. In Whitehead's process philosophy, each actual occasion arises from the tension between the prehension of data and their synthesis in a new aesthetic configuration through concrescence. Galanter's threshold of effective complexity, Goethe's dialectic of expansion and contraction, and Whitehead's principle of creativity can be read as converging, in different conceptual vocabularies, on a similar dynamic problem: complex and aesthetically meaningful form arises not in pure order or pure randomness but at their tense convergence. To the author's knowledge, this three-way connection has not been explicitly presented together in the literature and constitutes one of the chapter's original conceptual contributions.

DIGITAL PRACTICE: PROCEDURAL THINKING EMBODIED

All the major questions of the philosophical genealogy resurface in the software environment: form versus process, object versus system, and the object of mimesis. This section traces three principal embodiments of procedural thinking in contemporary digital tools and the aesthetic tension these embodiments produce. SideFX Houdini offers one of the clearest software expressions of procedural ontology. The artist designs a node network determining how data will flow and under what conditions geometry will be transformed. A key organizational form is the HDA (Houdini Digital Asset), which encapsulates the procedural logic the artist has built and exposes only high-level parameters: branching angle, building height, erosion amount. This structure echoes Goethe's *Urpflanze*: the artist does not model a specific and singular object but encodes the formal principles that make variations of the object possible. When a single parameter in the interface is adjusted, a new form that is structurally consistent but did not previously exist emerges from the immanent logic of the algorithm. The artist is the designer of the generative matrix from which form derives.

One of the clearest digital analogues to Spinoza's principle of necessity is *No Man's Sky* (Hello Games, 2016). The game contains 18.4 quintillion theoretical planets; not one of them was modeled individually by artists in the studio. All were derived from a single starting seed through algorithms based on L-systems and noise functions. The same seed and the same rules produce exactly the same result on every execution; when two different users travel to the same coordinates, they encounter the same environment. This bears a structural affinity with the Spinozist principle in Garrett's (2018) reading: the output is the necessary consequence of the rule, not of chance. But Spinoza's second principle is also at work here: necessity does not exclude infinite variety. In this sense, natura naturans operates and natura naturata emerges.

This procedural logic also finds expression in real-time environments. Unreal Engine 5's PCG Framework constructs game worlds through rule-based algorithms, while Oskar Stalberg's Townscaper (2020) demonstrates that procedural thinking can operate outside industrial-scale demands: constraint-solver algorithms derive aesthetically coherent scenes from simple user inputs (Karth & Compton, 2023). The organic quality of these environments rests on mathematical structures such as Perlin noise (Perlin, 1985), which generates controlled randomness to simulate natural textures. These algorithms do not simply mimic nature's outward appearance;

by modeling generative variation mathematically, they invite comparison with what Aristotle calls physis, the internal generative principle.

Yet this vast capacity for production confronts procedural art with an unavoidable aesthetic question: does variation, by itself, generate meaning? Compton's (2016) metaphor of "10,000 Bowls of Oatmeal" frames this problem sharply: a procedural algorithm can produce ten thousand mathematically distinct bowls. The position, orientation, and size of each grain differ from all the others. When these outputs are presented to human perception, however, the mathematical multiplicity collapses; what the viewer encounters is ten thousand identical, unremarkable bowls. Quantity does not automatically convert into quality or meaning. The tension points to the real weight-bearing center of procedural aesthetics: the problem is not technical but conceptual. The difference between a system that produces hundreds of thousands of variations and a system that generates meaning in the viewer lies not in the complexity of the rule but in the purpose for which the rule was written.

AUTHORSHIP, MEANING, AND EMERGENCE

What procedural creation looks like and what it means are not the same question. The philosophical genealogy and the examples from digital practice together suggest that procedural thinking reframes enduring questions. The first and most direct consequence of this reframing concerns the concept of authorship. The autonomy of procedural systems transforms the position of the author in traditional art theory. Whitelaw (2004) describes this transformation through a memorable metaphor: the author is no longer a sculptor but a gardener. The procedural artist plants seeds in a virtual ecosystem and sets the system's growth rules. At the same time, the artist acts as an aesthetic arbiter, making selections among the variations the machine produces. The act of creation has shifted from the construction of the object to the curation of a possibility space. This description, however, can seem too simple: the procedural artist is not always only the one who selects; in many cases the artist constructs the possibility space of the system with great precision in advance, and this prior construction is itself a creative act. The gardener metaphor does not exclude creativity; it relocates it to a different plane. This understanding is in alignment with Murray's definition of procedural authorship, in which the author writes the rules from which the work emerges rather than the work itself (Murray, 1997). It also resonates with Spinoza's framework: the artist becomes the author not primarily of *natura naturata but of natura naturans.*

This redefinition of authorship brings the problem of meaning with it. Compton's (2016) oatmeal problem showed that variation alone does not produce meaning. But it does not follow from this that procedurality lacks the capacity for meaning.

Ferreira (2015) positions procedurality as a semiotic resource: the meaning of a work resides not only in its visual output but also in the operative logic of the rules and constraints. Bogost's (2007) theory of procedural rhetoric carries this further: a system's rules directly encode its author's worldview and understanding of causality. Where meaning in traditional art is constructed through images or words, in procedural art meaning also resides in how the work behaves. This parallels the shift Brady (1987) identifies in Goethe: from reading the completed form (Gestalt) to reading the dynamic principles that produce it (Bildung).

When the questions of meaning and authorship are considered together, a third question opens: what kind of aesthetic experience arises when the distance between rule and output grows large? Procedural systems produce unpredictable complexity from the interaction of simple rules. This phenomenon of emergence prepares the ground for a specific aesthetic experience. According to McCormack and Dorin (2001), the viewer encounters this complexity, which comprehension cannot easily follow, with a double affect; the artist frequently experiences the same. This double affect can be read alongside two familiar categories in Kant's aesthetic theory (Kant, 1790/2000): the terror in the face of magnitude and force that characterizes the dynamical sublime, and the admiration arising from the capacity to comprehend infinity that characterizes the mathematical sublime. The computational sublime helps explain why procedural art cannot be reduced to a purely technical activity: when the distance between rule and output exceeds human comprehension, the resulting experience acquires a quality distinct from beauty, one proper to the sublime.

The conceptual genealogy approach adopted in this chapter has genuine strengths alongside real limits. The conceptual affinity is strongest where Spinoza's natura naturans/naturata distinction corresponds to the rule/output relationship in procedural systems, and where Goethe's Urpflanze corresponds to the axiom/production-rule logic of L-systems. This resemblance is not equally strong throughout, however. Applying Aristotle's dynamis concept to a contemporary algorithmic system requires bridging a gap of twenty-four centuries and carries a risk of anachronism. The chapter has attempted to reduce this risk by presenting these comparisons not as chains of direct influence but as recurring conceptual formations; even so, some parallels are more speculative than others and should be read accordingly. The distance between the complexity of procedural systems and the complexity of philosophy must also be preserved, without falling into the trap of technoeuphoria, the assumption that technology can formalize everything.

TOWARD A PHILOSOPHICAL FRAMEWORK FOR PROCEDURAL ART

Throughout this chapter, Aristotle's grammar of potentiality, Spinoza's immanent causality, Goethe's logic of morphological transformation, and Whitehead's process ontology formed the four stations of a conceptual genealogy. Each of the four philosophers approached the same problem from different directions: how does form come into being, and what is the relationship between generative principle and generated result? The chapter also traced the counterparts of these questions in the natural sciences, in art history, and in contemporary digital practice. The central finding is this: in procedural art, the object of mimesis shifts from natura naturata to natura naturans. The procedural practitioner does not copy the completed things of nature; the object of creative attention becomes nature's manner of bringing things into being, that is, the logic of rule-governed formation. This shift is also visible in Halliwell's (2002) reading of mimesis and in the Grossklaus formula relayed by Gebauer and Wulf (1995): from imitation (Nachahmung) to production (Erzeugung), from external copying to immanent generative logic.

This finding has practical consequences. Authorship is repositioned: the artist is the author not of the output but of the generative system that determines the character of the output. Whitelaw's (2004) gardener metaphor and Murray's definition of writing rules (1997) say this in different words. Criteria of evaluation also change: aesthetic judgment shifts from the singular output to the quality of the generative system. This quality can be discussed within the frame of Galanter's (2003) concept of effective complexity, but it cannot be reduced to a single measure. Finally, the natura naturans/naturata distinction offers a concrete analytical tool: it makes it possible to read procedural works not as completed objects but as rule-governed processes of formation. Mateas (2005) defines procedural literacy as the capacity to read and write processes and to engage with procedural representation and aesthetics. Within this framework, such literacy can be understood not merely as a technical skill but as an increasingly important form of conceptual equipment in contemporary digital culture.

FUTURE RESEARCH DIRECTIONS

The conceptual framework constructed in this chapter is not a closed system; it opens several lines of inquiry. The first concerns the semiotic dimension of procedurality. Ferreira's (2015) inquiry into how rules generate meaning could be developed through Bogost's (2007) concept of procedural rhetoric, enabling systematic examination of the cultural and ideological encodings embedded in rules. The second direction concerns the position of procedural thinking relative to artificial intelligence. The distinction drawn in the introduction raises new questions: how will explicitly rule-based procedural systems relate to statistical models built on learned parameter spaces, and how may hybrid approaches combine the two?

The third extends the geographical scope. Eglash's (1999) documentation of African fractal village planning, Indian kolam floor ornaments, and Japanese Zen garden design principles suggest a broader non-Western history of rule-governed form generation that warrants a comparative research program. A phenomenological extension, particularly through accounts of embodied perception, could examine how practitioners experience procedural systems not only as rule structures but as perceptual and bodily encounters with unfolding form, while gender-oriented analyses could investigate how procedural systems encode assumptions about authorship, labor, and creative agency. Finally, extending the fractal aesthetics findings of Taylor et al. (2001) and Forsythe et al. (2011) to procedural outputs raises a research question: does the preference humans show for fractal structures respond equally to artificial fractals generated through rule-governed production? Investigating this systematically would reinforce the theoretical framework and yield both pedagogical and practical design implications.

CONCLUSION

Returning to the artist working in a node-based procedural environment: as described in the introduction, this artist does not draw individual trees to build a forest; instead, a generative system is designed that defines topography, distribution zones, growth rules, and orientation parameters. The forest emerges as a consequence of the system's operation. The chapter's central argument is that such a creative disposition cannot be understood merely as a technical innovation; it is a contemporary expression of a longer philosophical problem, one that conceives of form not as a completed object but as a generative process.

To this end, the chapter has proposed a conceptual genealogy running from Aristotle's dynamis to Spinoza's natura naturans/natura naturata distinction, from Goethe's Urpflanze to Whitehead's process ontology. These recurring conceptual affinities make visible why procedural thinking should be treated not merely as a software technique but as a broader ontological and aesthetic orientation. The central conclusion is this: in procedural art, the object of mimesis shifts. Imitation is directed no longer only toward nature's completed products but toward nature's manner of producing form. The procedural practitioner, in most cases, models not direct copies of objects but the rules, relations, and logics of transformation that make those objects possible. The authorship of the procedural artist therefore lies not so much in producing a singular output as in designing the generative system and the possibility space from which outputs can be derived.

This framework also transforms criteria of evaluation. The aesthetic value of a procedural work lies not only in the singular output but in the explanatory power of the generative system, its capacity for variation, and its balance between constraints and emergence. One practical contribution of this genealogy is that the natura naturans/natura naturata distinction offers a concrete analytical lens for reading diverse examples, from Islamic geometric art to computational botany to contemporary node-based production, as rule-governed formations rather than completed objects. Procedural thinking is a mode of creation too broad to be reduced to a single software regime, yet too concrete to remain only an abstract metaphor. The procedural practitioner treats form not as something imposed from outside but as an event generated through immanent rules. This is not only a new method of production but a different way of thinking about form, authorship, and creation.

ACKNOWLEDGMENT

This research received no specific grant from any funding agency in the public, commercial, or not-for-profit sectors. AI-assisted tools were used solely for language refinement and readability improvements during the preparation of this manuscript. No AI tools were used to generate, create, or contribute to the scholarly content, arguments, or conclusions of this chapter. The author reviewed all output and takes full responsibility for the content of the manuscript.

REFERENCES

Aristotle, . (1984a). Metaphysics. In Barnes, J. (Ed.), *The complete works of Aristotle: The revised Oxford translation* (Vol. 2; Ross, W. D., Trans.). Princeton University Press.

Aristotle, . (1984b). Physics. In Barnes, J. (Ed.), *The complete works of Aristotle: The revised Oxford translation* (Vol. 1; Hardie, R. P., & Gaye, R. K., Trans.). Princeton University Press.

Aristotle, . (1984c). Poetics. In Barnes, J. (Ed.), *The complete works of Aristotle: The revised Oxford translation* (Vol. 2; Bywater, I., Trans.). Princeton University Press.

Barker, T. (2012). *Time and the digital: Connecting technology, aesthetics, and a process philosophy of time.* Dartmouth College Press.

Benjamin, W. (1977). *The origin of German tragic drama* (Osborne, J., Trans.). Verso. (Original work published 1928)

Bense, M. (1971). The projects of generative aesthetics. In J. Reichardt (Ed.), *Cybernetics, art and ideas* (pp. 57–60). Studio Vista. (Original German text published 1965)

Boden, M. A., & Edmonds, E. A. (2009). What is generative art? *Digital Creativity (Exeter)*, *20*(1–2), 21–46. DOI: 10.1080/14626260902867915

Bogost, I. (2007). *Persuasive games: The expressive power of videogames.* MIT Press. DOI: 10.7551/mitpress/5334.001.0001

Bommasani, R., Hudson, D. A., Adeli, E., Altman, R., Arora, S., von Arx, S., Bernstein, M., Bohg, J., Bosselut, A., Brunskill, E., Brynjolfsson, E., Buch, S., Card, D., Castellon, R., Chatterji, N., Chen, A., Creel, K., Davis, J., Demszky, D., . . . Liang, P. (2021). On the opportunities and risks of foundation models. *arXiv preprint arXiv:2108.07258.* https://arxiv.org/abs/2108.07258

Bonner, J. (2017). *Islamic geometric patterns: Their historical development and traditional methods of construction*. Springer. DOI: 10.1007/978-1-4419-0217-7

Brady, R. H. (1987). Form and cause in Goethe's morphology. In Amrine, R., Zucker, F. J., & Wheeler, H. (Eds.), *Goethe and the sciences: A reappraisal* (pp. 257–300). D. Reidel. DOI: 10.1007/978-94-009-3761-1_14

Burnham, J. (1968). Systems esthetics. *Artforum*, *7*(1), 30–35.

Burrell, J. (2016). How the machine 'thinks': Understanding opacity in machine learning algorithms. *Big Data & Society*, *3*(1), 1–12. DOI: 10.1177/2053951715622512

Compton, K. (2016, February 10). *So you want to build a generator* [Blog post]. Tumblr. https://galaxykate0.tumblr.com/post/139774965871

Della Rocca, M. (2008). *Spinoza*. Routledge. DOI: 10.4324/9780203894583

Dorin, A., McCabe, J., McCormack, J., Monro, G., & Whitelaw, M. (2012). A framework for understanding generative art. *Digital Creativity (Exeter)*, *23*(3–4), 239–259. DOI: 10.1080/14626268.2012.709940

Eglash, R. (1999). *African fractals: Modern computing and indigenous design*. Rutgers University Press.

Fazi, M. B. (2018). *Contingent computation: Abstraction, experience, and indeterminacy in computational aesthetics*. Rowman & Littlefield International. DOI: 10.5040/9798881812027

Ferreira, D. (2015). The meaning potential of procedurality. In *Proceedings of the 14th Brazilian Symposium on Computer Games and Digital Entertainment (SBGames 2015)*. SBC.

Forsythe, A., Nadal, M., Sheehy, N., Cela-Conde, C. J., & Sawey, M. (2011). Predicting beauty: Fractal dimension and visual complexity in art. *British Journal of Psychology*, *102*(1), 49–70. DOI: 10.1348/000712610X498958 PMID: 21241285

Galanter, P. (2003). What is generative art? Complexity theory as a context for art theory. In *Proceedings of the International Conference on Generative Art (GA2003)*. Politecnico di Milano.

Garrett, D. (2018). *Nature and necessity in Spinoza's philosophy*. Oxford University Press.

Gebauer, G., & Wulf, C. (1995). *Mimesis: Culture, art, society* (Reneau, D., Trans.). University of California Press.

Goethe, J. W. von. (1952). Versuch die Metamorphose der Pflanzen zu erklären. E. Trunz (Ed.) Hamburger Ausgabe, Vol. 13). C. H. Beck. (Original work published 1790)

Goethe, J. W. von. (1962). Italienische Reise. E. Trunz (Ed.) Hamburger Ausgabe, Vol. 11). C. H. Beck. (Original work published 1816)

Halliwell, S. (2002). *The aesthetics of mimesis: Ancient texts and modern problems*. Princeton University Press.

Hello Games. (2016). *No Man's Sky* [Video game]. Hello Games.

Kant, I. (2000). Critique of the power of judgment. (P. Guyer, Ed. & Trans., E. Matthews, Trans). Cambridge University Press. (Original work published 1790) DOI: 10.1017/CBO9780511804656

Kaplan, C. S. (2005). Islamic star patterns from polygons in contact. *Proceedings. Graphics Interface (Conference), 2005*, 177–185.

Karth, I., & Compton, K. (2023). Conceptual art made real: Why procedural content generation is impossible. In *Proceedings of the Foundations of Digital Games 2023 (FDG '23)*. ACM. DOI: 10.1145/3582437.3582470

LeWitt, S. (1967). Paragraphs on conceptual art. *Artforum*, *5*(10), 79–83.

LeWitt, S. (1969). Sentences on conceptual art. *Art-Language*, *1*(1), 11–13.

Lu, P. J., & Steinhardt, P. J. (2007). Decagonal and quasi-crystalline tilings in medieval Islamic architecture. *Science*, *315*(5815), 1106–1110. DOI: 10.1126/science.1135491 PMID: 17322056

Manovich, L. (2024). Separate and reassemble: Generative AI through the lens of art and media histories. *MATRIZes*, *18*(2), 7–18. DOI: 10.11606/issn.1982-8160.v18i2p7-18

Mateas, M. (2005). Procedural literacy: Educating the new media practitioner. *On the Horizon*, *13*(2), 101–111. DOI: 10.1108/10748120510608133

McCormack, J., & Dorin, A. (2001). Art, emergence and the computational sublime. *Proceedings of Second Iteration: A Conference on Generative Systems in the Electronic Arts* (pp. 67–81). CEMA.

Murray, J. H. (1997). *Hamlet on the holodeck: The future of narrative in cyberspace*. Free Press.

Perlin, K. (1985). An image synthesizer. *Computer Graphics*, *19*(3), 287–296. DOI: 10.1145/325165.325247

Petteni, O. (2022). The contemporary legacy of Goethean morphology: From *Anschauende Urteilskraft* to algorithmic pattern recognition, generation, and exploration. *Goethe Yearbook, 29*(1), 43–72. DOI: 10.1353/gyr.2022.0002

Prusinkiewicz, P., & Lindenmayer, A. (1990). *The algorithmic beauty of plants.* Springer-Verlag. DOI: 10.1007/978-1-4613-8476-2

Queloz, M. (2021). *The practical origins of ideas: Genealogy as conceptual reverse-engineering*. Oxford University Press. DOI: 10.1093/oso/9780198868705.001.0001

Roe-Dale, A., & Pfaff, C. (2019). Vera Molnar's machine imaginaire. *Journal of Mathematics and the Arts, 13*(3), 221–245.

Smith, G., & Whitehead, J. (2010). Analyzing the expressive range of a level generator. *Proceedings of the 2010 Workshop on Procedural Content Generation in Games (PCGames '10).* ACM. DOI: 10.1145/1814256.1814260

Spinoza, B. (1985). *The collected works of Spinoza* (Vol. 1; Curley, E., Trans.). Princeton University Press. (Original work published 1677)

Stiny, G., & Gips, J. (1975). *Shape grammars and their uses: Artificial perception, shape generation and computer aesthetics.* Birkhauser.

Taylor, R. P., Newell, B. R., Spehar, B., & Clifford, C. W. G. (2001). Fractals: A resonance between art and nature? *Symmetry: Art and Science, 1–2*, 194–197.

Thompson, D. W. (1942). *On growth and form* (2nd ed.). Cambridge University Press. (Original work published 1917)

Vlasopoulos, M. (2016). Spinoza's God in Goethe's leaf: Morphology as a theory of the attributes. *Goethe Yearbook, 23*, 117–140.

Weijers, O. (1978). Contribution a l'histoire des termes 'natura naturans' et 'natura naturata' jusqu'a Spinoza. *Vivarium, 16*(1), 70–80. DOI: 10.1163/156853478X00049

Whitehead, A. N. (1978). *Process and reality: An essay in cosmology* (D. R. Griffin & D. W. Sherburne, Eds., Corrected ed.). Free Press. (Original work published 1929)

Whitelaw, M. (2004). *Metacreation: Art and artificial life.* MIT Press.

Witt, C. (2003). *Ways of being: Potentiality and actuality in Aristotle's Metaphysics.* Cornell University Press.

Chapter 3
Agents of Innovation or Inequity?
Reimagining Possibility and Responsibility in Interdisciplinary Approaches to Design and Art

Nicole Simon
http://orcid.org/0009-0004-0678-1300
SUNY Nassau Community College, USA

ABSTRACT

This chapter investigates how color operates as a visual language in digital communication, particularly through a virtual exchange project linking students across cultural and disciplinary divides. Rather than viewing color as merely aesthetic, this chapter treats it as a vehicle of meaning, identity, and negotiation. It explores how design thinking, cultural semiotics, and emerging practices in design education intersect with virtual exchange to challenge existing color norms. Drawing on recent scholarship in digital design, educational exchange, and semiotics, the chapter uses qualitative data—including student artefacts, peer feedback, and reflective journals—to show how collaborative virtual environments reveal and reframe color literacies in culturally situated ways.

INTRODUCTION: COLOR, CULTURE, AND DIGITAL INTERACTION

Color is often treated in design education as a formal variable—hue, saturation, contrast—governed by perceptual or technical rules. Contemporary research, however,

DOI: 10.4018/979-8-3373-6680-7.ch003

demonstrates that color meaning is contextual, relational, and culturally situated. Color operates not only as an aesthetic choice but as a semantic system shaped by social convention, technological mediation, and cultural history.

These dynamics are especially consequential in higher education, where STEM disciplines remain structured by specialization, hierarchical knowledge systems, and enduring cultural biases (McIntyre & Delaney, 2020). While disciplinary specialization supports technical expertise, it can limit students' capacity to engage with complex problems that require ethical reasoning, cultural awareness, and systems thinking. This tension is intensified by the increasing reliance on digital visual communication in STEM learning environments, where color, imagery, and interactive visualizations function as primary modes of meaning-making rather than supplemental aids (Mukherjee et al., 2021; Schwarz, 2025).

As visual representations play a central role in the production and circulation of scientific knowledge, questions of interpretation, accessibility, and responsibility become integral to learning itself. Visualizations do more than support data analysis; they shape how relationships, uncertainty, and risk are perceived. Within this context, color operates as a critical visual language—one that encodes information, guides attention, and carries cultural and ethical implications.

Research in color perception and inference underscores this complexity. Schloss (2024), for example, demonstrates that color meaning emerges not from isolated attributes but from relationships among colors and their conceptual contexts. In digital environments, these meanings are further mediated by technological factors such as display systems, calibration, and color modes. Color, therefore, cannot be treated as a neutral or universal code; it is a site of interpretation and difference.

This chapter examines these dynamics through a virtual exchange project that brought together students from art, visual communication, and design programs across multiple countries. Working in culturally and disciplinarily mixed teams, students co-created digital artifacts addressing themes such as *Color and Emotion*, *Brand Hue Across Cultures*, and *Color in Protest and Identity*. Using shared platforms, palette tools, and structured critique, participants surfaced assumptions about color and negotiated meaning across cultural contexts. Through this process, students became not only designers of visual artifacts but interpreters of culturally embedded visual codes.

Situating this project within broader debates in design studies and visual communication, the chapter approaches interdisciplinarity not as neutral collaboration but as a situated practice shaped by institutional norms, power relations, and cultural assumptions (Buchanan, 1992; Margolin, 2002). Contemporary design and visual communication increasingly operate at the intersection of science, technology, and social inquiry, expanding creative possibility while intensifying ethical responsibility. Designers and artists function not simply as image-makers, but as mediators of knowledge and participants in public discourse.

Framed through this lens, the chapter explores how interdisciplinary practice reshapes both *possibility*—the capacity to imagine and construct alternative futures—and *responsibility*—the ethical obligations that accompany expanded creative agency. It argues that interdisciplinarity is not merely a methodological choice, but a critical stance toward authorship, representation, and impact in digitally mediated learning environments.

HEGEMONY, DECOLONIZATION, AND TRANSFORMATIVE PEDAGOGY IN STEM

Decolonizing pedagogy challenges epistemic hierarchies in STEM by recognizing learners' embodied experience, cultural knowledge, and collective histories as legitimate sources of insight (McIntyre & Delaney, 2020). Embodied learning strategies—such as makerspaces, interactive laboratories, fieldwork, and digital simulations—enable students to engage with scientific phenomena both cognitively and materially, fostering deeper understanding and critical awareness.

When aligned with Transformative Learning Theory (TLT), these approaches encourage learners to confront disorienting dilemmas, examine underlying assumptions, and develop perspectives that integrate ethical, cultural, and social dimensions of knowledge (Mezirow, 2000). Rather than treating learning as the accumulation of technical expertise, transformative pedagogy positions reflection and perspective change as central educational outcomes.

Historically, STEM disciplines have reinforced epistemic hierarchies that privilege dominant cultural and disciplinary perspectives while marginalizing alternative ways of knowing (Kidman & Tan, 2025). These hierarchies shape curricula, assessment practices, and norms of legitimacy, limiting opportunities for students to engage critically with complex social and environmental challenges. Addressing these limitations requires pedagogical forms capable of integrating multiple epistemologies—forms most effectively realized through transdisciplinary and representational practices. From this perspective, visual and color-mediated forms of representation are not supplementary to STEM learning but central to its transformation. They offer ways to hold complexity, difference, and relational meaning, supporting pedagogies that foreground ethical inquiry and cultural responsiveness alongside technical competence.

TRANSDISCIPLINARITY AND THE CREATION OF NEW REPRESENTATIONAL GENRES

Transdisciplinary pedagogy integrates multiple disciplines, epistemologies, and methods to produce knowledge artifacts that exceed traditional academic boundaries (Bardecki, 2019). In STEM education, this integration often involves the convergence of science, mathematics, engineering, technology, and design to create visual, interactive, and narrative forms of representation.

Color plays a pivotal role in these emergent genres, functioning as a visual language that communicates relationships, patterns, and hierarchies across quantitative and qualitative domains (Lyu, 2025). Heat maps, for example, use color gradients to convey environmental risk, while molecular visualizations rely on hue to differentiate structural components. Through the design of color-mediated artifacts, learners engage in embodied sense-making that supports cognitive comprehension, ethical reflection, and collaborative interpretation (Guan & Wang, 2022).

Transdisciplinary projects require students to negotiate shared vocabularies, integrate diverse forms of expertise, and produce artifacts that are simultaneously analytical, expressive, and communicative. In doing so, they reposition representation itself as a site of learning, where meaning is constructed through dialogue rather than transmitted as fixed knowledge.

COLOR, DESIGN, AND VISUAL COMMUNICATION IN CONTEMPORARY STEM

Design, art, and visual communication are increasingly practiced within conditions of complexity that exceed the capacity of any single discipline. Designers collaborate with scientists, artists work with data and algorithms, and visual communicators shape narratives across social, technological, and political systems. In this context, interdisciplinarity is no longer an exception or experimental add-on; it has become a defining condition of contemporary creative practice. Yet while interdisciplinarity expands what practitioners *can* do, it also raises pressing questions about what they *should* do.

Contemporary STEM education faces the dual challenge of fostering disciplinary mastery while also cultivating interdisciplinary, ethical, and creative competencies necessary for addressing complex real-world problems (McIntyre & Delaney, 2020). Traditional pedagogical approaches often reinforce hierarchical knowledge structures, privileging Western epistemologies and quantitative reasoning at the expense of marginalized perspectives. In response, educators are increasingly exploring critical, transdisciplinary, and embodied pedagogies, coupled with digital visual communication, as strategies to cultivate richer learning experiences.

Color-rich visualizations, interactive dashboards, and dynamic storytelling have emerged as essential tools in STEM education. Research indicates that visual representations may surpass textual explanations in their capacity to convey complex scientific information efficiently (Schwarz, 2025). By integrating color as a visual language, students can encode and interpret multidimensional data, detect patterns, and communicate insights across disciplinary and cultural boundaries. This chapter explores how TLT, transdisciplinary design, embodied learning, and visual literacy converge to foster critical, creative, and ethically grounded STEM education, particularly in the context of environmental problem-solving.

Interdisciplinary approaches fundamentally reframe both possibility and responsibility in design, art, and visual communication. Possibility refers not only to new tools, methods, or outputs, but to expanded ways of imagining futures, reframing problems, and producing meaning. Responsibility, by contrast, concerns the ethical, social, and ecological implications of these expanded capacities. As creative practices gain influence—often shaping public understanding, behavior, and policy—questions of accountability, power, and care become inseparable from the act of making.

TRANSFORMATIVE LEARNING THEORY (TLT) AND COLOR-MEDIATED VISUAL COMMUNICATION

Transformative Learning Theory provides a critical framework for understanding how visual communication—and color-mediated practices in particular—can function as sites of ethical reflection and interdisciplinary integration in STEM education. Rather than framing learning as the acquisition of technical knowledge alone, TLT emphasizes processes of critical reflection, perspective transformation, and reflective discourse (Mezirow, 2000).

When applied to design-oriented STEM practices, this framework foregrounds representation as an active driver of learning. Decisions about how data are visualized, how color encodes meaning, and how visual choices shape interpretation become moments of inquiry rather than neutral technical acts. Color-mediated visual communication thus functions not only as a means of conveying information, but as a medium through which learners negotiate meaning, responsibility, and disciplinary boundaries.

Color operates cognitively, semiotically, and culturally within this framework (Mukherjee et al., 2021; Lyu, 2025). It enables rapid perception of complex data, supports cross-cultural interpretation, and carries emotional and ethical significance. Developing visual and color literacy equips learners to design and critique representations responsibly, attending to issues of accessibility, clarity, and cultural context (Sun & Zhu, 2022; Schwarz, 2025).

CONCEPTUAL FRAMEWORK: COLOR, VISUAL LITERACY, AND TRANSFORMATIVE STEM LEARNING

This chapter proposes a conceptual framework that synthesizes Transformative Learning Theory, color as visual language, visual literacy, embodied pedagogy, and transdisciplinary practice within STEM education. Rather than treating these elements as discrete strategies, the framework models learning as an integrated and iterative process in which reflection, representation, and collaboration are mutually reinforcing.

The framework positions critical reflection and ethical reasoning as central outcomes of learning, activated through encounters with disorienting dilemmas such as environmental uncertainty or conflicting data. In parallel, color-mediated visual communication functions as a pathway for encoding and interpreting complex relationships, linking visual literacy to ethical awareness and cultural responsiveness.

Embodied and transdisciplinary practices connect these pathways by situating learning within collaborative, hands-on engagement. Through the creation of multimodal artifacts, learners integrate scientific analysis with design and visual communication, translating theoretical insight into socially responsive problem-solving. The framework thus conceptualizes STEM learning as a dynamic ecosystem in which meaning, responsibility, and action are continually negotiated.

The diagram represents learning as an iterative process in which critical reflection, color-mediated visual representation, and transdisciplinary collaboration inform one another. Transformative Learning Theory anchors the framework by positioning ethical reflection and perspective transformation as core outcomes of STEM education. Color functions as a visual language that supports interpretation, meaning-making, and cultural responsiveness, while embodied and transdisciplinary practices situate learning within collaborative, practice-based engagement. Together, these pathways converge toward socially responsive STEM problem-solving, emphasizing sustainability, equity, and responsibility.

Figure 1. Conceptual framework: Color, visual literacy, and transformative STEM learning

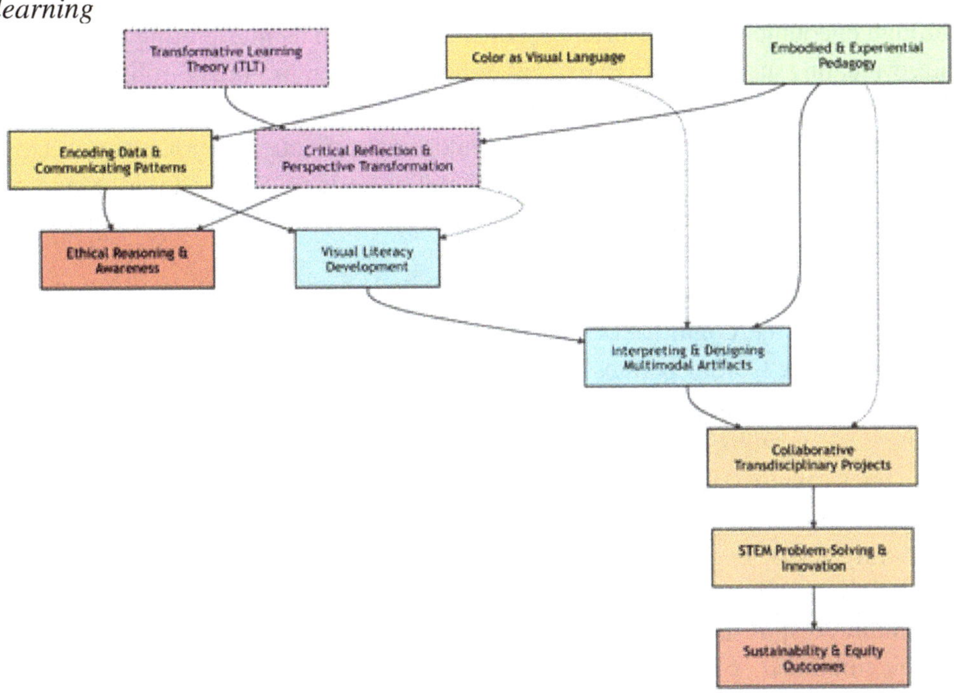

While Figure 1 visualizes learning as an interconnected and iterative process, it also functions as a diagnostic and pedagogical tool. Each pathway—critical reflection, color as visual language, and embodied transdisciplinary collaboration—represents a site where assumptions may be stabilized or unsettled. Movement across these pathways is not neutral: it surfaces tensions between efficiency and care, clarity and cultural specificity, innovation and accountability.

In practice, the framework is mobilized through cycles of making and critique in which students are prompted to ask not only how color communicates, but for whom, under what cultural conditions, and with what consequences. The diagram thus reframes visual representation as an ethical act embedded in systems of power, access, and interpretation rather than a purely technical response to data.

The conceptual diagram presents a top-to-bottom learning flow that visualizes how Transformative Learning Theory, color as visual language, visual literacy, embodied pedagogy, and transdisciplinary collaboration interact to support ethical, creative, and socially responsive STEM education (Figure 1). Rather than depicting learning as a linear progression, the model emphasizes interconnection and iteration, showing how reflection, representation, and collaboration continually inform one another across the learning process.

At the top of the diagram, TLT anchors the learning flow by foregrounding critical reflection, perspective transformation, and ethical reasoning (Mezirow, 2000). Through encounters with disorienting dilemmas—such as interpreting conflicting data, evaluating sustainability trade-offs, or confronting environmental uncertainty—learners are prompted to examine underlying assumptions and reconsider established ways of knowing. The pathway from critical reflection to ethical awareness illustrates how learning extends beyond cognition to include moral reasoning and responsibility, positioning ethical judgment as a core outcome of STEM education rather than an ancillary concern.

Running parallel to this reflective pathway, the color as visual language pathway highlights the cognitive, semiotic, and cultural functions of color in STEM communication. Color operates as a means of encoding complex data, revealing patterns, and supporting interpretation across disciplinary and cultural contexts. By linking data encoding to visual literacy development, the diagram emphasizes that proficiency in color-mediated representation is not merely aesthetic but foundational to meaning-making, accessibility, and ethical communication. The feedback loop connecting visual literacy to ethical awareness underscores that visual choices—particularly those involving color—carry consequences for interpretation, inclusion, and cultural responsiveness.

The embodied and transdisciplinary pathway reflects the role of hands-on engagement, collaboration, and cross-disciplinary integration in deepening learning. Embodied and experiential pedagogies feed into both critical reflection and the design of multimodal artifacts, demonstrating how physical engagement and experimentation enhance understanding and support reflective inquiry. Through collaborative transdisciplinary projects, learners synthesize perspectives from science, mathematics, technology, design, and art to create artifacts that are simultaneously analytical, expressive, and communicative. These activities foster cognitive integration, ethical reasoning, and creative problem-solving, enabling learners to translate theoretical insight into practical innovation.

The diagram culminates in STEM problem-solving and innovation, followed by sustainability and equity outcomes, highlighting the broader aims of the learning process. By integrating TLT, color-mediated visual literacy, and embodied transdisciplinary practice, learners develop the capacity to address complex, real-world challenges in ways that are scientifically rigorous, socially attentive, and ethically grounded. The diagram's cross-links reinforce the iterative nature of learning: reflection informs visual design, visual analysis deepens ethical awareness, and collaborative experimentation continually refines critical and creative competencies. In this way, the framework models STEM learning as a dynamic ecosystem in which meaning, responsibility, and action are continually negotiated rather than fixed.

Environmental STEM as an Illustrative Context

Environmental STEM education provides a compelling context for applying this framework, as it routinely confronts learners with uncertainty, risk, and ethical trade-offs. Color-mediated visualizations—such as heat maps, geospatial models, and narrative data representations—play a central role in shaping how environmental phenomena are interpreted and communicated. When embedded within embodied and transdisciplinary projects, these visual practices support critical reflection, visual literacy, and collaborative problem-solving. Environmental STEM therefore functions not as an exceptional case, but as a revealing context in which the relationships among color, ethics, and interdisciplinary learning become especially visible.

From Disciplinary Mastery to Relational Practice

Professional identity in STEM, design, and visual communication has traditionally been grounded in disciplinary mastery. While technical expertise remains essential, this model is insufficient for addressing complex challenges that are social, cultural, and ecological in nature. As color-mediated visual communication and transdisciplinary collaboration become central to meaning-making, professional competence is increasingly defined by relational practice: the ability to engage across disciplines, collaborate ethically, and remain accountable to the consequences of representational choices. This shift reframes designers and artists as sense-makers and facilitators rather than sole problem-solvers, expanding creative possibility while complicating questions of authorship and responsibility.

Pedagogical Strategies for Embodied and Transdisciplinary Learning

Responsibility in interdisciplinary creative work cannot be reduced to compliance with ethical guidelines or professional codes. Instead, it emerges through ongoing negotiation among intentions, contexts, and impacts. As Papanek (1985) observed, design choices—even when well-intentioned—can contribute to social and environmental harm, a concern amplified by the scale and reach of digital systems.

Practice-facing responsibility involves reflexivity: sustained attention to positionality, power relations, and the ethical implications of representation (Margolin, 2002). Participatory and co-design approaches offer strategies for redistributing agency and valuing lived experience as a form of expertise (Sanders & Stappers, 2008), though they require careful structuring to avoid tokenism or extraction. Rather than seeking to eliminate risk altogether, responsible interdisciplinary practice emphasizes attentiveness, dialogue, and adaptability throughout the creative process.

Design Thinking, Visual Semiotics, and Collaborative Exchange

The methodological frame for the project draws on design thinking (empathy, prototyping, iteration) and visual semiotics to allow students to explore meaning-making in color. Students conducted visual ethnography of color usage in their local contexts—both public media and digital platforms—and compared these across cultures. For example, one team compared branding palettes in Asian tech startups with Scandinavian minimalist design norms, discovering distinct differences in brightness, saturation, and symbolic associations.

Recent studies of virtual exchange show the potential for these settings to foster professional awareness, cultural reflexivity, and new design literacies. Symeonidis & Impedovo (2023) studied virtual exchange among student teachers across Europe and found that tasks involving multimodal digital artefacts fostered both creative and intercultural awareness. Meanwhile, Weaver, McDonald, Louie, & Woodman (2024) in a scoping review emphasize how international virtual exchange has expanded as a response to COVID-19, showing both promise and challenges in equitable participation and technological access (Weaver et al., 2024). These works provide a theoretical and practical backdrop for situating our color-focused virtual exchange. These theoretical insights were not abstract. They played out in the lived experiences of students negotiating color across cultural and disciplinary lines.

COLOR AS CODE: INTERCULTURAL VISUAL LANGUAGE IN A GLOBAL VIRTUAL EXCHANGE

Color, often treated as a fixed visual constant in design pedagogy, reveals itself in this chapter as an unstable, negotiated code—deeply shaped by cultural narratives, geopolitical histories, and the asymmetries of global visual culture. Within the virtual exchange project described here, students did not simply use color—they encountered it as a contested site of meaning, one that demanded critical reflection on their own positionalities and inherited design norms. In co-creating digital artefacts across borders, they engaged not only with hue and contrast, but with questions of symbolism, emotional resonance, and the politics of visual representation. What emerged were moments of friction and discovery: color palettes that carried joy in one culture signaled mourning in another; corporate blues that connoted trust in one context evoked state surveillance in another. Rather than flattening these differences into a universalist color theory, the project invited students to dwell in complexity—to see color not as neutral code, but as culturally charged visual language.

Yet this approach to color as intercultural code also raises deeper pedagogical questions about who defines visual norms, whose perspectives are centered in global design education, and what tools are available to surface these tensions. The chapter shows how students, guided by design thinking and visual semiotics, enacted an emergent form of critical visual literacy—one that was not only technical or aesthetic, but ethical. Importantly, the virtual nature of the exchange highlighted new forms of access and exclusion: while some students thrived in multimodal digital platforms, others encountered linguistic, temporal, or technological barriers that shaped their ability to participate fully. In this way, the exchange became a mirror of broader inequities in global education and creative industries. Still, the project offered more than critique—it pointed toward possibility: a model of visual communication that is collaborative, reflexive, and attentive to cultural specificity. By positioning color as code, not constant, the chapter reframes digital design as a space of intercultural negotiation and shared meaning-making.

IMPLICATIONS FOR EQUITY, INNOVATION, AND SUSTAINABILITY

Color-mediated visual communication and transdisciplinary pedagogies carry significant implications for equity in STEM education by expanding who can access, interpret, and contribute to scientific knowledge. Visual literacy, coupled with ethical reflection, enables students to communicate complex concepts to diverse audiences, challenging epistemic hierarchies that privilege technical or disciplinary expertise alone. When color is treated as a culturally situated visual language rather than a neutral design choice, visualizations become tools for inclusion, supporting accessibility, cross-cultural interpretation, and more democratic forms of knowledge production (Kidman & Tan, 2025).

In sustainability education, color-coded representations play a critical role in rendering environmental risk, resource distribution, and climate impacts perceptible and actionable. Heat maps, gradient scales, and narrative visualizations allow learners to engage with large-scale, abstract systems in ways that support sense-making and ethical decision-making. By integrating visual literacy with transdisciplinary design practices, students are better equipped to consider ecological, social, and cultural dimensions simultaneously, fostering forms of innovation that are responsive rather than extractive (Chang et al., 2024; Sun & Zhu, 2022).

More broadly, visual storytelling that leverages color encourages creative engagement while foregrounding responsibility. When technical mastery is integrated with semiotic awareness, learners develop the capacity to design solutions that are not only innovative but also ethically grounded and socially attentive. In this way, the integration of Transformative Learning Theory, color-mediated visual communication, and transdisciplinary pedagogy prepares students to navigate complex STEM challenges with reflexivity, care, and an expanded sense of accountability.

RESPONSIBILITY AS AN ONGOING PRACTICE

Responsibility in interdisciplinary creative work cannot be reduced to compliance with ethical guidelines or professional codes. Instead, it emerges through ongoing negotiation among intentions, contexts, and impacts. Victor Papanek's early critique of socially irresponsible design highlighted how seemingly benign artifacts can contribute to environmental degradation and social harm (Papanek, 1985). Today, these concerns are amplified by the reach of networked technologies and data-driven systems.

Practice-facing responsibility involves reflexivity—the ability to critically examine one's own role, assumptions, and limitations. It also involves recognizing that design and art are never neutral. Choices about what to visualize, whose voices to include, and which futures to imagine are inherently political, even when framed as technical or aesthetic decisions (Margolin, 2002).

Interdisciplinary collaboration can both mitigate and exacerbate these challenges. On one hand, diverse perspectives can surface blind spots and challenge dominant narratives. On the other, power imbalances among disciplines and institutions can marginalize certain forms of knowledge, particularly those rooted in lived experience or community practice. Participatory and co-design approaches attempt to address this tension by redistributing agency and valuing non-professional expertise (Sanders & Stappers, 2008). For practitioners, responsibility thus becomes less about avoiding harm altogether—an impossible task—and more about cultivating attentiveness, dialogue, and adaptability throughout the design or creative process.

Why a Practice-Facing Lens Matters

Much writing on interdisciplinarity remains abstract or institutionally focused, emphasizing frameworks, methodologies, or disciplinary boundaries. While valuable, such perspectives can feel distant from the realities of practice, where constraints, timelines, and stakeholder expectations shape decision-making. This chapter adopts a practice-facing lens to bridge that gap.

Rather than prescribing a single model of interdisciplinary work, the chapter explores patterns and tensions that recur across contexts. How do practitioners balance experimentation with accountability? How does visual communication function differently when it is explanatory, speculative, or activist? What kinds of educational and organizational structures support responsible interdisciplinary practice? By addressing these questions, the chapter aims to support reflective practitioners who seek to expand possibility without losing sight of responsibility. Interdisciplinarity, approached critically, becomes not a solution in itself but a means of engaging complexity with humility and care.

Education and Pedagogy for Interdisciplinary Futures

Reimagining possibility and responsibility necessitate corresponding changes in education. Traditional disciplinary silos often inadequately prepare students for the complexity and ambiguity of contemporary creative practice. Interdisciplinary pedagogy emphasizes collaboration, critical theory, and ethical reasoning alongside technical proficiency (Cross, 2006).

Studio-based learning environments that integrate research, making, and reflection support the development of systems literacy and ethical sensitivity. Engaging students with real-world contexts and diverse collaborators fosters an understanding of design and art as relational practices rather than isolated acts of creation (Manzini, 2015). Such pedagogical approaches encourage students to navigate uncertainty while remaining accountable to social and environmental concerns.

Importantly, interdisciplinary education must also interrogate power dynamics within knowledge production. Decisions about which histories, perspectives, and methods are taught reflect broader cultural values and exclusions. Recognizing design and art as culturally situated practices enables more responsible and inclusive forms of interdisciplinary engagement (Papanek, 1985).

Color, Emotional Associations, and Identity

Another area this chapter explores is how colors evoke emotional meaning and identity across cultures. A recent paper using a "fuzzy set" approach (Muratbekova & Shamoi, 2023) demonstrates strong associations between certain colors and specific emotions (for instance, yellow with happiness, gray with fear), and argues such associations are both statistically significant and culturally inflected. In the student exchange, similar associations emerged—yet with variations: in some cultural contexts, certain colors associated with political or religious symbolism altered the emotional resonance of a palette.

Color semiotics and grammar more broadly are also under discussion in current research. "Color Theory and Semiotics: Exploring the Relationship Between Visual Semiotics and Color," an article accepted in early 2024, advances models for "color grammar," "color harmony," and "color combinations," showing how general semiotic theory can help us understand color as part of a larger communicative system (Elhefnawy et al., 2026). These theoretical foundations inform how in our virtual exchange, students reflected not just on color choice, but on how color combinations, contrasts, and cultural palette norms function as implicit communicative grammar.

INTERDISCIPLINARITY AS A GENERATIVE FRAMEWORK

Interdisciplinarity in creative practice enables the integration of diverse epistemologies, methods, and value systems. Rather than blending disciplines superficially, meaningful interdisciplinary work often involves productive tension: differing assumptions about truth, aesthetics, evidence, and purpose are brought into dialogue (Cross, 2006). This friction can generate new forms of knowledge and novel modes of expression that are inaccessible within a single disciplinary framework.

In design and visual communication, interdisciplinary approaches have reshaped processes of problem framing. Buchanan (1992) characterizes design problems as "wicked," emphasizing their indeterminacy and resistance to linear solutions. Issues such as climate change, public health, misinformation, and social inequality exemplify this condition and demand collaborative approaches that integrate design with social science, policy, and community knowledge (Manzini, 2015).

Artistic practices have similarly embraced interdisciplinarity to challenge dominant narratives and propose alternative imaginaries. By incorporating scientific data, computational processes, and participatory methods, contemporary artists expand the scope of visual communication, transforming abstract or invisible phenomena into experiential forms that invite critical reflection and public engagement (Margolin, 2002).

REIMAGINING POSSIBILITY THROUGH SPECULATION AND SYSTEMS THINKING

One of the most significant contributions of interdisciplinary practice is its capacity to reimagine possibility. Speculative and critical design approaches draw from philosophy, futures studies, and science fiction to explore hypothetical scenarios that question present assumptions (Dunne & Raby, 2013). These practices do not aim to predict the future or offer immediate solutions; rather, they provoke ethical inquiry and expand the range of conceivable social, technological, and cultural outcomes.

Systems thinking further strengthens this speculative capacity by emphasizing relationships, feedback loops, and unintended consequences within complex environments. Designers who adopt systems-oriented approaches shift their focus from isolated artifacts to networks of interaction and influence (Findeli & Bousbaci, 2005). Visual communication plays a critical role in this process, translating complexity into diagrams, maps, and interactive visualizations that make systemic relationships legible to diverse audiences.

By integrating systems thinking with artistic experimentation, interdisciplinary practices resist reductive narratives of progress based solely on efficiency or innovation. Instead, they foreground uncertainty, plurality, and the coexistence of multiple futures, reinforcing the idea that design and art are cultural practices embedded in social and political contexts (Dunne & Raby, 2013). Interdisciplinary approaches significantly expand the realm of what is possible in design, art, and visual communication. Beyond enabling technical collaboration, they reshape how practitioners imagine futures, frame problems, and explore alternatives. Possibility, in this context, is not limited to innovation or novelty; it encompasses the capacity to challenge assumptions, visualize complexity, and open spaces for reflection and dialogue.

This section examines two closely related practice orientations—speculation and systems thinking—and how they function as tools for reimagining possibility in interdisciplinary creative work. Both approaches encourage practitioners to move beyond immediate solutions and engage with uncertainty as a productive condition.

SPECULATION AS A PRACTICE OF INQUIRY

Speculative approaches have gained prominence in interdisciplinary design and art practices as a way of engaging with emerging technologies and social change. Speculative design, critical design, and design fiction draw from disciplines such as philosophy, futures studies, and science fiction to explore "what if" scenarios rather than "what is" (Dunne & Raby, 2013). For practitioners, speculation provides a framework for thinking beyond current constraints without abandoning responsibility.

In practice-facing contexts, speculative work often takes the form of artifacts, narratives, or visual systems that materialize possible futures. These may include fictional products, imagined interfaces, or alternative policy scenarios. Importantly, such artifacts are not intended for direct implementation; they function as conversational devices that provoke discussion among stakeholders, audiences, and collaborators.

Speculation expands possibility by legitimizing ambiguity and imagination as integral to professional practice. It allows designers and artists to surface ethical tensions, question dominant trajectories, and explore consequences before they become irreversible. For example, speculative visualizations of data surveillance or climate futures can make abstract risks emotionally and cognitively accessible, fostering critical engagement rather than passive consumption.

However, speculative practice also raises questions of responsibility. Futures are never neutral; they reflect the values and assumptions of those who imagine them. Interdisciplinary collaboration can help mitigate this risk by bringing diverse perspectives into the speculative process, challenging singular or technocentric visions of the future.

VISUALIZING FUTURES ACROSS DISCIPLINES

Visual communication plays a central role in speculative practice, particularly in interdisciplinary contexts where collaborators may hold different assumptions and vocabularies. Visual artifacts serve as boundary objects—shared references that enable dialogue across disciplines without requiring full consensus. Diagrams, storyboards, prototypes, and scenarios help make speculative ideas tangible and debatable.

For practitioners, this function of visual communication expands its scope beyond persuasion or explanation. Visuals become tools for thinking together, enabling teams to externalize ideas, test assumptions, and explore alternatives. This collaborative visualization process often reveals conflicts or blind spots that might otherwise remain implicit.

Interdisciplinary speculative projects frequently blend artistic expression with informational clarity. The aesthetic dimension invites emotional engagement, while the communicative dimension supports analysis and critique. This hybrid quality enhances possibility by resisting binary distinctions between art and design, expression and utility. Yet this hybridity also complicates evaluation. Speculative visuals may be judged differently by different disciplines—valued for conceptual rigor in one context and dismissed as impractical in another. Practice-facing interdisciplinarity requires practitioners to navigate these tensions, articulating the purpose and value of speculative work in ways that resonate across domains.

SYSTEMS THINKING AND THE EXPANSION OF CREATIVE SCOPE

While speculation opens imaginative horizons, systems thinking grounds possibility in an awareness of complexity and interdependence. Systems-oriented approaches encourage practitioners to consider how elements interact over time, producing emergent effects that cannot be predicted by analyzing components in isolation (Findeli & Bousbaci, 2005).

In interdisciplinary practice, systems thinking often manifests through mapping and modeling activities. Stakeholder maps, causal loop diagrams, and journey maps help teams visualize relationships among actors, resources, and influences. These visual tools are particularly valuable in contexts where creative interventions intersect with social, ecological, or technological systems.

For designers and visual communicators, systems thinking expands possibility by shifting the unit of intervention. Instead of designing a single object or message, practitioners may design platforms, processes, or conditions that enable ongoing adaptation. This shift aligns with practice-facing realities, where long-term impact often depends on how work is taken up and transformed by others. Systems thinking also reframes failure and success. In complex systems, interventions rarely produce linear outcomes. Unintended consequences are not anomalies but expected features. Recognizing this dynamic encourages iterative experimentation and learning rather than premature closure.

MAKING COMPLEXITY LEGIBLE

One of the key contributions of interdisciplinary creative practice is its ability to make complexity legible without oversimplifying it. Visual communication plays a crucial role in this translation, transforming abstract systems into accessible forms while preserving nuance. For practitioners, the challenge lies in balancing clarity with openness. Simplified visuals can support understanding and decision-making, but they may also obscure uncertainty, power dynamics, or marginalized perspectives. Interdisciplinary teams can address this tension by layering information, incorporating multiple viewpoints, and designing interactive or participatory visualizations.

Artistic strategies are particularly effective in this context. Metaphor, narrative, and sensory engagement can convey complexity in ways that purely analytical representations cannot. By engaging audiences emotionally as well as cognitively, interdisciplinary visual practices expand the range of possible interpretations and responses. However, making complexity visible also entails responsibility. What is rendered visible becomes actionable; what remains invisible may be neglected. Practitioners must therefore consider not only how to visualize systems, but why certain aspects are emphasized and others omitted.

POSSIBILITY AS COLLECTIVE IMAGINATION

Interdisciplinary practice reframes possibility as a collective rather than individual endeavor. Speculation and systems thinking both rely on collaboration, dialogue, and shared exploration. Visual artifacts function as mediators in this process, enabling participants to imagine together across disciplinary and cultural boundaries. This collective orientation challenges traditional narratives of authorship and creativity. Possibility emerges from interaction rather than inspiration alone. For practitioners, embracing this shift can be both liberating and unsettling, as it requires letting go of control and acknowledging uncertainty. At the same time, collective imagination carries ethical weight. Who participates in imagining futures? Whose voices shape speculative scenarios? Interdisciplinary practice offers tools for inclusivity, but it does not guarantee it. Responsibility lies in designing processes that invite diverse perspectives and remain attentive to power dynamics.

TENSIONS BETWEEN POSSIBILITY AND CONSTRAINT

Practice-facing interdisciplinarity must contend with real constraints: budgets, timelines, institutional expectations, and client demands. Speculative and systems-oriented approaches may be perceived as risky or impractical, particularly in commercial or policy-driven contexts.

Successful practitioners navigate these tensions by framing expanded possibility as a resource rather than a distraction. Speculative artifacts can support strategic thinking; systems maps can inform decision-making; visual narratives can align stakeholders around shared values. By articulating the practical relevance of these approaches, interdisciplinary practitioners sustain space for imagination within constrained environments. Importantly, constraint itself can generate possibility. Working within limits forces prioritization and creativity, encouraging practitioners to focus on leverage points within systems rather than exhaustive solutions. Interdisciplinary thinking supports this strategic orientation by highlighting where small interventions may produce disproportionate impact.

FROM POSSIBILITY TO RESPONSIBILITY

Expanded possibility inevitably leads to questions of responsibility. Speculation can inspire, but it can also mislead or exclude. Systems thinking can illuminate, but it can also overwhelm or depoliticize. For practitioners, the challenge is not to abandon these approaches, but to engage them critically and ethically. The next section turns explicitly to this challenge, examining how interdisciplinary practice reframes responsibility through ethics, power, and participation. Building on the expanded possibilities discussed here, it explores how designers, artists, and visual communicators can remain accountable to the social and cultural consequences of their work.

RESPONSIBILITY, ETHICS, AND POWER IN CREATIVE PRACTICE

As interdisciplinary practices expand creative influence, they also heighten ethical responsibility. Design and visual communication shape perception, behavior, and belief, often at significant scale. Papanek (1985) famously argued that designers bear responsibility for the social and ecological consequences of their work, a concern that has become increasingly urgent in the context of data-driven systems and algorithmic mediation.

Responsibility in interdisciplinary contexts requires reflexivity—an ongoing awareness of positionality, assumptions, and power relations. Ethical practice is not reducible to compliance or technical standards; rather, it emerges through situated engagement with stakeholders and affected communities (Sanders & Stappers, 2008). Participatory and co-design methodologies exemplify this shift by redistributing authorship and recognizing lived experience as a legitimate form of expertise. Art, too, bears responsibility in how it frames social issues. While provocation and ambiguity are central to artistic freedom, interdisciplinary art practices increasingly grapple with questions of consent, representation, and care, particularly when working with data, biological materials, or vulnerable populations.

Artistic practices also confront ethical questions as they intersect with science, technology, and social research. While ambiguity and provocation remain central to artistic inquiry, interdisciplinary art increasingly grapples with issues of consent, representation, and care, particularly when working with personal data, biological materials, or marginalized communities (Margolin, 2002). Responsibility, in this sense, involves balancing critical expression with attentiveness to impact.

Responsibility Beyond Individual Intent

Practitioners often approach ethics through the lens of intention: aiming to do good, avoid harm, or act responsibly. While intention matters, interdisciplinary practice reveals its limits. Design and art operate within complex systems where outcomes are shaped by interactions among multiple actors, institutions, and technologies. As a result, well-intentioned interventions can still produce harmful or exclusionary effects.

Papanek (1985) argued that designers bear responsibility not only for what they create, but for the broader consequences of their work. Today, this responsibility extends to how creative outputs circulate, scale, and are interpreted. Visual communication, in particular, can influence public perception in ways that exceed the practitioner's control, especially in digital environments. For practice-facing professionals, this reality calls for a shift from outcome-based ethics to process-oriented responsibility. Rather than assuming that ethical intent guarantees ethical impact, practitioners must engage in ongoing reflection, dialogue, and adaptation throughout a project's lifecycle.

Power and Positionality in Interdisciplinary Teams

Interdisciplinary collaboration is often celebrated as inherently equitable, bringing together diverse forms of expertise. In practice, however, power dynamics persist—both among disciplines and within project structures. Certain forms of knowledge, such as technical or quantitative expertise, may be privileged over experiential or cultural knowledge. Institutional authority, funding sources, and professional status further shape whose contributions carry weight. For designers, artists, and visual communicators, recognizing positionality is a critical component of responsibility. Positionality refers to how one's social, cultural, and professional position influences perspective and authority. In interdisciplinary contexts, practitioners must be attentive not only to their own positionality, but to how it interacts with others'.

Visual communication can either reinforce or challenge these power dynamics. For example, who is represented in visual narratives, how data is categorized, and which stories are foregrounded all reflect underlying values. Margolin (2002) emphasizes that design is a cultural practice embedded in political and economic structures, making power an unavoidable dimension of creative work. Practice-facing responsibility involves making these dynamics visible and open to critique, rather than allowing them to operate implicitly.

Representation, Visibility, and Ethics of Visual Form

Representation is one of the most ethically charged aspects of visual communication. Images do not merely depict reality; they actively construct meaning. In interdisciplinary projects addressing social issues, representational choices can influence empathy, stigma, and policy decisions. Ethical representation requires practitioners to consider how visual forms frame subjects and audiences. Simplified or abstracted visuals may improve clarity, but they can also erase context and individuality. Conversely, highly emotive imagery may provoke engagement while reinforcing stereotypes or exploiting vulnerability.

Interdisciplinary collaboration can support more nuanced representation by integrating perspectives from social research, community engagement, and artistic practice. However, collaboration alone does not guarantee ethical outcomes. Responsibility lies in critically examining how visual strategies align with values such as dignity, agency, and respect. For practice-facing professionals, ethical representation is not a fixed standard but a contextual judgment that evolves through dialogue with those represented and affected by the work.

Participation as Ethical Practice

Participatory and co-design approaches have emerged as key strategies for addressing ethical challenges in interdisciplinary work. By involving stakeholders and communities directly in creative processes, participation seeks to redistribute agency and challenge hierarchical models of expertise (Sanders & Stappers, 2008). In practice, participation can take many forms, from workshops and co-creation sessions to long-term partnerships. When implemented thoughtfully, these approaches enhance both ethical accountability and creative richness. Participants contribute local knowledge, values, and priorities that may otherwise be overlooked.

However, participation is not inherently ethical. Tokenistic engagement, extractive research practices, and unequal decision-making power can undermine participatory intentions. Practice-facing responsibility requires practitioners to critically examine how participation is structured, who benefits, and how outcomes are shared. Interdisciplinary teams must also navigate tensions between participation and professional accountability. Designers and artists remain responsible for facilitating processes, translating contributions, and negotiating constraints. Ethical practice involves transparency about these roles and limitations.

Data, Technology, and Emerging Ethical Challenges

Interdisciplinary practice increasingly intersects with data-driven systems, algorithms, and emerging technologies. Visual communication often mediates these systems, translating complex data into accessible forms. While this mediation enables understanding, it also carries ethical risk. Data visualizations can obscure uncertainty, reinforce bias, or present contingent models as objective truth. Algorithmic systems may amplify inequities while remaining opaque to users. For practitioners, responsibility involves questioning not only how data is visualized, but how it is collected, categorized, and deployed.

Interdisciplinary collaboration can help surface these concerns by integrating technical expertise with ethical and cultural perspectives. Artists, in particular, have played a critical role in exposing the social implications of data and technology through critical and speculative practices. However, such interventions must balance critique with care, avoiding sensationalism or fatalism. Practice-facing responsibility in this domain requires ongoing learning, humility, and a willingness to challenge assumptions about progress and innovation.

Accountability in Open-Ended Practice

One of the defining characteristics of interdisciplinary creative work is its open-endedness. Speculative projects may not yield immediate outcomes; participatory processes may evolve unpredictably; systems-oriented interventions may produce delayed or diffuse effects. This open-endedness complicates traditional notions of accountability. For practitioners, accountability involves articulating the rationale behind decisions, documenting processes, and remaining engaged beyond the point of delivery when possible. It also involves creating feedback mechanisms that allow for reflection and course correction. Institutions and clients often seek clear metrics of success, yet responsible interdisciplinary practice may resist reductive evaluation. Practitioners must navigate this tension by advocating for forms of assessment that recognize learning, dialogue, and relational impact alongside tangible outputs.

Responsibility as a Collective Commitment

Ultimately, responsibility in interdisciplinary practice is not borne by individuals alone. It is a collective commitment shaped by teams, organizations, and cultural norms. Visual communication, design, and art operate within systems that reward certain behaviors and outcomes. Changing practice therefore requires engaging not only with methods, but with structures of value and power. For practice-facing professionals, embracing responsibility means accepting uncertainty and imperfection. Ethical practice is not about achieving moral purity, but about remaining attentive, responsive, and willing to adapt. Interdisciplinary approaches provide tools for this engagement by fostering dialogue across differences and exposing assumptions to critique.

PEDAGOGICAL REFLECTIONS: TEACHING COLOR CRITICALLY, TEACHING ACROSS BORDERS

From an educational perspective, this virtual exchange project foregrounds pedagogies that are cross-cultural, critical, and creative. Instructors scaffolded reflection sessions where students discussed not only their design choices but also cultural assumptions underlying them. They used peer critique, visual comparison, and reflective design journals. The findings align with recent studies such as *Immersive digital creation environments in design education* (Çoruh, 2025) which look at how new digital tools (VR and other immersive tools) reshape individual and group work in design education (Çoruh, 2025). Such environments offer potential for richer exploration of visual communication, including color, especially when combined with virtual exchange. Moreover, the chapter proposes integrating color semiotics, cultural theory, and digital tool literacy into curricula in art, design, and visual communication. Rather than treating color theory as a technical or perceptual exercise alone, it should be embedded in intercultural design tasks, collaborative critique, and ethical reflection.

Framing the Problem as a Shared Inquiry

One of the most significant shifts in interdisciplinary practice occurs at the level of problem framing. In traditional design workflows, problems are often defined externally—by a client brief, institutional mandate, or market need. Interdisciplinary contexts challenge this model by treating problem definition as a collaborative and iterative process. Practitioners frequently find that collaborators from different disciplines hold divergent assumptions about the nature of the problem, its causes, and its desired outcomes. Rather than resolving these differences prematurely, effective interdisciplinary teams treat them as sources of insight. Visual tools such as mapping exercises, concept sketches, and narrative scenarios help externalize assumptions and create a shared space for inquiry. This approach expands possibility by allowing problems to evolve as understanding deepens. It also supports responsibility by preventing narrow or biased framings from dominating the process. For practice-facing professionals, investing time in shared inquiry can feel risky under tight timelines, yet it often reduces conflict and misalignment later in the project.

Negotiating Roles and Expertise

Interdisciplinary practice destabilizes conventional professional roles. Designers may find themselves facilitating workshops rather than producing artifacts; artists may operate as researchers or critical commentators; visual communicators may act as translators between technical and public audiences. These role shifts can be generative, but they can also create uncertainty and tension. Successful interdisciplinary teams explicitly negotiate roles and expectations rather than assuming shared understanding. This negotiation is not a one-time activity; roles often evolve as projects unfold. For practitioners, responsibility involves remaining attentive to how authority and labor are distributed, and whether certain forms of expertise are consistently undervalued. Visual communication plays a key role in mediating these negotiations. Shared artifacts—prototypes, diagrams, and process documentation—help clarify contributions and make invisible labor visible. By foregrounding process rather than only outcomes, interdisciplinary teams can foster greater mutual respect and accountability.

Working With, Not Against, Institutional Constraints

Practice-facing interdisciplinary work unfolds within institutions that impose constraints on time, resources, and evaluation. Whether operating in corporate, nonprofit, academic, or community settings, practitioners must navigate funding cycles, reporting requirements, and organizational cultures that may not align with exploratory or participatory approaches. Rather than treating these constraints as obstacles to be overcome, effective interdisciplinary practitioners work with them strategically. For example, speculative artifacts can be framed as strategic foresight tools; participatory workshops can be aligned with stakeholder engagement goals; systems maps can support organizational learning.

This pragmatic orientation expands possibility by embedding interdisciplinary methods within existing structures. At the same time, it supports responsibility by avoiding performative innovation—projects that appear progressive but lack sustained impact. Practitioners play a crucial role in translating interdisciplinary value into institutional language, advocating for processes that prioritize learning, inclusion, and ethical reflection.

Iteration, Reflection, and Care in Process

Iteration is a defining feature of interdisciplinary practice. As projects evolve, new insights emerge, assumptions are challenged, and directions shift. While iteration is often associated with efficiency and optimization, practice-facing interdisciplinarity reframes it as a form of care. Reflection—both individual and collective—allows teams to assess not only what is being produced, but how and why. Reflective practices may include debrief sessions, documentation, or critical writing integrated into the creative process. These practices support responsibility by making values and trade-offs explicit. Care also manifests in how teams attend to emotional labor, conflict, and burnout. Interdisciplinary work can be demanding, particularly when addressing social or ecological issues. Acknowledging these challenges and designing supportive processes is an ethical concern as well as a practical one.

Engaging Communities and Publics

Many interdisciplinary projects extend beyond professional teams to engage communities or publics. These engagements introduce additional layers of responsibility, particularly around consent, representation, and reciprocity. Practice-facing professionals often navigate tensions between project goals and community needs. Responsible engagement involves transparency about intentions, limitations, and potential outcomes. It also requires practitioners to consider what participants gain from the process and how relationships are sustained beyond the project's conclusion. Visual communication is central to these engagements, shaping how projects are introduced, documented, and shared. Thoughtful visual strategies can foster trust and accessibility, while careless ones can reinforce exclusion or misrepresentation. Interdisciplinary practice supports more ethical engagement when it values community knowledge as integral to the creative process rather than as raw material for professional output.

Evaluating Impact and Sustaining Interdisciplinary Practice

Evaluating the impact of interdisciplinary creative work presents persistent challenges. Conventional metrics—such as deliverables, audience size, or market reach—often fail to capture learning, relationship-building, and shifts in understanding that emerge through collaborative, practice-based work. In response, practice-facing practitioners increasingly adopt mixed approaches to evaluation, combining qualitative and quantitative measures. Reflective writing, narrative documentation, and process artifacts complement measurable outcomes, offering a more nuanced account of impact.

Resisting reductive evaluation practices is itself an ethical stance. When assessment prioritizes visibility or scalability over depth, care, and relational learning, it risks undermining the values interdisciplinary work seeks to advance. Integrating perspectives from social research, education, and the arts supports alternative evaluation frameworks that better reflect the complexity of interdisciplinary practice.

Sustaining such practice over time requires more than individual commitment. It depends on organizational support, professional networks, and institutional recognition of interdisciplinary labor. Practitioners often face challenges related to authorship, career progression, and legitimacy within discipline-based systems. Practice-facing responsibility therefore includes advocating for structures that support collaboration, such as flexible roles, shared crediting, and long-term partnerships. Visual communication can play a strategic role in this advocacy by making interdisciplinary processes and impacts legible to decision-makers.

PEDAGOGY AND CONCLUSION: TOWARD RESPONSIBLE INTERDISCIPLINARY FUTURES

Interdisciplinary approaches to design, art, and visual communication are not only reshaping professional practice; they are also transforming how future practitioners must be educated. As creative possibility and ethical responsibility become increasingly intertwined, pedagogy plays a critical role in preparing students to navigate complexity with reflexivity, care, and collaborative skill.

Traditional disciplinary education has emphasized mastery within clearly bounded fields. While foundational skills remain essential, they are no longer sufficient. Interdisciplinary pedagogy prioritizes learning across contexts, positioning education as an iterative process of inquiry, experimentation, and reflection rather than the transmission of fixed knowledge (Cross, 2006). Studio-based and project-based learning environments mirror practice-facing conditions, exposing students to ambiguity, negotiation, and ethical decision-making.

In interdisciplinary contexts, the studio becomes a site of responsibility as well as production. Students encounter questions of representation, authorship, and impact as they engage with complex social, environmental, and technological themes. Critique, documentation, and presentation function not only to assess formal quality but to surface values, power relations, and consequences embedded in visual choices.

Collaboration, often assumed to be intuitive, must be deliberately taught. Interdisciplinary pedagogy cultivates skills in communication, role negotiation, and conflict navigation through structured collaborative projects. Reflection supports this learning by helping students articulate insights about process, power, and responsibility. Educators play a critical role in scaffolding collaboration ethically, ensuring equitable participation and making expectations explicit.

Interdisciplinary education also increasingly involves engagement with external partners and communities. These contexts introduce additional ethical considerations related to accountability, reciprocity, and representation. Responsible pedagogy emphasizes preparation, transparency, and care, reinforcing the chapter's central argument that responsibility is not abstract but developed through situated practice.

By framing interdisciplinarity as a practice of both possibility and responsibility, education prepares future designers, artists, and visual communicators to engage complexity without seeking premature closure. Graduates enter professional contexts equipped not only with skills, but with dispositions—curiosity, humility, and attentiveness to impact—that are essential for responsible interdisciplinary futures.

CONCLUSION: TOWARD A PLURAL, REFLECTIVE COLOR POLITICS IN DIGITAL DESIGN

This chapter has argued that color-mediated visual communication, when integrated with Transformative Learning Theory, embodied pedagogy, and transdisciplinary practice, can support more ethical, inclusive, and reflective forms of STEM education. As digital visual communication increasingly shapes how scientific knowledge is produced and interpreted, color must be understood not as decoration but as a critical cognitive, semiotic, and ethical resource. By foregrounding visual and color literacy, educators can enable learners to engage complex data responsibly, communicate across cultural and disciplinary boundaries, and confront real-world challenges with reflexivity and care. In this way, interdisciplinary approaches to design, art, and visual communication reframe STEM learning as a relational practice—one that expands creative possibility while deepening responsibility.

REFERENCES

Bardecki, M. J. (2019). Multi-disciplinarity. In Leal Filho, W. (Ed.), *Encyclopedia of sustainability in higher education* (pp. 1179–1184). Springer., DOI: 10.1007/978-3-030-11352-0_90

Buchanan, R. (1992). Wicked problems in design thinking. *Design Issues, 8*(2), 5–21. DOI: 10.2307/1511637

Chang, H.-Y., Chang, Y.-J., & Tsai, M.-J. (2024). Strategies and difficulties during students' construction of data visualizations. *International Journal of STEM Education, 11*(1), 11. DOI: 10.1186/s40594-024-00463-w

Çoruh, L. (2025). Immersive digital creation environments in design education. *International Journal of Technology and Design Education, 35*(5), 1841–1870. DOI: 10.1007/s10798-025-09961-6

Cross, N. (2006). *Designerly ways of knowing*. Springer.

Dunne, A., & Raby, F. (2013). *Speculative everything: Design, fiction, and social dreaming*. MIT Press.

Elhefnawy, H., Saada, M., Abdelkareem, S., Elemam, Y., Subaih, R., & Hassabo, A. (2026). Color Theory and Semiotics: Exploring the Relationship Between Visual Semiotics and Color. *Journal of Textiles. Coloration and Polymer Science, 23*, 9–15. DOI: 10.21608/jtcps.2024.259782.1322

Findeli, A., & Bousbaci, R. (2005). L'éclipse de l'objet dans les théories du projet en design. *The Design Journal, 8*(3), 35–49. DOI: 10.2752/146069205789331574

Guan, X., & Wang, K. (2022). Visual communication design using machine vision and digital media communication technology. *Wireless Communications and Mobile Computing, 2022*(1), 6235913. Advance online publication. DOI: 10.1155/2022/6235913

Kidman, G., & Tan, H. (2025). Interdisciplinary thinking in STEA+M: Cognitive integration, makerspaces, and knowledge creation. In *Knowledge generation in STEM and STEAM education* (pp. 89–121). Springer., https://link.springer.com/chapter/10.1007/978-3-032-03247-8_4 DOI: 10.1007/978-3-032-03247-8_4

Lyu, H. (2025). A study of the role of color in visual communication in the digital perspective. *Mediterranean Archaeology & Archaeometry. International Journal, 25*(1), 352–357.

Manzini, E. (2015). *Design, when everybody designs: An introduction to design for social innovation.* MIT Press. DOI: 10.7551/mitpress/9873.001.0001

Margolin, V. (2002). *The politics of the artificial: Essays on design and design studies.* University of Chicago Press. DOI: 10.7208/chicago/9780226518374.001.0001

McIntyre, P., & Delaney, K. (2020). Reimagining STEM education: Critical, transdisciplinary, and embodied approaches. In *STEM Education: New Directions in Theory and Practice* (pp. 1–18). Springer. https://link.springer.com/chapter/10.1007/978-3-030-29489-2_1

Mezirow, J. (2000). *Learning as transformation: Critical perspectives on a theory in progress.* Jossey-Bass.

Mukherjee, K., Yin, B., Sherman, B. E., Lessard, L., & Schloss, K. B. (2021). Context matters: A theory of semantic discriminability for perceptual encoding systems. *arXiv.* https://arxiv.org/abs/2108.03685

Muratbekova, P., & Shamoi, A. (2023). Color-Emotion Associations in Art: Fuzzy Approach. *arXiv preprint.* arXiv

Papanek, V. (1985). *Design for the real world: Human ecology and social change* (2nd ed.). Thames & Hudson.

Sanders, E. B.-N., & Stappers, P. J. (2008). Co-creation and the new landscapes of design. *CoDesign, 4*(1), 5–18. DOI: 10.1080/15710880701875068

Schloss, K. (2024). Color semantics in human cognition. Current Directions in Psychological Science, 33(1), 58–67. https://doi.org/, C. L. (2025). Postdigital visual literacy: Visual entanglements and dynamic learning processes in art education. *American Journal of STEM Education, 14*, 49–58. https://doi.org/DOI: 10.1177/09637214231208189Schwarz

Sun, Q., & Zhu, Y. (2022). Teaching analysis for visual communication design with the perspective of digital technology. *Journal of Educational Multimedia and Hypermedia, 31*(2), 145–160. PMID: 35903440

Symeonidis, V., & Impedovo, M. A. (2023). Where internationalisation and digitalisation intersect: Designing a virtual exchange to enhance student teachers' professional awareness as European teachers. *European Journal of Teacher Education, 46*(5), 821–839. DOI: 10.1080/02619768.2023.2243644

Weaver, G. C., McDonald, P. L., Louie, G. S., & Woodman, T. C. (2024). Future potentials for international virtual exchange in higher education post COVID-19: A scoping review. *Education Sciences, 14*(3), 232. DOI: 10.3390/educsci14030232

Chapter 4
Motion Design in Immersive Media:
A Critical Synthesis of Visual Storytelling Frameworks

Amir Ahmadoghlu
http://orcid.org/0009-0002-8798-0779
Koç University, Turkey

ABSTRACT

Immersive media environments are increasingly shaping how narratives are perceived, experienced, and interpreted through motion design . However, existing literature addresses motion design, immersive media, and narrative theory in a fragmented manner, often limiting motion to an aesthetic or technical role. This study proposes a conceptual and critical synthesis that repositions motion design as a narrative infrastructure integrating perceptual, spatial, and temporal dimensions. Drawing on interdisciplinary approaches, motion design is defined as a system that organizes attention guidance, spatial dramaturgy, and temporal sequencing within immersive environments. The proposed layered model demonstrates how motion determines perceptual priorities, structures narrative space, and regulates experiential rhythm. This approach moves motion design beyond a complementary visual element and frames it as a fundamental mechanism that ensures narrative coherence and experiential continuity in immersive storytelling.

INTRODUCTION

Immersive media fundamentally transforms how visual storytelling is constructed and experienced. Rather than functioning as a linear sequence unfolding over time,

DOI: 10.4018/979-8-3373-6680-7.ch004

narrative becomes a multi-layered structure situated within a spatial environment. In traditional screen-based media, stories are framed and temporally controlled, whereas in immersive contexts such as virtual reality (VR), augmented reality (AR), mixed reality (XR), and spatial installations, narrative emerges through the user's physical presence, spatial position, and perceptual orientation. The reality-virtuality continuum proposed by Milgram and Kishino (1994) provides a foundational framework for understanding this shift, while Ryan's (2015: 82-96) work on digital narrative and Murray's (2017: 71-92) concept of immersion demonstrate that immersion is not merely a technological feature but a condition that shapes how narrative is spatially and experientially organized.

This transformation is also reshaping the role of motion graphics within storytelling. Emerging through the expansion of graphic design into time-based media, motion graphics evolved from a static visual discipline into a dynamic system that integrates space, time, and movement (Krasner, 2013: 1-5). In immersive environments, movement functions not only as a visual enhancer but also as a structuring mechanism that organizes spatial relationships, temporal progression, and perceptual hierarchy. Research on visual perception demonstrates that motion plays a critical role in directing attention and guiding user focus, effectively shaping how information is experienced over time (Ware, 2013: 155-170).

However, the existing literature falls short of addressing this transformation within a comprehensive framework. Studies on immersive media are often technology-driven, focusing primarily on hardware systems and interaction techniques rather than pedagogical or narrative structures. Concepts such as presence and immersion are typically discussed in relation to system characteristics and user experience metrics (Slater, 2009: 3549-3552). Within this framework, motion is generally treated as a functional component, for example, through interface transitions or attention-guiding cues, while its role in structuring the spatial and temporal organization of narrative remains underdeveloped.

The literature on motion design has developed primarily within graphic communication and publication design, with limited discussion of motion's narrative-building potential. Wong's (1993: 222-226) principles on form and direction, and Lupton & Phillips's (2015: 18–19, 232-240) focus on temporal composition, highlight motion's role in meaning-making but remain confined to screen-based narratives. The influence of movement on spatial dramaturgy and experiential rhythm in immersive environments is addressed only fragmentarily. More recent contributions have begun to close this gap: Austin (2020: 2-3) frames space as an active medium of communication shaped by a deliberate sequence of movement through space and time, while Shaw and Colette (2023: 11-13) position rhythm, tempo, and continuity as the primary means through which a motion designer constructs meaning across a temporal arc. Despite these contributions, a unified framework integrating spatial, temporal, and perceptual dimensions under motion design as narrative infrastructure has yet to be established.

Conversely, narrative theory and game studies have explored the transformation of narrative structures through concepts such as spatial narrative and environmental storytelling. Jenkins's (2004: 118-130) notion of environmental storytelling demonstrates that narrative can be embedded within spatial configurations. Similarly, Murray (2017: 71-92) argues that digital narratives reconfigure the experience of time and space through immersion and interaction. Ryan's (2015: 82-96) work further emphasizes the importance of spatial and interactive dimensions in digital storytelling. However, within this body of research, movement itself is rarely theorized as a primary structuring system of narrative and is more often treated implicitly within broader discussions of interaction and immersion.

This interdisciplinary gap creates conceptual confusion about the role of motion design in immersive storytelling. As Bucher (2018) emphasizes, although immersive technologies have rapidly evolved, the narrative principles and structures for storytelling in virtual environments remain underdeveloped, and there is still no clear consensus on how stories should be constructed in these media (2018: 2-3, 5-6). This lack of a shared narrative framework leads to fragmentation in how core concepts are understood and applied. As a result, motion design is often reduced either to an aesthetic form of expression or to a technical tool for guidance, while a comprehensive understanding of how narrative operates across spatial, temporal, and perceptual levels has yet to be established.

This article explores the connection between motion design and immersive storytelling through a critical overview, addressing the previously mentioned gap. The study redefines motion as a narrative framework that comprehensively organizes attention guidance, spatial dramaturgy, and the creation of experiential rhythm. As illustrated in Figure 1, this approach places motion design at the crossroads of immersive media environments, narrative structures, and perceptual processes, viewing it not just as a supplementary visual technique but as a core narrative mechanism. Using selected sources from visual communication, narrative theory, immersive media studies, and cognitive psychology, this study seeks to clarify the fundamental role of motion design in immersive narratives.

Figure 1. The conceptual positioning of motion design at the intersection of immersive media, visual storytelling, and perceptual cognition

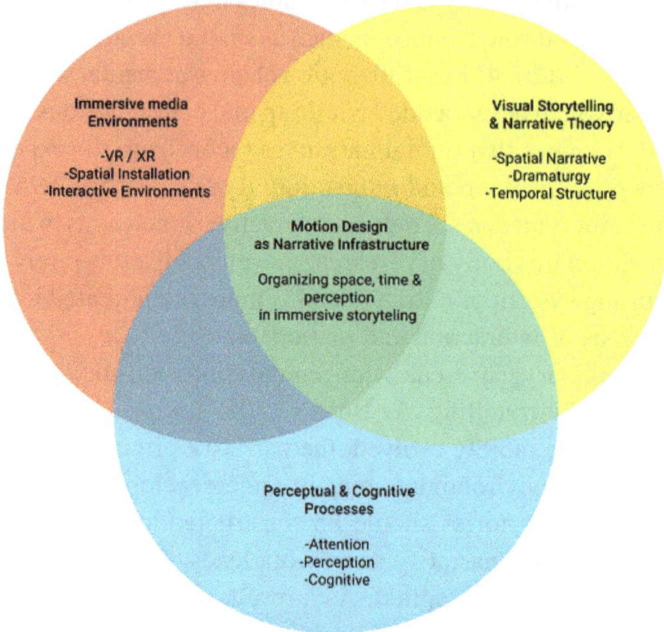

The rest of the article is organized as follows: The second section reviews the literature on motion design, immersion, and spatial narrative within an interdisciplinary framework. The third section compares existing approaches to visual storytelling through a critical synthesis and identifies common themes. The fourth section introduces an integrated conceptual framework that characterizes motion design as a narrative infrastructure within immersive media. In the final sections, the theoretical and practical contributions of this framework are discussed, along with recommendations for future research.

LITERATURE REVIEW

Motion Design and Time-Based Visual Narrative

Motion design can be defined as a design practice that emerged from the expansion of graphic design into the temporal dimension, transforming visual communication from a static arrangement into a process-based narrative. In this context, time-based visual narrative refers to narrative structures in which meaning is produced not only through form and composition but also through movement, rhythm, and transformation. Consequently, motion design should be regarded as a narrative system concerned not only with "what is shown" but also with "how the content unfolds."

In early studies of the field, motion was mainly viewed as an aesthetic and formal enhancement. Krasner defines this field as a reconfiguration of graphic design principles over time, emphasizing the impact of motion on visual hierarchy, emphasis, and continuity (Krasner, 2013: 21-25). Similarly, in her study focusing on the history of motion graphics, Betancourt shows how motion has served as a tool for attracting attention and guiding viewers in modern visual culture (Betancourt, 2013: 210-216). While these approaches highlight the significance of motion design in visual communication, they only partially address the narrative-building potential of motion.

From a time-based narrative perspective, motion graphics go beyond merely presenting sequential images; they establish a structure in which meaning develops over time. McCloud's analysis of closure demonstrates that viewers actively construct meaning by mentally filling the gaps between sequential images (McCloud, 1993: 94-110). While McCloud discusses this process in relation to static panels, these principles can be extended to motion design, where temporal elements such as continuity and transition guide the viewer's perceptual completion of the narrative.

At this point, a strong theoretical parallel emerges between motion design and film theory. While discussing the role of movement, editing, and rhythm in creating narrative meaning in cinema, Bordwell emphasizes the significant influence of time on dramatic structure (Bordwell, 2008: 85–110). However, unlike cinema, motion design constructs a temporal narrative through graphic elements and abstract forms without being tied to a single camera perspective. This feature makes it a narrative practice closely related to cinema but independent of it.

The literature on visual perception and cognition provides a crucial theoretical basis for understanding how time-based narratives affect viewers. Motion plays a central role in guiding visual attention, as dynamic stimuli are more effective in capturing perceptual resources than static images (Goldstein, 2014: 133-150, 184-196). Changes over time enhance the visibility and interpretability of objects, demonstrating that perception is highly sensitive to movement and temporal variation. Similarly, Ware (2013: 155-170) emphasizes that visual attention is strongly driven by dynamic visual features, which organize perceptual priorities in complex visual environments. These findings clarify why motion design is fundamental in time-based storytelling.

In motion design literature, temporal parameters such as duration, velocity, and transition are typically discussed in relation to formal and technical control, analyzed through variables like timing, speed, and interpolation, which determine how visual elements change over time (Krasner, 2013: 146-167). Shaw and Colette (2023:

11-12) extend this by arguing that the timeline is not merely a technical interface but a narrative instrument: knowing an animation's duration allows the designer to plan narrative structure, rhythm, and cadence. In this sense, temporal parameters are inseparable from the dramaturgical organization of content. While Lupton and Phillips (2015: 18-19, 232-247) address time and motion within visual form and composition, their approach emphasizes perceptual and formal effects rather than narrative construction. Consequently, the relationship between temporal design decisions and narrative meaning remains only implicitly addressed in the literature.

In the context of immersive media, time-based narrative takes on a more complex structure. Time ceases to be a predetermined flow and transforms into an experiential dimension shaped by the user's spatial movements and interactions. As Murray emphasizes, in digital narratives, time acquires an experiential and participatory quality rather than remaining strictly linear (Murray, 2017: 71–92). In this context, motion design emerges as one of the fundamental narrative tools that organizes this fluid temporal structure and makes the experience comprehensible.

Shaw and Colette (2023: 12-13) describe rhythm in motion design as an ordered alternation between slow and fast movement: slower moments allow viewers to process and emotionally register information, while faster motion introduces new narrative elements or transitions. The overall pacing of a motion design project, they argue, directly determines its emotional sensibility, functioning less as a stylistic choice than as a structural narrative decision. In this context, we can identify three fundamental functions of motion design: (1) preventing the narrative from being perceived as fragmented by providing visual continuity, (2) regulating the emotional flow through rhythm and tempo, and (3) making narrative progression visible through transformation. However, in existing literature, few studies examine these functions within a holistic narrative system. Most research examines these functions under separate headings and addresses the structural role of motion design in time-based narrative in a fragmented manner.

In conclusion, to fully grasp the role of motion design in immersive storytelling, it is necessary to re-examine time-based visual narratives. In this context, motion design should be viewed not merely as a visual technique that unfolds over time, but as a foundational narrative practice that determines how the story is experienced. In the next subsection, we will discuss how this approach integrates with the spatial dimension and relates to the concept of immersion.

The Concept of Immersion and Experiential Narrative Structures

The concept of immersion is a fundamental term used in the literature on immersive media to describe the extent to which a narrative is experienced "from within" by the user. However, the concept is approached with different layers of meaning across various disciplines and is often used interchangeably with technological realism. Yet immersion cannot be explained solely by high resolution, low latency, or hardware-based immersion; it is directly related to how the narrative is structured spatially, temporally, and perceptually (Ryan, 2015: 82-103).

In early virtual reality studies, immersion was primarily defined through the concept of presence. Slater and Wilbur (1997) described immersion in terms of technological envelopment and sensory consistency, framing immersive environments as systems that generate a sense of "being there." Slater's later work extends this perspective by distinguishing between system-based immersion and user experience, demonstrating that immersive environments can elicit not only perceptual responses but also realistic behavioral reactions through mechanisms such as place illusion and plausibility illusion (Slater, 2009: 3549-3553). This shift suggests that immersive experiences are shaped not only by technical features but also by how experiences are structured and perceived.

From the perspective of narrative theory, immersion is closely related to the concept of narrative presence. Ryan defines immersion as the user's perception of the narrative world as a mentally coherent and believable whole and emphasizes that it depends on the narrative's spatial and temporal coherence (Ryan, 2015: 145-172). When the rules of the narrative world, its spatial logic, or its temporal continuity are compromised, immersion inevitably weakens. This approach shifts immersion from being a technological outcome to a narrative condition.

In the context of experiential narrative structures, immersion assumes that the user's relationship with the narrative is an active process. Murray argues that in digital narratives, immersion is enhanced by the user's capacity to interact with the narrative world and perform meaningful actions within it (Murray, 2017: 71-90). Therefore, immersion should be understood not as a passive viewing experience but as being within and participating in the narrative.

At this point, motion design plays a critical role in establishing immersion. In immersive experiences, users encounter a multitude of visual and spatial stimuli; establishing a meaningful sense of direction within this density does not always happen spontaneously. Motion design ensures the perceptual consistency of the narrative world by establishing continuity and hierarchy among these stimuli. Ware's studies on visual perception highlight the decisive influence of motion in directing attention and establishing perceptual priority, thereby explaining why immersion is felt more strongly in dynamic visual structures compared to static ones (Ware, 2013: 155-170).

Experiential narrative structures encompass forms in which the linear flow of time is shaped by user actions. Calleja (2019: 222-234) critiques the ambiguity of the concept of immersion and proposes a more grounded understanding based on user involvement and experiential processes. This perspective suggests that immersion cannot be reduced to a single variable but emerges from multiple interacting dimensions of experience. In this context, motion design can be understood as a visual and temporal element that helps organize and connect these experiential layers.

In contrast, the concept of immersion in the literature is often reduced to an effect that "draws the user in," while the structural conditions that sustain this experience remain underexamined. Experiences that rely heavily on technological immersion but lack narrative coherence may generate short-term engagement yet fail to sustain a meaningful immersive experience. As Murray (2017: 71-90) emphasizes, immersion is closely linked to the user's active participation within a coherent narrative world. From this perspective, immersion should not be understood solely as a sensory effect but as a condition shaped by narrative organization. In this context, motion design can be reconsidered as a narrative-structuring tool that contributes to the continuity and intelligibility of immersive experiences.

In this context, immersion is not merely a simple output of experiential narrative structures, but rather an indicator of the extent to which these structures are established coherently and meaningfully. Motion design, meanwhile, serves as a fundamental tool that ensures the sustainability of immersion by organizing the narrative's spatial continuity, temporal flow, and perceptual guidance. In the next subsection, this relationship between immersion and space will be examined in greater detail, and the role of motion design will be discussed through the concept of spatial storytelling.

Spatial Storytelling and Immersive Media

Spatial storytelling refers to narrative forms in which the story is constructed not merely through a temporal sequence, but through the organization and experience of space. In the context of immersive media, space ceases to be a passive backdrop against which the narrative unfolds; instead, it becomes an active component that generates meaning, guides the narrative, and structures the experience. This transformation fundamentally alters how the narrative is perceived, shifting the user's relationship with the story from temporal tracking to spatial experience (Ryan, 2015: 60-88).

The concept of spatial narrative has become increasingly prominent in game studies and digital storytelling literature. Jenkins's (2004: 118-130) framework of environmental storytelling demonstrates that narrative can be conveyed through the organization of space, environmental cues, and design decisions. Within this framework, narrative is not structured as a fixed sequence of events but as a distributed system that unfolds through the user's exploration of the environment. Austin (2020: 2) formalizes this insight within the concept of narrative environments, arguing that the design of such spaces involves a triple, integrated unfolding of movement through space, through time, and through story content. In this framework, narrative is not overlain on space. Still, it is embedded in and expressed through the material and atmospheric qualities of the environment itself, making spatial form an active agent of storytelling rather than its backdrop (Austin, 2020: 19-20). This spatial structure enables non-linear narrative experiences, where meaning is constructed progressively as users navigate and interpret the space.

From the perspective of narrative theory, space plays a decisive role in establishing narrative presence. The spatial consistency and believability of the narrative world ensure that the user mentally perceives it as a "real" environment (Ryan, 2015: 82-103). Therefore, space should be considered not merely as the setting in which the narrative unfolds, but as a foundational structure that defines the narrative's logic and rules.

In immersive media environments, spatial narrative is closely related to the user's physical movements and perceptual orientation. As Bowman et al. (2004: 137-190) demonstrate, navigation in three-dimensional interactive environments involves the user's control over position and viewpoint orientation, which directly shapes how the environment is experienced. Where the user stands, which direction they face, and how they move within the space influence which elements of the environment become perceptually accessible, this indicates that spatial narrative is not a static arrangement but a dynamic and experiential process. Austin (2020: 15-16) reinforces this point from a phenomenological perspective, drawing on Merleau-Ponty's theory of embodied perception to argue that we 'read' spatial environments with our whole bodies, carrying with us a sense of depth, dimensionality, orientation, flow, and movement as perceptual-spatial qualities. This embodied reading of space is central to how narrative environments produce meaning, suggesting that spatial narrative cannot be reduced to visual information alone but must account for the full sensory and kinesthetic engagement of the user.

At this point, motion design plays a central role in establishing spatial narrative. In immersive environments, space is often complex and multi-layered; therefore, a meaningful sense of coherence does not always emerge spontaneously for the user. Motion design organizes this complexity by establishing visual continuity and perceptual hierarchy, thereby making the space narratively legible. As Ware has demonstrated, motion shapes the user's cognitive map of the space through direction, changes in scale, transitions, and visual rhythm (Ware, 2013: 155-170, 211-230). In this regard, motion design functions not only as an aesthetic tool but also as a cognitive organizing mechanism.

The concept of spatial dramaturgy provides an important framework for understanding the performative dimensions of immersive narrative structures. From a dramaturgical perspective, space can be understood as a staged narrative environment in which the user assumes an active, participatory role. Murray's (2017: 71-92) discussion of immersion and agency highlights that digital narratives position the user not as a passive observer but as an active participant navigating a responsive narrative world. Building on this perspective, motion design makes the dramatic intensity, transitions, and narrative thresholds within this spatial structure perceptible. In immersive narratives, such dramaturgical structures function as implicit systems that guide the user experience.

However, excessive guidance in spatial narrative risks undermining the sense of discovery, a fundamental characteristic of immersive experience. Overly directive structures can increase extraneous cognitive load and reduce user engagement. Cognitive load theory demonstrates that excessive instructional guidance may become counterproductive, particularly as user expertise increases, leading to what is known as the expertise reversal effect (Sweller, Ayres, & Kalyuga, 2011: 155-169). Similarly, the guidance fading effect suggests that instructional support should be gradually reduced to avoid cognitive overload and maintain active engagement (pp. 171-182). Therefore, spatial narrative must be designed through motion in a way that is directive yet non-coercive.

A general review of the literature reveals that spatial narrative is most often addressed within the frameworks of architecture, game design, and performance studies, while the role of motion design in this context is frequently relegated to the background. Yet in immersive media environments, the transformation of space into narrative is largely tied to the choreography of movement. Motion design transforms space into a temporal experience, making the narrative's spatial dimension visible and tangible.

In this context, spatial narrative should be regarded as one of the fundamental building blocks of immersive storytelling. Motion design, meanwhile, serves as one of the foundational narrative tools within this framework. In the next subsection, we will examine the concepts of visual dramaturgy and cognitive attention, which complement the relationship between spatial narrative and immersion; the role of motion design in guiding perception will be discussed in greater detail.

Visual Dramaturgy and Cognitive Attention

Visual dramaturgy refers to an approach in which a narrative is structured not merely through content or plot, but through decisions regarding visual composition, rhythm, transitions, and staging. In classical dramaturgy, the dramatic structure is typically built around characters and events. In contrast, visual dramaturgy focuses on narrative forms in which meaning is generated through visual organization and perceptual guidance. In the context of immersive media, this approach emphasizes the necessity of "enabling the audience to experience" the narrative through sensory and cognitive processes, rather than simply "showing" it to them.

The literature on cognitive psychology provides an important foundation for explaining the attention mechanisms underlying this approach. The human perceptual system operates with limited attentional resources, which are guided by visual features such as motion, contrast, change, and continuity. Research in perception demonstrates that visual attention is highly sensitive to temporal change and that dynamic stimuli exert a stronger influence on perceptual prioritization than static visuals (Goldstein, 2014: 177-185). This explains the central role of motion design within visual dramaturgy.

In immersive media environments, cognitive attention is not limited to a single screen or a fixed viewpoint. The user must continually select focal points, redirect their attention, and make perceptual decisions within the visual field. For this reason, attention management becomes one of the fundamental dramaturgical challenges of immersive narratives. Motion design functions as a tool that regulates the economy of attention in response to this problem; through motion, the viewer's perceptual priorities are determined, and the order in which information is perceived is implicitly structured (Ware, 2013: 155-170). Ware's studies on visual perception clearly demonstrate the decisive role of motion in this guidance.

From the perspective of visual dramaturgy, motion design provides a system for staging the narrative's dramatic structure over time. The acceleration, deceleration, or interruption of movement can elicit emotional responses in the viewer, such as tension, anticipation, or relief. In film theory, Bordwell emphasizes how temporal organization and narrative structure shape the viewer's experience (Bordwell, 2008: 85–110). In immersive environments, this effect is felt more intensely and physically because the viewer is directly situated within the narrative space.

Another critical function of motion design is maintaining narrative continuity. Immersive experiences often involve multiple simultaneous visual and spatial stimuli, which can challenge the coherence of the narrative. Motion design contributes to continuity by organizing transitions and establishing rhythmic relationships between elements. McCloud's analysis of visual sequencing shows that meaning is constructed through the relationships between sequential images and the transitions connecting them (McCloud, 1993: 94–106). Although originally formulated in the context of comics, these principles can be extended to time-based media, where motion guides the perceptual continuity of the experience.

Visual dramaturgy also encompasses the concepts of staging and choreography. In motion design, visual elements are often choreographed over time, allowing relationships between forms to emerge through movement rather than static composition (Krasner, 2013: 160-167). Rather than functioning as a purely formal device, motion enables the construction of meaning through the interaction of elements. In immersive narratives, this choreographic organization extends into spatial environments, where movement structures how viewers navigate space and perceive dramatic intensity.

In this context, cognitive load theory provides a critical framework for understanding the limits of motion usage. Excessive motion, frequent transitions, and uncontrolled visual changes can increase extraneous cognitive load, thereby hindering meaning production (Sweller, Ayres, & Kalyuga, 2011: 63-71). This risk is even more pronounced in immersive media environments, where users must process both spatial and temporal stimuli simultaneously, potentially leading to split-attention effects and working memory overload (2011: 68-71, 190-195). Therefore, motion design should be used not merely to attract attention, but to direct it in a balanced and purposeful manner.

A review of the existing literature reveals that the concept of visual dramaturgy is primarily addressed within the contexts of cinema, theater, and performance studies, and is applied only to a limited extent to the relationship between immersive media and motion design. However, in immersive narratives, motion design is not merely an aesthetic choice but a fundamental dramaturgical tool that regulates the viewer's perceptual and cognitive processes. Therefore, re-examining the perspective of visual dramaturgy within the context of motion design more clearly reveals the structural dynamics of immersive storytelling.

In conclusion, visual dramaturgy can be regarded as a fundamental theoretical tool for explaining the role of motion design in immersive storytelling. Motion simultaneously structures the narrative's cognitive and emotional framework through its functions of directing attention, creating perceptual continuity, and generating dramatic intensity. In the next subsection, this literature review will examine conceptual gaps and limitations and explain why current approaches require an integrated framework.

CONCEPTUAL GAPS AND LIMITATIONS IN THE LITERATURE

An examination of studies on immersive media, motion design, and visual storytelling reveals that, despite the field's rapid expansion, significant conceptual and theoretical gaps remain. The existing literature largely addresses these three fields in parallel; it falls short of discussing their relationships within a holistic narrative system. This situation often positions motion design's role in immersive storytelling as implicit, secondary, or instrumental. As shown in Figure 2, these fragmented approaches hinder the establishment of an integrated theoretical connection between motion design, immersive media, and narrative theory; they also limit the consideration of motion as a narrative-generating system that simultaneously organizes its spatial, temporal, and perceptual dimensions.

Figure 2. A diagram illustrating the conceptual gaps and the lack of an integrated framework in the literature on motion design, immersive media, and visual storytelling

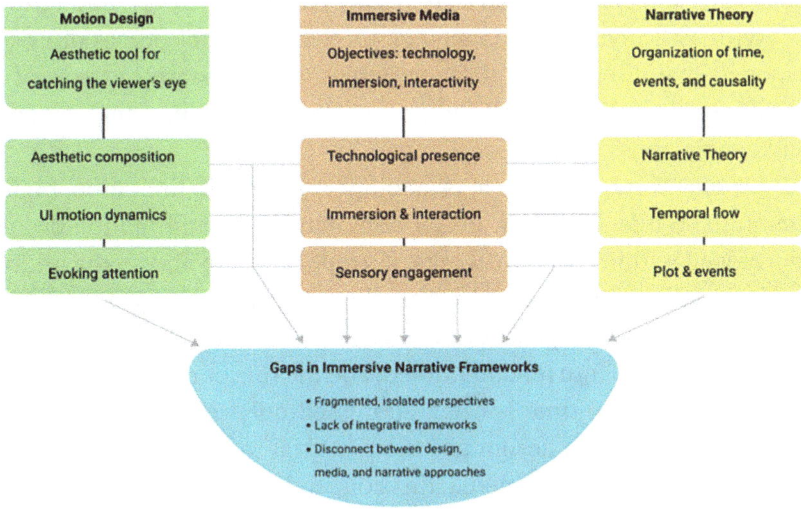

One of the fundamental issues in the literature is the lack of a common and consistent terminology. Motion design is defined across different disciplines using terms such as "motion graphics," "animation," "interface motion," or "transition design," and this diversity creates ambiguity regarding its narrative function (Krasner, 2013: 21-25). A similar conceptual ambiguity appears in immersive media literature, where terms such as "immersion," "presence," "engagement," and "embodiment" are often used inconsistently or interchangeably (Slater, 2009: 3549-3553; Ryan, 2015: 90-97). This terminological fragmentation makes it difficult to clearly define the levels at which motion design structures narrative meaning.

Another significant limitation is that motion design is often treated merely as a technical or aesthetic tool. While a significant portion of immersive media studies focuses on hardware performance, interaction techniques, and interface design, the visual and dramaturgical dimensions of the narrative remain in the background (Bowman et al., 2004: 137-190). The work of Bowman and colleagues, along with Manovich's media theory, clearly demonstrates how this technically focused approach has shaped the field. This approach prevents motion design from being evaluated as a system that structures narrative, rendering its strategic role in experience design invisible.

Another notable gap in the literature is the lack of systematic research into the narrative effects of motion design. Existing studies primarily rely on descriptive analyses, design examples, or case studies; variables such as user perception, cognitive load, and narrative presence are addressed only to a limited extent. While Ware's studies on visual perception emphasize how attention and perception are structured in visual environments (Ware, 2013: 5-12), and cognitive load theory demonstrates how excessive visual and temporal complexity can hinder information processing (Sweller, Ayres, & Kalyuga, 2011: 43-71), these approaches do not offer comprehensive models that directly link these variables to the narrative effects of motion design. This situation makes it difficult to translate the findings into generalizable theoretical conclusions.

Interdisciplinary fragmentation is another significant limitation highlighted in the literature. While studies in visual communication and motion design have largely developed within the frameworks of graphic design and media art, research on immersive media has progressed within the contexts of human–computer interaction, game studies, and cognitive science. The connections established between these two bodies of literature remain limited, and the role of motion design in spatial narrative and experiential time is often addressed only indirectly (Jenkins, 2004: 118-130). Although motion design has the potential to serve as a bridge between narrative theory and immersive media, this connection has not yet been sufficiently established in the literature.

Another conceptual limitation is the lack of a comprehensive theoretical framework that explains the role of motion design in immersive narratives. Current approaches focus on the individual functions of motion, such as attention guidance, emotional impact, or spatial organization, but do not sufficiently address how these functions cohere into a coherent narrative system. This fragmented approach leads to a reductive understanding of motion design's structural capacity within immersive storytelling.

Finally, it is evident that there are limited studies in the literature that address motion design as a narrative-building framework. However, in immersive experiences, motion is not merely a visual element; it is a fundamental organizational tool that simultaneously structures the narrative's spatial logic, temporal flow, and perceptual guidance. This situation indicates that motion design requires a deeper, more comprehensive conceptualization in the context of immersive media.

These conceptual gaps and limitations necessitate a critical synthesis that reevaluates motion design's role in immersive storytelling. In the next section, existing approaches to visual storytelling will be examined comparatively; the functions of motion design in attention guidance, spatial dramaturgy, and temporal sequencing will be discussed within a common framework. This critical synthesis aims to reposition motion design as a narrative infrastructure within the context of immersive media.

Figure 3. The interconnected structure of perceptual, spatial, and temporal layers through which motion design shapes immersive narrative experiences

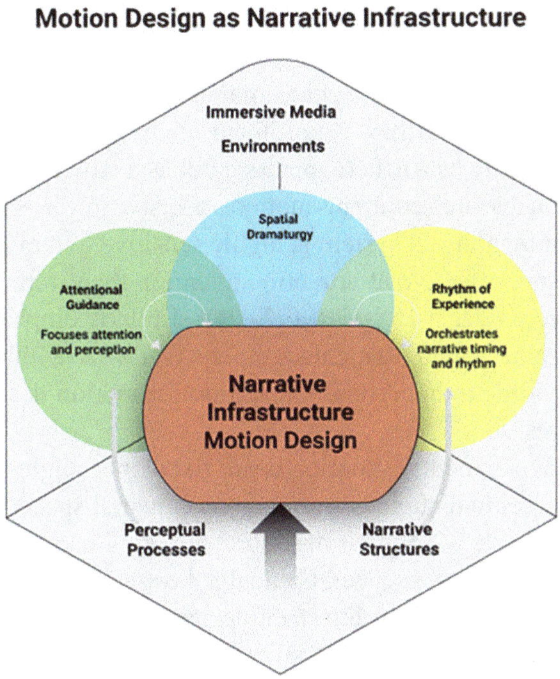

Critical Synthesis

This section re-evaluates the role of motion design in immersive storytelling through a critical synthesis approach, discussing theoretical concepts, which have been addressed in a fragmented manner across the literature, within an integrated framework. The studies examined in the previous sections have revealed that motion has been addressed in a fragmented manner across different disciplines in the contexts of attention guidance, spatial organization, and temporal flow. As conceptualized in Figure 3, this study positions motion design as an integrated system operating through the simultaneous interaction of perceptual, spatial, and temporal layers, and explains immersive narrative experiences through this multi-layered structure.

Kinetic Guidance: The Role of Motion in Attention and Meaning Production

Kinetic guidance describes motion design's capacity to regulate viewer attention, establish perceptual priorities, and direct narrative structure. In immersive media, it functions as a central narrative mechanism determining which elements the user perceives, when and how, within a multifocal environmental space, positioning motion design not merely as aesthetic practice but as a structural narrative tool.

Visual perception research confirms motion's decisive role in establishing perceptual priority. The human visual system is highly sensitive to temporal change, with dynamic stimuli more effective at attracting attention than static ones (Goldstein, 2014: 170-185). Ware (2013: 155-170, 173-180) similarly emphasizes that changes over time determine which elements are perceived first within complex visual environments, providing a theoretical foundation for motion design's centrality in immersive narratives.

In immersive environments, attention is not fixed on a single frame; users must constantly make perceptual choices across environmental space. Kinetic guidance functions as the narrative's "implicit narrator," directing users through movement they often do not consciously register. Critically, however, the concept is primarily addressed in the literature within interface design and information visualization, where motion is treated as a functional tool rather than a narrative one. In immersive storytelling, by contrast, motion determines not only "where to click" but "what is important" and "how it should be felt" (Murray, 2017: 71-90).

Kinetic guidance is also linked to symbolic meaning production. Wong's (1993: 223-227) analyses show that upward, downward, or circular movements evoke different conceptual associations, associations experienced more intensely when the user is physically present within the space. Yet uncontrolled kinetic navigation risks undermining perceptual coherence: excessive movement and inconsistent rhythms increase cognitive load and disrupt meaning production (Sweller, Ayres, & Kalyuga, 2011: 63-71), with split-attention effects compounding when focus is divided across multiple moving elements (2011: 190-195). Kinetic guidance should therefore be understood not as generating more movement, but as consciously organizing narrative priorities in balance. Considered as such, kinetic guidance constitutes one of the fundamental narrative layers of immersive motion design, an invisible system that directs attention, establishes perceptual priorities, and organizes semantic structure.

Spatial Dramaturgy: How Motion Transforms Space into Narrative

Spatial dramaturgy refers to dramaturgical structures in which the narrative is constructed not only through temporal progression, but through the staging and experiencing of space. With regard to immersive media, space ceases to be a passive ground on which the narrative occurs and instead becomes an active structure that generates and guides the narrative. This transformation necessitates treating space not merely as a physical or digital environment, but also as a system in which narrative relationships are organized.

Narrative theory and digital media literature increasingly emphasize the role of space in narrative production. As Ryan points out, existence is established not only through characters and plot but also through the spatial consistency of the narrative world (Ryan, 2015: 82-103). Similarly, Murray emphasizes that in immersive narratives, space is constructed as an experiential structure, and the user's sense of "being present" within this space becomes the cornerstone of the narrative (Murray, 2017: 71-90). These approaches reveal that space is not only the carrier of the narrative but also the site where it is directly produced.

In immersive media environments, space is continuously reconfigured through the user's physical position, line of sight, and movement. This indicates that spatial dramaturgy is not a static staging but a dynamic, process-based structure. As Bowman et al. (2004: 137-145) demonstrate, navigation in three-dimensional environments involves the user's control over position and viewpoint orientation, which shapes how the environment is experienced. Therefore, spatial dramaturgy can be understood as a narrative strategy that regulates how the narrative is perceived and navigated within space.

At this point, motion design plays a central role in establishing spatial dramaturgy. Immersive environments often contain multi-layered visual relationships, depth structures, and various spatial cues; this complexity does not always form a self-evidently meaningful whole from the user's perspective. Motion design organizes this complexity through visual continuity, orientation, and rhythm, and makes the space narratively legible. Motion shapes the user's cognitive map by structuring perceptual hierarchy and guiding attention across spatial elements, thereby making the narrative's spatial logic visible (Ware, 2013: 155-170, 211-230).

Spatial dramaturgy is closely related to staging and choreography. In motion design, visual elements are organized through choreographed movement, allowing relationships to emerge over time rather than through static composition (Krasner, 2013: 160-167). Variations in speed, direction, scale, and rhythm shape the viewer's experience of continuity and transition. In immersive environments, this choreographic logic extends into space, structuring how users navigate between experiential states. Austin (2020: 91-92) describes this as a triple movement: the body moves over time, through different atmospheres, and through successive representations of narrative content, arguing that sudden transitions without adequate spatial preparation disorient rather than engage audiences. From this perspective, spatial dramaturgy is not merely a visual concern but a fundamentally temporal and bodily one, reinforcing motion design's role as the key mechanism through which this layered spatial-temporal journey is orchestrated.

From a critical perspective, spatial dramaturgy is generally addressed in the literature within the contexts of architecture, theater, and performance studies; in immersive media studies, however, space is often defined as a technical container or the environment in which the experience takes place. This approach keeps the role of motion design in transforming space into narrative in the background. Yet, in immersive narratives, the dramaturgical function of space is largely related to how motion is designed.

On the other hand, an excessive emphasis on spatial dramaturgy risks weakening the narrative's exploratory structure. Overly directing the user's movements within the space may limit the sense of subjective exploration, which is a fundamental characteristic of immersive experience. Cognitive load theory demonstrates that overly directive visual structures can generate extraneous cognitive load and reduce user engagement (Sweller, Ayres, & Kalyuga, 2011: 63-71). This effect becomes particularly evident in the expertise reversal effect, where excessive guidance can hinder active exploration and learning (2011: 155-169). Furthermore, the guidance fading effect suggests that instructional support should be gradually reduced to maintain user agency and avoid cognitive overload (2011: 171-182). Therefore, spatial dramaturgy must be established through motion design in a balance that is guiding but non-coercive.

In this line, spatial dramaturgy can be defined as the second fundamental narrative layer of immersive motion design. Motion design offers a system that stages the space, regulates dramatic intensity, and structures the narrative relationships that the user establishes throughout the experience. In the next subsection, we will examine how these spatial structures are organized over time, considering temporal sequencing through the concepts of rhythm, tempo, and emotional flow.

Temporal Sequencing: Rhythm, Tempo, and Emotional Flow

Temporal sequencing is a fundamental concept that explains how a narrative is organized over time, the rhythm and tempo with which it is experienced, and how this organization elicits emotional responses in the viewer. While classical narrative theories approach time through the chronological or dramatic arrangement of the plot, in the context of immersive media, time becomes an experiential dimension that the user perceives and is physically engaged with throughout the experience. This transformation carries motion design to a central position as one of the main regulators of temporal narrative.

Cinema and visual narrative theories have long emphasized rhythm and temporal organization in the production of narrative meaning. Bordwell (2008: 121-148) shows how narrative structure and the organization of time shape viewer comprehension and expectations. Motion design extends these temporal principles beyond screen-based narratives into more abstract, graphic, and spatial contexts. Shaw and Colette (2023: 12) articulate this practically, describing how faster rhythms are emotionally stimulating while slower rhythms feel calmer and more reflective — functioning like musical tempo in determining the overall sensibility of a piece. This demonstrates that temporal sequencing in motion design operates simultaneously as a perceptual, emotional, and narrative mechanism, bridging formal design decisions and experiential outcomes. In immersive narratives, however, temporal structuring is experienced as a continuous environmental flow rather than along a single linear timeline.

In immersive environments, time assumes a flexible structure shaped by user actions and spatial exploration rather than following a strictly linear progression. In digital narratives, temporal experience is no longer confined to a sequence that is passively received, but emerges through active participation within the narrative world (Murray, 2017: 71-90). In this context, motion design becomes one of the primary tools for organizing experiential temporality. Variations in speed, rhythm, and pause structure how narrative phases intensify and shape how these phases are perceived by the user.

One of the most critical functions of temporal sequencing in immersive narratives is the structuring of emotional flow. Visual rhythm can produce emotional states such as tension, expectation, relief, or uncertainty in the viewer. As Wong notes, visual rhythm establishes not only a perceptual but also an emotional language, and the role of motion in meaning production is directly linked to formal decisions (Wong, 1993: 231-234). In immersive narratives, this emotional language combines with the user's physical and spatial experience to create a more intense impact.

The literature on perceptual psychology demonstrates that temporal organization plays a significant role in shaping perceptual coherence. Studies on visual perception indicate that changes over time and structured visual sequences support the perception of continuity and facilitate sustained attention (Goldstein, 2014: 177-185). In this context, motion design guides the perception of time through structured temporal patterns, making visual experiences more cognitively manageable and coherent.

From a critical perspective, it is evident that the literature on temporal sequencing often emphasizes technical parameters such as system performance, software operations, and interaction structures. As Manovich (2013: 8-10) argues, focusing only on the visible outputs of digital media risks overlooking the underlying software processes that generate them. In this sense, software-based cultural production shifts attention from static outcomes to dynamic systems and operations. However, while this perspective highlights process and transformation, the narrative and emotional dimensions of time remain largely underexplored in relation to immersive storytelling. From this viewpoint, motion design can be reconsidered as a narrative infrastructure that determines not only how time unfolds, but also how it is experienced.

However, the uncontrolled use of temporal sequencing can weaken the narrative's perceptual coherence. Rapid transitions, constantly shifting rhythms, and inconsistent pacing can increase the user's cognitive load, making the experience mentally demanding. Cognitive load theory demonstrates that unnecessary visual and temporal complexity can generate extraneous cognitive load and disrupt meaning production (Sweller, Ayres, & Kalyuga, 2011: 63-71). This effect is further intensified when attention is repeatedly divided across multiple temporal cues, leading to split-attention effects (2011: 190-195). Therefore, motion design should be approached as a narrative strategy that not only creates dramatic temporal effects but also ensures cognitive sustainability.

Consequently, temporal sequencing can be defined as the third fundamental layer of narrative in immersive motion design. Motion design regulates the narrative's emotional flow through rhythm, tempo, and continuity, enabling the user to perceive the experience as a meaningful, coherent whole over time. In the next subsection, these three narrative layers will be examined comparatively in the literature, and their common points and distinctions will be discussed.

COMMON CONCEPTS AND DISTINCTIONS: A COMPARISON OF VISUAL STORYTELLING FRAMEWORKS

When the literature on visual storytelling, motion design, and immersive media is evaluated together, it becomes evident that these fields take shape around similar conceptual issues but address them through different terminology and priorities. This situation leads to both strong areas of overlap and clear distinctions in the literature. From a critical synthesis perspective, a clear presentation of these common points and differences is crucial for situating the role of motion design in immersive storytelling with a holistic framework.

When common concepts are examined, attention guidance emerges as a primary factor. The literature on visual perception and cognition demonstrates that human attention operates as a limited resource, shaped by visual features such as motion, contrast, and change (Goldstein, 2014: 170-185; Ware, 2013: 155–170, 173–180). Narrative theory, in turn, emphasizes the organization of perceptual and cognitive focus in shaping narrative engagement and prioritization (Ryan, 2015: 142–155).

While motion design literature addresses this primarily through visual hierarchy and emphasis, immersive media studies approach attention in relation to spatial orientation and user awareness. Across these perspectives, motion emerges as a central mechanism for guiding attention, although its role is conceptualized differently within each framework.

The second common concept is the role of space in narrative production. Game studies and immersive media literature approach space as a structure experienced through exploration (Calleja, 2019: 222-234). In contrast, motion design literature primarily evaluates space in terms of visual composition and screen-based relationships. Narrative theory, on the other hand, emphasizes the importance of spatial coherence in constructing narrative worlds (Murray, 2017: 71-92). Despite these different perspectives, a shared understanding emerges: space is not a passive background but an active component that shapes narrative meaning. However, the role of motion design in organizing this spatial structure is often addressed only indirectly in the literature.

The third common concept is time and rhythm. Film theory, motion design, and digital narrative literature have long emphasized the role of temporal organization in the production of meaning. Bordwell (2008: 85-100) discusses how the structuring of time shapes narrative comprehension and viewer expectations in cinematic storytelling. In the context of immersive media, however, time is increasingly understood as an experiential dimension shaped by user interaction and participation (Murray, 2017: 71-90). From this perspective, a key distinction lies in how temporal experience is structured. While time is largely organized by the narrator in traditional narratives, immersive environments distribute this control through user engagement. Motion design, in this context, can be understood as a narrative tool that mediates between these two modes by structuring temporal experience through rhythm, pacing, and transition.

When these distinctions are examined, it becomes clear that the main difference lies in how motion is conceptualized. While the motion design literature typically considers motion as an aesthetic and formal language, studies in immersive media evaluate it within the context of interaction and guidance. Narrative theory, on the other hand, generally accepts motion as an implicit element and does not conceptualize it directly. This situation makes the narrative-constructing role of motion design insufficiently visible in the literature.

Another significant distinction concerns whether the narrative is linear. While traditional narrative theories are based on linear or semi-linear structures, the immersive media literature emphasizes non-linear, branching, and exploration-based narratives. Motion design works, however, often progresses along pre-determined timelines. This creates a conceptual ambiguity regarding how motion design positions between linear narrative and open-ended experiences.

This comparative analysis clearly highlights the lack of a comprehensive conceptual framework that explains the role of motion design in immersive storytelling in the literature. Despite common concepts that focus on attention, space, and time, how these concepts come together in motion design is not systematically addressed. Distinctions, meanwhile, reduce motion design to either an aesthetic or a technical tool, making the narrative's structural organization invisible.

At this point, motion design can be considered a potential conceptual bridge connecting different literatures. Motion simultaneously structures the narrative's perceptual, spatial, and emotional dimensions through functions such as attention guidance, spatial dramaturgy, and temporal sequencing. In the following section, drawing on this critical synthesis, an integrated conceptual framework that defines motion design as a narrative infrastructure within the context of immersive media will be presented in detail.

Figure 4. A conceptual model that positions motion design as a narrative infrastructure through the integration of layers of kinetic guidance, spatial dramaturgy, and temporal sequencing

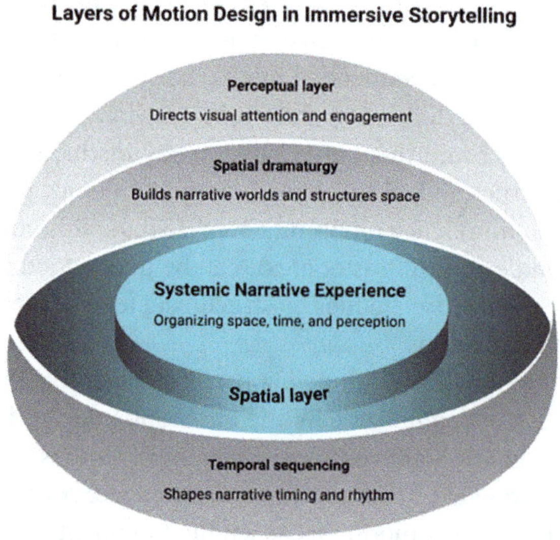

INTEGRATED CONCEPTUAL FRAMEWORK: MOTION DESIGN AS NARRATIVE INFRASTRUCTURE

Based on the literature review and critical synthesis presented in the previous sections, this chapter proposes an integrated conceptual framework that explains the role of motion design in immersive storytelling. The proposed framework positions motion design not merely as an aesthetic or technical application, but as a narrative infrastructure that simultaneously structures the spatial, temporal, and perceptual dimensions of the narrative. As shown in Figure 4, this framework explains how immersive narrative experiences are constructed through the interaction of the layers of kinetic guidance, spatial dramaturgy, and temporal sequencing.

In the existing literature, motion design is mostly discussed in the context of aesthetic composition, user interface motions, or attention-grabbing mechanisms. However, as demonstrated in the previous sections, the role of motion design in immersive narratives extends beyond these limited definitions. Motion becomes one of the fundamental organizational layers that determine how a narrative is perceived, experienced, and interpreted. Therefore, motion design should be considered a structural system that enables the narrative's functioning, not an element "added" to it afterward.

The proposed conceptual framework explains the role of motion design in immersive storytelling through three interrelated main layers:

1. Kinetic guidance
2. Spatial dramaturgy
3. Temporal sequencing

These layers do not form a hierarchical structure, but they create a dynamic narrative framework in which they interact and continually transform one another. This interaction enables the simultaneous organization of the perceptual, spatial, and temporal dimensions of the immersive narrative experience.

Kinetic Guidance Layer

Kinetic guidance refers to motion design's ability to regulate user attention and determine perceptual priorities. In immersive media environments, the user simultaneously encounters numerous visual and spatial stimuli; therefore, ensuring that the narrative remains understandable and followable depends on the conscious guidance of attention.

In this layer, motion design serves as an implicit narrator. The direction, speed, rhythm, and continuity of movement determine which narrative elements the user will notice first and which information will be perceived at a secondary level. Kinetic guidance offers a system that intuitively guides the viewer rather than directly explaining the narrative. In this way, the user protects their position as an active subject in the narrative while unconsciously following its structural priorities.

This layer has a critical role, particularly in limiting distractions in immersive experiences and preserving narrative integrity. While excessive or uncontrolled motion weakens this layer's function, the design of rhythmic, purposeful motion strengthens the narrative's perceptual continuity.

Spatial Dramaturgy Layer

The spatial dramaturgy layer defines the function of motion design in staging the space and transforming it into a narrative. In immersive media environments, space ceases to be a passive container in which the narrative occurs and becomes an active structure in which the narrative is produced and guided. Motion design dramatically organizes this spatial structure, making the narrative's spatial logic visible.

In this layer, motion facilitates narrative segmentation by creating spatial thresholds, transitions, and areas of dramatic intensity. As the user moves through the space, they not only follow a physical route but also experience a narrative journey. Motion design functions as a fundamental dramaturgical tool that determines the rhythm and direction of this journey.

Instead of completely controlling the exploration-based structure of narrative, spatial dramaturgy aims to offer the user a guided yet open-ended experience. This balance is critical to preserving the sense of subjective discovery, an essential characteristic of immersive experiences. Austin (2020: 92) makes a closely related observation in the context of narrative environments, arguing that anticipation is key to audience engagement and that designers must enable audiences to savor spatial transitions rather than imposing abrupt changes that disorient rather than immerse. In this sense, the balance between guidance and openness in spatial dramaturgy is not only a design preference but also a condition of sustained narrative immersion.

Temporal Sequencing Layer

The temporal sequencing layer defines the function of motion design in organizing the narrative's flow over time and its emotional rhythm. In immersive narratives, time ceases to be a predetermined linear structure and becomes an experiential dimension shaped by user actions. Motion design is one of the fundamental narrative tools that makes this fluid temporal structure readable and meaningful.

In this layer, motion regulates the narrative's emotional intensity through rhythm, tempo, and continuity. While accelerating motions create tension and expectation, slowing or pausing motions open up spaces for thinking and awareness. Temporal sequencing determines not only "when" the narrative occurs, but also "how it is felt."

Moreover, temporal sequencing plays a decisive role in cognitive sustainability. A balanced rhythm and consistent tempo facilitate the user's mental processing of the experience. Within this framework, motion design goes beyond producing dramatic effects and offers a system that regulates the narrative's cognitive ergonomics.

MOTION DESIGN AS AN INTER-LAYER INTERACTION AND NARRATIVE INFRASTRUCTURE

The layers of kinetic guidance, spatial dramaturgy, and temporal sequencing do not operate independently; they are in continuous interaction within immersive narratives. While kinetic guidance enhances the perceptibility of spatial dramaturgy, temporal sequencing regulates the emotional rhythm of this spatial structure. Motion design serves as the infrastructure that connects these layers and establishes the narrative's integrity.

With this integrated structure, motion design becomes a foundational system that enables the narrative's functioning, rather than merely an aesthetic choice in immersive storytelling. Without this infrastructure, the narrative may be fragmented, disjointed, or perceptually exhausting.

DISCUSSION

This study reconceptualizes the role of motion design within immersive media, moving it beyond instrumental and aesthetic approaches to treat motion as a narrative infrastructure that simultaneously structures spatial, temporal, and perceptual dimensions. While existing literature confines motion design to graphic design, animation, or interaction-level guidance, this framework positions it as a foundational system enabling narrative to function, bringing together attention guidance, spatial organization, and temporal flow into an integrated narrative structure rather than treating them as isolated functions.

One important contribution is the framework's potential to reduce interdisciplinary gaps, establishing common conceptual ground among visual communication, narrative theory, and immersive media. Motion is thus repositioned not as a visual effect but as a fundamental organizing principle shaping how narrative is perceived.

Central to the debate is the balance between control and user autonomy. Kinetic guidance, spatial dramaturgy, and temporal sequencing intuitively convey narrative priorities without explicitly directing the user — demonstrating motion design's ability to structure narrative without being didactic. This framework also provides a powerful analytical tool for explaining why immersive narratives feel impressive in some cases yet exhausting or disjointed in others.

For design practice, motion decisions, direction, rhythm, duration, and spatial relationships, must be treated as narrative decisions, not merely aesthetic ones. Motion design should therefore be considered a foundational component from the earliest stages of narrative design, redefining the motion designer's role in interdisciplinary teams as a strategic contributor to narrative architecture.

In educational contexts, motion design instruction should extend beyond technical skills to integrate narrative theory and experience design, pointing to a pedagogical transformation that could directly influence the quality of immersive experiences. As a conceptual study, the proposed framework has not been directly tested empirically. Future research should apply it through case studies across immersive formats, virtual reality, digital exhibitions, interactive installations, while quantitative and qualitative user experience studies could further examine how motion design affects attention, emotion, and spatial perception.

CONCLUSION

This article examines the relationship between motion design and immersive storytelling through a critical synthesis approach and conceptualizes motion not only as an aesthetic or technical element but also as a narrative infrastructure that enables immersive experiences. In the literature, motion design, immersive media, and visual storytelling are mostly studied as separate disciplines, and the relationships among these fields are discussed in a fragmented and indirect manner. In this study, beyond this fragmented structure, motion design is positioned as a foundational system that simultaneously structures the spatial, temporal, and perceptual dimensions of narrative.

The literature review and critical synthesis demonstrate that motion design focuses on three fundamental narrative functions in the context of immersive media: kinetic guidance, spatial dramaturgy, and temporal sequencing. These functions are treated as non-hierarchical yet mutually interactive layers; the decisive role of motion in directing attention, transforming space into narrative, and emotionally experiencing time is explained within a holistic framework. Thus, motion design moves to a structural and foundational position in immersive storytelling, beyond being a mere instrumental element.

The proposed integrated conceptual framework clearly demonstrates why motion design cannot be considered only as a visual embellishment or a guiding tool in immersive narratives. Motion is a fundamental organizational mechanism that ensures the narrative's legibility, supports the cognitive sustainability of the experience, and regulates the emotional flow. Therefore, motion design should be treated as an infrastructural system that enables the narrative to function, rather than as a layer added to it. One of the main contributions of this study is its positioning of motion design as a unifying concept across various fields of literature. This framework, drawn from visual perception, narrative theory, immersive media studies, and cognitive psychology, demonstrates that motion design can be understood as an interdisciplinary narrative language. Thus, motion should be reconsidered not only in the context of visual communication or interaction design but also as a foundational element of experiential narratives.

From the perspective of a design practice, this framework emphasizes that motion design decisions are not aesthetic choices left until the end of the process, but rather strategic decisions made in the early stages of narrative design. The rhythm, direction, and continuity of motion directly influence the narrative's tone, spatial legibility, and emotional impact. This carries the motion designer's role beyond visual production, making it a foundational component of narrative architecture.

In the context of education, the study shows that teaching motion design cannot be limited to technical skills alone. Designers who can grasp the perceptual, spatial, and dramaturgical effects of motion can create more coherent and effective immersive experiences. This approach provides a theoretical foundation for developing pedagogical models that integrate narrative theory and experience design within motion design and new media arts programs.

Because this study is a review and conceptual article, the proposed framework has not been directly tested with empirical data. However, this situation reveals a clear research agenda for future studies, rather than limiting the study's contribution. Future studies could focus on testing this framework through applied case analyses across different types of immersive media, supporting it with research on user experience, and measuring the perceptual and emotional effects of motion design.

In conclusion, this article proposes a framework for filling the conceptual gap regarding the role of motion design in immersive storytelling. Treating motion as an infrastructure that shapes narrative enables a reevaluation of both theoretical and practical approaches to immersive media design. Considering this perspective, motion design is a fundamental narrative language that determines not only how immersive experiences appear but also how they acquire meaning.

REFERENCES

Austin, T. (2020). *Narrative environments and experience design: Space as a medium of communication*. Routledge. DOI: 10.4324/9780367138073

Betancourt, M. (2013). Ideologies of the real in title sequences, motion graphics, and cinema. In Betancourt, M. (Ed.), *The history of motion graphics: From avant-garde to industry in the United States*. Wildside Press.

Bordwell, D. (2008). *Poetics of cinema*. Routledge.

Bowman, D. A., Kruijff, E., LaViola, J. J., & Poupyrev, I. (2004). *3D user interfaces: Theory and practice*. Addison-Wesley.

Bucher, J. (2018). *Storytelling for virtual reality: Methods and principles for crafting immersive narratives*. Routledge.

Calleja, G. (2019). *In-game: From immersion to incorporation*. MIT Press.

Goldstein, E. B. (2014). *Sensation and perception* (9th ed.). Cengage Learning.

Jenkins, H. (2004). Game design as narrative architecture. In Wardrip-Fruin, N., & Harrigan, P. (Eds.), *First person: New media as story, performance, and game* (pp. 118–130). MIT Press.

Krasner, J. (2013). *Motion graphic design: Applied history and aesthetics* (2nd ed.). Focal Press. DOI: 10.4324/9780240824703

Lupton, E., & Phillips, J. C. (2015). *Graphic design: The new basics* (2nd ed.). Princeton Architectural Press.

Manovich, L. (2013). *Software takes command*. Bloomsbury Academic. DOI: 10.5040/9781472544988

McCloud, S. (1993). *Understanding comics: The invisible art*. HarperCollins.

Milgram, P., & Kishino, F. (1994). A taxonomy of mixed reality visual displays. *IEICE Transactions on Information and Systems*, *77*(12), 1321–1329.

Murray, J. H. (2017). *Hamlet on the holodeck: The future of narrative in cyberspace* (Updated ed.). MIT Press.

Ryan, M.-L. (2015). *Narrative as virtual reality 2: Revisiting immersion and interactivity in literature and electronic media*. Johns Hopkins University Press. DOI: 10.1353/book.72246

Shaw, A., & Colette, J. (2023). *Motion design toolkit: Principles, practice, and techniques*. Routledge.

Slater, M. (2009). Place illusion and plausibility can lead to realistic behaviour in immersive virtual environments. *Philosophical Transactions of the Royal Society of London. Series B, Biological Sciences*, *364*(1535), 3549–3557. DOI: 10.1098/rstb.2009.0138 PMID: 19884149

Slater, M., & Wilbur, S. (1997). A framework for immersive virtual environments (FIVE): Speculations on the role of presence in virtual environments. *Presence (Cambridge, Mass.)*, *6*(6), 603–616. DOI: 10.1162/pres.1997.6.6.603

Sweller, J., Ayres, P., & Kalyuga, S. (2011). *Cognitive load theory*. Springer. DOI: 10.1007/978-1-4419-8126-4

Ware, C. (2013). *Information visualization: Perception for design* (3rd ed.). Morgan Kaufmann.

Wong, W. (1993). *Principles of form and design*. John Wiley & Sons.

Chapter 5
New Trends in Cinematic Space Design:
The Impact of Physical, Hybrid, and Digital Technologies on Set Construction in Film Productions

Tolga Gürocak
http://orcid.org/0000-0002-5284-8447
Faculty of Fine Arts, Afyon Kocatepe University, Turkey

Gamze Çoban
http://orcid.org/0000-0001-6524-3861
Faculty of Fine Arts, Afyon Kocatepe University, Turkey

ABSTRACT

Cinema constructs meaning through the organization of space, where mise-en-scène, camera, and production design operate as interdependent systems. This study examines how different modes of space construction—physical, digital, and hybrid—shape in-scene visual organization. Drawing on a comparative qualitative case study, it analyzes selected film scenes in relation to depth perception, light continuity, actor movement, and camera design. The findings suggest that physical setups rely on optically verifiable spatial coherence, while digital setups offer flexibility but depend on post-production accuracy. Hybrid systems, particularly virtual production and LED volume technologies, reduce spatial ambiguity by enabling real-time integration of physical and digital elements. Consequently, the production regime emerges as a decisive factor that not only conditions technical workflows but also directly influences the visual and narrative structure of cinematic space.

DOI: 10.4018/979-8-3373-6680-7.ch005

INTRODUCTION

Cinematic space is a primary means through which visual order is organized within the frame. Camera perspective, actor placement, light distribution, and depth perception depend on the spatial conditions available to the camera. Mise-en-scène names this coordination of decor, light, bodies, and movement in narrative production (Bordwell & Thompson, 2019). Space design should therefore be understood not only as physical construction, but as a cinematic operation shaping narrative, atmosphere, and visual hierarchy.

Production design gives the film world its atmosphere and visual identity, translating psychological states and emotional tones into spatial form (LoBrutto, 2002; Barnwell, 2004). Walls, thresholds, surfaces, light sources, and movement paths affect what the filmmaker can stage, block, illuminate, and frame (Affron & Affron, 1995; Block, 2008; Ettedgui, 1999). Space is therefore not secondary to narrative; it defines the relationships and movements through which narrative becomes visible.

Mise-en-scène is inseparable from how cinematic space is produced. A physically built set, digitally extended environment, and hybrid in-camera system each offer different conditions for composition, lighting, performance, and camera movement. The production method is more than a technical preference; it shapes scene-level visual order during filming. As production technologies diversify, hybrid systems and digital extensions have become common alongside physical sets (Okun & Zwerman, 2025). This shift makes the relation between spatial production and on-screen composition visible: the construction method affects both what appears in the image and how it is organized.

Recent scholarship has examined digital effects, virtual production workflows, screen performance, and film labor. Yet these discussions often focus on technological infrastructure or industrial consequences. Chung (2018) foregrounds the distributed labor behind digital environments; Bode (2017) examines special-effects performance and the actor's relation to absent or partially present environments; and Swords and Willment (2024) identify virtual production as an emerging field shaped by changing workflows and production cultures.

Less systematically addressed is how spatial-construction regimes produce distinct scene-level conditions for mise-en-scène. This study treats physical, digital, and hybrid setups not as technical alternatives but as production regimes that reorganize depth cues, light continuity, actor spatial awareness, camera movement, and on-set visibility. Its contribution lies in linking production method to on-screen composition and proposing a comparative framework for analyzing mise-en-scène across material, computational, and hybrid conditions.

The argument proceeds in four stages. First, the chapter clarifies the relation between cinematic space, mise-en-scène, and the profilmic order. Second, it defines the regimes structuring the comparison. Third, it explains the qualitative comparative case-study design, including scene selection and coding criteria. Finally, it applies four analytical clusters—depth, light, actor-camera organization, and on-set visibility—to the fifteen-film corpus to identify each regime's trade-offs.

BACKGROUND

Space in cinema functions both as an element that constructs the narrative world and as the material and technical foundation of the profilmic order — the physical set, actors, decor, and objects before the camera at filming (Lageira, 2025; Souriau, 1953). It does not merely provide a backdrop but integrates with the story to produce spatial, emotional, and psychological experience (Bachelard, 1994; Monaco, 2009; Tarkovsky, 1986). Thus, space makes the diegetic universe visible while determining the production conditions of scene-level visual order.

Theoretical discussions often focus on the relation between narrative space and production space. Space provides the narrative framework through which audiences perceive the film world, while also constituting the production field that determines the material or digital conditions of the profilmic order. André Bazin (1967) argued that cinema is the art form closest to reality, emphasizing long takes and deep focus as techniques that render space more authentic. Postmodern theories, by contrast, examine space through simulation and artificiality: Baudrillard's (1994) concept of simulation suggests that cinema presents not reality itself but a copy of it, with space — particularly in science fiction and dystopian films — constructed as part of that simulation. Bordwell's (1989; 2008) historical poetics positions space as a design field carrying production and perception simultaneously, showing how mise-en-scène and cinematography explain both the image and the production regime behind it.

Production design literature supports this constitutive role. Production design constructs the atmosphere, period, and visual identity of the film world (Barnwell, 2004), making characters' social positions, psychological states, and narrative atmosphere visible. Set design need not reproduce a real location; building only the required portion of the story, omitting ceilings, or scaling the space are fundamental practices (İnceoğlu, 2022). According to LoBrutto (2002), set design is not merely decor but narrative architecture shaping camera movement, lighting, and actor blocking. Prince (2012) treats digital visual effects as a toolkit expanding cinema's perception of reality, noting that spatial representation has changed with technological transformation.

Against this background, cinematic space production can be examined under three operational regimes. Physical setup refers to materially produced studio sets or real locations (Bordwell & Thompson, 2019; LoBrutto, 2002). Digital setup describes spaces created largely in post-production through CG environments, set extensions, and compositing (Okun & Zwerman, 2025; Prince, 2012). Hybrid setup refers to the collaboration of physical and digital production during filming, using real-time engines, camera tracking, and LED volume/ICVFX technologies (Epic Games, 2019). These regimes are not mutually exclusive — many productions combine them within the same film or scene — yet they remain productive analytical categories because they foreground the structural conditions under which spatial configurations are produced.

Over the last decade, digitalization has transformed cinematic space construction. Linear workflows have increasingly evolved into parallel and feedback-driven structures (Swords & Willment, 2024), as real-time rendering moves space production from post-production into pre-production and production. The clearest example is the On-Set Virtual Production (OSVP) approach defined by SMPTE (2023), which describes the real-time merging of physical and digital worlds on set and brings virtual production into industrial standardization.

THE FUNCTION OF CINEMATIC SPACE

Cinematic space functions as a field of meaning production: it determines where the narrative world becomes visible and how that world is experienced. Three frameworks are especially useful here: the organizing logic of mise-en-scène, the phenomenological dimension of spatial experience, and the relation between space and the profilmic order.

Mise-en-scène defines the visual order created by decor, light, actor placement, and movement within the frame. It positions space as the structure organizing spatial relations, depth, movement, and visual narration (Bordwell & Thompson, 2019; Brown, 2016; Elsaesser & Hagener, 2015; Gibbs, 2002; Monaco, 2009). When space, light, actors, and objects are arranged together, space becomes more than a backdrop. It becomes an atmospheric narrative device that can externalize character psychology and shape the viewer's emotional relation to the story (Adanır, 2003; Pallasmaa, 2001).

From a phenomenological perspective, cinematic space is not merely a container for action but an experiential environment mediating between the viewer's bodily dispositions and the film world. Tarkovsky (1986) described cinematic time and space as inseparable from the physical conditions in which they are recorded; the authenticity of a filmed environment — its material weight and sensory specificity — was central to cinematic expression. Bachelard's (1994) analysis of inhabited space similarly argues that space is charged with psychological and imaginative meaning: the poetics of space emerges from how space is lived, feared, desired, and remembered. Applied to production, these frameworks suggest that whether space is constructed materially, computationally, or in hybrid form affects the meanings and experiences it can carry.

This phenomenological argument can be connected to cognitive accounts of cinematic perception without reducing spatial experience to psychology alone. Continuity, attention, and embodied orientation shape how viewers follow movement, infer depth, and maintain spatial relations across shots (Anderson, 1996; Gibson, 1979; Smith, 2012). Thus, depth cues, light behavior, and camera movement are not merely formal features; they are perceptual supports that help viewers organize the cinematic world.

The relationship between space and the profilmic order adds a further dimension. The profilmic denotes everything before the camera at shooting: actors, costumes, props, sets, and the physical or optical conditions of the environment (Lageira, 2025; Souriau, 1953). When space is physically constructed, the profilmic order is tangible and co-present with actors; when digitally extended or generated, it becomes partial or conditional. Hybrid setups occupy an intermediate position: the profilmic order includes a real background image projected on LED panels, yet this image is a digital representation updated in real time. Each configuration structures mise-en-scène differently.

PRODUCTION REGIMES: PHYSICAL, DIGITAL, AND HYBRID SETUP

In the most comprehensive form of digital setup — full CG environment — actors are positioned during filming only in front of a blue or green screen (chroma key), while space is created in post-production through three-dimensional modeling, texture mapping, light simulation, and rendering (Stump, 2021; Wright, 2024). The visual effects team models the digital environment according to the camera's viewpoint, lens characteristics, and reference light conditions recorded during filming — including HDRI measurements, color calibration, and camera tracking data — and integrates it with the footage. As Hye Jean Chung (2018) emphasizes, digital cinema environments consist of heterogeneous layers produced in multiple locations and later assembled. The visual coherence of the scene is therefore the product of a globally distributed production network.

Set extension — a hybrid method between full CG environment and physical setup — involves building only the portion of the set where actors interact and the camera frames closely, while the rest is completed digitally in post-production (Dinur, 2017; Prince, 2012). This approach allows actors to move within a partially real environment, providing an important advantage for performance authenticity and spatial awareness (Bode, 2017). However, integrating physical and digital layers visually and consistently — particularly in terms of light matching, color continuity, and perspective coherence — still creates a significant post-production burden (Wright, 2024).

Historically, this hybrid logic predates LED volume technology. Cinema has long combined material and represented space through rear projection, front projection, matte painting, miniatures, traveling mattes, optical compositing, and later digital set extensions. What distinguishes contemporary LED volume/ICVFX is not the mere combination of physical and non-physical space, but the real-time synchronization of represented space with camera movement, lens data, and on-set light. In this sense, virtual production is a new operational form of an older hybrid impulse: it relocates background integration from optical or post-production pipelines into the moment of shooting (Prince, 2012; Dinur, 2017; Okun et al., 2025).

A hybrid setup defines the production model in which physical and digital processes work together in real time, at or near the moment of filming. Often discussed under virtual production, this approach was developed to bring digital setups' post-production-heavy workflow onto the set, centering on LED volume and ICVFX workflows (Okun et al., 2025). Wide audiences became aware of this approach through *The Mandalorian* (2019), where the StageCraft system developed by Industrial Light & Magic (ILM) was implemented; since then, it has been used in many high-budget film and series productions (Epic Games, 2019; Kavakli & Cremona, 2022).

The LED volume system refers to a circular or semi-circular filming environment composed of high-resolution LED panel arrays. In this setup, the digital background is continuously rendered on the LED panels by real-time render engines, most commonly Unreal Engine (Epic Games, 2019). The dynamic update of the background is achieved through camera tracking, the technical core of ICVFX: by tracking camera position and orientation in real time, it sends positional data to the render engine, synchronizing the LED image's perspective with the camera's viewpoint (Epic Games, 2019; SMPTE, 2023). From only three LED volume facilities in 2019 to more than 300 installed systems by late 2022, this growth reflects the pace of industrial adoption (Kavakli & Cremona, 2022).

The distinctive features of hybrid setup are organized around four core technical components. First, real-time visualization systems — primarily game engines such as Unreal Engine — render three-dimensional virtual environments during filming and project them onto LED panels, transferring traditional post-production workflows onto the set (Kavakli & Cremona, 2022; Zhang, 2024). Second, camera and lens tracking: without this technology, the visual continuity of a hybrid setup would be impossible. Third, color management and calibration: in hybrid environments, this issue goes beyond a technical problem to shape cinematographic language (AMPAS,

2020; Long et al., 2025). Fourth, synchronization, artifact management, and data processing: artifacts such as moiré effects, flicker, color shifts, parallax errors, and depth-of-field inconsistencies can affect production quality, making careful calibration necessary (ARRI, 2022; James et al., 2021; LeGendre et al., 2022; Netflix, 2023).

For readers approaching this discussion from film theory rather than production practice, four technical terms require clarification. Real-time rendering refers to generating the digital background during filming rather than after the shoot; camera tracking continuously measures camera position, orientation, and lens data so the virtual background shifts correctly with the shot; compositing combines separately produced image layers into a single final frame; and ACES is a color-management framework used to keep color decisions consistent across cameras, software, and display systems. These terms matter not as isolated engineering details, but because they determine what filmmakers can evaluate, adjust, and control at the moment of shooting.

The effect of hybrid setup on actor performance is a particularly important area of inquiry. Unlike the actor in chroma key filming — who faces an empty, flat-colored background — the actor in an LED volume environment is surrounded by a visible environment. Light, color, and spatial atmosphere are physically perceptible; this supports the claim that sensory dimensions of spatial context contribute directly to performance (Bode, 2017). The performing-in-the-void phenomenon in chroma key filming is structurally transformed in LED volume. Rather than producing a symbolic performance in an absent space, the actor exists within a visually and photometrically active environment. Some industry professionals have also noted that the technical structure of LED volume can occasionally interrupt the actor-director dialogue (Boutellier & Raptis, 2023; Zhang, 2024).

THE SPACE-MISE-EN-SCÈNE-CAMERA RELATIONSHIP

The relationship between space, mise-en-scène, and the camera can be stated as follows: when the production model of space changes, the arrangement of the camera, the actor, and the light also changes. Across physical, digital, and hybrid models, mise-en-scène appears not only as an aesthetic preference but also as an outcome shaped by technical and operational conditions.

Bordwell's (2005; 2008) staging-focused approach emphasizes that narrative information is conveyed through shot design, actor placement and movement, and spatial relationships within the frame. From this perspective, space becomes the plane on which visual hierarchy is organized. As the production regime changes, so do the mechanisms of that organization: depth cues, light and color continuity, and camera movement constraints are configured differently. Two scenes may look similar on screen, even though they are produced under very different conditions.

In physical setup, mise-en-scène is constructed through the movement and contact possibilities offered by real geometry. Actor placement and camera movement are planned in concert with the set's material scale, physical obstacles, and real lighting conditions. Depth cues such as overlap, perspective diminution, real parallax, reflections, and shadows, and depth of field derive from the physical world, giving spatial consistency an observable, optically verifiable foundation at the moment of filming (Bazin, 1967; Burch, 1973). The physical setup in this respect situates the camera's framing decisions within a more predictable spatial infrastructure; the environment speaks back to the filmmaker, imposing and enabling decisions simultaneously (Anderson, 1996; Block, 2008; Gibson, 1979).

In a digital setup, the placement of actors and the design of camera movement are often planned with reference to an environment that will be produced later; this leads to limited spatial feedback and defers ambiguity to the post-production phase. Spatial consistency depends on the accuracy of the data and references collected on the set, as well as on the quality of matching in the compositing process. While digital setup generates creative flexibility by producing physically impossible environments, the inability to see the final look at the moment of filming can introduce delays and consistency risks in mise-en-scène decisions (Okun & Zwerman, 2025).

Hybrid approaches aim precisely to reduce this spatial ambiguity. The LED volume/ICVFX system, by showing the background in the correct perspective for the camera in real time, offers a more integrated mise-en-scène and a shooting environment closer to the final image in a single exposure (Epic Games, 2019; Okun et al., 2025). The simultaneous update of camera movement and virtual background ties cinematic decisions more directly to the set. This represents a structural shift in the temporal organization of mise-en-scène: decisions that, in a digital setup, must be deferred can now be evaluated, rejected, or modified on the day of shooting. However, this advantage of a hybrid setup must be evaluated within the framework of technical constraints — color calibration, panel-camera matching, artifact management — which function as production variables that shape mise-en-scène reliability (ARRI, 2022; Long et al., 2025). The introduction of these constraints means that the on-set team in hybrid production includes not only the director, DP, and production designer, but also real-time rendering specialists, color scientists, and LED calibration engineers — expanding the circle of authorship over mise-en-scène decisions.

Actor experience also varies across production models. In chroma key work, the actor often performs without a fully visible environment; in LED volume production, by contrast, the actor is surrounded by an image that is visually and photometrically active. Light from the LED walls affects faces and costumes in real time, and the background shifts with camera movement. These cues can strengthen spatial awareness in ways that a flat chroma background cannot provide (Bode, 2017; Chen, 2024).

Virtual production also changes the timing of creative decisions. As more choices move from post-production into pre-production, the familiar "fix it in post" logic (Swords & Willment, 2024) increasingly gives way to "fix it in pre." This shift is not only about efficiency. Choices made in advance through previsualized environments differ from choices made spontaneously in response to a physical or quasi-physical set during shooting. The same shift also raises access questions for small- and medium-budget productions, where specialized labor, workflow knowledge, and infrastructure costs can become barriers to adoption (Bodini et al., 2024).

These access questions also have labor and sustainability dimensions. LED volume workflows may reduce travel to some locations and some post-production corrections. Still, they also shift costs and responsibilities to pre-production asset creation, stage rental, data infrastructure, calibration work, and specialized real-time teams. This redistribution aligns with production-culture research, which shows that technical innovation often reallocates labor and authority rather than simply eliminating them (Caldwell, 2008; Curtin & Sanson, 2016; Zhang, 2024). Environmental trade-offs should be approached with similar caution: physical set construction and location shooting generate material waste and travel demands, while rendering infrastructures and LED stages require energy-intensive hardware and display systems. For this reason, access, labor, and sustainability should be treated as production variables that shape which spatial regime is practically available to a given project, not as external issues added after the aesthetic analysis (Bodini et al., 2024; Kääpä, 2018; Silva Jasaui et al., 2024). Because cost data for LED stage rental, render infrastructure, physical construction, and location logistics vary sharply by region, project scale, and contract structure, this study treats economic access as a structural condition rather than as a universal numerical comparison.

AIM AND METHODOLOGY

Different methods of constructing space make visible the close relation between production practice and scene-level composition. Physical sets and real locations long served as the dominant modes of cinematic space. Still, digital imaging technologies have made hybrid in-camera systems and post-production-based extensions increasingly common (Okun & Zwerman, 2025). This transformation affects not only how space is produced, but also how light, depth, performance, and camera movement are organized within the scene.

Mise-en-scène provides the main conceptual framework for addressing this relation, as it explains how decor, lighting, actor placement, and movement participate in narrative production (Brown, 2016; Elsaesser & Hagener, 2015; Gibbs, 2002; Monaco, 2009). The construction of space shapes the quality of on-screen composition, from in-frame depth relations to camera movement possibilities (Barnwell, 2004; Bordwell & Thompson, 2019; Brown, 2016). A physically built space and a digitally extended environment do not provide the same conditions for actor movement, camera placement, or lighting design; camera tracking, real-time visualization, and compositing make these differences especially visible (Okun et al., 2025). Yet existing literature has most often treated cinematic space through its aesthetic and narrative functions, while the scene-level effects of different production methods have received more limited attention (Barnwell, 2004; James et al., 2021; Monaco, 2009; LeGendre et al., 2022; Silva Jasaui et al., 2024; Whitehead, 2017).

This study examines how different methods of space construction shape scene-level visual arrangement in cinema. It focuses on the effects of physical spaces, hybrid in-camera systems, and digitally extended setups on mise-en-scène, depth perception, light continuity, actor performance, and camera movement.

Accordingly, the study asks how the production mode of cinematic space affects the organization of depth, light, movement, and camera placement. The following questions guide the research:

1. How do different space construction methods (physical, hybrid, and digital) affect the way in-scene visual organization is formed?
2. What differences emerge between physical sets, hybrid in-camera systems, and digital extensions in terms of depth perception, perspective relationships, and light continuity?
3. What effect do space construction methods have on actor performance, scene blocking, and the design of camera movement?
4. What advantages and limitations do different space construction methods contain in terms of cinematic narrative, production control, and visual consistency?

This study examines cinematic space across physical, hybrid, and digital production regimes and asks how these regimes transform mise-en-scène and camera organization. Rather than treating the film scene as a self-contained text, the analysis treats the production logic that generates the visible image as part of the object of study.

The methodological premise is production-sensitive. Visual style analysis is incomplete when detached from the material, computational, or hybrid conditions that enable the image. Conversely, an account of production technology remains limited if it does not identify observable consequences for depth, light, performance, and camera organization.

The research is designed as a qualitative comparative case study, with the space-construction regime (physical, digital, or hybrid) as the principal unit of comparison

(Yin, 2018). The model proceeds on two connected planes. The descriptive plane clarifies the technical and workflow-based equivalents of the three regimes. The analytical-comparative plane examines how those regimes produce different scene-level conditions through structured coding (Neuendorf, 2017; Rose, 2016).

Each selected scene was coded through four categories: (1) depth cues and spatial continuity, including foreground-background layering, parallax, scale consistency, and perspective coherence; (2) light behavior and color continuity, including motivated light sources, color spill, shadow direction, and foreground-background matching; (3) actor placement, movement, and camera movement design, including blocking, bodily orientation, and the spatial feedback available to performers; and (4) on-set visibility and technically induced artifacts, including the degree to which the final image could be evaluated during shooting and the risks of compositing seams, moiré, flicker, color mismatch, or calibration error.

The sample consists of 15 films selected through purposive sampling (Patton, 2015) and grouped into three production categories. The aim is not statistical representativeness, but the selection of information-rich cases in which the relationship between spatial production and visual arrangement can be clearly observed. Four criteria guided the selection: the film had to be widely discussed or documented in relation to a dominant spatial-production regime; the selected scenes had to foreground at least two analytical categories, such as depth construction, light continuity, actor-camera organization, or on-set visibility; production-contextual materials such as interviews, VFX breakdowns, making-of sources, or technical documentation had to be available for cross-validation; and the corpus had to include variation in period, genre, budget scale, and production culture.

Table 1. Comparative summary of physical, digital, and hybrid space-construction regimes

Analytical dimension	Physical setup	Digital setup	Hybrid setup
Depth cues	Derived from real geometry, optical parallax, and material surfaces.	Produced computationally through modeling, rendering, and compositing.	Produced through a combination of real foregrounds and tracked digital backgrounds.
Light and color continuity	Largely established by practical light sources and the material environment during shooting.	Matched primarily in post-production through digital lighting and color workflows.	Partly established on set because LED backgrounds serve as both images and light sources.
Actor spatial feedback	High: performers interact with a fully present environment.	Limited: performers often work against absent or partial environments.	Intermediate: performers see a visible environment, but not always a fully physical one.

continued on following page

Table 1. Continued

Analytical dimension	Physical setup	Digital setup	Hybrid setup
Camera movement and blocking	Shaped by the actual geometry and physical constraints of the set or location.	Flexible in principle, but often dependent on previs and deferred spatial verification.	Allows real-time evaluation of camera-background relations, while introducing technical constraints.
On-set visibility of final look	Highest, although subject to uncontrollable physical variables such as weather or reflections.	Lowest, because many visual decisions are finalized later in post-production.	Higher than a digital setup, because background imagery is visible during filming.
Typical production risk	Uncontrollable environmental variation, practical-light inconsistency, or set-specific artifacts.	Compositing mismatch, perspective inconsistency, and delayed problem detection.	Calibration demands, moiré, color shifts, and panel-camera synchronization issues.

The physical setup group consists of *There Will Be Blood* (2007), *No Country for Old Men* (2007), *The Dark Knight* (2008), *Mad Max: Fury Road* (2015), and *Barbie* (2023). The digital setup group consists of *Sin City* (2005), *300* (2006), *Avatar* (2009), *Gravity* (2013), and *Dune: Part One* (2021). The hybrid setup group consists of *The Batman* (2022), *Top Gun: Maverick* (2022), *Thor: Love and Thunder* (2022), *Bullet Train* (2022), and *Dune: Part Two* (2024).

Table 1 summarizes the study's comparative logic and serves as a roadmap for the analysis that follows. It does not replace scene analysis; rather, it condenses the main dimensions along which the three production regimes are compared.

Data collection operates on two levels. First, audiovisual data are treated as primary sources: each selected scene was viewed repeatedly, with close attention to foreground-background junctions, lighting transitions, camera movements, blocking patterns, and visual details that reveal or conceal spatial depth. Frame freezing and slow playback were not used purely as descriptive devices but as tools for identifying how spatial organization is constructed within the image. Second, contextual data were compiled from director and director of photography interviews, production designer statements, VFX breakdowns, studio documentation, and making-of materials, allowing scene-level observations to be cross-validated against production context (Flick, 2018). The analysis is organized by criteria rather than by film to compare how the same visual problem is handled across different production regimes. Not every film is therefore given identical weight in every subsection; instead, each case is used where the available scene evidence and production documentation most directly illuminate the criterion under discussion. This procedure is intended to avoid unsupported generalization while preserving the comparative logic of the study.

To strengthen the link between claims and evidence, the analysis distinguishes between three levels of support: directly observable scene features, documented production practices, and theoretical interpretation. Claims about foreground-background relations, camera movement, lighting transitions, and visible artifacts are grounded primarily in repeated audiovisual viewing. Claims about workflow, calibration, rendering, and production organization are used only when supported by production-contextual sources. Theoretical sources are therefore not treated as general proof for every scene-level observation, but as frameworks that explain why the observed production differences matter for mise-en-scène analysis.

ANALYSIS AND FINDINGS

Depth Cues and Spatial Continuity

Depth cues and spatial continuity most clearly reveal how production regimes affect mise-en-scène. Physical, digital, and hybrid models differ in how depth is constructed, how foreground, middle ground, and background are layered, and how spatial continuity is maintained across shots. To address the corpus's comparative balance, the following analysis uses all 15 films across the four clusters, while assigning the greatest analytical weight to the scenes that most clearly expose each criterion.

Physical Setup: The opening mining sequence in *There Will Be Blood* is a strong example of how physical depth cues operate within mise-en-scène. Daniel Plainview works alone in a rocky landscape during this long sequence; the mostly static or slow-moving camera lets depth emerge from the geometry of the location. Anamorphic lenses and high-speed film stock create a shallow depth of field that separates the foreground actor from the wide desert background. Overlap, perspective diminution, and atmospheric haze all stem from an optically verifiable spatial ground. Production designer Jack Fisk's integration of the set with the location — including structures placed within the topography and the use of the horizon line — ties depth order to real terrain. In *No Country for Old Men*, the opening scene in which Llewelyn Moss tracks game across the Texas desert follows a similar spatial logic: foreground/background layering is produced by the flat, expansive geography, while the actor's small figure creates depth perception integrated with the landscape. Roger Deakins's practical light and natural sunlight maintain consistent shadow and reflection relationships across surfaces, reinforcing spatial continuity. *The Dark Knight* shows how depth cues can be organized in a constructed interior: the bank lobby's architecture — columns, staircases, teller partitions — naturally produces foreground, middle-ground, and background layers, while the IMAX camera records physical texture and perspective lines with exceptional clarity. Nolan's use of large-scale practical sets confirms that this depth order is achieved through actual construction. In *Mad Max: Fury Road*, the initial convoy attack presents a complex arrangement of vehicles and characters moving simultaneously across open desert terrain; wide-angle shots create a layered depth order through the placement of vehicles across foreground, middle-ground, and background planes. Because the stunts and vehicles occupy real desert space, perspective relationships and scale consistency are maintained optically without computation. *Barbie* offers a contrasting example in which depth cues are deliberately flattened by the physical set. Gerwig's design creates an artificial but coherent spatial logic: even the absence of depth cues becomes a consistent visual language, demonstrating the physical setup's direct and controlled influence over depth order.

Digital Setup: In *Sin City*, the sequence in which Hartigan searches the harbor demonstrates the structural effect of digital setup on depth cues in its purest form: depth layering is produced not by real geometric relationships but through the post-production arrangement of color, contrast, and light, within a composition built largely on a black background. Conventional depth cues such as overlap and perspective diminution are deliberately minimized; spatial continuity is established through graphic design principles. In *300*, the first major battle at Thermopylae follows a similar structure with a different aesthetic aim: while the actors' physical performances provide foreground data, the background is digitally constructed. Because depth layering is produced by render decisions, perspective relationships derive from post-production choices rather than real optical space. *Avatar* offers the most comprehensive example of depth staging through digital setup: the multi-planar depth order of the bioluminescent forest is created through render technology, while digital depth cues — overlap, atmospheric haze, and perspective diminution — are convincingly simulated. Yet since scale and perspective relationships derive from design decisions rather than physical laws, spatial consistency depends on data integrity. *Gravity* represents an extreme case in which depth cues are severed from physical reference: because the space environment contains no real surface, depth order is produced through Earth's spherical surface, spacecraft geometry, and character placement, all coordinated in post-production. *Dune: Part One* presents a mixed pattern: Greig Fraser's lens selection and color management preserve scale consistency between physical and digital layers, but large-scale background data remain dependent on render decisions, sustaining reliance on post-production perspective relationships.

Hybrid Setup: In *The Batman*, the wet asphalt and vehicles are physically present in the foreground, while Gotham's nighttime skyline is projected in real time on the LED volume background. Camera tracking provides parallax synchronization that links the background's perspective to camera movement, producing depth perception that differs sharply from the static background of chroma key. Yet the transition boundary between physical foreground and digital background remains a production variable requiring careful monitoring. In *Top Gun: Maverick*, the film enables comparison between two depth-production mechanisms: real aerial shots, where depth cues derive from the physical world, and LED-volume cockpit scenes, where sky and ground are digitally projected. The LED volume's parallax update creates a convincing cockpit depth illusion, but this depth depends on render-engine calculations rather than optical data from real space. In *Thor: Love and Thunder*, physical foreground vegetation produces real depth cues while the background forest is projected from LED panels; ILM's documentation shows that making the physical/digital vegetation boundary imperceptible was a central aim, demonstrating the analytical importance of boundary management in hybrid setups. In *Bullet Train*, the constructed train car limits where the digital background enters the frame, making depth-continuity issues more controllable than in larger LED-volume productions. In *Dune: Part Two*, real-location shots in Jordan and Abu Dhabi contrast with studio LED-volume scenes, showing how scale and perspective consistency are managed across different production conditions.

The comparison of depth cues shows that the differences between production models are not incidental. In the physical setup, depth cues derive from real geometry, optical surfaces, and light behavior; spatial consistency can therefore be checked during filming. In a digital setup, depth cues depend on computational decisions, which makes depth highly controllable but also dependent on data integrity and compositing precision. The case studies clarify this contrast. *Sin City* and *300* demonstrate that the transformation or reduction of depth cues can serve as an aesthetic strategy. At the same time, *Gravity* demonstrates the possibilities and limits of a spatial language largely detached from physical reference. The hybrid setup occupies an intermediate position: LED volume parallax synchronization reduces the ambiguity of chroma key backgrounds, but the boundary between the physical foreground and the digital background remains a continuing risk to spatial consistency.

Light Behavior and Color Continuity

Light behavior and color continuity are organized differently across regimes. In physical setup, they are largely shaped by the material environment; in digital setup, they are determined through post-production decisions; and in hybrid setup, the LED volume operates both as background and as light source, bringing part of the light-matching process into the moment of filming (Debevec & LeGendre, 2022). This distinction affects how far the cinematographer can read, evaluate, and adjust the light during the shoot.

Physical Setup: The oil-well fire scene in *There Will Be Blood* reveals both the possibilities and limitations of physical light continuity. Elswit and Anderson's deliberate rejection of digital intervention, using the fire as a real practical light source, means the flickering orange light on actors' faces and costumes derives entirely from the fire itself. Yet the inability to control the fire produced changing sky color and light intensity throughout the night, which the crew managed by minimizing camera angles rather than correcting in post. This exemplifies a physical setup in which cinematic authenticity and limited production control are experienced simultaneously. In *No Country for Old Men*, Deakins lit the motel room confrontation with only a room lamp and a streetlight, without additional lighting sources; because direction, contrast, and shadow relationships derive from the geometry of physical sources, color temperature and tonal continuity are organically preserved across frames. This makes practical lighting directly convey the space's atmosphere into the image. In *Mad Max: Fury Road*, John Seale adopted a "don't worry about light continuity, just shoot" principle for daylight scenes, leaving color and light consistency largely to post-production grading. Particularly in day-for-night shots, the image was overexposed by 2 stops and pulled back in post. This demonstrates that physical light continuity can be managed through an integrated production/post-production strategy, with the two stages complementing each other. *Barbie* shows that light continuity can also operate as a deliberate aesthetic tool: its pink and pastel palette comes not from natural light but from an artificial lighting scheme ensuring that surfaces reflect the same color temperature, creating a "fake but consistent" visual language. However, actual light reflected from the pink surfaces caused unwanted color spill on actors' faces, forcing DP Rodrigo Prieto to cover surfaces outside the camera's view with neutral grey cloth; this shows how set design can generate visual artifact risk. *The Dark Knight* adds another physical-set example in which light continuity is tied to the built architecture itself: interior light sources, reflective surfaces, columns, and glass partitions remain spatially fixed across camera angles. As a result, the relation between light direction, shadow, and architectural depth remains readable during filming rather than reconstructed later.

Digital Setup: In *Sin City*, selective color accents over a black-and-white composition — such as isolating yellow within a single character — are produced entirely through post-production color decisions. No consistency derives from a real physical light source; light and color continuity are established through graphic design principles. This shows that digital setup can free light design from physical spatial constraints. In *300*, the lighting of actors' physical footage is matched with the digitally simulated background in post-production. The golden-sepia tone creates tonal continuity between foreground and background, yet this continuity depends on data-matching quality, distinguishing it from the organic unity of physical light. In *Avatar*, every light source's color, intensity, and direction are determined at the rendering stage, producing exceptional consistency; however, this consistency comes from a computational model rather than real physical light behavior. DP Mauro Fiore's decisions on depth of field and light orientation were applied within the render engine, revealing light continuity's dependence on data integrity. In *Gravity*, sunlight in space is simulated according to physical laws, while reflections on costumes and equipment derive from render-engine calculations. In this single-shot-like long take, light continuity cannot be measured in real space and depends entirely on the digital environment's internal consistency. Greig Fraser's ACES color-management strategy in *Dune: Part One* shows how light continuity can be managed systematically: aligning practical desert footage with digital set extensions makes foreground-background light matching structurally dependent on post-production decisions.

Hybrid Setup: In *The Batman*, Greig Fraser used the LED volume both as background and light source, allowing Gotham's orange and purple night tones to reflect onto actors' faces and vehicle surfaces. This LED spill shaped physical objects in the scene, establishing foreground-background light matching largely during filming rather than in color grading. Fraser's principle — that every light source must be explicable within the scene's internal logic — is directly supported by the LED volume, since the background motivating the lighting is visible to both actor and camera. In *Top Gun: Maverick*, LED-volume cockpit scenes appear alongside real aerial footage, creating a within-film comparison between natural atmospheric light and digitally controlled sky and ground tones. Achieving seamless color continuity between these very different production conditions became one of the film's major post-production challenges. In *Thor: Love and Thunder*, the LED volume's spill on dense physical foliage shows how differently colored LED light interacts with real organic surfaces; production records confirm that synchronizing the light color of physical and digital vegetation required real-time render adjustments and dedicated calibration sessions, while narrow-band RGB LED output created challenges for costume and skin-tone accuracy. In *Dune: Part Two*, the transition from Jordan's harsh desert sunlight to the controlled LED-volume environment required a color-management strategy sustained from pre-production through shooting, ensuring the visual difference remained imperceptible to audiences. *Bullet Train* offers a more contained hybrid setup: because the train-car interior is physically built and the digital environment enters mainly through windows and exterior views, foreground lighting remains under tighter practical control, though the moving background still introduces color and exposure cues that must be matched to the car interior.

The analysis of light behavior reveals changes in the source and the management of continuity. In a physical setup, light from real surfaces can provide color continuity and an organic relationship to the shooting environment. *There Will Be Blood* and *No Country for Old Men* show how practical light can carry spatial atmosphere into the image; *Mad Max: Fury Road* and *Barbie* show that physical setup also includes deliberate strategies for managing or stylizing light continuity. In a digital setup, light design can be controlled with great precision, as *Sin City* and *300* demonstrate, but foreground-background matching depends on data quality and compositing decisions. *Avatar* and *Gravity* represent the extreme of this dependency, where light behavior is produced almost entirely through computational modeling. A hybrid setup offers a different compromise: LED light spill helps establish foreground-background matching during filming, yet color calibration and narrow-band RGB output require demanding technical management. Across the three models, light continuity remains a mise-en-scène variable whose source, reliability, and management responsibility change with the production regime.

Actor Placement, Movement, and Camera Movement Design

Actor placement, movement, and camera movement design bring the performance dimension of the comparison into focus. This cluster addresses the actor's spatial awareness, the body's relation to the environment, and the camera's available movement paths.

Physical Setup: In *There Will Be Blood*, the restaurant's actual architecture — the arrangement of tables, the scale of the interior, the presence of other customers — directly shaped the placement and movement of actors; the camera was integrated into this physical order across three key setups. In *No Country for Old Men*, narrow corridors, low ceilings, and door frames constrain actors' movement paths — these constraints function not as production limitations but as the visual architecture of tension, directly shaping Deakins's camera angles and framing. In *The Dark Knight*, the IMAX camera's wide field of view captures the spatial relationships of actors and vehicles moving in real space within a single frame, demonstrating how camera movement is designed in concert with the set's actual geometry. In *Mad Max: Fury Road*, cameras mounted on vehicles and operators positioned beside drivers create a production condition in which camera movement is directly tied to the physical dynamics of the location — speed, vibration, G-force. *Barbie* illustrates how actor movement in a physical set can be orchestrated in complete alignment with the set's construction. Every physical element of the set was designed to define the limits of choreography.

Digital Setup: In *Sin City*, actors' movement paths and placements rest not on a physical spatial framework but on compositional decisions made in post-production — directly exemplifying performing in the void. In *Gravity*, the entire film was animated scene by scene and frame by frame during previs; Sandra Bullock was guided on a 12-wire rig with a puppeteer. As Cuarón stated, "due to the technological process, very little space remained for improvisation and instant decision"; actor movement and camera design were produced together within a digital production pipeline rather than a physical space. In *Avatar*, James Cameron directed the virtual camera in real time using a controller similar to a game pad, moving it as a crane, dolly, or handheld — enabling a camera design completely independent of physical constraints, while structurally perpetuating the problem of actors lacking real spatial feedback. *300* further clarifies this condition: combat choreography is physically performed, but the surrounding battlefield, spatial scale, and atmospheric pressure are supplied after the shoot. *Dune: Part One* complicates the same category by retaining more practical foreground reference; yet the scale of Arrakis and the final camera-space relation still depend on digital extension, so blocking remains partly oriented toward a space completed later.

Hybrid Setup: In *The Batman*, Greig Fraser's ability to see the LED volume's color and light spill in real time as he designed camera movement creates a production condition in which the actor-camera-space relationship can be assessed on set in the moment. In *Top Gun: Maverick*, real aerial shots — where actors must manage the camera themselves under actual G-forces — represent the most extreme example of the actor-camera relationship in physical setup; in the LED volume studio scenes, actors are surrounded by visual context but lack the physical spatial pressure of real G-forces, offering within the same film a direct opportunity to compare the spatial awareness dimension of actor performance. In *Bullet Train*, the foreground train car's physical construction means the actors are in contact with real surfaces, keeping the fight choreography anchored to spatial reference points; the set directly constrains the camera's movement in the narrow corridor. *Thor: Love and Thunder* and *Dune: Part Two* extend this hybrid pattern in different directions. In the former, actors and practical foreground elements can be coordinated with a visible LED environment, but the performer's bodily relation to depth remains mediated by the volume. In the latter, the alternation between desert locations and controlled stage environments foregrounds the need for blocking to remain consistent across physically distinct production conditions.

The physical setup provides actors with a concrete framework for movement and anchors camera design within the set's physical limits. Digital setup, by contrast, often deprives performers of environmental reference; *Gravity*'s wire-rig arrangement and *Avatar*'s previs dependency support performing in the void. A hybrid setup provides a visible, photometrically active environment that can strengthen spatial awareness. Still, it does not replace the bodily contact and physical pressure available in a material space. For camera movement, LED volume parallax synchronization allows the camera-space relation to be assessed on set, reducing some of the post-production dependency associated with digital setup.

On-Set Visibility and Technically Induced Visual Artifacts

This final cluster concerns the technical traces left by each production model and the degree to which the final look can be assessed during filming. In a physical setup, these traces come from the shooting environment itself; in a digital setup, the final look is largely deferred to post-production; and in a hybrid setup, on-set visibility improves while new artifact risks emerge.

Physical Setup: The oil-well fire scene in *There Will Be Blood* exemplifies the direct and irrevocable effect of shooting conditions on visual outcome: the uncontrollable fire produced a changing sky color and light intensity throughout the night, conditions the crew accepted rather than correcting afterward, adapting staging decisions accordingly. On-set visibility in physical setup is, in this sense, complete; yet uncontrollable variables simultaneously persist in the scene. *The Dark Knight* shows how large-scale physical sets naturally ensure technical visual consistency: the fact that the physical set exists in a single condition structurally excludes digital-setup-specific risks such as composite boundaries or color mismatch. *Barbie* presents the most analytically apt example of a deliberate technical artifact in the physical setup: the real light reflecting from the set's pink surfaces created unwanted color spill on actors' faces, and DP Rodrigo Prieto was forced to cover every surface outside the camera's view with neutral grey cloth. *No Country for Old Men* and *Mad Max: Fury Road* demonstrate two other forms of physical visibility. In the former, the motel interiors allow the crew to evaluate tension, shadow, and spatial restriction directly within the built environment; in the latter, real vehicles, dust, sunlight, and stunt movement make many visual risks visible on set, even when later grading and effects refine the final image.

Digital Setup: In *Sin City*, the final look does not exist in any form during filming. Three separate VFX studios working independently on the same film could have introduced stylistic inconsistencies at compositing boundaries; Rodriguez mitigated this risk by assigning each studio a separate segment and consciously adopting isolation as an aesthetic decision. In *Gravity*, pre-programming all scenes through previs left no room for improvisation during filming; over 80 minutes of VFX content was produced in post-production. On-set visibility is lowest in this model. In *Dune: Part One*, the integration of digital set extensions with physical footage deferred color and perspective matching to post-production; Fraser's ACES color management strategy addressed this risk systematically, but many decisions were finalized in post-production. *Avatar* and *300* show that digital setup can increase previsual control while still limiting final-image visibility during live-action performance. Virtual camera tools and previs provide a designed spatial plan, but the finished integration of bodies, light, background, and atmosphere becomes fully testable only after rendering and compositing.

Hybrid Setup: In *The Batman*, the most critical technical artifact risk highlighted by Fraser is light-motivation continuity: his principle that every light source should be explicable by the audience requires precise management of color calibration and panel-camera matching. However, the LED volume's ability to produce a result close to the final look at the moment of filming significantly reduced post-production surprises. In *Thor: Love and Thunder*, moiré effects and color shifts are explicitly documented as technical artifacts in production records; ILM's StageCraft infrastructure's management of color deviations from narrow-band RGB LED output through calibration processes concretely demonstrates the hybrid setup's dependency on the calibration team. In *Dune: Part Two*, the mixing of real-location shots with LED volume scenes required managing technical artifact risk in a continuously shifting production environment. *Top Gun: Maverick* and *Bullet Train* indicate how hybrid setups can reduce this uncertainty without eliminating it. Cockpit and train-car interiors provide actors and cinematographers with visible context during filming. Still, synchronization between practical foregrounds and projected or digitally rendered backgrounds remains a technical condition that must be continuously checked.

Physical setup offers the greatest on-set visibility, but uncontrollable conditions such as changing light, set-specific reflections, and weather can still shape the image. Digital setup provides flexibility, yet it lowers on-set visibility and shifts decisions into a time- and cost-intensive post-production pipeline. Hybrid setup increases proximity to the final image during shooting, but color calibration, moiré management, and panel-camera matching add a new layer of technical responsibility. Technical artifact risk, therefore, does not disappear across the three models; its source and management strategy change.

CONCLUSION

This study examined how cinematic space is produced under physical, digital, and hybrid setup models and how these conditions shape scene-level visual arrangement. Across the four analytical clusters, the same pattern emerges: the production model is not merely technical, but a decision that organizes mise-en-scène.

The first research question asked how different space-construction methods affect visual order. Each regime organizes depth cues, light behavior, and camera movement differently. In the physical setup, visual order is established through the material reality of the space during filming. In the digital setup, it is distributed across post-production. In the hybrid setup, these processes merge in real time while introducing constraints. These findings support Bordwell's (2005; 2008) argument that film form cannot be evaluated independently of production conditions: what appears as style is also shaped by the chosen regime.

Differences in depth perception, perspective relationships, and light continuity emerge as structural features rather than incidental variations. In the physical setup, depth cues derive from real optics, providing a verifiable basis for spatial consistency. In the digital setup, consistency depends on data integrity and compositional decisions. This extends Prince's (2012) argument that digital effects restructure cinema's relationship with reality through the mechanisms that produce spatial consistency.

The findings also support and qualify Bode's (2017) concept of performing in the void. LED volume gives actors a visible, photometrically active environment, yet cannot reproduce all sensory layers of bodily contact and physical pressure available in material space. *Top Gun: Maverick* demonstrates this distinction: real G-forces shape acting choices in aerial footage, while such pressure is absent in studio conditions. LED volume parallax enables on-set evaluation of the camera-space relation, but does not fully reproduce physical space.

Regarding production control and visual consistency, the findings suggest a trade-off framework rather than a hierarchy: physical setup offers optical continuity but imposes spatial constraints; digital setup provides flexibility but increases post-production dependency; hybrid setup offers on-set visibility but requires calibration. These trade-offs vary according to content type, budget, infrastructure, labor capacity, and narrative demands.

Theoretically, the findings extend the framework in two ways. First, the space-mise-en-scène-camera relationship appears dynamic and production-dependent rather than fixed. Second, the distinction between "fix it in post" and "fix it in pre" (Swords & Willment, 2024, p. 1567) changes workflow and redistributes authority among production design, cinematography, VFX, color science, and real-time rendering (Caldwell, 2008; Curtin & Sanson, 2016; Zhang, 2024). A key implication is that hybrid setup is not automatically superior to digital setup: LED volume can complicate wide depth-of-field shots, while physical setup can generate artifact risks.

In conclusion, spatial production is inseparable from mise-en-scène analysis. Physical, digital, and hybrid setup models organize depth cues, light continuity, actor spatial awareness, and camera movement in distinct ways. This study does not rank these models, but clarifies the conditions each creates for staging and visual composition.

Future Research Directions

Several directions emerge from these findings. First, future research could examine the factors that determine which production model is preferred under which conditions, including genre conventions, budget thresholds, and dramatic function. Second, as LED volume technology becomes more accessible, the evolution of mise-en-scène in small- and medium-budget productions deserves independent study. Third, the audience-reception dimension remains underexplored. Whether viewers can perceive the difference between optically grounded and computationally derived depth cues, or between practical and LED-volume light, is an empirical question suited to cognitive film research and eye-tracking methods. Fourth, longitudinal studies could track how the redistribution of creative authority across production stages—from director to production designer, VFX supervisor, color scientist, and real-time rendering team—reshapes authorial practice over time. Finally, future research should examine the environmental consequences of each regime, since physical sets, location shooting, rendering infrastructures, and LED volumes distribute material waste, travel demand, hardware dependence, and energy use differently.

REFERENCES

Adanır, O. (2003). *Sinemada anlam ve anlatım* (2nd ed.). Alfa Yayınları.

Affron, C., & Affron, M. J. (1995). *Sets in motion: Art direction and film narrative.* Rutgers University Press. DOI: 10.36019/9781978813199

AMPAS. (2020). *ACES overview.* Academy of Motion Picture Arts and Sciences. https://www.oscars.org/science-technology/aces

Anderson, J. D. (1996). *The reality of illusion: An ecological approach to cognitive film theory.* Southern Illinois University Press.

Anderson, P. T. (Director) (2007). *There Will Be Blood* [Film]. Paramount Vantage.

ARRI. (2022). *LED wall shooting guide: On-set virtual production.* ARRI.

Bachelard, G. (1994). *The poetics of space* (Jolas, M., Trans.). Beacon Press.

Barnwell, J. (2004). *Production design: Architects of the screen.* Wallflower Press.

Baudrillard, J. (1994). *Simulacra and simulation* (S. F. Glaser, Çev.). The University of Michigan Press.

Bazin, A. (1967). *What is cinema?* (Vol. 1). University of California Press.

Block, B. (2008). *The visual story: Creating the visual structure of film, TV and digital media* (2nd ed.). Focal Press.

Bode, L. (2017). *Making believe: Screen performance and special effects in popular cinema.* Rutgers University Press.

Bodini, A., Manohar, A., Colecchia, F., Harrison, D., & Garaj, V. (2024). Envisioning the future of virtual production in filmmaking: A remote co-design study. *Multimedia Tools and Applications, 83*(7), 19015–19039. DOI: 10.1007/s11042-023-16308-7

Bordwell, D. (1989). Historical Poetics of Cinema. In Palmer, R. B. (Ed.), *The cinematic text: methods and approaches.* Georgia State Literary Studies.

Bordwell, D. (2005). *Figures traced in light: On cinematic staging.* University of California Press. DOI: 10.1525/9780520938007

Bordwell, D. (2008). *Poetics of cinema.* Routledge.

Bordwell, D., & Thompson, K. (2019). *Film art: An introduction* (12th ed.). McGraw-Hill.

Boutellier, A., & Raptis, P. (2023). Teaching virtual production: The challenges of developing a formal curriculum. *Film Education Journal*, *6*(2), 69–81. DOI: 10.14324/FEJ.06.2.01

Brown, B. (2016). *Cinematography: Theory and practice* (3rd ed.). Focal Press. DOI: 10.4324/9781315667829

Burch, N. (1973). *Theory of film practice*. Princeton University Press.

Caldwell, J. T. (2008). *Production culture: Industrial reflexivity and critical practice in film and television*. Duke University Press.

Cameron, J. (Director). (2009). *Avatar* [Film]. 20th Century Fox.

Chen, M. (2024). The impact of virtual technology on film and television performance: A paradigm shift in performance from green screen to virtual production. *Economic Society and Humanities*, *1*(6), 56–62. DOI: 10.62381/E244609

Chung, H. J. (2018). *Media heterotopias: Digital effects and material labor in global film production*. Duke University Press. DOI: 10.1215/9780822372158

Coen, J., & Coen, E. (Directors). (2007). *No Country for Old Men* [Film]. Miramax Films.

Cuarón, A. (Director). (2013). *Gravity* [Film]. Warner Bros. Pictures.

Curtin, M., & Sanson, K. (Eds.). (2016). Precarious creativity: Global media, local labor. In M. Curtin & K. Sanson (Eds.), *Precarious creativity: global media, local labor*. University of California Press.

Debevec, P., & LeGendre, C. (2022). HDR lighting dilation for dynamic range reduction on virtual production stages. *arXiv*. https://doi.org//arXiv.2205.07873DOI: 10.1145/3532719.3543243

Dinur, E. (2017). *The filmmaker's guide to visual effects: The art and techniques of VFX for directors, producers, editors and cinematographers*. Routledge.

Elsaesser, T., & Hagener, M. (2015). *Film theory: An introduction through the senses* (2nd ed.). Routledge. DOI: 10.4324/9781315740768

Epic Games. (2019). *Unreal Engine for virtual production*. Epic Games. https://www.unrealengine.com/en-US/uses/film-television

Ettedgui, P. (1999). *Production design & art direction screencraft*. RotoVision.

Favreau, J. (Creator). (2019-). *The Mandalorian* [TV series]. Disney+.

Flick, U. (2018). *An introduction to qualitative research* (6th ed.). SAGE.

Gerwig, G. (Director). (2023). *Barbie* [Film]. Warner Bros. Pictures.

Gibbs, J. (2002). *Mise-en-scène: film style and interpretation*. Wallflower Book.

Gibson, J. J. (1979). *The ecological approach to visual perception*. Houghton Mifflin.

İnceoğlu, S. (2022). Mimarlık ve sinema arakesitinde bir yönetmenin analizi: Wes Anderson. Master's thesis, Mimar Sinan Güzel Sanatlar University, Türkiye.

James, O., Achard, R., Bird, J., & Cooper, S. (2021). *Color-managed LED walls for virtual production.* SIGGRAPH: International Conference on Computer Graphics and Interactive Techniques, New York.

Kääpä, P. (2018). *Environmental management of the media: Policy, industry, practice*. Routledge., DOI: 10.4324/9781315625690

Kavakli, M., & Cremona, C. (2022). The virtual production studio concept: Analysing the impact of LED volume technology on film and television production. In *2022 IEEE Conference on Virtual Reality and 3D User Interfaces (VR)* (pp. 29-37). IEEE. https://doi.org/DOI: 10.1109/VR51125.2022.00020

Kosinski, J. (Director). (2022). *Top Gun: Maverick* [Film]. Paramount Pictures.

Lageira, J. (2025). Imaginary Subject. In Chateau, D. (Ed.), *Subjectivity: filmic representation and the spectator's experience* (pp. 161–184). Routledge., DOI: 10.4324/9781003704515-13

LeGendre, C., Lepicovsky, L., & Debevec, P. (2022). Jointly optimizing color rendition and ın-camera backgrounds in an rgb virtual production stage. *arXiv*(July), 1-12. https://doi.org//arXiv.2205.12403DOI: 10.1145/3543664.3543681

Leitch, D. (Director). (2022). *Bullet Train* [Film]. Columbia Pictures.

LoBrutto, V. (2002). *The filmmaker's guide to production design*. Allworth Press.

Long, D., Bogart, R., Stephens, S., Kennel, G., & Fazakerley, A. (2025). Color management principles for LED panels in on-set virtual production. *SMPTE Motion Imaging Journal, 134*(2), 43–52. DOI: 10.5594/JMI.2025/XEJK1138

Miller, G. (Director). (2015). *Mad Max: Fury Road* [Film]. Warner Bros. Pictures.

Monaco, J. (2009). *How to read a film: Movies, media, and beyond* (4th ed.). Oxford University Press.

Netflix. (2023). *What is Virtual Production?* Netflix Technology Blog. https://partnerhelp.netflixstudios.com/hc/en-us/articles/1500002552642-What-is-Virtual-Production

Neuendorf, K. A. (2017). *The content analysis guidebook* (2nd ed.). SAGE.

Nolan, C. (Director). (2008). *The Dark Knight* [Film]. Warner Bros. Pictures.

Okun, J. A., Zwerman, S., & Thurmond O'Neal, S. (2025). *The ves handbook of visual effects: industry standard vfx practices and procedures* (4th ed.). Routledge., DOI: 10.4324/9781003534259

Pallasmaa, J. (2001). *The architecture of image: Existential space in cinema.* Rakennustieto Publishing.

Patton, M. Q. (2015). *Qualitative research & evaluation methods* (4th ed.). SAGE.

Prince, S. (2012). *Digital visual effects in cinema: The seduction of reality.* Rutgers University Press., https://www.jstor.org/stable/j.ctt5hj5pv

Reeves, M. (Director). (2022). *The Batman* [Film]. Warner Bros. Pictures.

Rodriguez, R., & Miller, F. (Directors). (2005). *Sin City* [Film]. Dimension Films.

Rose, G. (2016). *Visual methodologies: An introduction to researching with visual materials* (4th ed.). SAGE Publications.

Silva Jasaui, D., Martí-Testón, A., Muñoz, A., Moriniello, F., Solanes, J. E., & Gracia, L. (2024). Virtual Production: Real-Time Rendering Pipelines for Indie Studios and the Potential in Different Scenarios. *Applied Sciences (Basel, Switzerland), 14*(6), 2530. DOI: 10.3390/app14062530

Smith, T. J. (2012). The attentional theory of cinematic continuity. *Projections (New York, N.Y.), 6*(1), 1–27. DOI: 10.3167/proj.2012.060102

SMPTE. (2023). *The On-Set Virtual Production initiative will be the first RIS from SMPTE.* Society of Motion Picture and Television Engineers. https://www.smpte.org/

Snyder, Z. (Director). (2006). *300* [Film]. Warner Bros. Pictures.

Souriau, E. (1953). *L'univers filmique.* Flammarion.

Stump, D. (2021). *Digital cinematography: Fundamentals, tools, techniques, and workflows* (2nd ed.). Routledge. DOI: 10.4324/9780429468858

Swords, J., & Willment, N. (2024). The emergence of virtual production: A research agenda. *Convergence (London), 30*(5), 1557–1574. DOI: 10.1177/13548565241253903

Tarkovsky, A. (1986). *Sculpting in time: Reflections on the cinema* (Hunter-Blair, K., Trans.). University of Texas Press.

Villeneuve, D. (Director). (2021). *Dune: Part One* [Film]. Warner Bros. Pictures.

Villeneuve, D. (Director). (2024). *Dune: Part Two* [Film]. Warner Bros. Pictures.

Waititi, T. (Director). (2022). *Thor: Love and Thunder* [Film]. Marvel Studios.

Whitehead, J. (2017). *Creating interior atmosphere: Mise-en-scène and interior design*. Bloomsbury Visual Arts.

Wright, S. (2024). *Digital compositing for film and video: Production workflows and visual effects* (5th ed.). Routledge. DOI: 10.4324/9781032418070

Yin, R. K. (2018). *Case study research and applications: design and methods* (6th ed.). SAGE.

Zhang, T. (2024). *From digital visual effects to emerging in-camera visual effects: investigating the change of workflow, occupational roles and common challenges in Southeast Asian and East Asian countries*. Master's thesis, Nanyang Technological University, Singapore. https://hdl.handle.net/10356/174920

Chapter 6
Reflexive Thematic Analysis Through Reflective Drawing in Design Research

Fırat Küçükersen
http://orcid.org/0000-0002-5795-7300
Istanbul Technical University, Turkey

ABSTRACT

This study aims to present a design research approach for integrating reflective drawings into the reflexive thematic analysis method developed by Virginia Braun and Victoria Clarke. To this end, I will discuss how I used reflective drawings in the reflexive thematic analysis I employed in two case studies on design education and explore the contributions of this type of reflective thinking, comprising sketches, diagrams, and brief notes, to my analysis. As a result, this study, following the concretization of the visual thinking process within my analysis, offers insights into visual analysis strategies that design researchers can apply in their research.

INTRODUCTION

Thematic analysis is widely used to analyze data and is applied in three different ways: coding reliability, codebook, and reflexive. This study focuses on the reflexive one. This analytical method is referred to in the literature as "thematic analysis, thematic content analysis, Braun and Clarke's thematic analysis, and reflexive thematic analysis." Since this is the terminology preferred by Braun and Clarke (2024), the founders of this analytical approach, and because it has become more

DOI: 10.4018/979-8-3373-6680-7.ch006

widely used in recent times, the term "reflexive thematic analysis (RTA)" will be used in this study. RTA is entirely qualitative. In this analytical process, researchers assume the role of a storyteller. Therefore, the narrative constructed around the data incorporates the researchers' personal perspectives, life experiences, assumptions, and expectations. Researchers are not expected to be neutral or unbiased observers or reporters; consequently, they play an active role in shaping the results (Braun & Clarke, 2021). RTA does not provide a set of rules for researchers; rather, it creates a dialogic environment that allows them to chart their own course. This dialogue takes place in two distinct ways. The first is the reflective dialogue the researcher engages in with themselves. The second is the dialogue they will engage in with other researchers. For this reason, it is suggested that the first-person singular, rather than the third person, which obscures the researchers' roles in studies, be employed in the RTA process (Braun et al., 2022). Similarly, Lazard and McAvoy (2020) consider it standard practice for researchers to explicitly indicate their active role in the research process through first-person narration. Based on these arguments, in this study, which examines RTA within the context of design research and reflective drawing, I mainly use the first-person singular to emphasize my positionality, and particularly my reflexive position.

Qualitative researchers require action-oriented thinking tools during the analysis process. Writing is the most common of these tools and is, in fact, an integral part of qualitative analysis. It is not merely a reporting process that occurs only in the final stages of the analysis, but rather a form of thinking that begins with note-taking and potential coding schemes and extends across all stages of the analysis (Braun & Clarke, 2006). The inclusion of visual and creative data and analysis tools in research is not only possible but is an expected approach. However, in research in the social sciences and design research, I have observed that traditional text-based approaches dominate RTA processes and that visual forms of thinking are not incorporated. Furthermore, the literature remains silent regarding the inclusion of creative, reflective, and visual practices in the RTA process. Nonetheless, the role of reflective drawing in the RTA process goes beyond mere documentation; it can establish and enrich interpretation through reflexivity. Building on this gap in the literature, this study aims to offer insights into how reflective drawings can be incorporated into the analysis of collected data. In this vein, this study opens a discussion, using examples, on how forms of visual thinking, such as those facilitated by reflective drawing, can be integrated into the six stages of RTA: "familiarization," "coding," "initial theme generation," "reviewing and developing themes," "refining, defining, and naming themes," and "report" (Braun et al., 2022), and discusses, with examples, how forms of visual thinking mediated through reflective drawing can be integrated. Consequently, this study raises the research question: "How can design researchers integrate reflective drawing into their reflexive thematic analysis process?"

Following the abstract and introduction, I discuss the concepts of positionality and reflexivity in the context of design research and examine RTA in detail. I then explain the notion of reflective drawing, which consists of sketches, diagrams, and brief notes, and reveal the role of reflective drawings that I used during the analysis phase of two case studies on design pedagogy. In this way, I present the results of how reflective drawings, as a form of visual thinking, can be integrated into the RTA stages of design research. Finally, I present insights and recommendations to help design researchers using RTA make their analysis processes more active through reflective drawings. As a result, this research presents findings on how design researchers can integrate reflective and creativity-stimulating visual thinking tools into their RTA processes. This study offers experience-based insights that guide design researchers in using tools commonly used in design processes, such as sketches and diagrams, in the context of reflexivity during the RTA phases of their research. Consequently, this study may contribute to the literature on qualitative design research, reflexive thematic analysis, and reflective drawing.

POSITIONALITY AND REFLEXIVITY: ACKNOWLEDGING RESEARCHER SUBJECTIVITY

The incorporation of positionality and reflexivity as fundamental elements in qualitative research has become a conventional practice. Since the 1990s, the notion of positionality has been increasingly significant in the social sciences and humanities (Moser, 2008). This idea is often referred to in research as "position" and "positionality statements" (Ríos & Patel, 2023). Researchers consistently adjust their positions, especially in qualitative investigations (Bott, 2010; Skukauskaite et al., 2022). Positionality is not a fixed declaration of identity but rather an analytical foundation of research that elucidates how researchers perceive, understand, and engage with the environment (Rinchen et al., 2025). This notion concerns the recognition of researchers' personal experiences, values, beliefs, and identities, as well as their influence on research (Piedra, 2023; 2025). Although it is contended that researchers' positionality affects research design, data collection methods, and analysis (Rinchen et al., 2025), ambiguity persists regarding the potential contributions of discussions of researchers' positionality to research, as well as the obstacles they may pose (Moser, 2008). Positionality is frequently neglected in research (Ríos & Patel, 2023); however, it can take on a critical dimension when researchers disclose their methodological, ethical, and epistemological underpinnings, particularly their biases and assumptions. In this context, positionality analysis recognizes that there is no singular truth or reality and that various perspectives can influence research and analysis processes in diverse ways (Zembylas, 2025).

Positionality is often discussed alongside reflexivity (Piedra, 2023). Reflexivity was initially developed in anthropology (Guillemin & Gillam, 2004; Macbeth, 2001) and has since become increasingly prevalent in the social sciences over the past century (Bott, 2010; Cardwell, 2025). In terms of self-observation and consideration of other stakeholders' perspectives, the impact of positionality on research is like that of reflexivity (Rinchen et al., 2025). Nevertheless, reflexivity transcends mere identification of the researchers' position and cultural context (Trainor & Bundon, 2021; Yip, 2024) and transforms researchers into the subjects of their own research (Bright et al., 2024) by emphasizing the researchers' active roles in knowledge production. In this context, reflexivity, as both a concept and a practice, can be considered a research component that is becoming more prevalent and addresses the gaps in post-positivist research. Reflexivity serves three primary functions in research. Researchers' primary objective is to consider variables such as gender, race, and social class. The second approach is to consider the intersubjective dynamics of the researcher-participant relationship as essential elements of the research. Third, this notion enables researchers to recognize their biases, attitudes, emotional responses, and motivations, thereby transforming these potential obstacles in qualitative research into essential components of the study (Bright et al., 2024; Probst & Berenson, 2014). Researchers' critical engagement with the three core parameters I have delineated is associated with reflexivity. This process activates data related to the researchers' identities and positions, thereby emphasizing personal and context-specific experiences (Jamieson et al., 2023).

In a nutshell, researchers employ subjectivity as a research resource. They engage in the production of knowledge by conceptualizing meaning and knowledge as partial, situational, and contextual (Braun & Clarke, 2021). Consequently, qualitative researchers are unable to operate without the influence of their biases and assumptions (Berger, 2015). To summarize this perspective, positionality is the initial concept that systematically frames qualitative research. It involves defining our knowledge and beliefs, while reflexivity pertains to the effective application of this knowledge (D'Cruz et al., 2007).

REFLEXIVE THEMATIC ANALYSIS

Thematic analysis is often presented as an introductory qualitative analysis technique for researchers. As a relatively accessible form of analysis, it enables early-career researchers to articulate their epistemological positions and address their research questions (Braun & Clarke, 2006). Widely used for analyzing qualitative data, thematic analysis is also commonly perceived as a time-consuming and solitary process.

Reflexivity is a dynamic and ongoing process that affects every phase of qualitative research (Guillemin & Gillam, 2004), as I emphasized in the section "Positionality and Reflexivity: Acknowledging Researcher Subjectivity." In this vein, I am focusing on the concept's role during the analysis phase, given this study's extensive scope. Reflexivity, a critical element of qualitative research, is a continuous and recurring process that occurs during the analysis phase (Trainor & Bundon, 2021). Throughout the research process, reflexivity entails the researcher critically evaluating their values, assumptions, expectations, and choices to ascertain the extent to which these parameters are included or excluded. This concept holds that knowledge cannot be generated without the involvement of researchers. The knowledge generated is explicitly contextualized by the assumptions and values expressed. In this context, knowledge is not discovered; rather, it is generated (Braun et al., 2022). Consequently, the RTA approach posits that the researchers actively construct themes through an interpretive approach. The researcher can maintain transparency regarding analytical decisions and acknowledge their role in shaping meaning and research outcomes through reflexivity (Ozuem et al., 2025).

The reflexive approach is among the most comprehensive and widely used approaches to thematic analysis. However, there is uncertainty about how this analytical method needs to be conducted, depending on the research context (Byrne, 2022). For example, a large research team is not a requirement for RTA—in fact, it is not preferred. In such cases, the inability to control the researcher's decisions may lead to ambiguity. Furthermore, it is difficult to consider RTA as a finished product, as this concept requires assumptions to be repeatedly questioned (Braun et al., 2022). On the other hand, the RTA process offers a structurally flexible and organic roadmap. There is no requirement for RTA stages to be applied sequentially within strict boundaries. Furthermore, the stages of this analytical method are intertwined. In this context, the researcher revises the process by revisiting previous stages and repeatedly reflecting on decisions. In essence, the dataset, theoretical framework, and the researcher's analytical skills/resources are the fundamental components in the analysis process. An RTA report in the format of an 8,000-word paper, with 2 to 6 themes and subthemes, can be sufficient as the output of the RTA process (Braun & Clarke, 2013).

In summary, RTA does not provide qualitative researchers with clearly defined boundaries or a strict set of analytical steps or rules to follow. The six stages it encompasses—"familiarization," "coding," "initial theme generation," "reviewing and developing themes," "refining, defining, and naming themes," and "report" (Braun et al., 2022)—are inseparable parts of a holistic analysis process. The aim here is to deepen understanding, establish connections with the theoretical framework, and ultimately construct a thematic structure that answers the research question: "How can design researchers integrate reflective drawing into their reflexive thematic analysis process?"

REFLECTIVE DRAWING

As a transformative intellectual endeavor, reflexivity (Bright et al., 2024) can also be embodied through visual approaches during the research analysis phase. Given the increasing prevalence of visual methodologies and analytical approaches in social research, drawing can be used in this context as a form of thinking for designers. On the other hand, although drawing is a fundamental practice in the discipline and education of design, it is surprising that it is not widely used in the analysis phase of design research. This may stem from the fact that written reporting is often considered a requirement in thematic analyses, as well as from the need to express research findings primarily in writing.

Despite the preconception that it has a narrow scope of application, drawing as a research tool can offer design researchers an unconventional way to see and think. In other words, drawing can facilitate the generation of knowledge. In this context, drawings can provide a rich and insightful environment for research and analysis, helping to concretize how people understand and perceive their worlds. In short, when drawing is considered not merely as a final product but also for the contributions it makes during the production process, it can be used to construct knowledge and meaning (Guillemin, 2004; Gürer & Küçükersen, 2021). Hence, drawings transcend mere results or representations and acquire analytical qualities.

In summary, within the scope of this study, I define the drawings I used during the analysis phase of my research as reflective drawings with analytical properties. This type of drawing consists of sketching, diagramming, and brief notes. Since reflexivity inherently involves reflection (Jamieson et al., 2023), the diversity of reflective thinking and practice can enrich the analysis process. In particular, the use of drawings, which designers frequently employ in their design practice, may enrich analytical and reflective perspectives in the analysis phase of design research.

REVISITING THE SIX STEPS OF REFLEXIVE THEMATIC ANALYSIS

This research is built on two main case studies with RTA, and I developed an experimental and innovative analytical process by integrating reflective drawing into this process. In the first study, which I revisit here in detail in relation to the analysis process, I examined the experience- and dialogue-based interactions of first-year design students through reflective unsolicited diaries that I kept as a teaching assistant. By revisiting the reflective drawings, I produced during the analysis of these diaries, which were written between 2021 and 2024, I reconsider their content and functions (Küçükersen & Özemir, 2025). In the second study, I investigated how first-year design students learn by reflecting on their educational experiences through reflective diary and journal tools within the framework of Kolb's (2015) experiential learning theory. I revisited my RTA process, which includes the solicited diaries and journals of 12 volunteer first-year students over 13 weeks, especially the reflective drawing parts, and I clarified their role in my RTA process (Küçükersen et al., 2026).

To sum up, this research addresses the stages of RTA through two diary-based studies: one based on unsolicited diaries and the other on solicited diaries and journals. Since the methods used in these studies were parallel in structure, both focused on the learning experiences of first-year students, and both were developed as parts of a doctoral study structured over an extended period (Küçükersen, 2026). Notably, their analytical processes were sequential and complementary. Therefore, rather than examining my RTA processes separately for each case study, I address them here as an integrated whole. In doing so, I aim to clarify the analytical role of reflective drawing across these interconnected studies.

Familiarization

In qualitative research, data collection and analysis do not always proceed as clearly separated phases; rather, analysis may begin while data are still being collected, allowing the researcher to identify potential patterns, meanings, and relationships and, in turn, to refine or redirect the data collection process in line with the research question. In this sense, qualitative analysis is often not a linear process that begins only after data collection, but a dynamic process intertwined with it. The starting point of this process is immersion, that is, becoming deeply familiar with the data to begin noticing meanings, relationships, and possible patterns that are not immediately visible (Braun & Clarke, 2013; Braun et al., 2022). Developing insights relevant to the research question requires repeated reading, examination, and reflection on the data (Byrne, 2022). This familiarity involves not only understanding words or visuals but also beginning to see them as analyzable data; for this reason, particularly in RTA, even processes such as transcription can be understood as analytically productive steps that support interpretation rather than as merely technical tasks performed before analysis begins (Braun & Clarke, 2013).

In my case studies, reflective drawing supported this stage by enabling me to engage with the data not only through reading but also through sketching, marking, and visually responding to what I noticed. In this sense, familiarization became an interpretive and reflexive activity rather than a purely descriptive preliminary step. Figure 1 shows how I used reflective drawing while engaging with my notes in a direct and exploratory way. Across the page, I produced quick sketches, simple figures, arrows, spatial relations, short written comments, and fragmentary conceptual cues. These marks did not function as polished illustrations; rather, they helped me remain inside the data and think through it visually. Through these page-based responses, I began to identify recurring educational situations, interaction patterns, and possible conceptual tensions. The visual, therefore, represents familiarization as an active process of noticing, in which drawing helped me externalize early interpretations and remain attentive to meanings that were still forming (Figure 1).

Figure 2 reflects a diagrammatic form of familiarization. Here, I worked directly on a hard copy of the data, adding handwritten notes, underlining specific expressions, circling words, and connecting different parts of the text with lines and visual emphasis. This transformed the hard copy into an analytical surface. Instead of treating the printed page as a stable document to be passively read, I used it as a space for dialogue with the data. My annotations helped me slow down my reading and focus on specific statements, silences, and relationships in the text. In this way, the act of reading became materially visible through visual traces (Figure 2).

Figure 1. Field notes for the familiarization phase

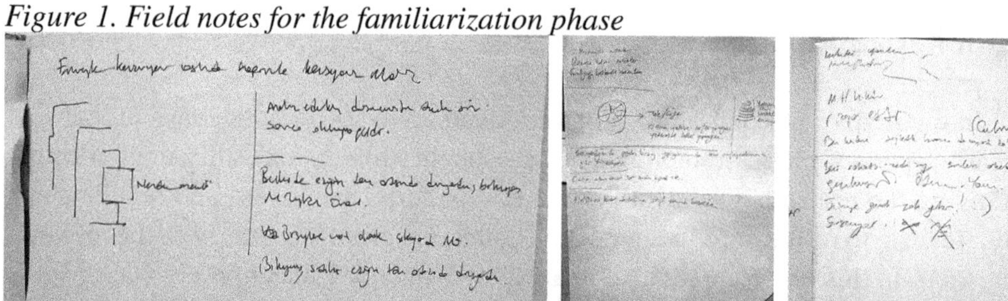

Figure 2. Diagrammatic familiarization phase

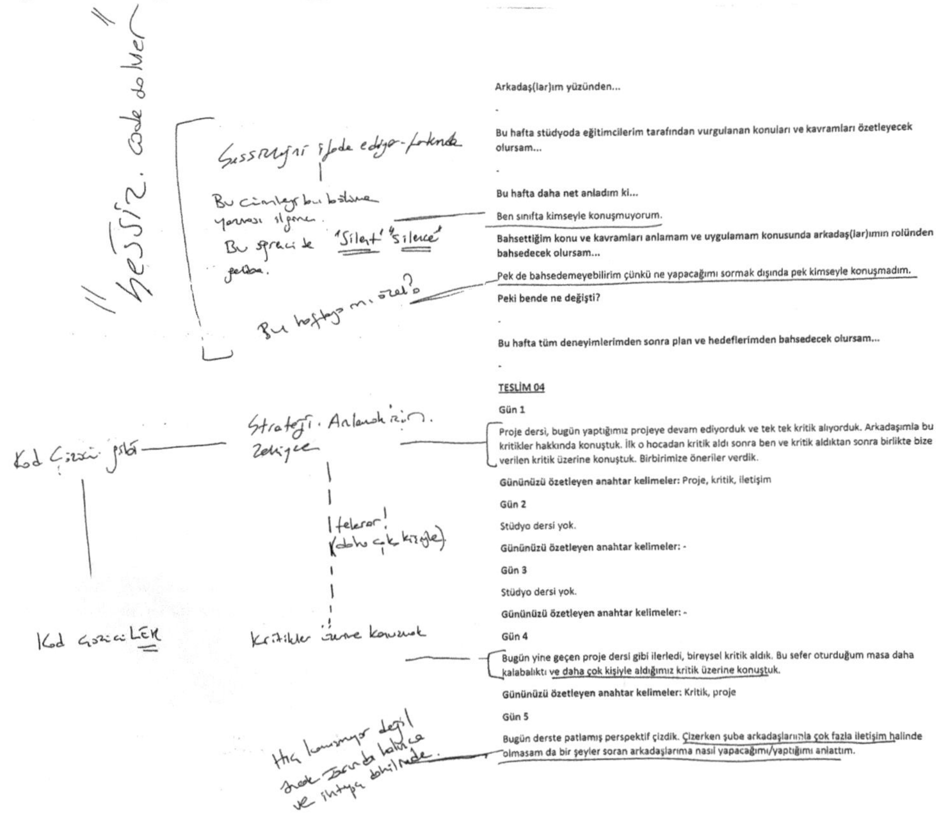

Overall, these two visuals indicate that familiarization in my analysis was supported by reflective drawing in two interconnected ways: first, through exploratory visual note-making, and second, through direct annotation on hard copies of the dataset. Both practices helped me become more deeply immersed in the material and supported the transition from initial reading to early interpretation. Reflective drawing, therefore, functioned not as an additional diagrammatic activity after reading, but as one of the ways through which familiarization itself was carried out. This is consistent with the understanding of familiarization in RTA as a recursive process of reading, reflecting, and beginning to see the data as analytically meaningful.

Coding

Coding, the second stage of RTA, involves engaging with the data in a more detailed, systematic, and analytical way. Rather than simply marking striking elements in the dataset, this stage requires the researcher to attend to the structure, texture, and possible layers of meaning within the data, thereby demanding a higher degree of analytical effort than familiarization (Braun et al., 2019). Codes are labels assigned to data segments that may be relevant to the research question, and they may be semantic or latent, as well as inductive or more theoretically driven. In this sense, codes constitute the building blocks of analysis and provide the basis for later theme development. However, in RTA, coding is not understood as the mechanical application of a fixed framework. Instead, it is an open, organic, and evolving process within a situated, interpretive, and reflexive analysis, and therefore does not rely on a predefined codebook. Themes are not the starting point of this process, but rather interpretive outcomes developed through sustained and iterative engagement with coded data. For this reason, the use of consensus coding, inter-coder reliability, or codebook procedures is not aligned with the assumptions of RTA (Braun et al., 2022). Accordingly, coding in RTA is not a linear or closed phase, but one that develops through repeated movement across the dataset. As each new segment of data is coded, the researcher evaluates whether an existing code remains appropriate or whether a new one is needed; thus, codes may be revised, expanded, merged, or renamed as analysis progresses. This iterative character also means that earlier phases may need to be revisited as new interpretations emerge, since thematic analysis often involves moving back and forth between stages rather than proceeding in a straightforward sequence (Byrne, 2022).

In my case studies, reflective drawing became an important part of this process. Rather than coding only through typed labels or separate coding tables, I worked directly on hard copies of the data by underlining excerpts, circling key expressions, drawing arrows between related statements, and adding handwritten notes, visual marks, and tentative conceptual labels in the margins. In this way, coding became not only a textual practice but also a visual and spatial one. Figure 3 shows how the printed pages functioned as an active coding surface. Different colors, shapes, lines, and marginal sketches helped me distinguish between excerpts, emerging emphases, and possible patterns across the text. At this stage, I was not simply identifying repeated words or summarizing participants' statements. Instead, I was asking what excerpts suggested analytically, how different statements could be linked, and what kinds of tensions, positions, or educational issues they pointed to. The annotations, therefore, supported an interpretive engagement with the data rather than a mechanical labeling procedure. This visual working page also demonstrates that coding was recursive and provisional. Some notes took the form of short code-like phrases, while others appeared as questions, visual connectors, or quick sketches that helped me think through possible meanings. These marks allowed me to test early interpretations, reconsider initial assumptions, and compare extracts across the page. In some places, several excerpts were visually grouped, suggesting the formation of broader coded patterns; in others, a single statement was expanded through notes and diagrams, showing that coding could develop from a single extract into a broader conceptual direction.

In sum, reflective drawing was particularly useful here because it enabled me to externalize analytic thinking while remaining close to the materiality of the dataset. The page became a space where reading, coding, questioning, and interpretation occurred simultaneously. This helped me see coding not as a separate technical stage, but as an evolving dialogue with the data. Accordingly, this coding style shows that RTA coding was carried out through a combination of textual attention and visual reasoning, allowing codes to develop through repeated interaction with the data and through the gradual construction of analytical connections across excerpts.

Figure 3. Visual coding phase

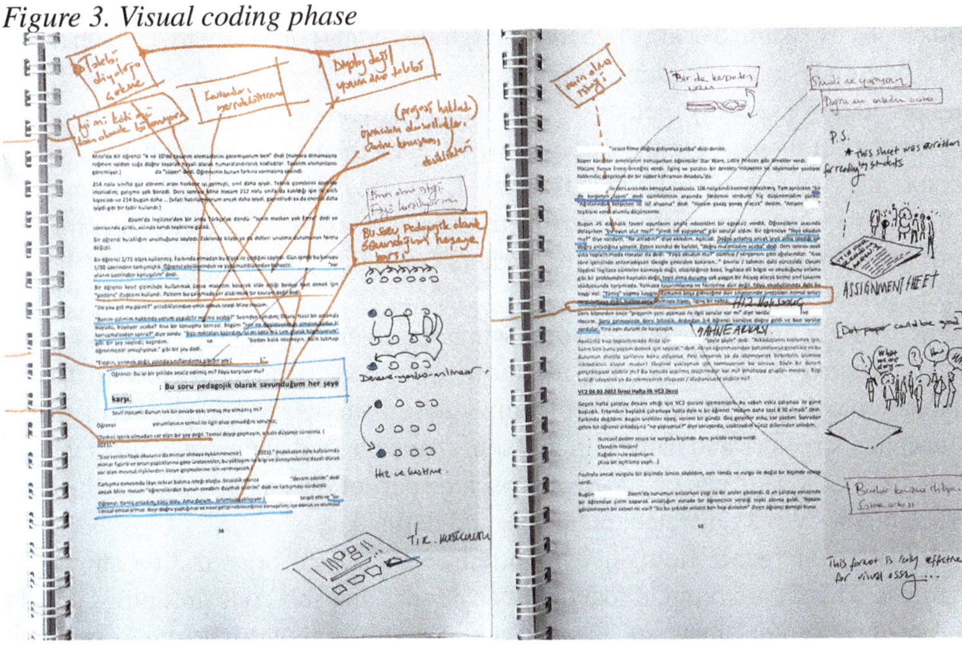

Initial Theme Generation, Reviewing and Developing Themes, and Refining, Defining, and Naming Themes

In RTA, themes are not understood as pre-existing structures hidden within the data and awaiting discovery. Rather, theme development is an active and interpretive process in which the researcher constructs patterns from codes and coded data segments; for this reason, describing themes as if they "emerge from the data" risks presenting analysis as passive and obscuring the researchers' analytical role. Instead, themes in RTA are better understood as meaning-centered interpretive narratives developed through the researchers' situated engagement with the data. This is also why the shift from "searching for themes" to "generating initial themes" is important, as it more clearly reflects the active and provisional nature of the process (Braun & Clarke, 2021; 2024).

This understanding shapes not only how themes are developed but also how the analysis is written. The use of thematic analysis needs to be justified in relation to the research topic, theoretical framework, and context, rather than through broad or generic statements, and the writing itself should make the researchers' analytical role visible, rather than relying on passive or objectifying language (Braun & Clarke, 2023). In this sense, theme development is not merely a technical act of classification but a cognitive and interpretive process that requires systematic rigor, reflexivity, and creativity (Ahmed et al., 2025). Although subthemes may help to develop more specific dimensions of a central theme, they are not necessary in every analysis, and producing too many themes can weaken analytical depth. What matters is not the number of themes, but the extent to which each theme is robustly developed to capture the richness of meaning in the data. Likewise, naming themes is not merely a formal step but a meaningful part of the analysis, as the chosen notions reflect both the theme's content and the researchers' analytic approach (Braun & Clarke, 2013, 2019).

In my RTA processes, reflective drawing played an important role across three interconnected stages by helping me move from coded fragments toward larger thematic patterns, then test and reorganize those patterns, and finally refine their conceptual structure and names. In this sense, drawing did not merely illustrate the analysis after it had been completed; it became part of the analytical work through which themes were generated, reviewed, and defined.

Initial theme generation was supported by the visual organization shown in Figure 4. This figure brought together many codes and sub-code groupings across clustered conceptual areas, such as individual cognitive tools, dialogue, self, limit, collaboration, affective expression, and acquisition. Rather than presenting themes as already finalized, the diagram functioned as an exploratory map in which coded material was visually gathered, grouped, and tentatively related to broader domains and cycles. The use of boxes, color-coded divisions, connective spacing, and grouped labels helped me see which codes appeared to gravitate toward each other and which clusters might begin to form more meaningful interpretive patterns. At this stage, reflective drawing helped me shift from coding individual segments to asking broader analytical questions: Which codes belong together? Which clusters have conceptual density? Which patterns appear central to the research question?

Figure 4, therefore, captures the provisional and generative nature of early theme development.

Reviewing and developing themes became more visible in Figure 5, where the thematic structure was no longer presented as a broad code map but as a more selective conceptual arrangement. In this drawing, categories such as self-awareness, self-assessment, critique, self-critique, tutor, peer critique, and individual acquisition were reorganized into a more coherent interpretive framework. This stage involved questioning whether the initial thematic groupings held together, whether some clusters needed to be merged or separated, and whether certain concepts functioned better as subthemes, dimensions, or transitional elements rather than as standalone themes. The handwritten phrases and arrows suggest that this was a stage of active conceptual testing. For example, the movement "from awareness to critical thinking" indicates that theme development was not only classificatory but also relational and process oriented. In this sense, Figure 5 reflects a deeper level of analytical synthesis, in which themes were reviewed not only for internal coherence but also for how they related to one another within a broader interpretive narrative.

Refining, defining, and naming themes was further developed through the visual experimentation shown in Figure 6. Here, the drawings become increasingly abstract, diagrammatic, and structural. Circular forms, layered rings, directional axes, and alternative schematic arrangements indicate that I was working not simply on grouping data, but on clarifying the conceptual logic, boundaries, and emphasis of the themes themselves. At this stage, reflective drawing allowed me to test multiple ways of understanding the thematic structure: as cycles, layered relations, intersecting domains, and movement across stages. These repeated diagrammatic trials helped me refine the scope of themes, distinguish central themes from notions, and evaluate whether the names I was considering adequately represented the interpretive story I wanted to tell. The drawings also show that naming was not a superficial final act, but part of the conceptual labor of analysis. Through this process, I worked toward thematic labels that were not only descriptive but also analytically meaningful and consistent with the study's developing structure.

Figure 4. Initial theme generation phase

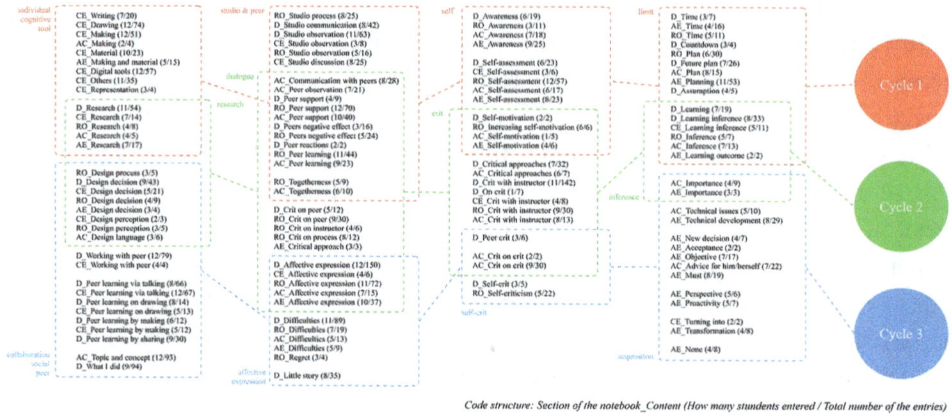

Figure 5. Reviewing and developing themes phase

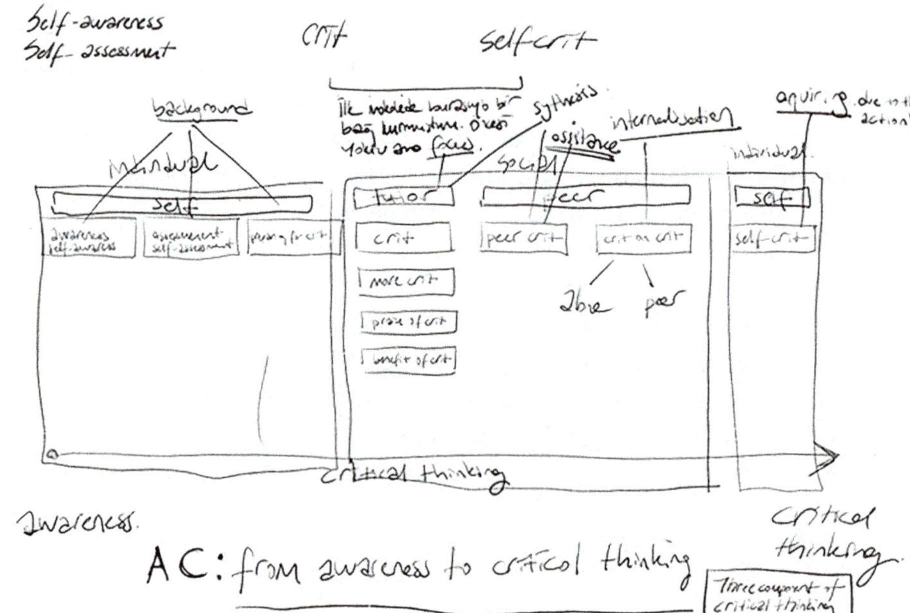

Figure 6. Refining, defining, and naming themes phase

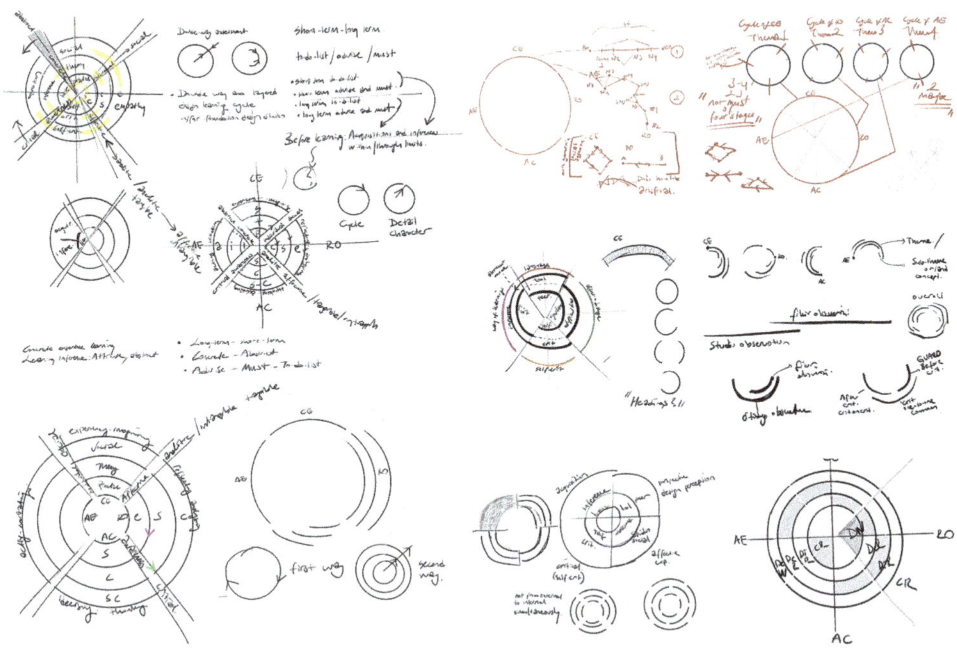

Overall, these three visuals show that reflective drawing supported theme development as a recursive progression from clustering codes, to reviewing conceptual relations, to refining the interpretive structure of the analysis. Figure 4 externalized the first stage of pattern construction; Figure 5 supported the review and development of those patterns into a more coherent structure; and Figure 6 enabled further refinement through repeated conceptual and visual testing. Across these stages, drawing functioned as a mode of analytical reasoning that helped me think spatially, relationally, and processual about the data. It therefore contributed not only to the presentation of themes, but to their actual formation, stabilization, and definition within the RTA process.

Report

In reflexive thematic analysis, writing is not an externally added final stage that follows data collection, but a fundamental process through which the analysis is developed. Qualitative analysis cannot be fully realized without writing, because it relies on words to construct a narrative of meaning around textual and visual data. For this reason, writing should be understood not as a secondary task undertaken after analysis, but as a creative and iterative process through which analysis takes its final form. In this sense, writing is not merely a summary of the data, but a space in which analytical insights are developed, and data are interpreted in relation to the research question. A robust analysis does more than restate the data; it deepens interpretation and connects it to the relevant literature, thereby situating the analysis within the existing body of knowledge and showing how the study contributes to or extends current understanding (Braun & Clarke, 2013; 2021).

The sixth stage begins when sufficiently developed themes are in place and involves shaping the final written form of the analysis. At this point, the aim is to present the complex story of the data in a way that demonstrates the analysis's strength and validity. This requires writing that is concise, coherent, logical, and engaging, and sufficient data extracts support that to illustrate the prevalence and interpretive power of the themes. However, such extracts should not stand alone; they need to be embedded within an analytical narrative that interprets the data, relates it to the research question, and develops a clear argument (Braun & Clarke, 2006). Writing in this sense is also a craft and an iterative practice rather than a one-off linear task. It often develops through revisiting, rethinking, and restructuring. It may benefit from being approached in smaller, regular sections, alongside periods of reflection away from the computer, where ideas often become clearer (Braun et al., 2019). In RTA, the report should not be understood as a merely technical final stage appended to an already completed analysis. Rather, as emphasized in this study, writing is integral to qualitative analysis itself, since analysis is realized through the construction of an interpretive narrative around textual and visual materials. In this sense, the report stage is the phase in which analytical insights are consolidated, clarified, and communicated in relation to the research question and relevant literature. Reflective drawing remained significant at this stage, not because it generated new codes or themes, but because it supported the articulation and presentation of the final interpretive structure.

Figure 7 demonstrates one way in which reflective drawing contributed to the report stage through an illustrative and metaphorical visual language. Composed of simplified figures, speech bubbles, symbolic forms, and scene-based arrangements, this drawing visualizes analytical ideas such as design elements, analytical reasoning, simplicity, comparison, criticism, critical thinking, and the challenge of acting "without tools." Such a representational mode is relatively uncommon within academic papers, where findings are more often communicated through conventional prose, tables, or standardized diagrams. Nevertheless, the rarity of this visual language within academic publications should not be regarded as a methodological limitation. On the contrary, it productively opens a space for reconsidering how research may be thought through and communicated. It suggests that analytical reporting in design research can benefit from modes of representation that emerge from the intertwined practices of thinking and making. From this perspective, Figure 7 contributes to expanding research practice by showing that reflective and design-based visual forms may serve not merely decorative functions but also intellectually generative ones within scholarly communication.

Figure 7. Reporting through sketching

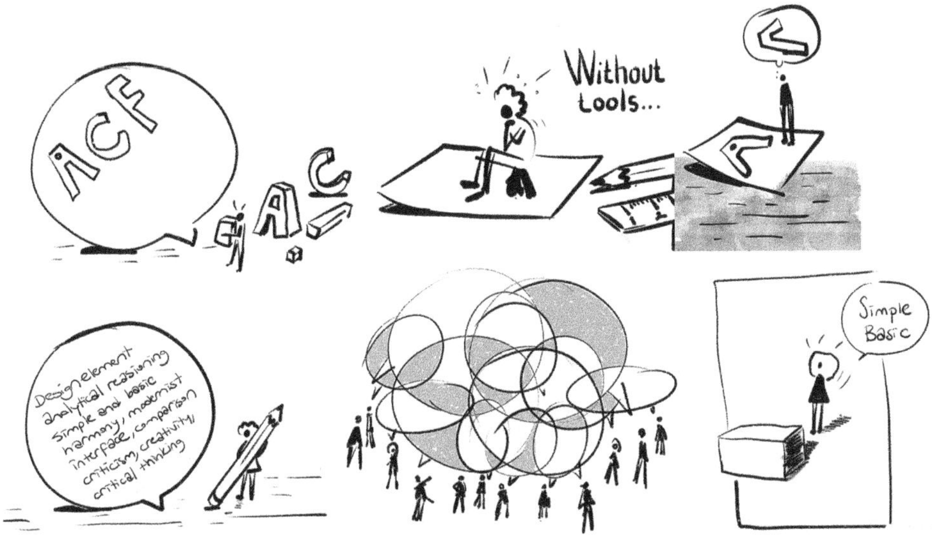

Figure 8. Reporting through diagramme

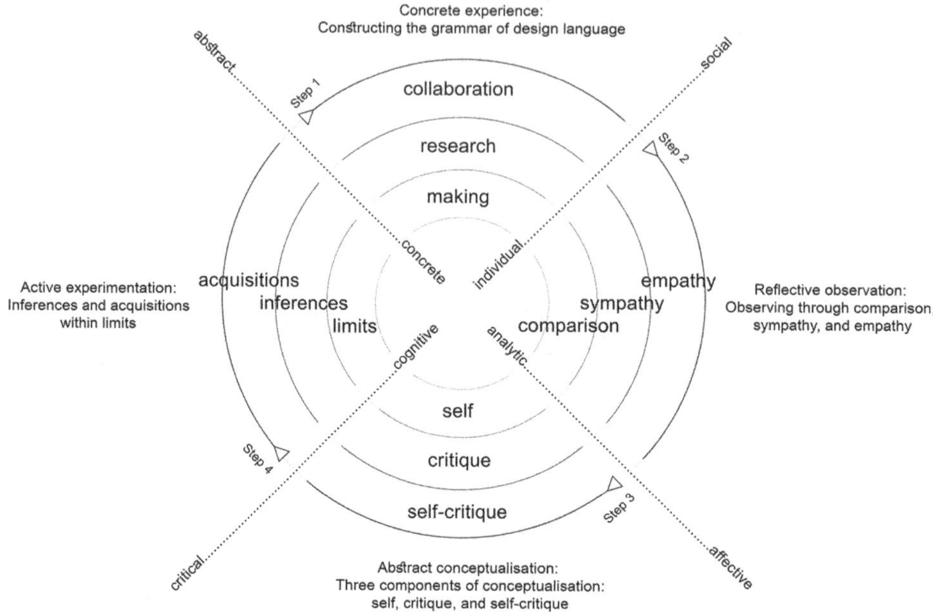

Figure 8, by contrast, presents the findings in a more formalized and conceptually stabilized structure. Organized into concentric circles, directional axes, and four experiential stages, the diagram presents the study's final thematic structure in relation to concrete experience, reflective observation, abstract conceptualization, and active experimentation. Notions such as collaboration, research, making, empathy, sympathy, comparison, self, critique, self-critique, acquisitions, inferences, and limits are positioned relationally within a coherent interpretive system. Compared with the open, illustrative, and exploratory language of Figure 7, Figure 8 performs a different reporting function: it synthesizes the findings into a legible conceptual model and clarifies the internal relations among the themes within the broader framework of the Design Learning Cycle. In this respect, it supports the written report by making the analytical structure more explicit and by helping translate thematic interpretation into a concise visual schema.

To sum up, Figures 7 and 8 show that reflective drawing supported the report stage in two complementary yet distinct ways. Figure 7 expanded the representational possibilities of academic reporting through an uncommon but productive visual language grounded in design practice, while Figure 8 consolidated the final analysis into a more systematic conceptual model. Accordingly, reflective drawing contributed not only to the presentation of findings but also to the shaping of how those findings could be intellectually communicated, interpreted, and situated within the final written account.

CONCLUSION

This study has aimed to discuss how reflective drawing can be integrated into reflexive thematic analysis (RTA) within the context of design research. Building on the understanding that RTA is not a mechanical procedure of coding and categorization but a situated, interpretive, and reflexive process of meaning-making, the study has argued that reflective drawing can serve as an analytical resource across the six stages of RTA. In this sense, sketches, diagrams, and brief notes were not treated merely as supplementary illustrations or post hoc visualizations of already completed findings. Rather, they were approached as part of the thinking process through which familiarity with the data was deepened, codes were developed, themes were generated and refined, and the final analytical narrative was communicated.

The study is positioned, first, within the literature on RTA. Braun and Clarke's work has consistently emphasized that themes do not simply emerge from data but are actively developed through the researcher's interpretive engagement with the dataset. Similarly, RTA has been framed as a flexible and recursive analytical process rather than a linear sequence of fixed procedural steps. This research aligns with that methodological position but extends it by showing that the interpretive labor of RTA can also be carried out visually. In other words, it suggests that the analytical dialogue may be conducted not only through writing, but also through drawing-based forms of reflection. In this respect, the study contributes to RTA scholarship by making visible how visual thinking can participate in the construction of themes and in the development of analytical coherence.

Second, this study is positioned within broader discussions of reflexivity and positionality in qualitative research. Studies on positionality and reflexivity have shown that qualitative research cannot be separated from the researcher's assumptions, values, choices, and subjectivities. Reflexivity, in this sense, is not only a declaration of the researcher's position but a continuing process through which knowledge is critically produced. This research supports that understanding and argues that reflective drawing may deepen this reflexive process by giving the researcher additional ways to externalize analytical uncertainty, conceptual relations, and interpretive movement. Thus, reflective drawing is presented not as an aesthetic addition to research, but as a reflexive practice through which the researcher's analytical role becomes more explicit.

Third, the study is situated within the literature exploring visual and arts-based approaches to research. In this sense, drawing can be used as a research method that generates insight rather than simply representing experience and artistic and arts-based practices can deepen reflexivity in qualitative inquiry. However, the present study differs from these contributions in one important respect: rather than discussing art-based reflexivity in general terms, it places reflective drawing directly into the analytical stages of RTA. In doing so, it offers a more process-oriented account of how visual practices may function during familiarization, coding, theme development, refinement, and reporting. Therefore, the research contributes to the literature not only by affirming that visual practices may enrich qualitative inquiry, but also by showing, more specifically, how they may operate within an established analytical approach such as RTA.

The contribution of this research to design research is also significant. Drawing is already a fundamental mode of thinking in design practice and design education, yet it has rarely been discussed as an integral part of the analysis phase of qualitative design research. This is a notable gap, especially given that design disciplines routinely rely on sketches, diagrams, and other visual tools to support conceptual development. By foregrounding reflective drawing as an analytical practice, this study suggests that design researchers can mobilize one of the discipline's most familiar ways of thinking within the reflexive analysis process itself. In this respect, the study helps bridge design practice and qualitative methodology, showing that the tools used to develop design ideas may also support the development of research interpretation.

Another contribution of the study concerns the reporting of analysis. Writing is not an external, final stage added after analysis, but a creative, iterative process through which analysis takes form. This research has extended that argument by showing that reporting may also be supported by reflective drawing. In particular, the contrast between the sketch-based and diagrammatic visualizations in the final stage demonstrates that academic communication need not be limited to conventional prose and standardized diagrams alone. Although some of the visual language presented in this research may appear unusual within academic publications, this should not be understood as a weakness. On the contrary, it may open a productive space for rethinking how scholarly arguments in design research can be constructed and communicated. In this sense, reflective drawing expands not only analytical practice but also the representational possibilities of academic reporting.

At the same time, the study has certain limitations. The approach presented here has been developed through my own experience of analyzing design pedagogy case studies. Therefore, it should not be assumed that reflective drawing will function in the same way, or with the same analytical value, in every qualitative context. Its usefulness may depend partly on the researcher's familiarity with visual thinking and their willingness to work iteratively across textual and visual modes. Future studies may therefore examine how reflective drawing can be adapted in non-design fields, how it may function for researchers with different methodological backgrounds, and how its use may further enrich reflexive and interpretive forms of qualitative analysis.

In conclusion, this study has argued that reflective drawing is a meaningful component of RTA in design research. Rather than treating drawing as a marginal or decorative activity, the study has shown that it can support the construction of knowledge by helping the researcher think, question, connect, refine, and communicate analysis. Accordingly, this research contributes to the literature on reflexive thematic analysis, reflexivity, and design research by offering an experience-based account of how visual thinking may be integrated into qualitative analysis. In this respect, it opens a methodological discussion on the role of reflective and creative visual practices in the production of knowledge.

REFERENCES

Ahmed, S. K., Mohammed, R. A., Nashwan, A. J., Ibrahim, R. H., Abdalla, A. Q., Ameen, B. M. M., & Khdhir, R. M. (2025). Using thematic analysis in qualitative research. *Journal of Medicine, Surgery, and Public Health, 6*, 1–6. DOI: 10.1016/j.glmedi.2025.100198

Berger, R. (2015). Now I see it, now I don't: Researcher's position and reflexivity in qualitative research. *Qualitative Research, 15*(2), 219–234. DOI: 10.1177/1468794112468475

Bott, E. (2010). Favourites and others: Reflexivity and the shaping of subjectivities and data in qualitative research. *Qualitative Research, 10*(2), 159–173. DOI: 10.1177/1468794109356736

Braun, V., & Clarke, V. (2006). Using thematic analysis in psychology. *Qualitative Research in Psychology, 3*(2), 77–101. DOI: 10.1191/1478088706qp063oa

Braun, V., & Clarke, V. (2013). *Successful qualitative research: A practical guide for beginners*. SAGE Publications.

Braun, V., & Clarke, V. (2019). Reflecting on reflexive thematic analysis. *Qualitative Research in Sport, Exercise and Health, 11*(4), 589–597. DOI: 10.1080/2159676X.2019.1628806

Braun, V., & Clarke, V. (2021). One size fits all? What counts as quality practice in (reflexive) thematic analysis? *Qualitative Research in Psychology, 18*(3), 328–352. DOI: 10.1080/14780887.2020.1769238

Braun, V., & Clarke, V. (2023). Is thematic analysis used well in health psychology? A critical review of published research, with recommendations for quality practice and reporting. *Health Psychology Review, 17*(4), 695–718. DOI: 10.1080/17437199.2022.2161594 PMID: 36656762

Braun, V., & Clarke, V. (2024). A critical review of the reporting of reflexive thematic analysis in Health Promotion International. *Health Promotion International, 39*(3), 1–12. DOI: 10.1093/heapro/daae049 PMID: 38805676

Braun, V., Clarke, V., & Hayfield, N. (2022). 'A starting point for your journey, not a map': Nikki Hayfield in conversation with Virginia Braun and Victoria Clarke about thematic analysis. *Qualitative Research in Psychology, 19*(2), 424–445. DOI: 10.1080/14780887.2019.1670765

Braun, V., Clarke, V., Hayfield, N., & Terry, G. (2019). Thematic analysis. In Liamputtong, P. (Ed.), *Handbook of research methods in health social sciences* (pp. 843–860). Springer. DOI: 10.1007/978-981-10-5251-4_103

Bright, D., McKay, A., & Firth, K. (2024). How to be reflexive: Foucault, ethics and writing qualitative research as a technology of the self. *International Journal of Research & Method in Education, 47*(4), 408–420. DOI: 10.1080/1743727X.2023.2290185

Byrne, D. (2022). A worked example of Braun and Clarke's approach to reflexive thematic analysis. *Quality & Quantity, 56*(3), 1391–1412. DOI: 10.1007/s11135-021-01182-y

Cardwell, M. E. (2025). Through the looking glass: A step-by-step guide to arts-based reflexivity. *Qualitative Research, 26*(1), 208–227. DOI: 10.1177/14687941251398971

D'Cruz, H., Gillingham, P., & Melendez, S. (2007). Reflexivity, its meanings and relevance for social work: A critical review of the literature. *British Journal of Social Work, 37*(1), 73–90. DOI: 10.1093/bjsw/bcl001

Guillemin, M. (2004). Understanding illness: Using drawings as a research method. *Qualitative Health Research, 14*(2), 272–289. DOI: 10.1177/1049732303260445 PMID: 14768462

Guillemin, M., & Gillam, L. (2004). Ethics, reflexivity, and 'ethically important moments' in research. *Qualitative Inquiry, 10*(2), 261–280. DOI: 10.1177/1077800403262360

Gürer, E., & Küçükersen, F. (2021). Performing a new agenda for a first-year interior architecture studio: Theatre space. In Garip, E., & Garip, S. B. (Eds.), *Handbook of research on methodologies for design and production practices in interior architecture* (pp. 218–256). IGI Global Scientific Publishing. DOI: 10.4018/978-1-7998-7254-2.ch011

Jamieson, M. K., Govaart, G. H., & Pownall, M. (2023). Reflexivity in quantitative research: A rationale and beginner's guide. *Social and Personality Psychology Compass, 17*(4), 1–15. DOI: 10.1111/spc3.12735

Kolb, D. A. (2015). *Experiential learning: Experience as the source of learning and development.* Pearson Education, Inc. (Original work published 1984)

Küçükersen, F. (2026). A design learning cycle: Transforming experience into foundational design learning through reflection. (Doctoral dissertation). Istanbul Technical University, Graduate School, Istanbul.

Küçükersen, F., & Özemir, P. (2025). Dialogic interactions in foundation design studio: An unsolicited diary research. *International Journal of Art & Design Education, 44*(3), 728–742. DOI: 10.1111/jade.12599

Küçükersen, F., Özemir, P., Dinçer, D., & Demirbilek, O. (2026). Beyond Kolb: Constructing a design learning cycle for the foundation studio. *Journal of Experiential Education, 49*(1), 158–191. DOI: 10.1177/10538259251362141

Lazard, L., & McAvoy, J. (2020). Doing reflexivity in psychological research: What's the point? What's the practice? *Qualitative Research in Psychology, 17*(2), 159–177. DOI: 10.1080/14780887.2017.1400144

Macbeth, D. (2001). On 'reflexivity' in qualitative research: Two readings, and a third. *Qualitative Inquiry, 7*(1), 35–68. DOI: 10.1177/107780040100700103

Moser, S. (2008). Personality: A new positionality? *Area, 40*(3), 383–392. DOI: 10.1111/j.1475-4762.2008.00815.x

Ozuem, W., Willis, M., Ranfagni, S., & Omeish, F. (2025). Thematic analysis in an artificial intelligence-driven context: A stage-by-stage process. *International Journal of Qualitative Methods, 24*, 1–15. DOI: 10.1177/16094069251362982

Piedra, L. M. (2023). Positionality-An analytical building block. *Qualitative Social Work: Research and Practice, 22*(4), 611–618. DOI: 10.1177/14733250231183294

Piedra, L. M. (2025). Paradigms, positionality, and the responsibilities of inquiry. *Qualitative Social Work: Research and Practice, 24*(6), 641–649. DOI: 10.1177/14733250251384424

Probst, B., & Berenson, L. (2014). The double arrow: How qualitative social work researchers use reflexivity. *Qualitative Social Work: Research and Practice, 13*(6), 813–827. DOI: 10.1177/1473325013506248

Rinchen, K., Banham, V., & Pelden, S. (2025). Reflexive researcher: Navigating positionality while interviewing participants in a close-knit community for a deeper exploration of their lived experiences. *International Journal of Qualitative Methods, 24*, 1–12. DOI: 10.1177/16094069251371471

Ríos, C. D. L., & Patel, L. (2023). Positions, positionality, and relationality in educational research. *International Journal of Qualitative Studies in Education : QSE, 36*, 1–12. DOI: 10.1080/09518398.2023.2268036

Skukauskaite, A., Yilmazli Trout, I., & Robinson, K. A. (2022). Deepening reflexivity through art in learning qualitative research. *Qualitative Research, 22*(3), 403–420. DOI: 10.1177/1468794120985676

Trainor, L. R., & Bundon, A. (2021). Developing the craft: Reflexive accounts of doing reflexive thematic analysis. *Qualitative Research in Sport, Exercise and Health, 13*(5), 705–726. DOI: 10.1080/2159676X.2020.1840423

Yip, S. Y. (2024). Positionality and reflexivity: Negotiating insider-outsider positions within and across cultures. *International Journal of Research & Method in Education, 47*(3), 222–232. DOI: 10.1080/1743727X.2023.2266375

Zembylas, M. (2025). Rethinking positionality statements in research: From looking back to building solidarity. *International Journal of Research & Method in Education, 48*(5), 1–13. DOI: 10.1080/1743727X.2025.2475762

Chapter 7
Satirizing Contemporary Art and the Neoliberal Subject in Ruben Öslund's The Square (2017)

Işıl Tombul
http://orcid.org/0000-0002-7793-7227
Independent Researcher, Turkey

ABSTRACT

This study examines the relationship between the abstract and conceptual dimension attained by contemporary art in the digital age and the fragmented ontological and epistemological existential experience of the subject within the neoliberal system. The Square, Ruben Östlund's satirical critique of contemporary art, reveals the parallel between the conceptual structure of contemporary art and processes of social disintegration. To this end, the study employs descriptive content analysis to analyze the reflection of social transformation in art. The parallel between the process of abstraction in contemporary art and the existential loneliness, ontological and epistemological fragmentation, the ethical and moral crises of the neoliberal individual in the digital age, is examined from a phenomenological perspective. In this context, the study opens up for discussion the question of whether the point reached by art constitutes a reflection of the stage humanity itself has reached.

DOI: 10.4018/979-8-3373-6680-7.ch007

INTRODUCTION

The global, digital, and neoliberal transformations of the twenty-first century have fundamentally reconfigured socio-economic structures, culture, and consequently the ontological and epistemological status of art. With the dissolution of the modernist paradigm grounded in representation, progress, and the production of meaning, contemporary art has moved beyond stylistic coherence, historical continuity, and formal classification. In place of these principles, it has evolved toward forms structured by multiplicity, contingency, and indeterminacy, shifting from object-based representation to conceptual and abstract modes of practice.

Accordingly, in the new era art can no longer be regarded merely as an aesthetic object; rather, it has become a critical instrument that reveals the fractures embedded within contemporary life. In this sense, contemporary art functions as a diagnostic apparatus that renders visible the ethical, political, and existential conditions of the present age. Thus, art reflects a broader restructuring of the relationship between the human subject and the world. The erosion of meaning, the instability of representation, and the dissolution of boundaries correspond to the fragmented and fragile experience of contemporary subjectivity.

Since the spirit of the age is inevitably reflected in artistic production, the nature of prevailing values gains particular significance at this point. Contemporary society manifests itself through fragmented values, institutions, and structures. Postmodernism, as the period in which the first ruptures and fragmentations emerged, constituted a transitional phase between modernism, which represented the old order, and digitalism, which represents the new era. The cultural structures of the old world have begun to dissolve, while the world itself seeks to redefine its position within a new eco-socio-political process. Consequently, issues such as loneliness, disconnection, migration, economic uncertainty, and fragile political structures etc. have come to the forefront.

The Square by Ruben Östlund transfers this trajectory into the socio-cultural domain by offering an ironic and critical perspective on the contemporary condition. The film situates the discourse of contemporary art within a framework shaped by ethical crisis, class inequality, migration, and existential anxiety. In this context, the metaphor of "The Square," which represents these tensions within the public sphere, exposes the contradictions of neoliberal society through the social reflections of art, while sarcastically interrogating the role of art itself. From this perspective, the film may be interpreted not only as a satire of the contemporary art world but also as a phenomenological inquiry into the condition of contemporaneity.

Within this theoretical framework, the study first examines debates concerning what the phenomenon of contemporary art is—or is not—and attempts to conceptualize and frame the highly ambiguous notion of contemporary art through a review of relevant definitions and discussions. Subsequently, the eco-politics of contemporary art and, accordingly, the role of art galleries within the new system are analyzed. Finally, the study proceeds to an analysis of the film, undertaking a contextual examination of the phenomenology of contemporary art.

FRAMING CONTEMPORARY ART

When we speak of contemporary art, a series of questions without definitive answers inevitably arises: how should the term "contemporary" be defined, how many years back should be considered contemporary, and whether the artist being alive affects the contemporaneity of the work (An & Cerasi, 2020). The claim that contemporary art is too complex and diverse to be fully grasped has become a widely accepted orthodoxy in the art world. In addition to traditional media such as painting, sculpture, and printmaking, contemporary art encompasses installation and digital media, ranging from online art to computer-controlled sound environments. A wide array of themes is addressed, including feminism, identity politics, mass culture, consumerism, and trauma (Stallabrass, 2004: 101).

Contemporary art also includes works that push the limits of imagination by incorporating the human body, blood, and organs. It demonstrates a rupture not only from the conventions of art but also from the norms and traditions of everyday life. Moreover, it does not remain confined to an intellectual playground; it may assume carnivalesque, barbaric, or protest-oriented attitudes. Accordingly, debates surrounding contemporary art range from interpretation and philosophical deviation to condemnation, ridicule, and outright rejection (Stallabrass, 2004: 1). The term "contemporary" thus functions as an umbrella category encompassing the diverse forms art takes today—from Lucian Freud's portraits to Jeff Koons's balloon sculptures, Marina Abramović's performances, and Joseph Kosuth's conceptual works (An & Cerasi, 2020).

Public perception of contemporary art is marked by considerable confusion. Many people, when confronted with contemporary art, claim that it is not art (Nancy, 2010: 93). When considered as an internal source of definition and differentiation, the term contemporary signifies the multiplicity of existing in time—feeling aligned with one's era and experiencing it both individually and collectively. Therefore, contemporary art no longer represents a single type of art. It neither possesses a limited set of common characteristics that ensure continuity with the past, nor is it a style that represents a specific historical moment. Like contemporaneity itself, contemporary art is multifaceted, mutable, and unpredictable. The condition of contemporaneity refers to a broader conception of the present that differs from modernity (Smith, 2011: 176).

The temporal framing of the term "contemporary" varies significantly across authors and institutions. Taylor (2005) subtitles his book Contemporary Art as Art Since 1970. Christie's categorizes works from the 1950s and 1960s under "20th Century Sale," while Sotheby's defines works produced between 1945 and 1970 as "early contemporary" and those after 1970 as "late contemporary." "Old Masters" refers to art produced before the nineteenth century, whereas modern art—including Abstract Expressionism and Pop Art—covers the twentieth century up to 1970. Another definition equates contemporary art with works produced by living artists; however, this excludes many influential figures such as Andy Warhol, Joseph Beuys, Martin Kippenberger, Roy Lichtenstein, Donald Judd, Yves Klein, and Jean-Michel Basquiat. Alternatively, defining contemporary art as works by artists born after World War II excludes others such as Kippenberger and Basquiat. Considering major auction houses Sotheby's uses a historical classification while Christie's employs the broader category "Post-War and Contemporary Art" (Thompson, 2008: 10). On the other hand The Museum of Contemporary Art (MOCA) in Los Angeles considers works produced after 1940, whereas Tate Modern's contemporary collection largely consists of works created after 1965 (Medina, 2010).

The relationship between art and contemporaneity can be traced back to the late eighteenth century in the writings of Friedrich Schiller, who described the relationship between the artist and their time as timeless and referred to the artist as a "citizen of the century" (Antoine, 2013: 28). Since then, art has never been as contested as it is today. In the West, claims about contemporary art are often shaped by the density of theoretical discourse, which operates through practices that presume a certain level of general intelligibility (Medina, 2010). However, unlike historical movements such as Impressionism, Fauvism, Cubism, Surrealism, and the avant-garde, contemporary art is not a fixed category but one in constant motion (Nancy, 2010: 91).

The traditional concept of a work of art was characterized by formal harmony, mastery of craftsmanship and technique, and a balanced relationship between order and complexity. However, the classical criteria that distinguished works of art from other objects fell out of favor with the advent of modernity (Saehrendt & Kittl, 2007). Now, the term contemporary signals the death of the modern (Medina, 2010). It is no coincidence that concepts, institutions, and artistic forms associated with the contemporary have replaced those linked to modernity (Smith, 2011: 176). After modernity, art was left with a single option: to be contemporary. While every artwork is inherently tied to its time, never before have currency and contingency been so dominant. The concept of *contempus* emerged to describe the multiplicity of relationships between being and time (Smith, 2009: 1-4).

Agamben (2009: 40), drawing on Nietzsche's (1874) Unzeitgemässe Betrachtungen, shows that contemporaneity contains a disconnect with its own time. Nietzsche wrote that his meditation was also untimely, because he saw the historical culture of the age as a defect. Nietzsche understood that we are consumed by the spirit of the age. Those who adapt to the age are not contemporary because they fail to see it. Contemporaneity is a relationship that one establishes with one's own time, remaining bound to it while simultaneously distancing oneself from it. In other words, it is a relationship established with time and remaining bound to it through anachronism (Agamben, 2009: 41). Therefore, those who are contemporary have a critical attitude.

After 1945, many artists moved away from concrete representation (Saehrendt & Kittl, 2007). Throughout much of the twentieth century, modern art was defined by cyclical tensions: between acceptance and rejection of modern life, between high and popular culture, between traditional practices and mechanical reproduction, and between formal and political avant-gardes. The transition from modern to contemporary art began in the 1950s, emerged in the 1960s, was debated in the 1970s, and became clearly visible in the 1980s (Smith, 2009: 4-5). With the advent of postmodernism, institutional structures were increasingly questioned. One might argue that the first decisive step in this transformation was taken by Marcel Duchamp. When Duchamp submitted a urinal signed "R. Mutt" to the Society of Independent Artists in New York in 1917, it was rejected on the grounds that it was not art. Because art had long been understood as a refined craft requiring skill, the readymade directly challenged conventional notions of artistic creation (An & Cerasi, 2020).

The condemnation of art for breaking rules is not new; what demands attention is the transformation itself. While some changes originate from internal artistic concerns, others respond to broader economic and political shifts (Stallabrass, 2004: 1). Pop Art in the 1960s and 1970s marked a major rupture. Postmodern responses to Pop Art arose from features that could not be accommodated within formalist or realist critical frameworks, most notably anonymity (Harrison, 2003: 11).

After the 1970s, postmodernism evolved into a broader worldview (Jencks, 1992: 10). It was constructed both as a reaction against modernity and as an intensification of its qualities (Negri, 2008: 23). While Lyotard (1979) defined postmodernism as the end of grand narratives, Jameson (1983; 1991) described it as the cultural logic of late capitalism. Yet contemporary art possesses a level of institutional concreteness—museums, art centers, journals, academic programs, and market niches—that postmodern art did not (Esanu, 2012: 6).

The new world order of the 1980s globalized the art world, while art in developed societies came under increasing pressure from mass culture. After the 1990s, neoliberal policies became more pronounced (Stallabrass, 2004: 51–52). The collapse of the Soviet Union and political transformations in Eastern Europe accelerated the development of contemporary art. While contemporary art has a long institutional history in the West, it is also a product of post-socialist transition. In these regions, the rapid transfer of new artistic practices into existing cultural environments rendered contemporary art more susceptible to critical scrutiny (Esanu, 2012: 8).

The events of 1989 and their aftermath—German reunification, the dissolution of the Soviet Union, the rise of global trade agreements, and China's partial shift toward capitalism—profoundly reshaped the art world. Previously structured by Cold War divisions between East and West, the art world underwent a reconfiguration as these oppositions diminished. Postmodern critique exposed the white male figure behind the universalist façade of high culture, highlighting the importance of feminist and non-white artistic struggles. Consequently, artistic discourse, institutions, and practices rapidly transformed. The proliferation of biennials and the expansion of museums in the 1990s further commercialized the art world, aligning it more closely with consumer culture and transforming museums into hybrid spaces resembling stores and theme parks (Stallabrass, 2004: 7–9). Post-9/11 developments, ongoing wars, global inequalities, institutional crises, and the proliferation of alternative networks have generated a pervasive sense of "ground zero," while simultaneously inspiring adaptive forms of resistance (Smith, 2008: 2–3).

In short, the process leading to contemporary art involves a long period of modernism followed by postmodern change. Especially in today's world, digital culture, neoliberalism, and consumerism have a significant impact on shaping contemporary art.

THE POLITICAL ECONOMY OF CONTEMPORARY ART

The political economy of contemporary art—formed together with galleries, auction houses, and the new global wealthy class—constitutes its the most fundamental ontology. Considering the high proportion of international trade in the art market, it is clearly evident that art is closely related to the financial capitalist economy. Art prices and the volume of art sales closely correspond to stock market dynamics, and major financial centers are also the primary centers of art sales (Stallabrass, 2004: 3–4). Contemporary art refers to specific conditions of artistic production that have developed in the latest stage of global capitalism. This stage is known in some contexts as neoliberalism, in others as neoconservatism, corporatism, free-market ideology, or laissez-faire economics (Esanu, 2012: 7).

The global historical events of 1989 transformed the foundations of the art institution. Artists and curators sought new alternative discourses and frameworks beyond museums, which were directly connected to the idea of the modern nation-state (Griffin, 2013: 9). In the 1990s, the end of the Cold War, the collapse of totalitarian regimes in Eastern Europe, and the fall of the apartheid regime in South Africa triggered a critical reassessment of the conditions of artistic production and the systems through which such production was legitimized, bringing about new developments in curatorial practice. Whereas earlier questions around identity, difference, and multiculturalism were often discussed by curators through the most basic oppositions present in artists' works, in the 1990s postcolonialism and globalization shifted the reference systems of curatorial practice—its aesthetic and cultural canons—from twentieth-century modernity toward twenty-first-century tendencies (Enwezor, 2007: 382–383).

In relation to contemporary global capitalism, the art world has become a worldly global religion, abandoning more anachronistic aura-producing tools such as the cult of the artist, nationality, or creativity in order to manifest the contemporary. Being part of global art is less about aesthetic interest and more about keeping pace with the frenzy of the times. The main reason for this is the horizontal expansion of the market. As the bourgeoisie—who once purchased works within local art circles—became part of a new global elite consuming the same branded artistic products, this horizontal expansion of the market increased sales, and contemporary art came to define the aesthetic philanthropy identity of the global elite. Thus, through interaction with a new social service economy carried out by artists, critics, and curators, contemporary art becomes a social structure defined by the dialectic between the new jet class and its proletariat (Medina, 2010).

In describing the old and new art systems, Shiner (2001) views the artist in the new system as operating within a more liberal environment. In the old art system, there were many patronage and commission relations, some of which resembled features of a market economy. Patrons or clients typically commissioned poems, paintings, or musical compositions for specific places or contexts. Even in cases where producers were granted considerable freedom, artists still created their works according to the wishes of their clients. The criteria for success in this system included not only how well the work served its purpose, but also traditional standards of beauty such as harmony and proportion. The price of the resulting work was generally determined by materials, difficulty, and time, as well as the reputation of the workshop or master and the function of the work. By contrast, in the market system, artists produce works in advance and then attempt to sell them—often through dealers or intermediaries—to a largely anonymous body of buyers. The absence of a predetermined order gives the impression that artists are free to follow their own inclinations. Criteria of success depend on intrinsic qualities such as originality, expressive power, and formal excellence, as well as on the artist's reputation and fashion. Historians have often described the transition from the old art system to the new fine arts system as a "liberation." In the old system, patrons were usually in a superior position and artisans/artists were obliged to comply with their demands; in the new market system, artists and buyers are thought to have come closer to an equal standing (Shiner, 2001: 126–127).

However, Thompson (2008) demonstrates that the freedom mentioned by Shiner is entirely dependent on money. After the aristocracy and monarchy abandoned patronage of the arts in the mid-eighteenth century, the relationship between money and the artist's fame came to determine the value of the artwork. Works gained value not according to their intrinsic success or merit, but insofar as they became expressions of status. Therefore, today artists are influenced by the market—since they must sell their works to dealers, collectors, and speculators, whose status concerns and investment motivations shape artistic selection. The importance of an artwork is often tied to the size of the collector's bank account (Thompson, 2008: 178–179).

Dealers support and promote non-traditional art because they represent the art world equivalent of what is called disruptive innovation in business. The branded dealer manages the long-term career of a mature artist, bringing works to collectors, fairs, and museums (Thompson, 2008: 30). In the contemporary art market, pricing is largely determined by intermediaries—those who operate between the producer (artist) and the consumer (collector). Primary market sales, meaning new artworks entering the market for the first time, occur mainly through galleries that represent selected artists and manage their sales (An & Cerasi, 2020). Alongside auction houses and galleries, art fairs are a crucial enterprise for generating sales in the visual arts market. Art fairs provide vital infrastructure for both local and international art markets worldwide and have become a significant industry in their own right (Morgner, 2014: 318).

A popular artist is one who has already passed through several gatekeepers. The artist has been accepted, exhibited by a mainstream gallery, and is often represented by a superstar dealer. Their works are cleverly marketed, placed within branded collections, and exhibited in branded art museums. The works appear in evening auctions at Christie's or Sotheby's. It is not aesthetic judgment that defines a popular artist, but this process in the market. The value of art often relates less to the artwork itself than to the branding of the artist, dealer, or auction house, as well as the ego of the collector. The market is driven by high-status auctions and art fairs that have become events in themselves—forms of entertainment for the ultra-wealthy and public spectacle. The value of a work of art also depends on whether it sells for a high price (Thompson, 2008: 228).

Art spaces form a network encompassing different fields and economies such as the studio, gallery, museum, art criticism, art history, and the art market. To dismantle and recode institutional traditions reveals how institutions shape the meaning of art, modulate its cultural and economic value, expose the illusion of the autonomy of art and its institutions, and demonstrate their relationship with broader socio-economic and political processes of the present (Kwon, 2002: 14).

According to Duncan (1995: 7–20), Western museums serve the construction of Western society. Visitors, consciously or unconsciously, perform a ritual within the museum's own structure. However, in modern art museums, the transformation of the traditional structure of the museum—such as the shift to the white cube form, the abandonment of historical grandeur, and the use of different visual codes—has led to the disruption of this ritual. Thus, the new museum design has produced a sense of alienation, distancing visitors from processes of Western subject formation. As modernism ages, context turns into content. In a strange reversal, the object placed in the gallery frames the gallery and its laws. A gallery is constructed as meticulously as a medieval church (O'Doherty, 1976: 15).

The museum's architecture corresponds to the logic of contemporary galleries. Galleries are typically windowless and consist of plain white-walled rooms known as the "white cube." This neutral environment reinforces the idea that what is seen is art and that galleries are elitist. The art trade is one of the least transparent and least regulated major commercial activities in the world. What an art dealer needs is money and a strong network. Art dealing also confers class status by signaling superior aesthetic understanding and negotiation skills (Thompson, 2008: 27-29).

The contemporary art market demonstrates that contemporary art is more than just art itself. The traditional understanding of art and museology has changed in this new era, with a shift from museums to galleries and auctions. The political economy of contemporary art shows that it cannot be evaluated solely on the basis of art; it encompasses much more.

THE SARCASTIC SATIRE OF CONTEMPORARY ART AND HUMANITY IN THE SQUARE

In the film "The Square," Ruben Östlund critically and satirically questions the world we live in through Western values, Christian values, modern values, ethics, morality, and social classes. Because art is one of the clearest areas where social change is reflected, he draws a parallel between contemporary art and cultural change. The fact that the museum used as the main setting in the film is a Royal Museum (Royal Palace) represents the historical values and imperial power of the West, while the renaming of this museum as "X" anonymizes these representations (Figure 1).

Figure 1. X-Royal Museum

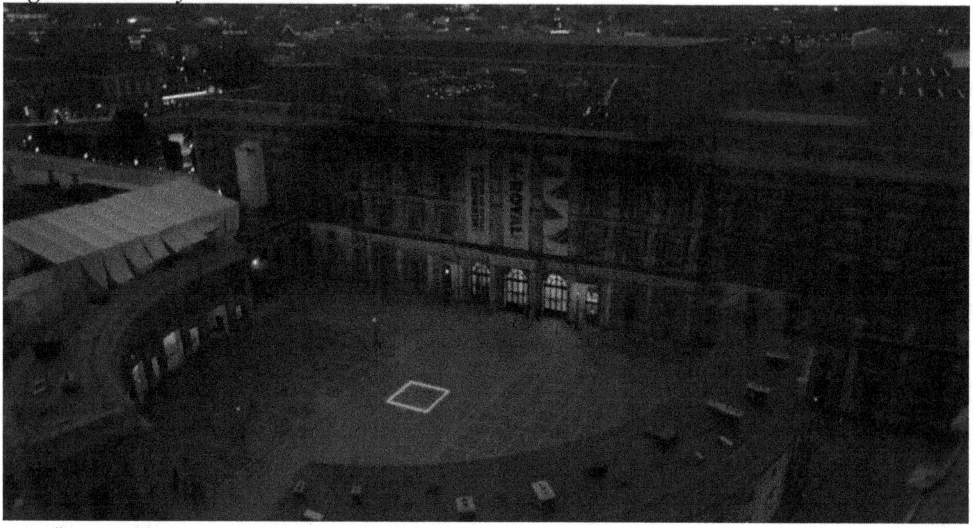

(Östlund, 2017)

Since the film is a critique of modern Western values, the director employs symbols belonging to this culture. The protagonist's name, Christian, signifies Christianity. As a setting, Stockholm is chosen as a city representing Western and modern values. Scandinavian countries generally rank at the top of the Human Development Report. According to the 2025 Human Development Report, Iceland ranks first, followed by Norway, Switzerland, and Denmark. As the capital of Sweden—one of the most developed Scandinavian countries—Stockholm represents both economic and social welfare, while also serving as a cultural symbol of Western civilization as the city where the Nobel Prizes, among the most prestigious awards in science, literature, and medicine, are awarded.

In The Square, Ruben Östlund draws attention to neoliberalism as the cause of the hypocritical and insensitive world in which his characters exist. He not only contextualizes their anxieties within a capitalist system, but also satirizes this economic system as the fundamental cause of social conflict. What Östlund had previously described as "man guilt" in relation to the social pressures to conform to Swedish white masculinity norms is now transformed into "liberal guilt." Many problems that should be addressed by the state have today been shifted onto the conscience of individuals (Gullette, 2018: 73–74).

While socially critical cinema typically attempts to present the narrative and perspective of the migrant, Östlund portrays the encounter with the Other from the perspective of either the guest or the host (Fernández Jiménez et al., 2020: 224–228). Östlund's cinema presents an aesthetics of vulnerability. He is one of the leading narrators of social unease and moral precarity in Scandinavian cinema. A common feature of all his films is an unusual sensitivity to how everyday life can be overturned by unexpected events that pose an existential threat to characters and their worldviews. In Östlund's cinematic universe, the most examined condition is that of exposure: the loss of (cultural and material) protection privileges and the feeling of being defenseless against unpleasant and invasive external forces. In Caché (Michael Haneke, 2005), which addresses a similar theme, the bourgeois life of a successful television host is disrupted by invasive threats from his own past (Grønstad, 2020: 20). As in Haneke's films, the transformation of the rigid masculinity of the white male character in Östlund's films requires a kind of catalyst that can be described as an external threat—such as a mysterious videotape, an avalanche, or a primate (Grønstad, 2020: 29).

Christian, the curator of a prestigious modern art museum called X-Royal Museum in Stockholm, is an intellectual, well-presented, Tesla-driving, divorced father of two who strives to fulfill all the requirements of the modern world. In fact, Christian shares characteristics with director Ruben Östlund, and in a sense, the director criticizes the Western individual through himself (Carew, 2018: 50–51). The mistake Christian makes following a theft incident leads him into a moral crisis, while simultaneously initiating the chain of events that compels us to question modern Western values. Christian's moral crisis is, in fact, a typical Scandinavian sensibility. He experiences such ethical discomfort that he records a video message apologizing to the immigrant child he falsely accused of theft. Experiencing global privilege as a problem is based on the perception of distributive injustice and transnational inequalities of power. In Scandinavian public discourse, however, this perception does not emerge primarily as a political concern; rather, the issue is addressed in different ways: "Is this okay?" Because recognizing one's privilege as a problem requires sensing an exploitative global infrastructure shaped by complex histories and lasting effects such as capitalism, imperialism, racism, neocolonial violence, the Capitalocene, neoliberal hegemony, and white supremacy. Yet within Scandinavian public culture, this historical-political infrastructure appears more as a collection of fragmented and incomplete histories of injustice. Although sensitivity to privilege is not unique to Scandinavia, it has gained particular significance in twenty-first-century Scandinavian societies, where the postwar welfare state model has fostered a popular egalitarian imagination in which socio-economic privilege is not fully acceptable (Sharma, 2024: 11).

Christian's decision to distribute threatening letters to residents of an apartment building in a marginal neighborhood—where he traced his stolen phone signal—leads to conflict with the family of an innocent immigrant child, pushing Christian into a Western moral crisis. On the one hand, there is the successful yet selfish intellectual Christian; on the other, there is a refugee child forced to seek asylum in a foreign country and work at a young age simply to survive. When he confronts the child, Christian is accompanied by his daughters and is still wearing the tuxedo from the previous night's event.

Christian struggles with the problem of his relation to the lack of completeness in the Other. After a dinner attended by the elite, Christian, wearing a tuxedo, rummages through the trash behind his apartment trying to find a piece of paper with the immigrant child's number written on it. What he's actually searching for in the trash is the conscience of an era that has long been lost (Figure 2). In the video message he records to send to the child, after admitting his prejudice, he connects the issue to structural problems and the unequal distribution of assets. This scene foreshadows the loss of his symbolic identity on the eve of his formal resignation from his professional role. Also, there is another scene that depicts an encounter with the Other. During a meeting attended by a man with Tourette's syndrome, a member of the audience reminds others that they should show tolerance toward this condition. Here, explicit instruction regarding the correct symbolic response to an unexpected event intervenes to control the possibility of a destabilizing encounter with the enjoyment of the Other (Friedlander, 2020: 96-97).

Figure 2. Christian searching for paper among the trash

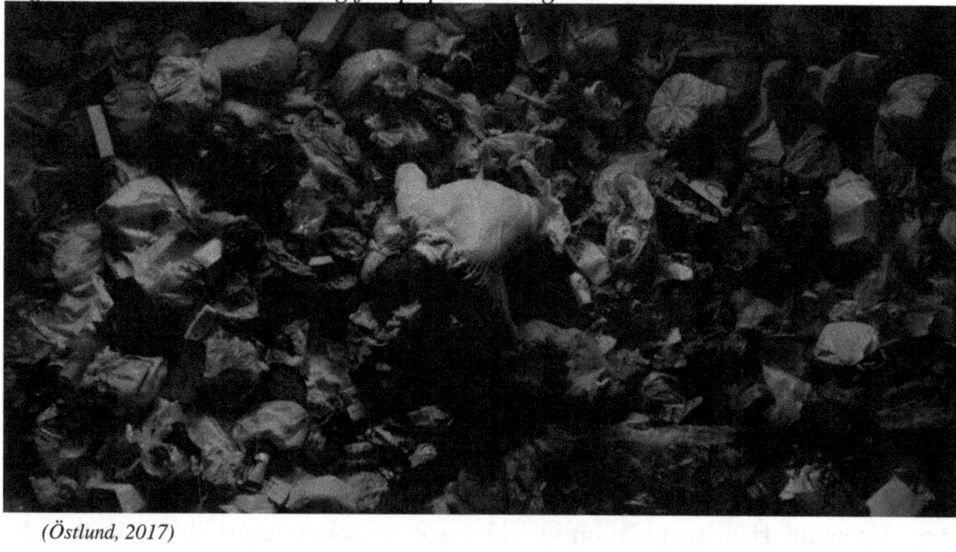

(Östlund, 2017)

In Östlund's films, the phenomenon of contemporary technological control is evident. Mobile phones lead not to easier communication but to communication failure. Male protagonists are symbolically castrated by digital technology. After his phone is stolen, Christian experiences a series of negative events, while also being forced to resign following the viral video (Lynch, 2020: 108). In the viral video prepared by young Generation Y marketers for The Square installation, a blonde child representing the Western archetype explodes like a bomb upon entering the square. What makes the image provocative is precisely the use of a blonde child (Figure 3).

Figure 3. Child in The Square

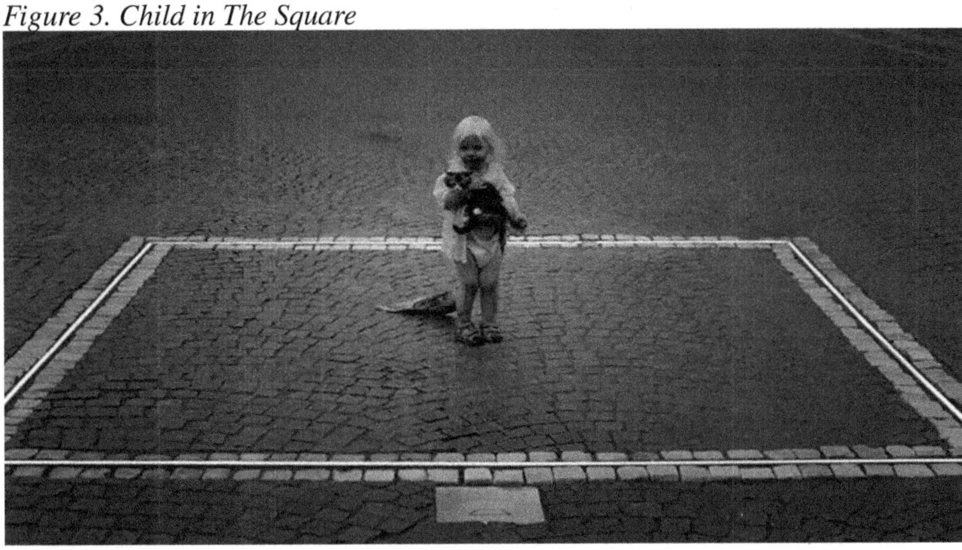

(Östlund, 2017)

Throughout the film, the phrase "Do you want to help save a human life?" is heard at random intervals. The film establishes a relationship between philanthropy and hypocrisy. No one in the film pays attention to those asking for help. The selectiveness of the homeless woman surprises Christian, who expects to be hailed as a hero for his charitable act (Smith, 2021: 45). As Christian walks through a crowd in central Stockholm where everyone is looking at their phones, the Word "help" is heard again, yet no one pays attention. Later, Christian helps a woman together with another man. After rescuing her, he laughs, feeling like a hero. In a context where migrants have fled war and beg in the streets, and in a country where criminal incidents are relatively rare, for Western individuals this act of rescuing a woman appears as an extraordinarily significant event.

The installation titled "The Square," exhibited in front of the museum, is geometrically a square but metaphorically represents public space and people from different social classes. The 4x4 meter square is introduced with idealistic statements suggesting that everyone within it has equal rights and responsibilities and that those in need will find trust. It is described as: "A sanctuary of trust and caring. We all share, within its boundaries, equal rights and obligations." The Square essentially represents the social contract at the center of democracy and civilization. However, this modern contract has become extremely fragile. It is being punctured by theft, slang, migration, and issues of trust. In this context, the problem of trust becomes central—a question that follows the viewer throughout the film. At the beginning, when Christian helps a woman asking for assistance, he is actually lured into a theft trap. On the other hand, he doesn't trust the female journalist he had sex with and doesn't want to give her the condom.

The film presents contrasts. The director stated in an interview that he creates dilemmas in his films (Billard, 2017). Similar to the contradictions within individuals in Russian literature, these oppositions reveal human existence in its most naked form. However, Östlund presents these contradictions not with Russian seriousness or Scandinavian depression, but rather with a Western ease and a sense of absurdity. While Haneke addresses the migrant issue in a tragicomic way by contrasting it with the elite class, Östlund does so sarcastically. We see this opposition first in the name of the museum. While it is a royal museum, it is also anonymized by the name "X." In Sweden—one of the countries with the highest levels of welfare—beggars wander the streets. Scenes where people from different social classes and cultures coexist are striking. While some people discuss art, homeless individuals ask them for help. On the one hand, migrants and homeless individuals struggling to survive are shown; on the other, the absurd behaviors of elite museum-goers are depicted. When Christian loses his daughters in a shopping mall, he entrusts his valuable belongings to a beggar while searching for them. In an art talk conducted in an elite language, the swearing of a person with Tourette's syndrome sabotages this elite language. A male employee attends a workplace meeting with his baby. The chimpanzee in the journalist's home questions normality. While elite art consumers rush toward the catering without waiting for the chef to finish speaking—revealing their lack of genuine interest in art—a homeless person asking Christian for a chicken ciabatta without onions appears more selective than the elites. As a curator, Christian is unable to explain the texts in his own museum, implicitly referencing the "unknowable" nature of contemporary art.

In the dinner scene—featuring real billionaire donors (Kelly, 2018) —we watch the primate performance of a performance artist named Oleg (a reference to Oleg Kulik, known for animal performances) (Figure 4.). Östlund may have increased the risks of the conflict between the "civilized" and the "uncivilized" by inviting real elite donors from the Swedish art world to play themselves (Friedlander, 2020: 100). This scene confronts people with their most primitive states within the most sublimated environment of culture. However, when the primate attacks a woman, the guests fail to maintain the composure that "civilized society" prides itself on (Trujillo, 2018: 508). They realize that no one is safe unless they take the risk of acting together rather than passively hiding within the herd. All claims to civility vanish with the shout of "kill him" (Friedlander, 2020: 99). The beating of Oleg by the men leads to a violation of social norms that is no less disturbing than Oleg's behavior (Grønstad, 2020: 28).

Figure 4. Oleg's performance

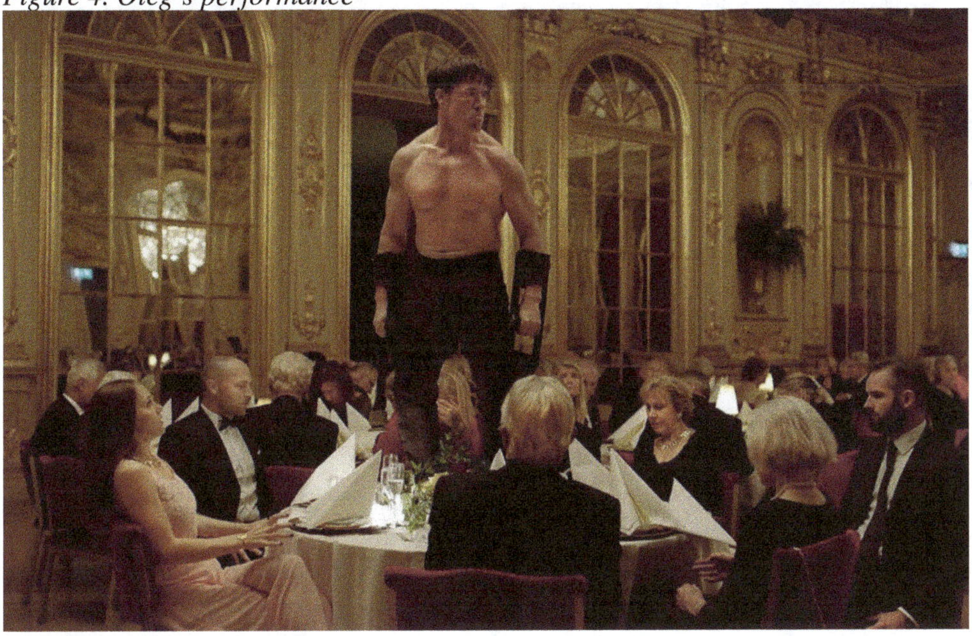

(Östlund, 2017)

Throughout the film, the primate motif is repeatedly used to emphasize the primitive nature of human beings (Figure 5). However, this motif also serves a function of ambiguity. After its first appearance, we see Christian and Anne engage in sexual intercourse with tense determination. Toward the end of the film, in its second appearance in Anne's apartment, the pickpocketing incident reaches its climax. Christian pushes the child he falsely accused down the stairs of his apartment building. This raises the question of what happened to the child—or whether the child is merely a product of Christian's guilt (Riis, 2024: 294–295).

Figure 5. The chimpanzee at Anne's home

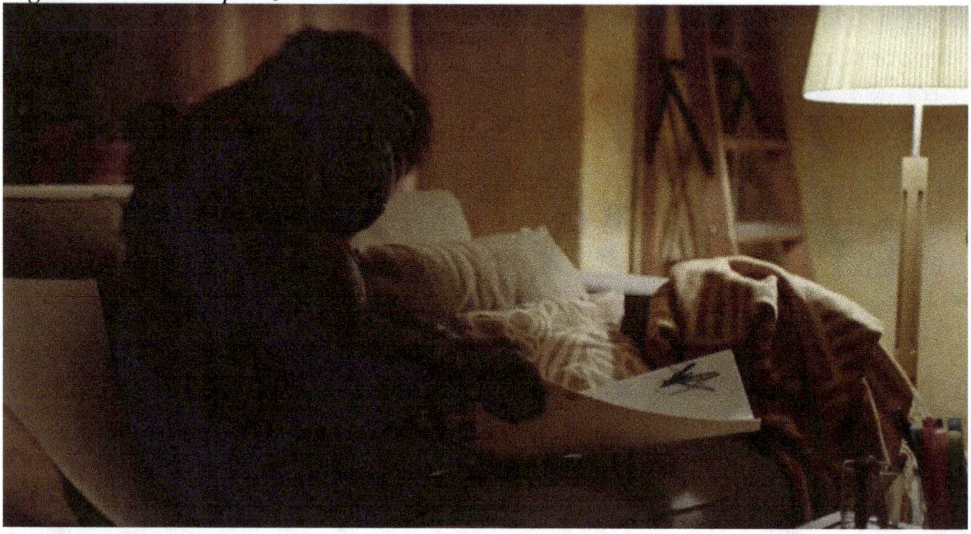

(Östlund, 2017)

In short, these are all events that – when considered in terms of the old world order – shouldn't be happening. Migrants are not in their own countries; high and low culture coexist side by side in the city; men bring babies to work; profanity is uttered in spaces of elevated discourse; objects that are not art have become art, and so on. The director opens up for debate what is acceptable. The square represents this in the public sphere. Boundaries have become highly blurred. Where do normality, acceptability, limits, and tolerance begin and end?

The absurd interview scene about art at the beginning of the film reflects the most conceptual consciousness of the Western individual. Christian emphasizes the commercial aspect of art. The phrase "You have nothing" on the wall points to the stage of nothingness humanity has reached (Figure 6). The journalist asks Christian whether he can explain, in layman's terms, a highly theoretical statement published on the museum's website: "Exhibition, non exhibition. An evening conversation that explores the dynamics of the exhibitable and the construction of publicness in the spirit of Robert Smithson's sight, non-sight. From non-sight to sight from non-exhibition to exhibition, what is the topos of exhibition, non-exhibition in the crowded moments of mega exhibition?" The text read by Anne is a direct quotation from a colleague of Östlund who teaches at the Academy of Fine Arts at the University of Gothenburg. This is an issue of jargonization (Nazarbaeva, 2018: 26–27).

Figure 6. The state "you have nothing" on the wall

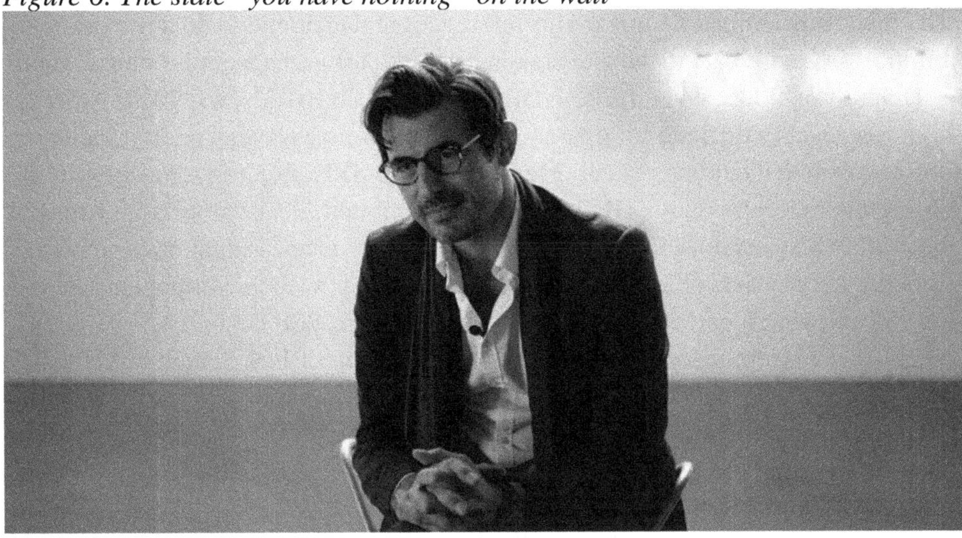

(Östlund, 2017)

The film suggests from the outset that one must know this jargon to understand art; however, the curator himself, who cannot answer this question during the interview, does not fully understand it either. At the same time, the complexity and incomprehensibility of contemporary art are emphasized. He responds to the question with another question: "When—I mean, if you place an object in a museum, does that make this object a piece of art? For instance, if we took your bag and placed it here, would that make it art?" His answer (or question) implies that anything can be a work of art in contemporary art. What matters here is the context in which the object is framed. Within the context of a museum or art gallery, an object can become an artwork.

The viewer is usually aware that civilizing mechanisms are at work when the museum creates a public stage where rituals are openly displayed. For example, when the X-Royal Museum is open to the public, a person who makes noise and disrupts discussion is perceived as crossing the boundaries of politeness. However, when the museum hosts a private party for staff and special guests, attendees dance to loud music (Nazarbaeva, 2018: 61). The visitor experience in the museum is often shaped by audience participation. Therefore, within the museum walls, we see wealthy sponsors donating money to purchase installations. At the same time, just outside those walls, we see how Christian is robbed in the middle of the square. Thus, when art moves outside museum doors, interaction with an artwork is no longer governed by museum behavior (Nazarbaeva, 2018: 72).

The museum's cleaning staff accidentally cleans up an installation made of gravel piles, mistaking it for trash. This references real incidents in contemporary art exhibitions where cleaners have mistaken artworks for garbage and removed them (see Donaldson, 2025; Wright, 2024; BBC News, 2015; BBC News, 2014; Alberge, 2004). Because it's difficult to separate modern art from everyday reality, incidents prone to misunderstandings occur. Members of the SPD, holding a meeting in the building where Joseph Beuys's Badewanne was exhibited, cleaned the bathtub to cool their drinks (Saehrendt & Kittl, 2007). Additionally, since contemporary artworks are contingent physical objects, issues arise regarding how their components should be stored and which parts belong to the work (Buskirk, 2003: 15–16).

The Square is reminiscent of Malevich's Black Square. Black Square was actually a drawing for the opera "Victory over the Sun". The theme of this opera perfectly captured the spirit of the time: the victory of technology over nature, of modern man over the sun, and Malevich's Black Square, which he called the zero point, reflected this spirit (Lynton, 1980: 78-80). Malevich (1959: 68) analyzes the spirit of the time with his work as follows: "This was no 'empty square' which I had exhibited but rather the feeling of non-objectivity. I realized that the 'thing' and the 'concept' were substituted for feeling and understood the falsity of the world of will and idea." Östlund, however, a century later, shows that the zero point that Malevich saw as the starting point has today become a ground zero within the context of the human condition.

Baudrillard (2005) argued that images no longer represent reality but replace it. In today's digital age, the artwork itself has become an object that exists only at the level of the image, to be exhibited and consumed—it no longer truly exists. Through all these absurdities, social decay, and individual disconnections, Östlund ultimately depicts the collapse of the social contract through art. The current stage of society—marked by advanced digital technology—also brings a period of collapsing values. This collapse of values finds expression in art. Perhaps this is most dramatically seen in the removal of the statue of King Karl XIV Johan—who lived in the nineteenth century, when modernism was at its strongest—from in front of the museum, and its replacement with an empty square. While the statue represents the art and values of the old world, it is replaced by the digital void and nothingness of the new world. The fact that workers filmed the removal of the statue with their cell phones and that the square installation in its place was framed with neon lights is a nod to the new era (Figure 7 and Figure 8).

Figure 7. Removal of the statue

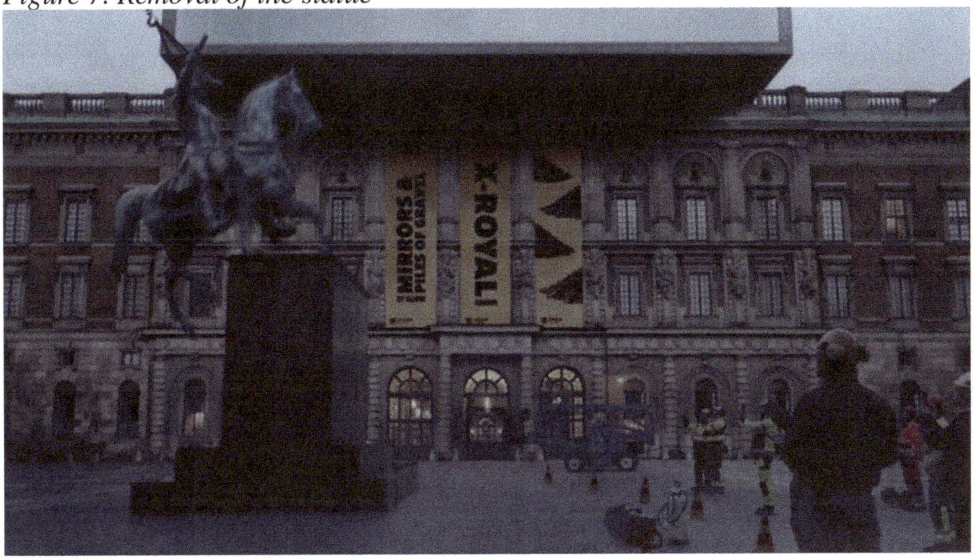

(Östlund, 2017)

Figure 8. The square installation

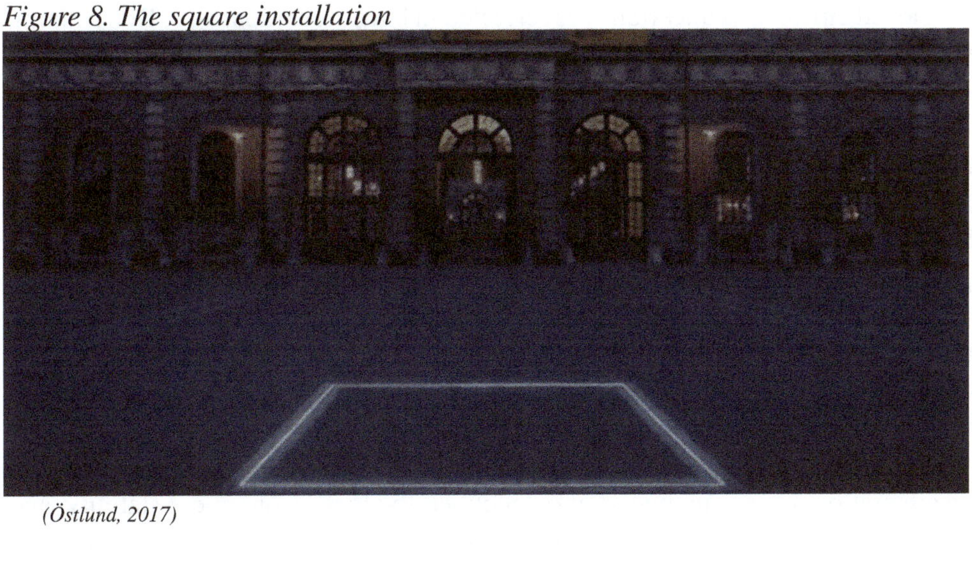

(Östlund, 2017)

CONCLUSION

Ruben Östlund's film demonstrates that the transformation of contemporary art is not limited solely to aesthetic paradigms; it functions as a critical space reflecting the ontological, ethical, and social crises of the contemporary subject and representing the contradictions of neoliberal society, such as class inequality, ethical concerns, and trust issues.

While the characters in the film articulate a fragmented and unstable subjectivity, the "Square" installation symbolically represents an idealized shared public space. However, the socio-political stage the world has reached and the neoliberal values within which humanity finds itself show that the social contract constituting this public space is dissolving. Östlund illustrates this dissolution and fragmentation through the example of art. In this sense, Östlund establishes a relationship between the logic of contemporary art and the dissolution of the social contract. Accordingly, art ceases to be a representational tool and instead becomes a symptomatic manifestation of this dissolution.

The new world order is a neoliberal order where borders are dissolving and old structures are dismantling. In this world, the definition of geography and space has changed. The cultural confusion manifests itself in the digital realm, ranging from the blurring of boundaries to the boundless reality of migrants in Europe's most developed cities. This uncertainty is reflected in human relationships. Determining where ethical boundaries begin and end has become both a personal and public issue.

Contemporary art, instead of producing aesthetic pleasure, confronts the viewer with the tension and fragility of meaning. Therefore, in the film, the often-criticized incomprehensibility of contemporary art emerges as a reflection of the epistemological uncertainty and ontological instability that define our time. Consequently, boundlessness and uncertainty are directly reflected in art itself. Art no longer presents itself through concreteness, but through abstraction.

The subject, within a void and nothingness further clarified by digital culture, is adrift in a vast emptiness in a digitally mediated and commodified neoliberal world characterized by loneliness and alienation. In this context, the subject, trapped within market values and digital culture, appears to be in a serious moral and ethical crisis. The film treats contemporary art as a space reflecting semantic collapse, social disintegration, economic uncertainty, neoliberal values, economic instability, and ethical contradictions. Therefore, contemporary art appears as a representation of the stage humanity has reached. The nothingness of contemporary art is nothing other than the nothingness within humanity itself.

REFERENCES

Agamben, G. (2009). *What is an apparatus? and other essays* (Kishik, D., & Pedatella, S., Trans.). Stanford University Press.

Alberge, D. (2004, August 27). Cleaner thought Tate exhibit was a load of rubbish. *The Times*.

An, K., & Cerasi, J. (2020). *Who's afraid of contemporary art?: An A to Z guide to the art world.* Thames & Hudson.

Antoine, J.-P. (2013). The historicity of the contemporary is now! In Dumbadze, A., & Hudson, S. (Eds.), *Contemporary art: 1989 to the present* (pp. 28–36). John Wiley & Sons.

Baudrillard, J. (2005). *Le complot de l'art: Entrevues* [The Conspiracy of Art: Interviews]. Lotringer, S., Ed.). Galilée.

BBC News. (2014, February 20). Cleaner throws out "rubbish" Sala Murat artwork.

BBC News. (2015, October 25). Art binned by cleaner in Italy "restored".

Billard, J. (2017, November 16). 8 times Ruben Östlund's *The Square* accurately portrayed the art world and embarrassed us all. *Artspace*.

Buskirk, M. (2003). *The contingent object of contemporary art.* MIT Press. DOI: 10.7551/mitpress/2139.001.0001

Carew, A. (2018). Art attack: Social responsibility and discomfort in the square. *Screen Education*, (91), 50–57.

Donaldson, M. (2025, November 10). Museum volunteer ruins artwork by "cleaning" display with toilet paper. *GB News*.

Duncan, C. (1995). *Civilizing rituals: Inside public art museums.* Routledge.

Enwezor, O. (2007). Artforum. *Artforum, 46*(1), 382–386.

Esanu, O. (2012). What was contemporary art? *Art Margins, 1*(1), 5–28. DOI: 10.1162/ARTM_a_00003

Fernández Jiménez, M., Martinicorena Zaratiegui, S., & Paris Arranz, I. (2020). Políticas europeas de la "hostipitalidad" en el cine de Ruben Östlund: el caso de *The Square* (2017) [European Policies of "Hostipitality" in the Cinema of Ruben Östlund: The Case of *The Square* (2017)]. *Fotocinema. Revista Científica De Cine Y Fotografía*, (21), 221-245. https://doi.org/DOI: 10.24310/Fotocinema.2020.v21i.10041

Friedlander, J. (2020). Repeating the square: From satisfaction to jouissance. *Crisis and Critique*, *7*(2), 91–103.

Griffin, T. (2013). Worlds apart: Contemporary art, globalization, and the rise of biennials. In Dumbadze, A., & Hudson, S. (Eds.), *Contemporary art: 1989 to the present* (pp. 7–16). John Wiley & Sons.

Grønstad, A. (2020). Conditional vulnerability in the films of Ruben Östlund. In Dancus, A. M., Hyvönen, M., & Karlsson, M. (Eds.), *Vulnerability in Scandinavian art and culture* (pp. 19–31). DOI: 10.1007/978-3-030-37382-5_2

Gullette, C. M. (2018). *Challenging Swedishness: Intersections of neoliberalism, race, and queerness in the works of Jonas Hassen Khemiri and Ruben Östlund* [Unpublished doctoral dissertation, University of California, Berkeley]. UC Berkeley Electronic Theses and Dissertations.

Harrison, S. (2003). *Pop art and the origins of post-modernism*. Cambridge University Press.

Human Development Report (2025). Human Development Report 2025, May 6, 2025 https://hdr.undp.org/content/human-development-report-2025

Jameson, F. (1983). Postmodernism and consumer society. In Foster, H. (Ed.), *The anti-aesthetic: Essays on postmodern culture* (pp. 111–125). Bay Press.

Jameson, F. (1991). *Postmodernism, or, the cultural logic of late capitalism*. Duke University Press.

Jencks, C. (1992). The post-modern agenda. In Jencks, C. (Ed.), *The post-modern reader*. Academy Editions.

Kelly, S. (2018, March 1). Artist Terry Notary explains that uncomfortable dinner scene in Oscar contender *The Square*. *Los Angeles Times*.

Kwon, M. (2002). *One place after another: Site-specific art and locational identity*. MIT Press. DOI: 10.7551/mitpress/5138.001.0001

Lynch, J. (2020). "Please leave a message": The media ecology of Ruben Östlund's *Play, Force Majeure*, and *The Square. Journal of Scandinavian Cinema, 10*(2), 145–160.

Lynton, N. (1980). *The story of modern art*. Phaidon.

Lyotard, J.-F. (1979). *La condition postmoderne: Rapport sur le savoir* [The Postmodern Condition: A Report on Knowledge]. Éditions de Minuit.

Malevich, K. (1959). *The non-objective world*. Paul Theobald.

Medina, C. (2010, January). Contemp(t)ory: Eleven theses. *e-flux*, (12). https://www.e-flux.com/journal/12/61335

Morgner, C. (2014). The evolution of the art fair. *Historical Social Research (Köln), 39*(3), 318–336. DOI: 10.12759/hsr.39.2014.3.318-336

Nancy, J.-L. (2010). Art today (C. Mandel, Trans.). *Journal of Visual Culture, 9*(1), 91–99. DOI: 10.1177/1470412909354265

Nazarbaeva, N. (2018). *Thinking inside and outside of The Square: Barriers, audience engagement, and contemporary art in Ruben Östlund's film The Square* [Unpublished master's thesis]. Lund University.

Negri, A. (2008). Contemporaneity between modernity and postmodernity. In Smith, T., Enwezor, O., & Condee, N. (Eds.), *Modernity, postmodernity, contemporaneity* (pp. 23–29). Duke University Press.

Nietzsche, F. (1874). *Unzeitgemässe Betrachtungen* [Untimely meditations]. Verlag von E. W. Fritzsch.

O'Doherty, B. (1976). *Inside the white cube: The ideology of the gallery space*. Lapis Press.

Östlund, R. (Director). (2017). *The Square* [Film]. Plattform Produktion

Riis, J. (2024). Symbolic purposes of style: Ruben Östlund's *The Square. Journal of Scandinavian Cinema, 13*(3), 283–297. DOI: 10.1386/jsca_00100_1

Saehrendt, C., & Kittl, S. T. (2007). *Das kann ich auch!: Gebrauchsanweisung für moderne Kunst* [I can do that too!: A user manual for modern art]. DuMont Buchverlag.

Sharma, D. (2024). Skeptimentality: The Square And The Aesthetics of Complicity. *The Nordic Journal of Aesthetics, 2024*(68), 10–32. DOI: 10.7146/nja.v33i68.152362

Shiner, L. (2001). *The Invention of Art: A Cultural History*. University of Chicago Press. DOI: 10.7208/chicago/9780226753416.001.0001

Smith, M. (2021). *Degrees of artificiality in the works of: Roy Andersson, Aki Kaurismäki, Ruben Östlund, Thomas Vinterberg, and Lukas Moodysson* [Unpublished master's thesis]. Queen's University.

Smith, T. (2008). Introduction: The contemporaneity question. In Smith, T., Enwezor, O., & Condee, N. (Eds.), *Modernity, postmodernity, contemporaneity* (pp. 1–19). Duke University Press.

Smith, T. (2009). *What is contemporary art?* University of Chicago Press. DOI: 10.7208/chicago/9780226131672.001.0001

Smith, T. (2011). Currents of world-making in contemporary art. *World Art, 1*(2), 171–188. DOI: 10.1080/21500894.2011.602712

Stallabrass, J. (2004). *Contemporary art: A very short introduction*. Oxford University Press.

Taylor, B. (2005). *Contemporary art: Art since 1970*. Pearson Prentice Hall.

Thompson, D. (2008). *The $12 million stuffed shark: The curious economics of contemporary art*. Palgrave Macmillan.

Trujillo, P. (2018). Desbordando los cuadrados: *La forma del agua* de Guillermo Del Toro y *The Square* de Ruben Östlund [Overflowing the Squares: *The Shape of Water* by Guillermo del Toro and *The Square* by Ruben Östlund]. *Orillas: Rivista d'ispanistica*, (7), 505–508.

Wright, G. (2024, October 8). Dutch museum finds beer can artwork in bin. *BBC News*.

Chapter 8
Reclaiming the Gaze:
Photographic Narratives of "Home", Memory, and Female Identity

Eva Katsaiti
http://orcid.org/0009-0002-1840-7178
University of West Attica, Greece

ABSTRACT

Chapter examines how women photographers transform the photographic act into a political and personal language of self-narration. Drawing on Laura Mulvey's male gaze, Judith Butler's gender performativity, and Hélène Cixous's écriture féminine, it argues that photography functions as a site of resistance and belonging — a visual "home" where identity is authored rather than assigned. Through close readings of Briony Campbell, Riti Sengupta, Carolle Benitah, Anna Fox, Helen Chadwick, and Maria Papadimitriou, the chapter traces how auto-ethnographic intimacy, archive intervention, material disruption, and collective practice each enact a reclaiming of the gaze. What unites these diverse practitioners is a shared refusal of the patriarchal visual order and a commitment to constructing narratives of selfhood on their own terms. Photography, understood here as writing with light, becomes the means by which women break the mirror of Medusa — rejecting silence and spectacle in favor of an embodied, rebellious, and generative act of becoming "home".

DOI: 10.4018/979-8-3373-6680-7.ch008

PHOTOGRAPHY AS "HOME", MEMORY, AND GENDER NARRATIVES

Taking pictures is an act of "homecoming". It is because women are traversing the ruthless pressures of a gender discriminating visual civilization, that they genially turn their photography practice into both a personal language and a vital political act. This chapter studies how directing the lens towards the outside or inwards towards the self permits people to negotiate rigid societal roles, recover their identity and construct a visual-scape they can finally call "home". At the core of this analysis is a focal question: in a culture flooded with given images of gender, how do photographers especially women recover their own stories and claim a space where they can stay intact? The lines of thought that follow observe how photographic storytelling becomes an influential means for reinstating authenticity, for speaking truths that social norms have long pursued to silence, and for building a language of belonging that is largely one's own.

CONTRIBUTION AND SCHOLARLY SIGNIFICANCE OF THIS CHAPTER

Despite the considerable body of scholarship on feminist visual theory and on women's photographic practice, a noteworthy gap persists: the literature has seldom examined how the photographic act itself - as a at the same time corporal, performative, and narrative practice -creates a method of "homing", a retrieval of identity, and belonging in response to the male-controlled ordering of the gaze. Present analyses tend to either study canonical feminist theory in removal from current practice or, in opposition, to discuss individual practitioners without grounding them in a merged theoretical framework. In this chapter we will connect Mulvey's politics of the gaze, Butler's performativity, and Cixous's écriture féminine. The present chapter addresses this gap by offering an original synthesis: it reads a carefully selected cross-section of women photographers working across auto-ethnography, archival intervention, materiality, and collective art making- through a combined theoretical lens that is applied constantly and relatively, and that is further extended by Johanna Frueh's "erotics of criticism" and Maria Gasouka's counter-discourse. In doing so, it creates a new analytical category, the photograph as "home", that is not formerly articulated in the existing literature.

This chapter makes three interrelated contributions to the field. First, it advances a new structure in which the photographic image is theorized not as representation or resistance, but as a site of existential belonging- a "home" structured through the act of vision itself. Second, it brings into creative dialogue a set of practitioners who have not previously been read together— Briony Campbell, Riti Sengupta, Carolle Benitah, Anna Fox, Helen Chadwick, and Maria Papadimitriou — demonstrating that their formally and culturally diverse practices share a shared epistemological project: the reclamation of the gaze as self-authorship. Third, and crucially this analysis does not remain within a Western-centric framework; by including Papadimitriou's collaborative practice with family marginalized communities and drawing on Gasouka's Greek feminist thought, it spreads the conversation into cross-cultural and postcolonial scopes that are largely absent from the dominant anglophone literature. The chapter is therefore not only a study of individual photographic practices but a methodological intervention: it proposes that embodied, auto-ethnographic, and counter-archival modes of photography constitute a distinct and under-theorised form of knowledge production, one that challenges the normative epistemologies of both academic research and visual culture.

Photography is far from just being an impersonal instrument of documentation, in the images - work of the practitioners reviewed here it functions as: an arena of memory, self identity, and active resistance. The practitioners discussed here use the camera not merely as a recording device but as a means of returning to themselves, a way of locating authenticity within and against the social roles that culture has assigned them. Through their own photographs they engage in a form of proactive storytelling that does not simply reflect reality but actively rewrites it. In doing so they challenge sometimes subvert the cultural stereotypes that have long governed representations of gender, using sarcasm, irony, and symbolic disruption as tools for undoing normalized representations of femininity and domesticity.

If photography can be a place of constraint, it can likewise become a site of freedom and nowhere is this more convincingly proved that in the methodical act of reclaiming the gaze. Principal to this evaluation is the act of reclaiming the gaze, the calculated creative decision to turn the camera toward oneself and one's own world on one's own terms. This is both a personal and a political gesture. When photographers generate their own images with artistic intentionality, they are composing a visual language that challenges who has historically been allowed to tell stories, and whose stories have been considered of being told. This trajectory hints how this retrieval unfolds across different registers: through auto ethnographic intimacy, through the manipulation of family archives, through sarcasm directed at domestic limitation, and through joint art making with marginalised peoples. What connects these varied procedures is the shared drive to assert a space, spatial, narrative, expressive, where identity can be held intact, where the self is not an object of the gaze but it's author.

We must synthesize how these diverse photographic practices operate against the historical background of the gaze. To understand how these photographic acts of reclamation resonate across time, it is worth returning to one of Western culture's oldest myths of the female gaze — and its punishment. Ovid (1916) describes

Medusa as a beautiful woman. Athena, Goddess of wisdom punishes Medusa, (the rape victim), for being violated by God of the sea Poseidon in one of the Goddess' temples. Medusa is the matriarchal victim that needs to be exemplarily raped by Poseidon and then decapitated by Perseus, for patriarchy to show off its power on her body. The clear and loud message for her and the strong lineage of womanhood she represents is that her body does not belong to her. Medusa's monstrosity-punishment alluding to matriarchy and the irrational is afflicted by another masculinized female, Athena. Moreover, in one of the versions of the myth Medusa dies when she looks at herself in the mirror. It is after the rape that the woman is turned into a monster with snakes for hair and the ability to turn everyone into stone. She has no power over her vision and especially the vision of herself that turns blind.

METHODOLOGY AND ANALYTICAL FRAMEWORK

This chapter assumes a qualitative interpretive methodology grounded in feminist art historical analysis and visual cultural studies. The analytical approach is not ever purely iconographic nor directly biographical; rather, it is theoretically driven, examining each photographic practice through a layered critical lens that is compiled exclusively for the purposes of this study. The primary theoretical tools are four: Mulvey's concept of the male gaze concept (1975), which provides the structuring condition against which all the practitioners here operate; Butler's theory of gender performativity and reiteration (1990, 1993), which furnishes a vocabulary for understanding how photographic acts can simultaneously duplicate and rapture normative identity; Hélène Cixous's notion of écriture féminine (1975), which reframes photography as a bodily, affective form of writing that exceeds patriarchal discourse; and crucially Johanna Frueh's "erotics of criticism", which authorises an embodied, partial, and passionate mode of scholarly engagement that mirrors the auto-ethnographic stance of several practitioners examined here . The four frameworks are not applied sequentially or in isolation: they are read in dialogue with one another and with Maria Gasouka's counter-discursive feminist thought which extends the analysis beyond its anglophone coordinates and anchors it in a cross-cultural critical tradition.

The selection of case studies was guided by three criteria. First, formal and methodological diversity: the six practitioners chosen represent, obviously different photographic modes (auto-ethnography, archival intervention, materiality and the book object, body based installation and participatory community practice), ensuring that the analytical framework is tried across a wide range of artistic strategies rather than long-established by a single type of practice. Second, thematic coherence: despite their formal differences, the six practitioners share the central gesture identified in this chapter as essential- the reclamation of the gaze as a means of creating a narrative "home"- which makes comparative analysis both meaningful and productive. Third, representational range: the selection deliberately includes practitioners working across different national and cultural contexts (British, Indian, French -Moroccan, Greek-Roma), different historical moments from the mid-1980s to the present, in different degrees of institutional recognition, from established canonical figures such as Chadwick to contemporary practitioners whose work has not yet received sustained scholarly attention. The analytical process moves from close visual reading of specific works to theoretical interpretation, and then outward to the broader questions of gender, memory, belonging, and knowledge production that frame the chapter as a whole. In line with Frueh's "erotics of criticism", this methodology does not claim impartial distance; it recognizes that the researcher's own situated perspective -as a woman, a scholar and a practitioner of visual culture-is itself part of the analytical apparatus, and that this partiality is source of epistemological strength rather than a limitation to be managed away.

FEMINISM VISUAL ART FRAMEWORK

To grasp how these photographic narratives function as both likeness and oppositional resistance, it is central to place this analysis in recognized feminist visual theory. This part defines the combination of viewpoints of Mulvey, Butler Cixous, Frueh and Gasouka which will operate as the lens system for exploring the examples presented later on.

Laura Mulvey's concept of the male gaze developed in "Visual pleasures and narrative cinema" (1975) describes how classical film uses a solely male spectator position to describe how women are excluded from their autonomous gaze, looking back at themselves. Women are depicted by the male gaze as a spectacle with the filter of the male desire, mediating their bodies, and their identities. In that sense women, when women look at themselves, they see themselves through the patriarchal filter. They are prevented from seeing themselves with, and in, their own eyes. The images of the female body reproduced widely propagate male desire, in that they are made for the male gaze. Women have no way to see themselves in their own eye as they have been dominated by the male perspective. Women are either forced to internalise the male gaze or not allowed to have a vision of themselves at all, much like Medusa who was not able to see her own image. When it comes to women looking at the mirror, does not signify self-knowledge but results in death as with Medusa. The other negative portrayal of women who dare to look at themselves is that they are vain and or narcissistic. Think of the iconic phrase "Mirror, mirror on the wall, who's the fairest of them all?" Yet there are women photographers, some of whom we will see later who bravely turn the mirror of the camera towards themselves and rewrite who they see —themselves — in new and exciting ways.

Complimenting Mulvey's analysis of the gaze, Butler's theory of reiteration provides a context for interpreting how identity is structured through perpetual performance. Butler describes that gender identity, is not something we are, but rather something we do over and over again. Thus, reiteration indeed proposes that we copy performances of norms over time. Butler expresses that when we reflect on being male or female gender as natural, we perform masculinity or femininity. She goes on to say that gender is a performed identity. The recurring acting establishes shared norms, and those repetitions make those norms and matches natural and categorical. The important component to Butler's system is a paradoxical detail that replication matters since it has two disparate effects: it stabilises identity and equally unlocks the opportunity for transformation because things can be repeated otherwise in slight discrepancies.

Finally, Cixous proposes the perception of 'écriture féminine' (feminine writing) as a process of disturbance. Cixous persuades towards conquering and altering through rewriting those norms. In "The Laugh of Medusa" (1976), she requests a method of writing that breaks stable shapes of language. Whilst Butler works on the norm arrangement by showing how they are generated, Cixous mentors women to write themselves differently, to source their bodies, and desires, to originate a new, fluid language that challenges linear, patriarchal reasoning.

To fully combine these academic readings into sound method, I drew up on Johanna Frueh's notion of the "erotics of criticism". Frueh meets the old disconnected art historical style, which often asks for a fruitless, detached space between the researcher and the study. Instead, she encourages a practice deep-rooted in partiality passion and the body. By implementing an "erotics of criticism", I am confirming the auto-ethnographic methods employed by the practitioners in this study. This approach indicates that the scholars or the artist's own venture—their joy, anger, grief and tenderness—is not an indicator of academic weakness or narcissism but a demanding, authentic pathway of knowing. When artists like Briony Campbell or Sengupta (we will see them later) place their own bodies and domestic lives within the frame, they are engaging in this kind of "erotic" research: a visceral, embodied form of knowledge that resists the clinical, patriarchal gaze.

As Maria Gasouka proposes, this original feminine language-writing centres in the body, the senses, and the rhythm of lived experience, refusing the binary reasoning that historically reduced in importance women and pushed them to the margins. By controlling how the past is archived and how the present is performed, these artists are not merely looking back; they are constructing a future. They have destroyed the "Mirror of Medusa", which previously denoted entrapment or death and now swap it with a camera, which develops into a tool for self-knowledge. In this opening of overflow and multiplicity, the digitised world as a site of non-stop scrutiny, is converted into a "home", a place of belonging, intervention, and a continuous, rebellious becoming.

NARRATIVE INTERVENTIONS IN PERFORMATIVE ART

From these theoretical grounds, we investigate how women practitioners employ photography to assemble identity, people having a place, and dispute regulating authority formations. The following case studies show how these photographers, in their art practice, interfere in and review old, gendered meanings. Here we examine how photography is used by practitioners to build identity—belonging and being excluded from belonging as well as to construct or to deconstruct the meaning—making process. Photographic practice is put to the test to negotiate and transform meanings that are normative and strictly repeat patriarchal power. Kelly asserts: "It is very difficult to articulate our oppression as women through a medium that is misused daily to exploit us." (Kelly, 2008). Women photographers meet women viewers on the surface of the photograph, thus forming an enduring togetherness. The following practitioners chosen are creating subversions that transform gender preconceptions and leave nothing unchanged.

AUTOETHNOGRAPHY: THE INTIMACY OF GRIEF AS RESISTANCE

Briony Campbell, "The Dad Project" 2011: The self-portrait as an act of integrity

Campbell photographed her father dying from cancer at hospital. She shot her father's pictures and made some self-portraits and was torn between being the photographer and the daughter. Campbell identified her dual positioning as both an artist-researcher and a bereft person who has been recuperating from losses, she quotes: "I'd prove (to myself or my parents? I'm not sure which was the necessity) that I was a daughter before a photographer" (Campbell 2011a).

Figure 1. Briony Campbell, "The Dad Project"

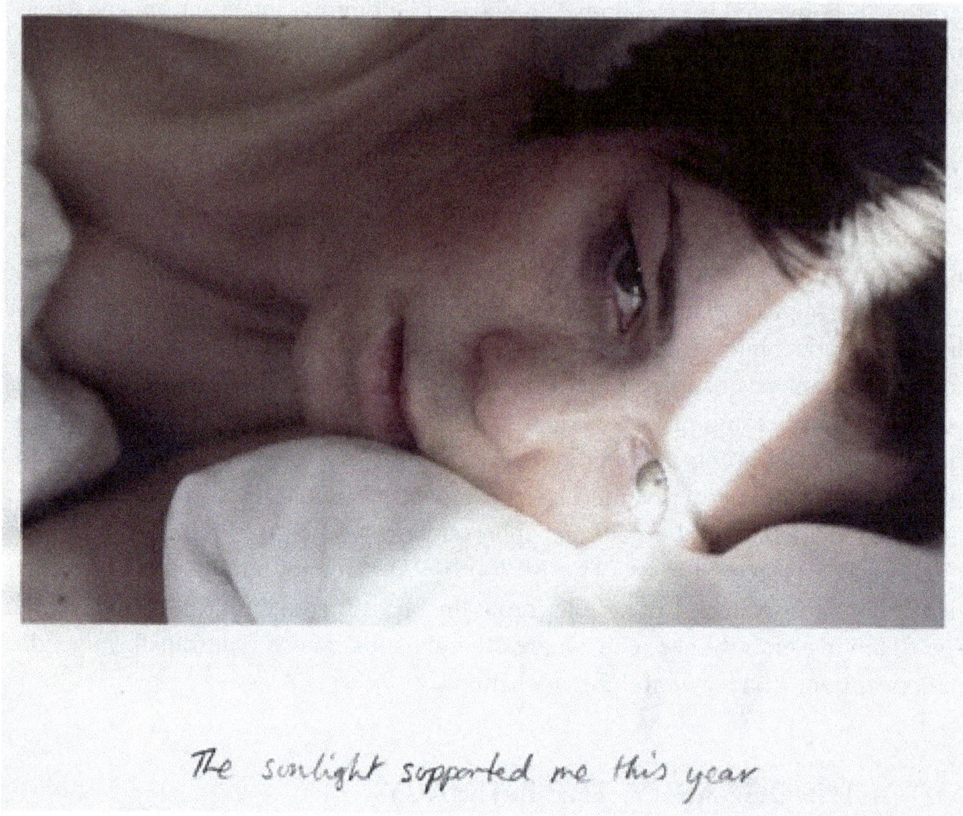

(Campbell, 2011b)

To admit the duality, it is to open to the potential of managing it. It is a project with an auto-ethnographic approach. She used herself, her Dad and their relationship as the subject and object of her photographic observation. Auto-ethnography is defined as a "blend of ethnography and autobiographical writing that incorporates elements of one's own life experience when writing about others" (Scott-Hoy, 2002), an autobiographical narrative that places the self within a social context (Reed- Danahay, 1997) Nevertheless auto-ethnography is "both a method and a text" (Etherington, 2004).

Creative languages such as photography are often assimilated into auto-ethnographic research. The most interesting point is when she felt split between the two roles of the photographer and the daughter, she comments:" Being a good daughter to my dying dad was tricky. I struggled to find the balance between dedication to his needs and distraction from my grief".

Figure 2. Briony Campbell, "The Dad Project"

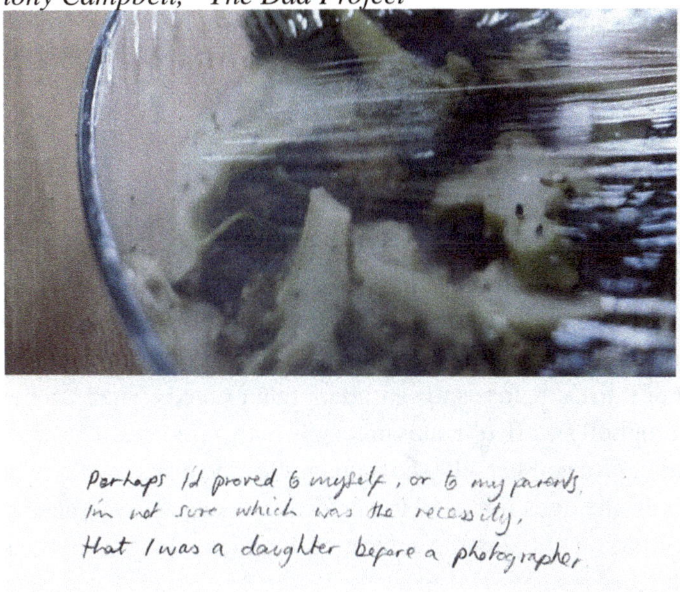

(Campbell, 2011b)

Let us consider how women or femininities that work with personal experiences are discounted as narcissistic and seen as incompetent. The element of self-disclosure incorporated in auto-ethnography (as defined above) is precisely the reason such a research method has been characterized as "self-indulgent solipsistic and narcissistic" Mykhalovskiy (1996). Indeed, there are many risks involved in this type of research, such as when one is talking about a personal experience of vulnerability. Nevertheless, Walkerdine explains that self-disclosure in auto-ethnography is meant to be a way of understanding subjectivity, and that is when "the confessional becomes reactionary" (Walkerdine, 1997: 58).

Like Campbell, Panourgia is an anthropologist (1995) who discusses social practices and family changes having to do with her grandfathers' death in the context of Modern Athens. She wrote as both a self (a part of her family, writing about her feelings) and another (an ethnographer, contextualizing the occurrences and rituals). In this "native" anthropology project, Panourgia conducted ethnographic research on her own family and faced concerns about the nature of belonging or having an insider's perspective.

In Campbell's work, her father and her relationship with him became the "home", her belonging in the intimacy of her picture taking which influences her performance of identity. Her father's imminent death was what disrupted that intimacy and created the strong potential of her exclusion from her Dad in herself. Bravely, she was working to bring forth her inner struggles to the conservative public by recording her internal emotional experience. This experience was shared for the viewer to see. In a simple and performative manner, she asked to be seen and witnessed throughout the entire process, even at the most vulnerable moments. Campbell created an alternative album that equally records her dad's passing and her own grief. In the process she uncovered some of the invisible social structures of seeing in the context of her background.

Campbell managed to bring forth a piece of work in which she eventually no matter the emotional intensity of the situation, she sees herself in grief while connecting to her father. As Brown and Phu (2014) argue in *Feeling Photography*, the photographic image is never merely a visual object but an affective one — it carries the tactile weight of intimacy, loss and sentiment that exceeds what can be consciously articulated. Campbell's work operates precisely in this register. Through that process of photographing him and herself, she manages to find a space of structure opposed to him. She finds she does not need to perform roles again. She need only observe herself in the situation of being the creator of the image. In that space she could feel free to integrate her sadness and grief for losing her father. Even before she loses him, the photographs are full of the integrity of a person who is photographing their deep affection and love for one who is departing. That she allows herself to take pictures of herself in order to console herself while her father is dying is an act of resistance and shows deep integrity in her belief in photography, in herself, in love and in her father.

Riti Sengupta "Things I Can't Say Out Loud" 2020: Covert Gender Inequality

Riti Sengupta's work provides a convincing search of the pressure between independence and family duty since it is moving from the context of loss of self to the context of domestic tension. Sengupta went back to live with her parents when she was left without a job during the pandemic, only to feel displaced and unseen in her own family. In doing so, she realized she had lost her autonomy. In turn, she started this work of photographing herself in the tension between the need for a self in her parents' space. She recalls: "There was a lot of friction because my parents didn't quite get how I wanted to live my life." (Sengupta, as cited in Warner, 2026) In that process she saw the double standards applied to women who had to manage both work and the household. She realized how this cultural demand caused her mother to be overloaded with responsibilities. Sengupta finally appreciated and understood her mother's position and the example of how she was living. Even though both her parents were working, it was her mother who was exhausted because of the cultural expectations. Sengupta's mother would work and then after she returned home, she would wash clothes, clean, cook and keep working nonstop to take care of the household right up until she finally went to bed.

Through her photography, Sengupta claimed her vision and her visibility as a language of writing herself as a home despite the surroundings. The dual threshold position of being the photographer and daughter all the way through her observation gave her images an element of unease, a kind of hypnotic dreamy absence. Sengupta observed the gender inequalities that worked in covert ways. She explains: "I was frustrated, and I felt a lot of anger inside… There weren't instances of violence, but it was present in subtle ways, like, 'Why does the food not have enough salt today?' This became such a huge part of my daily life that I needed to express it in some way," she says. "That's when I thought, 'why not try making photographs of how I'm feeling?' (Sengupta, as cited in Warner, 2026) Her photographic work is poetic; it has an element of hypnotic dreamy absence. She seems to be both in the family and at the same time outside of it. She is the insider and the detached observer of the family and what is fascinating is that she can keep that threshold position whilst being completely submerged within the family. Throughout her observation, Sengupta consistently maintains this theme of duality—of being both the photographer and the daughter. A powerful image which depicts a tomato split in half between the palms of mother and father symbolizing marriage. This is one of family stories that is also a story of covert oppression.

Sengupta becomes close to her mother and supports her to say no to the father. Both women reach a level of autonomy through their bonding. Their relationship transforms. The daughter's photography allows for the photographer and her mother to be seen in a fair way, in a way that they can truly regard each other without performing old, prescribed roles they both felt they had to keep playing. Her series is full of poetry and the simplicity of the poses; the dress and the symbols are disarming. For example, the implications of motherhood in the picture with the eggs where the mother has many eggs in the basket and the daughter only one right at the level of where the ovaries would be, is a subtle allusion to the photographer's concerns about motherhood and its burdens.

The cultural expectation for the daughter to follow her mother and become a mother herself, to repeat her mother's role without question is symbolized by the bird on the head of the mother. This signifies the mother's (soon to be followed by the daughter's) lack of freedom, a commentary on the gender role performance of motherhood. Caring for their children, women become so preoccupied and isolated due to socially imposed gender roles which dictate that this is a mother's sole purpose – to care for her offspring. Society is intolerant of a mother's need to take time for herself, the mother experiences a sense of time stagnancy. Her personal needs must never override the tasks inherent in motherhood. Consequently, mothers lose themselves and their time seems to disappear. So, Sengupta in her photography, observes her mother who has no time for herself. She fantasizes about herself as a mother. Through her art, in the role of photographer, she brings her mother the gift of time by so doing, creates a new space for both. It is a suggestion to her mother to claim time from the father, head of the family. In the very act of creating these photographs, Sengupta, the daughter finds her own purpose and claims her own creative role. Paying attention to the lessons of her own art, she arrives at a way to see motherhood as an experience of self-knowledge and a re-negotiation of the self. Not only she and her mother, but those who view her photographs can be freed from the violence of relegating the identity of "mother" to a confinement of the self, done by controlling the body, sexuality, values and ideas of what a "good mother" does and must not do. Her creative narrative practice brings forth a fertile space for the self, as she wishes to define it.

Figure 3. Riti Sengupta, "Things I Can't Say Out Loud" 2020

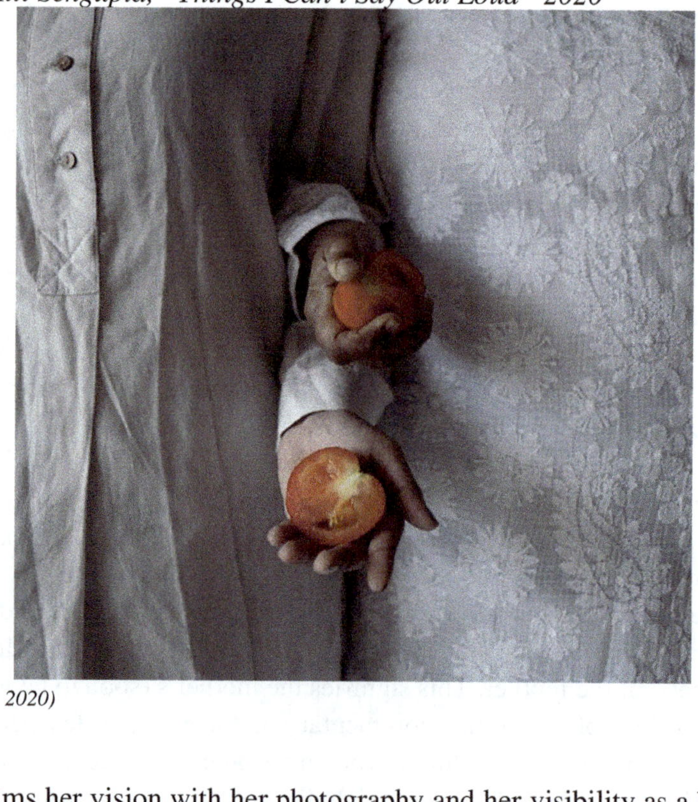

(Sengupta, 2020)

She claims her vision with her photography and her visibility as a language of writing herself as a "home", despite the eggs in the basket and the bird on her mother's head. Strangely, it is a playful image. It is also a meditation on the experience of motherhood. "Having watched my mother so closely, I'm scared of motherhood now. I feel like having a child won't let me have my autonomy; it's going to take something away". (Sengupta, as cited in Warner, 2026)

Motherhood as an institution is a mechanism of control over women's body sexuality and labor that controls women through motherhood. The most violent part of that is that women identities are reduced to a reproductive role defined by self-sacrifice and moral purity. By photographing herself and her mother within these structures, Sengupta transforms constraint into a negotiation space — reclaiming for both women the time and selfhood that domesticity had erased. This reading resonates with Susan Bright's observation, in her curatorial study of photography and motherhood, that personal and highly intimate photographic practice can challenge stereotypical representations of the maternal body and reframe domesticity as a site of power negotiation rather than passive confinement (Bright, 2013).

There is intolerance around mothers that need to take time for themselves or need to keep things that make them feel themselves if that overrides the task of being a mother. And it always does.

Mother and daughter, eggs, ovaries, the power of the feminine, concepts of fertility and reproduction resonate as well as creativity as a subversion mechanism of all of the above, they sit side by side, one facing forward, the other looking back, together mending a common identity. They belong to themselves. They belong to each other. They both belong. Remarkably, the artist' s mother found the courage to rebel. She spoke her truth to her husband. Ultimately, Sengupta's photographs helped both women rewrite their stories.

Figure 4. Riti Sengupta, "Things I Can't Say Out Loud" 2020

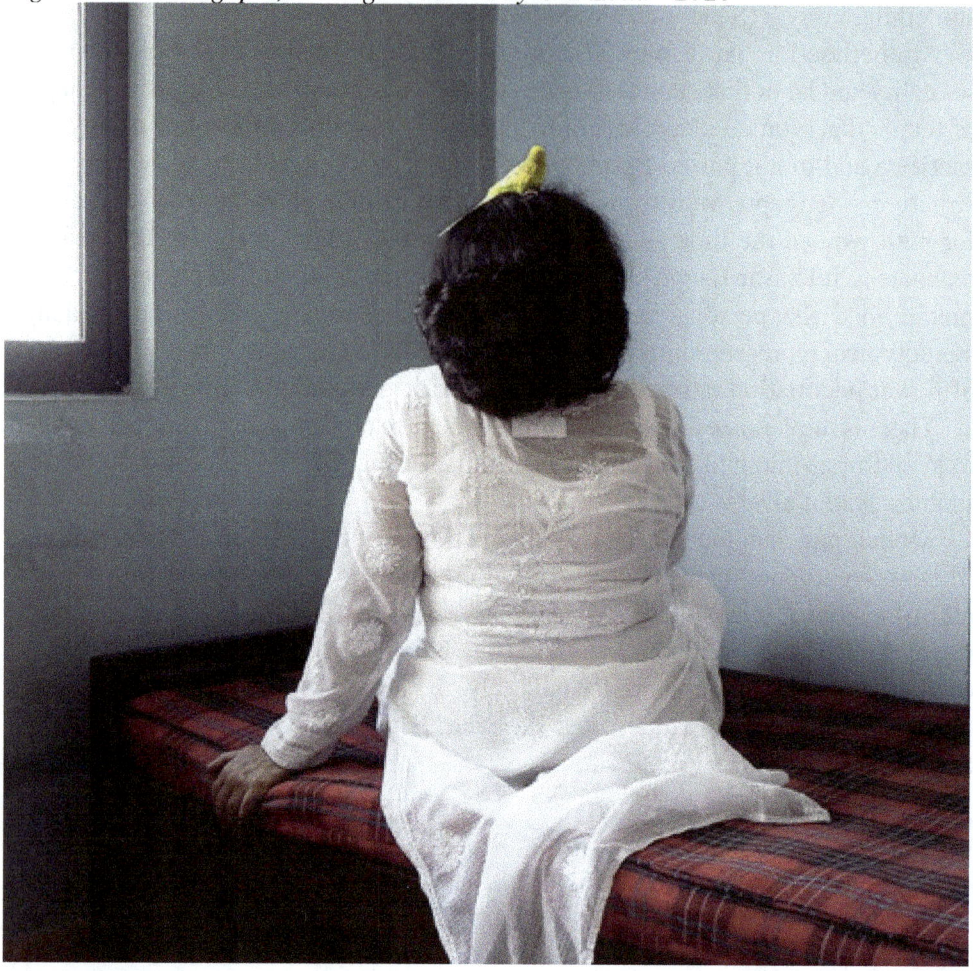

(Sengupta, 2020)

Figure 5. Riti Sengupta, "Things I Can't Say Out Loud" 2020

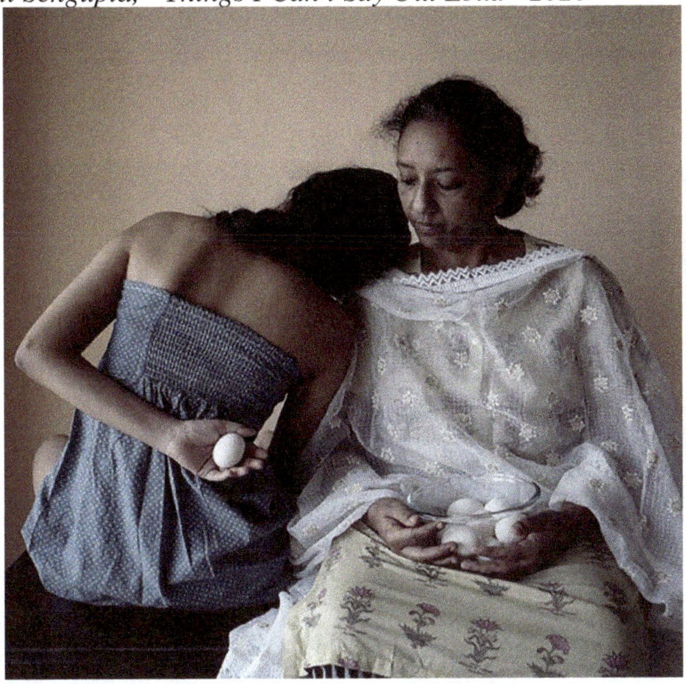

(Sengupta, 2020)

REWRITING MEMORY: THE FAMILY ARCHIVE, TRAUMA, AND MATERIALITY

Carolle Benitah, "Photos-Souvenirs" 2011: Destructive Restorative Gestures

While Sengupta explores the surviving, present domestic space, Carole Benitah focuses on the archive of the past, materially prevailing in the family album to review inherited trauma.

Benitah describes how she was overwhelmed by an emotion for which she could not trace the origin. She then worked with photographs from her family album. She declares: 'those moments, fixed on paper, represented me, spoke about me and my family, told things about my identity, my place in the world, my family history and its secrets.' Benitah talks about fears that have constructed her, and that they have stayed very well hidden in the family album along with many other things that contributed to who she was.

Photographs are inextricably bound to the way we remember because we cannot remember without objects. In and through the family album we explore memories of childhood to understand who we are and define our identities.

Figure 6. Carolle Benitah, "Photos-Souvenirs" 2011

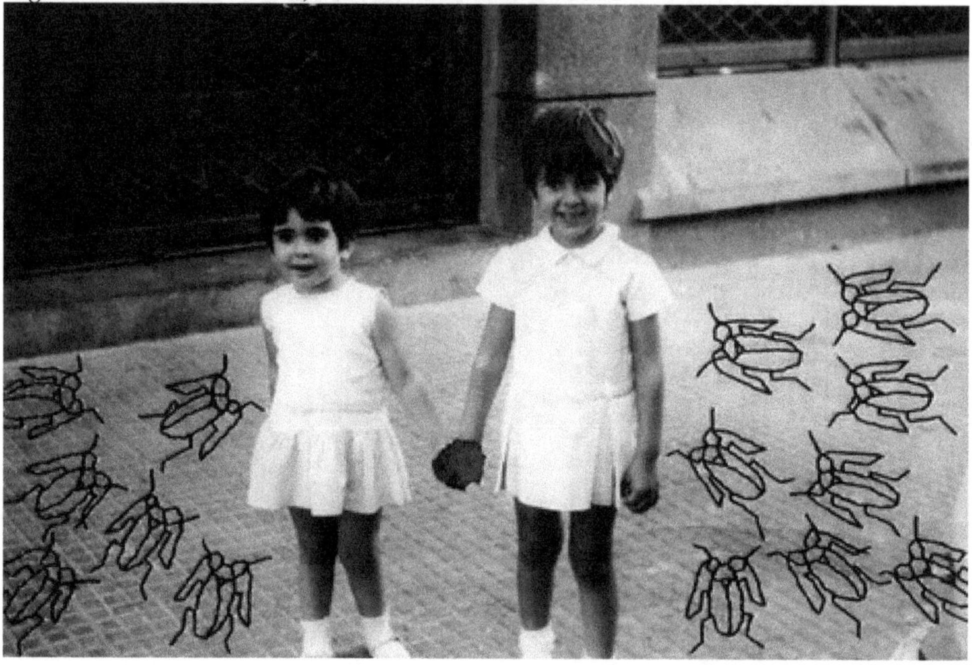

(Benitah, 2011)

Butler's (1990, 1993) concept of 'reiteration' is directly at work in Benitah's practice. As established in the theoretical framework above, gender identity is not something we are but something we do: a performed identity stabilized through the ceaseless repetition of social norms, yet always open to being done differently in small variations. It is precisely this opening — where repetition becomes rupture — that Benitah's embroidery exploits.

Thus, Benitah's exploration of the family album rephotographing it and destroying the faces by putting embroidery on them is a gesture that shows her intention to recontextualize, to reiterate, to even rewrite her identity and return to herself as a "home". By creating a new album, the photographer creates a parallel memory. Embroidering has always been associated with being virtuous. Considered a primarily feminine activity, women who embroidered did so waiting patiently or anxiously for the man of the house to return.

Girls raised in a "good family" used to learn how to sew and embroider. These were essential activities for "perfect women". Benitah's work brings the two activities, interpretation and needlework to dispute: embroidery is the sign of a good education: "yet the words that I speak don't show me to be what I was supposed to be: a well-behaved girl, a wise spouse and a loving mother".

Figure 7. Carolle Benitah, "Photos-Souvenirs" 2011

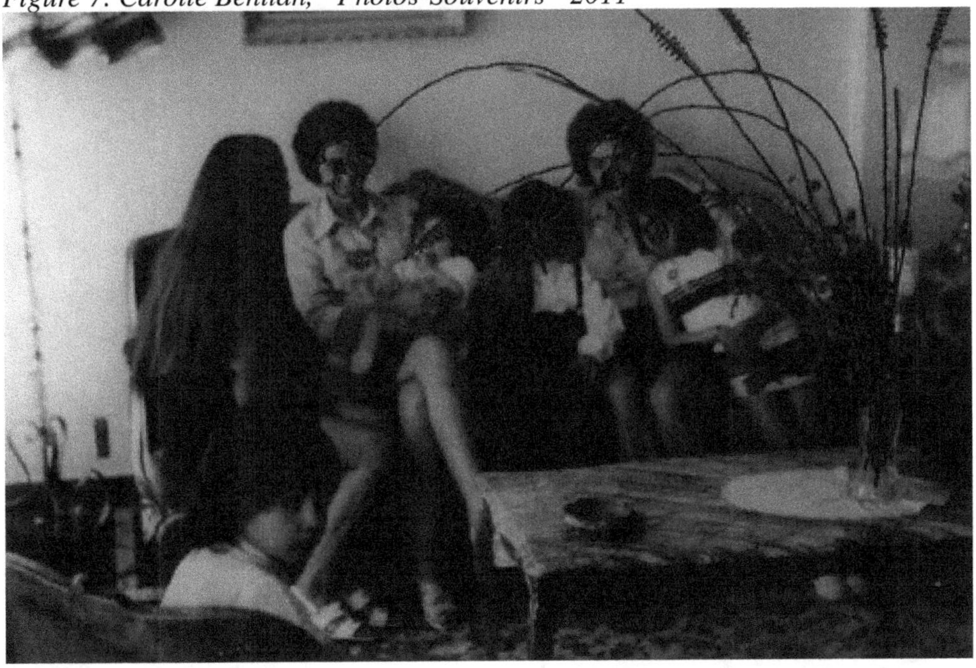

(Benitah, 2011)

Benitah's work resonates with Cixous', since her approach uses the conventional ideas of feminine writing such as embroidery as a gesture of irony to undermine the conventions of family photographs. "There is nothing subversive about this activity (embroidery), but I pervert it with my purpose. I use its decorative function to re-interpret my own history and to expose its failings". By defacing the people in the photos, she demonstrates how the performative quality of the fragmented evokes something wonderfully beautiful and at the same time disturbingly violent in the use of the loose red thread that signifies some kind of danger. The new changed works of art only function as aesthetic objects. The family album as a reference to family history and the family history as a story of trauma is presented to the public. Talking about trauma gives Benitah a kind of belonging back to her authentic self and family. The healing power of restoration happens by being witnessed. The artist says: "with each stitch I make a hole with a needle. Each hole is a putting to death of my demons. It's like an exorcism. I make holes in paper until I am not hurting any more"

Figure 8. Carolle Benitah, "Photos-Souvenirs" 2011

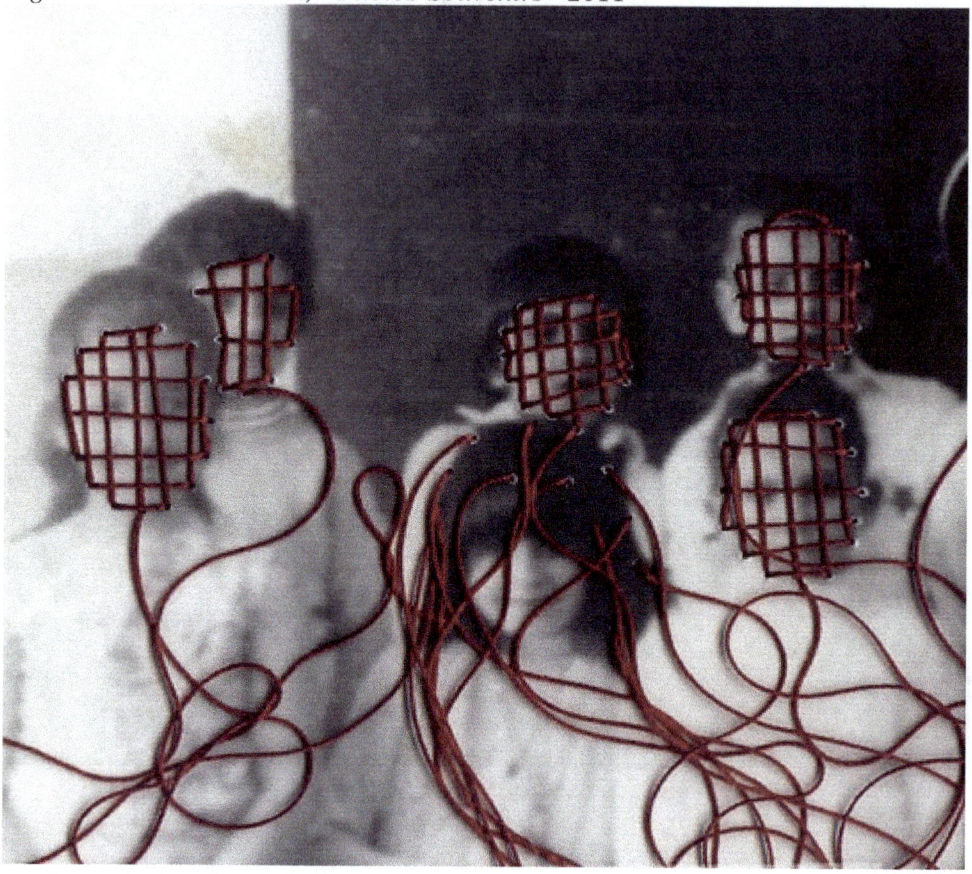

(Benitah, 2011)

Photography plays a significant role in mediating specific forms of remembering. The family album as a depiction of "home" negotiates issues of spatiality, power and belonging and in Benitah's work because of her destructive gesture of embroidering it, the manipulated album reveals inner life experiences of attachment and loss in a struggle from submission to power. The family album as an object for memory is not just a storage device but was produced in most families (close and extended) to be shown potentially to the wider circle of friends, of acquaintances. Most importantly, the album 's purpose was to influence and be communicated to the coming generations, organizing a historical context for the family, its whereabouts, and the personality of its members. Most important of all it gave a sense of self to the individual, referring to it for identifying their place. Personal memory organizes how one perceives oneself, how one understands their past and themselves - how they stand in the world.

Anna Fox, from the series 'My Mother's Cupboards & My Father's Words' 2000: The Somatic Reading Experience

In contrast to Benitah's physical, decorated retrieval, Anna Fox uses the domestic object to feature the acute division between maternal orderliness and paternal explosiveness.

'My Mother's Cupboards & My Father's Words' is a miniature book. The viewer has to get close to be able to read the text and to register the details in the photographs. It was created in 2000, for the Shoreditch Biennale, at a time when Anna Fox was inspired to make work "close to home", challenging the notion of the documentary photographer as outsider.

The book pairs words by her father – gruesome outbursts by a man who had a rapidly debilitating disease. These tirades towards the women in the house are matched with claustrophobic images of her mother's neatly organized cupboards. The result is one of Fox's most powerful and intimate bodies of work.

While at the peak of her documentary series, Anna Fox decides to take a grant to go back home and work on a piece in the family's house. She juxtaposes her father's words, which are very violent and her mother's drawers that look compulsively orderly. What comes out is this vulgar patriarchal logos in the words of the father. This book is exceedingly small and intimate. While it's being read one must bring the pictures very close to one's face. The entire book is roughly the size of a palm. It is designed to be looked at very privately and very closely, a most excruciating experience. These very big words are suffocating. Anna Fox, in this big space, is making way for herself to get out together with the mother. An exceptionally good tracker, she guides us first through the big entrapping space of patriarchy and then out. Resistance.

Figure 9. Untitled from the series My Mother's Cupboards and My Father's Words

You toad.
Pity
I got rid of the well;
you could have
gone down there
and
been cemented over

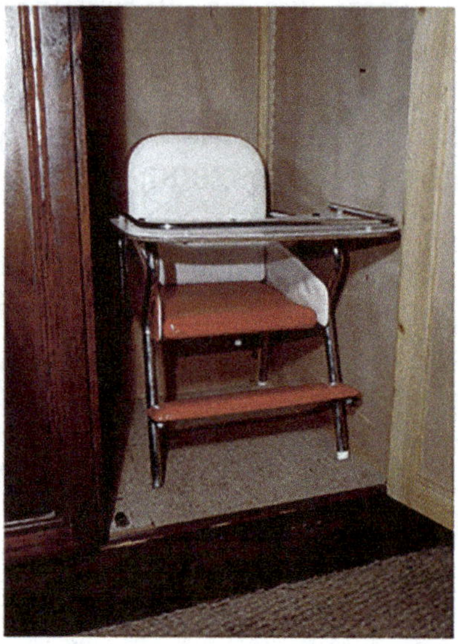

Figure 10. Untitled from the series My Mother's Cupboards and My Father's Words

I'll cut
your bum off
and serve it
in slices,
like raw ham

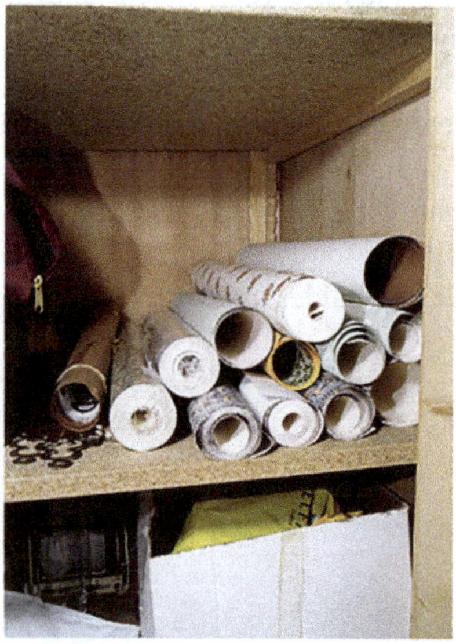

Cixous talks about performativity and writing as transformation, whereas Butler's "reiteration" focuses on how identities are produced through repeated norms. Cixous pushes towards breaking, overcoming and rewriting those norms. The two theories meet at the specific view that repetition can cause rupture, the rapture of socially regulated norms used to define identity. For Butler, identity exists because norms are repeated socially and are regulated. In her view we reiterate but only what already exists as language. Cixous takes the case further since she believes that there is writing beyond the norm. In 'The Laugh of the Medusa' (1975) she calls for a form of writing that escapes fixed structures of language. She defines these as patriarchal, directly emerging from the male desire of the body. Cixous resists linear rational control discourse; in other words, she is trying to overflow the system of repetition itself. Butler shows that norms depend on repetition and Cixous confirms that repetition can be disrupted through excess fluidity and embodied expression. Butler works inside the system of norms, whereas Cixous pushes at the edges of the system and sees change happening through overflow, multiplicity and things that cannot be said. So Cixous' writing can be regarded as a radical form of reiteration that refuses to stabilize. Identity is formed through repetition, and every repetition has the possibility of rupture and a poetic re-inscription, meaning reiteration can also become an act of writing otherwise. Fox is rewriting the home of the father logos by making the mother image.

The tactile physicality characteristic of both Benitah and Fox is crucial in understanding how materiality in photography can become resistance. It feels like there is an actual body of the photograph that we watch being pierced in Benitah and a suffocating space we enter in the case of Fox. Benitah puts holes in the photos treating them as objects that have a body. In doing so Benitah reclaims the body that is stolen from women as explained by the concept of Mulvey's internalized male gaze.

Benitah is using the album that has traditionally been used by women in order to unite generations as a connective thread enforcing identity of people that have left the family home to immigration or emigration. The album has been employed to unite the public image of the family with a private life while carrying the values of this public world conveyed in silence in the images which evoke emotions. The segregation of the two spaces the public and the private has been dealt by feminist theory within the desire of reframing and re-historizing the family. The album became the main performative narrative medium of telling stories of motherhood and domestic space, of children, of community and of belonging. Since women have been often marginalized in most public narratives, compiling their family albums offers a way they could be included and control some of the stories about their lives. Benitah's gesture of embroidery is one that uncovers the absences, the involuntary fragmentation, the exclusion from the self as a home for authenticity and desire, the lack of belonging of women from the narratives that concern and define them.

This gender injustice trauma is pointed here by the piercing trauma that is trans-generational and that is transferred to us through the photos that ancestors have left behind in the album. That is the post memory trauma (Hirsch, 2002) that Benitah embroiders upon. Silent trauma becomes visible on the red threading, visible in the dialogue between the private story of the family performance and its public display in Benitah's wounded album.

On the other hand, Fox creates something to be held intimately, a miniature book, and that way she creates a claustrophobic space of viewing. There is more in her entrapping space than what is immediately apparent to the eye. She creates a stage of performing the feminine in the mother cupboards and the masculine in the father's words. Once the viewer reads the text, a dramatic shift happens to the quality of that space even though that space looked innocent or domesticated or mundane or even boring, it now becomes a space of abuse, a space of entrapment, a space of suppression; a space of oppression. In those parameters then, the photograph is not just a two-dimensional image, but it is an object that describes space that can destroy, distort and ultimately can reclaim qualities of the space described, physically, mentally and psychologically. The photograph in this case has a somatic effect as it becomes a body, a space.

PERFORMATIVITY AND VISION

Helen Chadwick, "The Oval Court" 1986: The Joy Of Looking At Oneself In The Multiplied Body.

Helen Chadwick's work offers a connection between the domestic inferiority of Fox and the performative, body-centric identity politics of Cixoussian thought. Helen Chadwick creates a large garden in the oval court using her body in multiplicity in consecutive photocopies of her body, as well as animals and fruits. She creates a large space on paper, an environment that signifies nature in which her body- desire- is spread through the photocopier in deep blue color. The whole image in its totality looks like a lagoon that is made from small fragments of pictures. The fragments comprise the whole. This is a sequence of a silence in water, not unlike a silence in the depths of a lake, that becomes auditory. Even though Chadwick later suffered and died from cancer, she was determinated to look at herself through the mirror and cross to the other side. It is not a work for the faint-hearted to see and interpret Chadwick, naked in the midst of plants, fruits and animals. Like a child and a mistress as well, at the edges of it she cries: "Art, like crying, is an act of self-repair to shed the tears that free us, make us strong." (Chadwick, n.d., as cited in Warner, 2022) The artist's grief for and with herself and that is also an act of resistance.

Cixous's notion of a discourse she calls 'feminine writing', in which she argues for a positive ebullient representation of woman. She develops this idea in the essay 'The Laugh of the Medusa' (1975). She encourages women to write and thus reclaim their desire their bodies their pleasure. She sees writing as a counterattacking assertion of presence from the male-controlled politics of omissions of women's bodies. She urges: "Write yourself. Your body is yours." (Cixous, 1975: 323). Photography derives from the Greek word photographia which means the writing of light. I assert that photography has been this kind of writing for me and many other photographers, particularly the ones that I mention in this chapter, the writing with which we could reciprocally write (make a mark - photograph) with our body (vision) onto the world (viewers) and receive back the world (images) through our body (eyes). Cixous' description of this feminine emancipatory writing incorporates the idea of the pleasure of jouissance (bliss) which combines connotations of sexual orgasm and polysemic speech. "Jouissance" unsettles the reader's historical cultural and psychological assumptions and brings a crisis to her relationship with language. The text of feminine writing eradicates repressions weaving male dominated discourse and directs society to a new type of sexuality. The point is to imagine the possible "language", (code of communication) rather than describe those which already exist.

In navigating the patriarchal structures of visual culture, Maria Gasouka's insights into "female writing" present a vital connection between academic theory and societal experience. Gasouka argues that écriture féminine acts as a vital counter discourse, a structural intervention that disrupts what she terms as a male-centered sphere of literature and in addition, visual communication. For Gasouka the act of reclaiming narrative is not just a poetic gesture; it is a pedagogical and social need. It is a method to contest the prevalent covert violence of normative gender narratives that label women's experiences as subordinate. By framing the artistic interventions of photographers like Maria Papadimitriou, Riti Sengupta, through Gasouka's lens, we are enabled to see these photographic series as deeds of social recuperation. They are pedagogical spaces that teach the viewer and the participants themselves how to exist outside the regulated, male-centred boundaries of the archive and the home.

Figure 11. Helen Chadwick, "The Oval Court" 1986

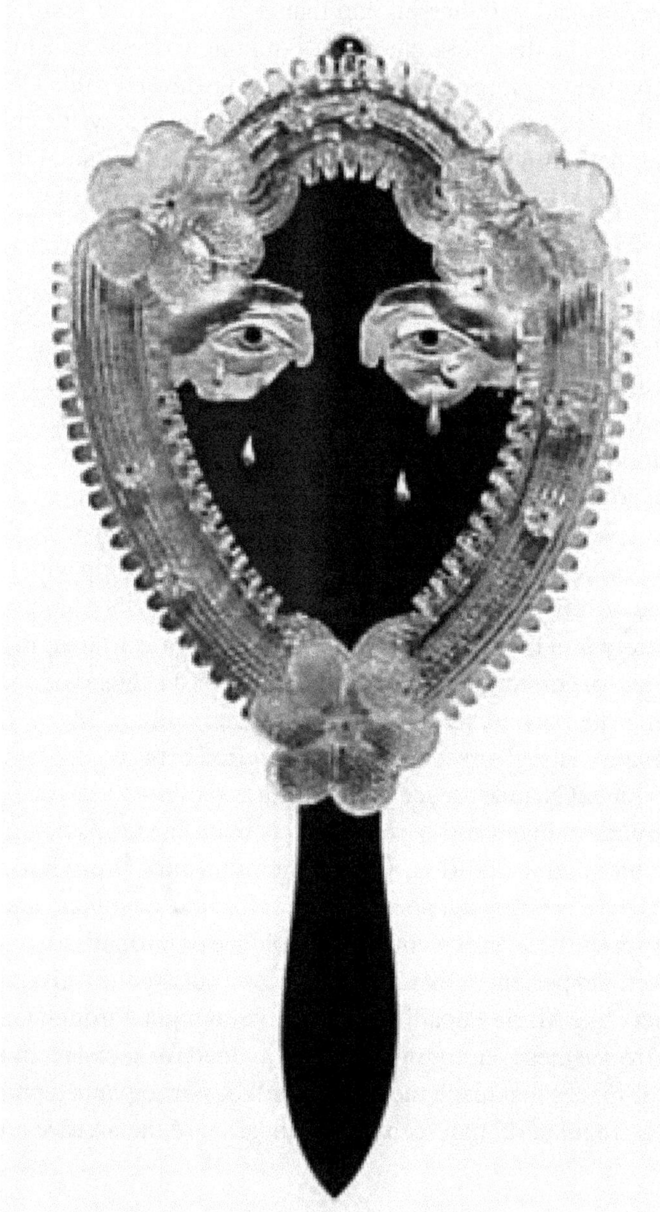

(Chadwick, 1986)

Figure 12. Helen Chadwick, "The Oval Court" 1986

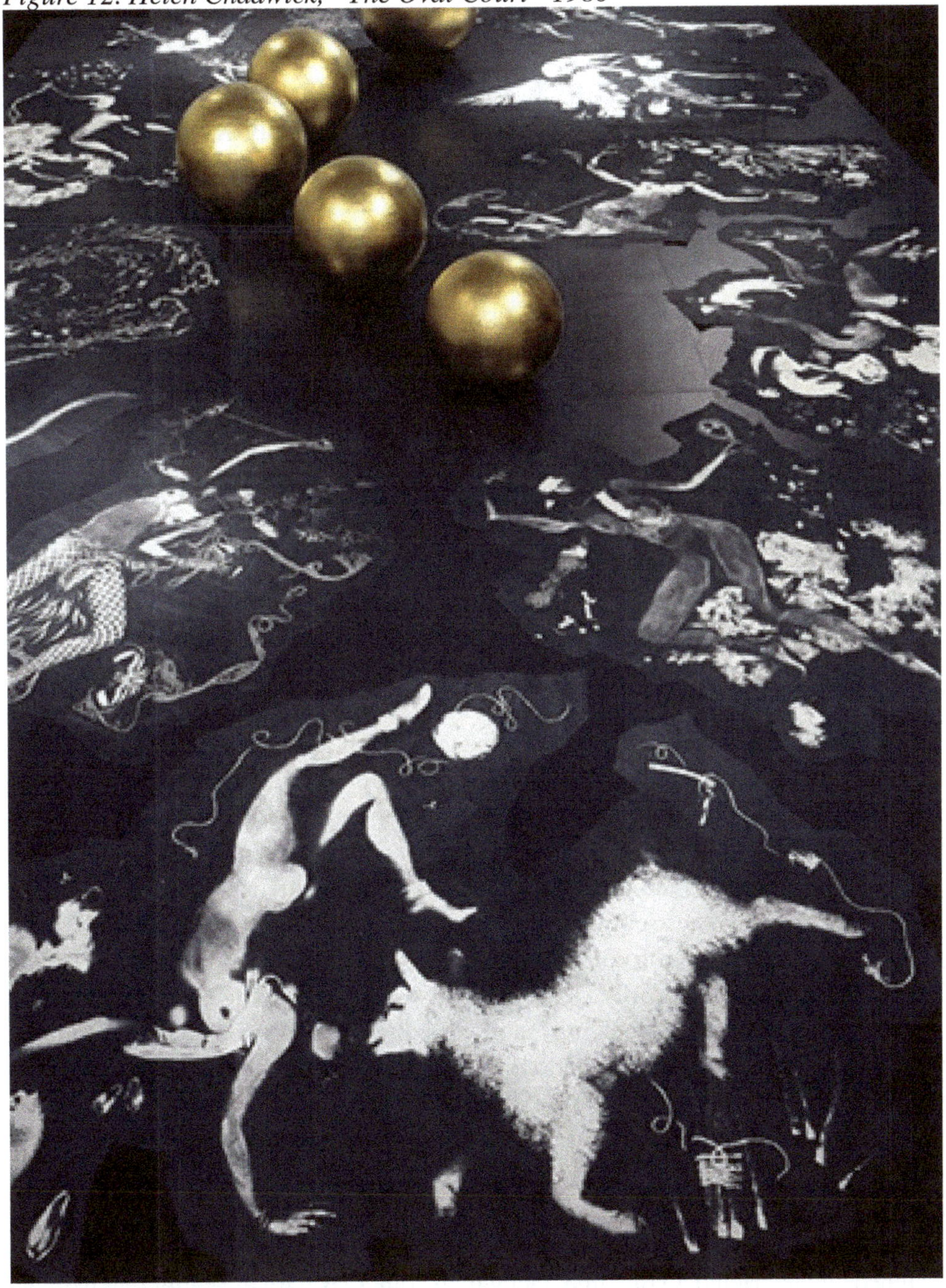

(Chadwick, 1986)

BEYOND THE SELF: COLLECTIVE IDENTITY AND CONTEMPORARY VISUAL CULTURE

Maria Papadimitriou T.A.M.A. (Temporary Autonomous Museum for All, est. 1998): Art as a Votive for the Doubly Marginalised

Papadimitriou in T.A.M.A. demonstrates how art acts as an "ex-voto" for marginalized populations. with the intention to expand from the individual domestic sphere, that women artists are often controlled in, to the community.

The word "Tama" in Greek means offering and in the Greek Orthodox tradition "Tama" is used to describe oblation, the small metal dedication, votive offering is an ex- voto. It also means ceremonial pilgrimage walk, which is also the promise of an offering to a saint in return for his or her help, a vow and a pledge. The artist shrewdly uses that word T.A.M.A. (Temporary Autonomous Museum for All) as a playful pun since she works in Avliza an area in Western Athens, 10 km from the center of the capital and very close to the new Olympic village. Traveling, impoverished populations such as Gypsies and Black Romanians from North of Greece use this area as a temporary Maria Papadimitriou from the series T.A.M.A. They use it as a shelter, their second home, one close enough to the big city, hopeful for work. But they are ostracized. This community is living in poverty because it is hard for the young people of that community to find employment. In her work T.A.M.A. (Temporary Autonomous Museum for All, est. 1998) the title meaning religious offering, pilgrimage the T.A.M.A. (Temporary Autonomous Museum for All) then becomes the quest of helping these people or dedicating religiously to them to them the museum as an act of inclusion and cultural exchange. They live in ghetto-like conditions, and they are ostracised by their surrounding communities. Living nomadically, these communities have no access to education, health or paid work. Thus, there is much criminal activity such as drug dealing, thievery and more. Young children do not usually have access to school and young girls are forced to marry early and have children. In a lot of ways, the level of expansionism is forcing the community to a colonised and conservative victimhood. Families constantly with packed suitcases, stories of poverty and sleeping in one-bedroom houses with parents and eldest siblings because of lack of room, and the obsessive need to own a family home are examples that point to "a semi-nomadic society that has partly adopted settled norms" (Bada 2005: 212).

Women's oppression in these nomadic societies is mainly about feeling regulated, watched and restricted all the time, fact which coincides with the belief that women should not go alone to public spaces, unescorted (Bada, 2005: 210). Marginalized women are doubly raised one by society and by internalized patriarchal structures of the gaze.

Figure 13. Maria Papadimitriou from the series T.A.M.A. 1998

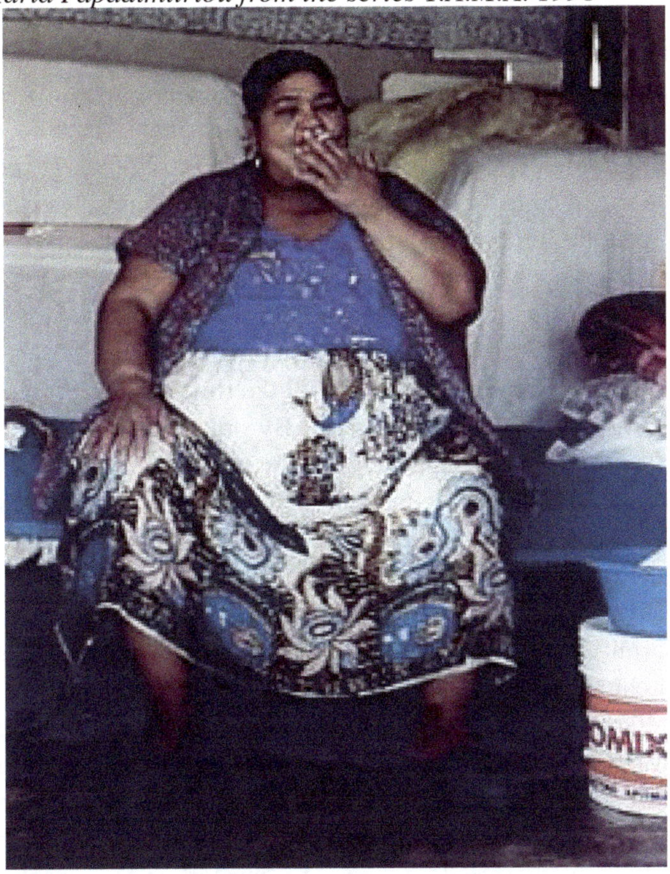

(Papadimitriou, 1998)

Papadimitriou bases T.A.M.A. in Bey's Instant' Zones of Autonomy. (1991) that are preferred performative moments in which another shape of identity and community are created. The temporary autonomous zone is a short-lived space where people organize themselves freely. It is the impermanent space of freedom that functions independently for a period of time and then dissolves before it can be controlled or institutionalized. The characteristic of those spaces is that they encourage autonomy, self-organization, resistance and aim to decentralize authority in an ephemeral community, through art imagination and cultural experimentation. The point that Papadimitriou is making with the experiment of T.A.M.A is that freedom can exist in small fleeting moments.

The artist has the ability to investigate collaborative projects and collective activities which highlight the interconnection between art and social reality. She examined the themes of belonging and chronic dislocation through her photographic series focused on displaced women. Her images tell the story of women's expatriation, marginalization, and isolation as nomads. Papadimitriou coordinated visiting artists, sociologists, anthropologists, filmmakers, and architects to build relationships with the local people and develop this place of social rejection into a "Social Facility." of T.A.M.A. (Temporary Autonomous Museum for All, est. 1998).

The women photographers that we have seen not only look at themselves but also look at the social construction of the self and view themselves through it with courage and freedom. In doing so they construct a space: the space of the photograph as a new body, as a "home" for their identity. Through vision they reclaim this "home", which is really a narrative practice of telling the story again while taking photos in the way they wish to be seen and telling the stories they wish to be told. This is a living home that changes all the time and is not shy to talk about desire, vision, blindness, loss and freedom. By practicing this new photography, women create ruptures where the new story, the new language, the new process of narration can be born. Usually, women are denied the knowledge they produce by narrating their stories. Research denies women that meaning making experience as knowledge. In other words, academia serves only one type of experience, only one type of knowledge— the normative one. Women's photography is a new way of researching narrative knowledge and producing methods. Through such different ways of researching if we change our epistemological orientation and allow for "multiplicity, elasticity, ambiguity, in the process of meaning making" (Jipson & Paley, 1997) we can subvert the covert violence of normative gender narratives. In doing so we have to reinvent what knowledge is and what we need it to do. In other words, as Bell Hooks states: "I suggest that we do not need to hear and know what is stated in its entirety, that we do not need to 'master' or conquer the narrative as a whole, that we may learn from spaces of silence as well as speech" (Jipson & Paley, 1997).

CONCLUSION

Gender Performativity and the Visual Construction of Identity

Mulvey's idea of an internalized male gaze in women, the idea of reiteration of Butler and the idea of rewriting of Cixous meet on the performance of the spectacle in the stage of social media everyday practices like the selfie, the story, the post and the reel. Women who look at themselves as they stage themselves to be looked at, all mediated by the patriarchal gaze of photography; women perform for the camera as they become spectacles, and they become blind to their own desire. Mulvey's idea of the gaze helps us explain why these performances then follow particular visual conventions and how norms are reproduced in everyday life. Only this time the performer is the director of the gaze. Identity depends on constant repetition. The interruption point then is to learn to repeat differently, discover a way that adds another layer by emphasizing expression and multiplicity. Those everyday digital practices are particular in the formation of subjectivity. Posting, scrolling, liking and photographing oneself are not trivial activities, but small performative gestures through which individuals negotiate ability, recognition and belonging in the everyday culture. A timeline becomes a stage where identities continuously rehearse themselves. Thus, the structuring power of the gaze of Mulvey in the uninterrupted performative repetition by Butler hopefully grows to become the potential overflow of Cixous in which social media is available for operating simultaneously as a space of dysregulation and experimentation.

Visual communication is the most powerful tool that we have for learning the roles we were told to perform -gender identity through memory. Owning one's memories and past is about being able to place one self in the future. To restore photographs as an empowering individual language is to control one's own performance of identity and memory production and thus a political act affecting the realm of the personal. As Guyas (2007) puts it: "I am searching for a language and knowledge that will help me to question the limitations of the perceived self and to continue to explore and develop my female identity".

The artists presented here use photography as a language in an empowering way to aid generative new narratives of the self with the goal of reclaiming their losses.

Reclaiming the Gaze, Rewriting the Self

The search of gendered photographic narratives traversing from the physical family archive to the fluid, omnipresent landscape of digital visual culture reveals the profound shift in the way the self is viewed as a construction. By synthesizing the foundational theories of Laura Mulvey and Judith Butler with the transformative potential of Hélène Cixous's écriture feminine and grounding these in Johana Frueh's "erotics of criticism" and Maria Gasouka's counter-discourse, we can conclude that the photographic act constitutes a vital site of political and existential struggle.

As this exploration has recognised, the "Male gaze" conceived by Laura Mulvey has not disappeared; it has been adapted and automated. Even though fully absorbed in the digital nowadays, panopticon the sample of art photography practitioners such as Campbell, Benitah, Fox, Chadwick, and Papadimitriou reveal that while digital platforms boost the replication of stereotyping prettiness ideals, they could also deliver the set-up to repeat differently disrupting direct patriarchal expectations through performative subversion. Even the family album, traditionally the repository for normative history, has been fundamentally repurposed by Carol Benitah's superimpositionitive embroidery, that acts as a forceful, exorcistic gesture. Briony Campbell's auto-ethnographic work transmutes the helplessness of grief into shared resistance; and Anna Fox's comparison of paternal violence and maternal order initiates a bodily involvement that impacts the viewer to recognise their own autonomy.

Hélène Cixous's écriture féminine delivers the crucial diversion path from the restrictions described by Mulvey and Butler. Photography literally "writing with light" develops into a corporal genre of inscription. By embracing the "personal as political", the digital selfie and the photographic narrative cease to be insignificant visual objects and surface as performative actions of self-identity authoring.

In this chapter, we have followed the development of the different roles of the female body in photography from being just an inactive "spectacle" of the male gaze to becoming a dynamic agent of its own narrative. We surveyed the theories of Mulvey, Butler and Cixous, and we have moved beyond the ordinary account of male-controlled photographic constructs into a space of committed "writing". Photography, in the hands of the women practitioners discussed here, is a bodily, performative, genuinely political act of self- "homing".

The journey from Briony Campbell's auto-ethnographic exploration of grief to Riti Sengupta's poetical uncovering of family unease uncovers a common thread: the application of photo narration to assert a place where the person can decisively belong to itself. We have observed how Carol Benitah and Anna Fox use the physicality of the photograph and the book through the punctuation of the needle or the claustrophobia of the miniature to materially interrupt the order of inherited distress. These are not merely images; they are tactile sides of resistance where the "body of the photograph" reflects the lived experience of the woman behind the lens.

At last, this chapter states that when a woman turns the camera toward her own life, she effectively breaks the mirror or of Medusa. She rejects the demise of silence and vanity, choosing instead the "writing of light". The undertaking of observing is recovered as a practice of learning - making in this new visual landscape. By integrating multiplicity and the "erotics of criticism", these artists prove that the personal is not only political it is the foundation upon which a new present language of belonging is built. The "home" they have constructed is not made of walls, but of vision, memory, and the brave integrity of a gaze that finally looks back.

REFERENCES

Bada, E. (2005). *Performance and Greek Roma identity: A visual anthropological study* [Doctoral dissertation, Napier University].

Benitah, C. (2011). Photos-Souvenirs [Embroidered photographs]. Retrieved May 22, 2026, from https://www.carolebenitah.com

Bright, S. (Ed.). (2013). *Home truths: Photography and motherhood.* Art/Books.

Brown, E. H., & Phu, T. (Eds.). (2014). *Feeling photography.* Duke University Press.

Butler, J. (1990). *Gender trouble: Feminism and the subversion of identity.* Routledge.

Butler, J. (1993). *Bodies that matter: On the discursive limits of 'sex.* Routledge.

Campbell, B. (2011a). *The Dad Project* [Personal essay]. Briony Campbell Photography & Film. https://www.brionycampbell.com/wp-content/uploads/2013/03/The_Dad_Project_Briony_Campbell.pdf

Campbell, B. (2011b). The Dad Project [Photograph]. Retrieved May 22, 2026, from https://www.brionycampbell.com

Chadwick, H. (1986). The Oval Court [Photographic installation]. © The Estate of Helen Chadwick.

Chadwick, H. (n.d.). Art, like crying, is an act of self-repair [Artist's notes]. As cited in Warner, M. (2022). *Helen Chadwick: The Oval Court.* Afterall Books/MIT Press.

Cixous, H. (1976). The laugh of the medusa (K. Cohen & P. Cohen, Trans.). *Signs: Journal of Women in Culture and Society, 1*(4), 875–893. (Original work published 1975)

Cixous, H. (1998). *Stigmata, escaping texts.* Routledge.

Etherington, K. (2004). *Becoming a reflective researcher: Using our selves in research.* Jessica Kingsley Publishers.

Fox, A. (2000). My Mother's Cupboards & My Father's Words [Artist's book/Photographs]. Retrieved May 22, 2026, from https://www.annafox.co.uk

Frueh, J., Raven, A., & Langer, C. L. (Eds.). (1988). *Feminist art criticism: An anthology.* Routledge.

Gasouka, M. (2026, March 7). Gynaikeia grafi ston androkentriko kosmo tis logotechnias [Female writing in the male centered world of literature]. *I Efimerida ton Syntakton*. https://www.efsyn.gr/nisides/503284_gynaikeia-grafi-ston-androkentriko-kosmo-tis-logotehnias

Guyas, A. S. (2007). Re-constructing self within the family: Re-building the family album. *Visual Culture & Gender*, *2*, 14–23.

Hirsch, M. (2002). *Familial frames: Photography, narrative and post memory*. Harvard University Press.

hooks, b. (1994). *Teaching to transgress: Education as the practice of freedom*. Routledge.

Jipson, J. A., & Paley, N. (Eds.). (1997). *Daredevil research: Re-creating analytic practice*. P. Lang.

Kelly, C. J. (2008). Personal is political. In O'Brien, J. (Ed.), *Encyclopedia of gender and society* (pp. 643–644). SAGE Publications.

Mulvey, L. (1975). Visual pleasure and narrative cinema. *Screen, 16*(3), 6–18. DOI: 10.1093/screen/16.3.6

Mykhalovskiy, E. (1996). Reconsidering table talk: Critical thoughts on the relationship between sociology, autobiography and self-indulgence. *Qualitative Sociology, 19*(1), 131–151. DOI: 10.1007/BF02393251

Ovid. (1916). *Metamorphoses* (F. J. Miller, Trans.). Harvard University Press. (Original work written c. 8 CE)

Panourgia, N. (1995). *Fragments of death, fables of identity: An Athenian anthropography*. University of Wisconsin Press.

Papadimitriou, M. (1998). T.A.M.A. (Temporary Autonomous Museum for All) [Photography/Installation]. Retrieved May 22, 2026, from https://www.mariapapadimitriou.com

Reed-Danahay, D. E. (1997). *Auto/ethnography: Rewriting the self and the social*. Berg.

Scott-Hoy, K. (2002). The visitor: Juggling life in the grip of the text. In Bochner, A. P., & Ellis, C. (Eds.), *Ethnographically speaking: Autoethnography, literature and aesthetics* (pp. 274–294). Altamira Press.

Sengupta, R. (2020). Things I Can't Say Out Loud [Photographs]. Retrieved May 22, 2026, from https://www.ritisengupta.com

Walkerdine, V. (1997). *Daddy's girl*. MacMillan Press.

Warner, M. (2022). *Helen Chadwick: The Oval Court*. Afterall Books/MIT Press.

Warner, M. (2026, March). Things I can't say out loud [Essay on Riti Sengupta]. In LensCulture Editors (Eds.), *Women shaping photography today — 19 artists to discover*. LensCulture. Retrieved May 22, 2026, from https://www.lensculture.com/articles/lensculture-editors-women-shaping-photography-today-19-artists-to-discover

Chapter 9

The Use of Variable Typefaces in Visual Identity Design:
The IBM Plex Variable Example

Dide Akdağ Satı
http://orcid.org/0009-0002-0593-2643
Yildiz Teknik University, Turkey

ABSTRACT

This chapter examines the IBM Plex variable typeface family as a case study in the intersection of algorithmic typography, parametric design, and corporate identity. As digital platforms multiply and communication environments grow increasingly complex, typeface systems have evolved from static forms into dynamic, data-driven design infrastructures. Per the authors, this chapter traces that transformation by analyzing the technical foundations of variable font technology alongside the formal and communicative properties of the IBM Plex Sans, Serif, and Mono sub-families. Through comparative typographic analysis, the chapter demonstrates how each sub-family fulfills a distinct communicative function within a unified brand system: Sans for digital legibility, Serif for textual authority, and Mono for technical precision. The chapter further situates IBM Plex within broader developments in generative and algorithmic design, arguing that contemporary corporate typography is no longer a neutral carrier but a strategic, meaning-producing layer of visual communication.

DOI: 10.4018/979-8-3373-6680-7.ch009

INTRODUCTION

In line with the desire to make its global brand identity more distinctive, accessible and consistent, IBM has decided to transition to its own proprietary corporate typeface, the IBM Plex Variable Font. The IBM Plex typeface family is a key example of contemporary corporate typography, thanks to its open-source structure, multilingual support and adaptability to various design applications. In this context, the technical foundations of variable typeface technology are outlined, and the axis structure of the "IBM Plex Variable Font", along with its capacity to support different writing systems, is examined in detail. By explaining how IBM Plex enables effective use in multilingual and multi-platform communication environments, it is evaluated in terms of design language, legibility, readability, licensing model and brand strategy, in comparison with other open-source corporate typefaces. This comparison demonstrates that the IBM Plex typeface is not merely a technical tool, but also a functional and aesthetic brand indicator. The aim is to explore variable typefaces by focusing on the opportunities they offer in the fields of algorithmic typography, responsive interface design and multi-channel corporate communication, whilst seeking answers to the questions: "How does parametric typography differ from classical typography? How is the design process of algorithmic typography transformed? How can the balance between flexibility and identity integrity in visual identity be maintained?" As a method, the analysis of the primary characteristic criteria that play a significant role in the transformation of the typography comprising the IBM Plex variable typeface family has been preferred. The scope of the research comprises the IBM variable typeface family, whilst the sample consists of the IBM Plex Sans, Serif, and Mono typefaces, along with italic options in specific cases. Moving beyond a singular form that preserves tradition, a common visual identity typography across different communication layers is evaluated, and the limitations of the system's transformation process are examined. These typographic developments in visual communication design are regarded as a significant turning point from both an aesthetic and functional perspective. The analysis of the IBM variable typeface is significant for its contribution to fostering an awareness of parametric typography design- a shared need that is evolving and developing across different communication layers of branding.

A NEW UNDERSTANDING OF FORM IN DIGITAL DESIGN AND THE DIGITAL TRANSFORMATION OF TYPOGRAPHY

In the rapidly evolving landscape of digital design and visual communication, the transformation of typography-shaped by letters, algorithms, data and artificial intelligence systems-represents not merely a form of visual expression, but also a dynamic field of interaction between information and form. Design perspectives looking towards the future are also exploring this transformation.

Since the advent of the printing press, typography has played a significant role as one of the fundamental means of expression in the field of visual communication; however, the transformations in digital technologies have reshaped not only the visual characteristics of typography but also its production processes and modes of use. In the traditional typographic approach, typefaces designed around fixed and unchanging structures have, under the influence of code-based systems, variable fonts and generative design approaches, evolved into more adaptable and dynamic structures (Lupton, 2010).

This transformation is not merely viewed as a change in typographic aesthetics; it also signifies an ontological shift that redefines the logic of typeface production and operation. In this context, the letter ceases to be merely a static form that ensures legibility, transforming instead into a process-oriented structure capable of interacting with data and exhibiting variability within specific systems. This approach not only facilitates a re-evaluation of typography's traditional boundaries but also establishes the concept of generative typography as a significant field of research. The generative approach refers to the creation of design outputs through specific algorithms, rule-based systems, or data-driven processes; it shifts the designer's role from that of a direct form-producer to that of a system architect who defines production processes (Galanter, 2003).

This transformation is not merely aesthetic but also ontological: the letter is no longer merely a 'readable' form but an 'operating' one. At this point, it offers a conceptual framework that facilitates a rethinking of typography, particularly for 'generative typography'. The concept of "generative" refers to the automatic production of design by an algorithm, a set of rules, or a data system (Galanter, 2003). In the design process, the role of the designer is shifting away from the direct practice of form-making towards the design of systems and rules that will produce formal outputs. This approach brings to the fore the conceptual framework defined as "algorithmic aesthetics" in the fields of art and design. Within the understanding of algorithmic aesthetics, formal order, visual balance and aesthetic value are not shaped solely by the designer's subjective intuition; rather, they emerge as a result of defined parameters, computational processes and interactions between systems. This situation, whilst redefining the logic of design practice, positions the designer not as the individual who directly creates the final output, but rather as an actor who structures the production mechanism (Bohnacker et al., 2012).

Writing has evolved through the alphabets and symbol systems developed by different cultures throughout history; it underwent a radical transformation with the advent of the printing press and has entered a new phase of change alongside digital technologies. This transformation is assessed within the context of changes in communication forms and technological advancements. Among current typographic developments, variable typefaces stand out for their flexible structure, capable of containing multiple weight and style variations within a single file. This axis-based system offers efficiency in terms of file size whilst adapting to different screen environments. With web browsers and design software supporting this technology, its scope of application has expanded; this has enabled designers to develop more experimental and innovative applications. This approach, which became evident with the introduction of the OpenType 1.8 standard in 2016, has contributed to the emergence of a new design philosophy in typography; in particular, it has accelerated the spread of parametric and experimental design methods.

Alongside Berlow (2017a) and Berlow (2017b), Van Halem (2017), Ross (2017), Mickel & Imas (2018) produced in collaboration with Huot-Marchand (2018) and Hanzer (2018), these exemplary works highlight the possibilities offered by variable typefaces through axes such as weight, width and optical dimensions. These examples demonstrate that variable typefaces are not merely a technical innovation; they have become a tool that transforms contemporary typographic forms of expression. Furthermore, this approach makes a significant contribution in that it can provide flexibility whilst maintaining consistency across different media environments (Kaplan, 2022).

Figure 1. Helvetica Now Variable font family displaying weight, width, and optical size axes (Penney, 2016)

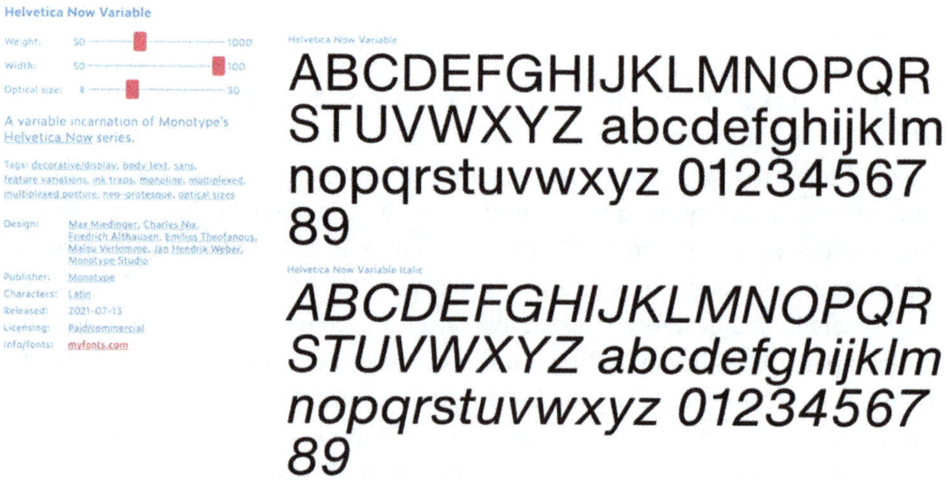

This project, developed for WPP, is regarded as one of the first logo (Figure 2) examples where variable font technology has been integrated into corporate identity design. The early involvement of Fontsmith in the design process enabled the systematic development and refinement of typographic elements in line with the creative concept originally conceived (Garnham, 2021).

Figure 2. Amsteldok WPP campus variable font logo designed by Fontsmith and VBAT (Monotype, 2019)

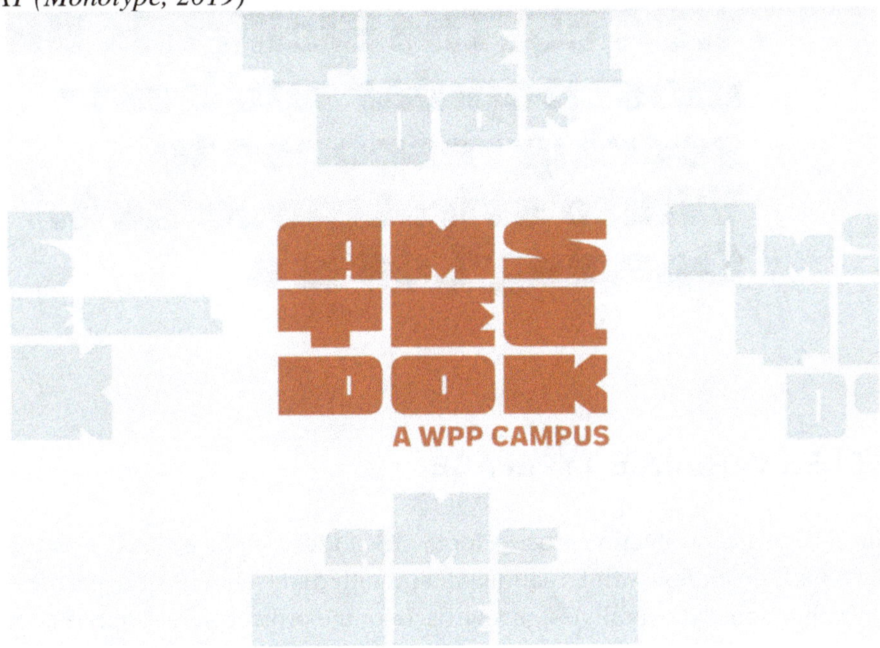

In the process of developing a typeface that strongly reflects the corporate identity, IBM's historical legacy was taken as the primary reference point. The role the company has assumed since its inception can be defined as creating an interface between human and machine, naturalness and engineering, emotional expression and rational thought, and traditional and innovative approaches. Designed within this context, the IBM Plex typeface aims to produce a visual language that reconciles these dual opposites. In the construction of the letterforms, a balanced structure reflecting both technological precision and human expression has been sought; thus, typography has transcended its role as a mere communication tool to become a holistic design element representing the organisation's values.

Figure 3. ABC Whyte Plus variable font axes demonstrated in Dinamo Font Gauntlet (Dinamo Typefaces, 2018)

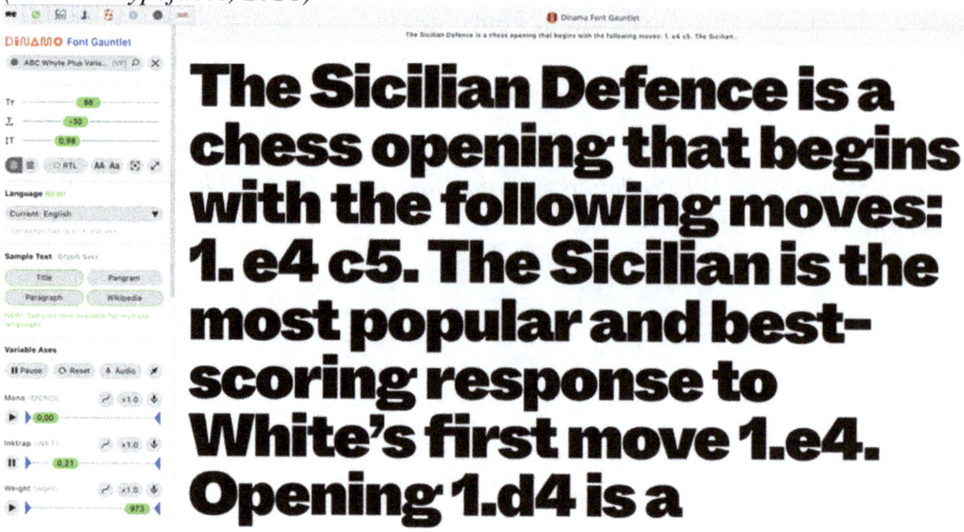

IBM PLEX VARIABLE TYPEFACE

The design and production process for the IBM Plex typeface family was carried out by a multidisciplinary, international team with diverse areas of expertise. The creative direction and overall design approach for the project were shaped under the leadership of Mike Abbink, within the IBM Design framework. The typographic direction and character design were developed by Paul van der Laan and Pieter van Rosmalen, in collaboration with Bold Monday. The production and design processes for the Latin alphabet typeface were brought to a technically and aesthetically cohesive structure with the contributions of experts such as Barbara Bigosińska, Diana Ovezea, Edgar Walthert and Jasper Terra. In addition, the Cyrillic and Greek character sets were designed by Aleksandra Samuļenkova; Marko Hrastovec and Pablo Gámez were involved in the production processes. In the development of non-Latin writing systems, the Arabic alphabet was handled by Wael Morcos and Khajag Apelian; the Devanagari script was designed by Erin McLaughlin, Hebrew characters by Yanek Iontef, and the Thai alphabet by Ben Mitchell and Mark Frömberg. The Korean alphabet (Hangul), meanwhile, was directed and produced by Wujin Sim, Chorong Kim and Dohee Lee in collaboration with Sandoll (IBM, n.d.). This multi-layered production structure demonstrates that the Plex typeface is conceived not merely as an aesthetic design product, but as a global typographic infrastructure encompassing diverse alphabetic systems. The simultaneous contribution of different areas of expertise is among the key elements that enhance the typeface's technical accuracy, cultural sensitivity and multilingual usability (Figure 4).

The IBM Plex typeface family offers extensive typographic flexibility through its structure comprising four sub-families, eight different weight options, and two basic style variations: roman and italic. Supporting over a hundred languages, this system possesses a comprehensive character set capable of meeting multilingual and multi-platform design requirements. In this respect, it can be regarded as a functional tool capable of addressing communication needs arising in various contexts. The typeface can be activated by integrating it into font management systems after download and utilised in various design processes.

The IBM Plex typeface family features an expanded character set that goes beyond the Latin alphabet to meet the needs of multilingual and multicultural communication. In this context, adapted versions have been developed for various alphabets, including Cyrillic, Greek, Arabic, Hebrew, Devanagari, Japanese, Korean (Hangul) and Thai, incorporating both loopless and looped variants of the Thai script (IBM, n.d.). This diversity reflects IBM Plex's objective of creating a consistent visual identity language on a global scale. Whilst preserving the structural and cultural characteristics specific to different writing systems, a common design approach is maintained in terms of typographic integrity and brand language. This ensures that the typeface is positioned not merely as a technical tool, but as a holistic design system that supports cross-cultural communication. (Figure 5- 6- 7)

Figure 4. IBM Plex typeface family multilingual character set (IBM, 2017)

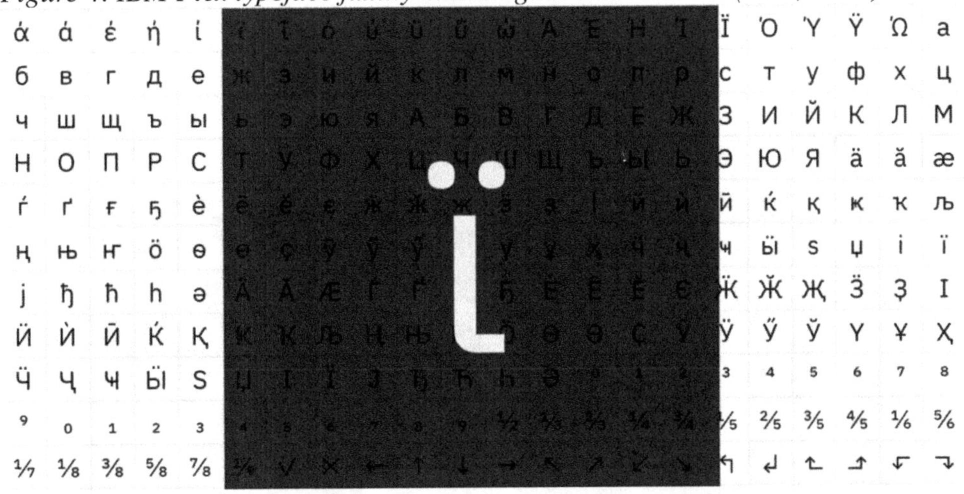

Figure 5. IBM Plex Cyrillic script letterforms with typographic guidelines (IBM, 2017)

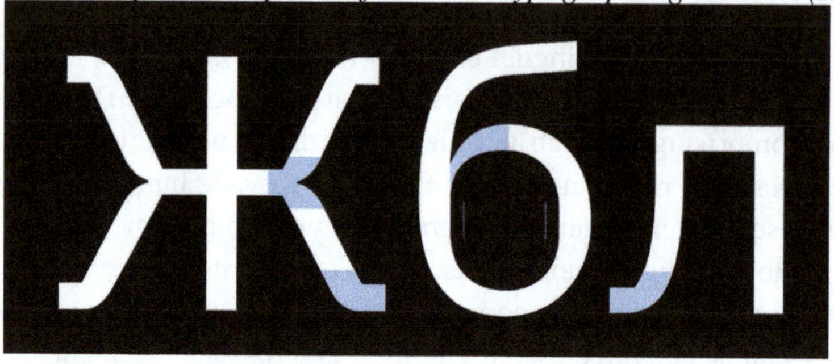

Figure 6. IBM Plex Arabic script letterforms with typographic guidelines (IBM, 2017)

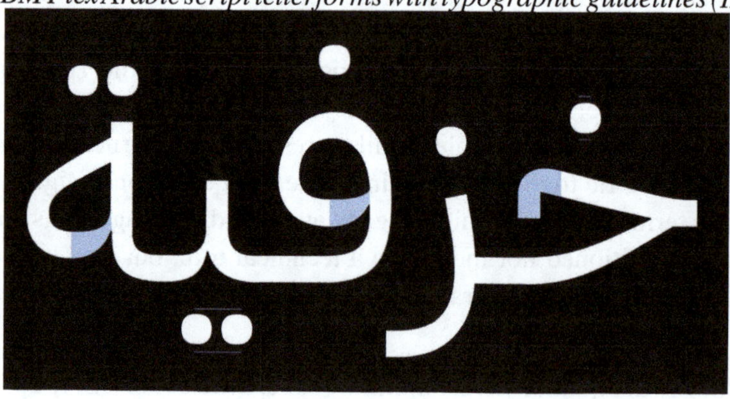

Figure 7. IBM Plex typeface design concept showing key letterform characteristics (IBM, 2017)

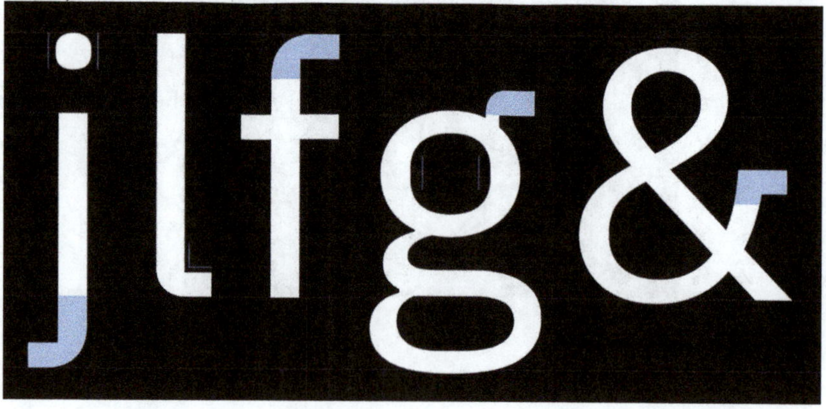

The digitalisation processes that gained momentum following the 1960s paved the way for multi-layered and multi-dimensional transformations in written communication and design practices. During this period, typographic production processes underwent a structural transformation; as techniques related to type production shifted from physical environments to digital platforms, they gradually moved away from centralised and static production models. Advances in computer technology and the widespread adoption of software-based tools have enabled typography to be redefined as an interactive, flexible and dynamic system, moving away from being a static form of expression.

From the second half of the 20th century onwards, developments in digital technologies contributed to the widespread use of computers and laid the groundwork for the emergence of new forms of production in design processes. Increased technological accessibility has created experimental research areas for designers and software developers, making it possible to integrate algorithmic systems into design processes. The parametric design studies and experimental applications carried out during this process provided a significant foundation regarding the potential applications of different design approaches prior to the development of variable typefaces.

With the announcement of the OpenType 1.8 standard in 2016, variable typefaces were incorporated into the typographic production process. As this technology developed, web browsers such as Chrome, Safari and Firefox began to support variable typefaces; subsequently, design software such as Illustrator, Photoshop, InDesign, Sketch and Figma also integrated this support into their systems. This technical compatibility across browsers and design tools has expanded the scope of variable typeface usage and increased its prevalence in digital design processes. Furthermore, the growing availability of variable typeface options on open-source typography platforms demonstrates the level of adoption of this technology in typographic applications.

Changing communication environments and new digital platforms have necessitated a re-evaluation of design processes across different platforms. Thanks to their adaptable structure, variable fonts provide designers with flexibility across various usage scenarios. This structure, which has a wide range of applications in both print and digital environments, makes design processes more efficient. Furthermore, current experimental studies suggest that variable typefaces may also have potential applications in augmented reality (AR) and virtual reality (VR) technologies.

The integration of digital technologies into the design field has led to significant structural changes in design production processes. This transformation has not been limited to the evolution of production tools; it has also reshaped the conceptual and methodological foundations of design. With the incorporation of computational thinking and algorithmic approaches into design processes, design practice has moved away from a static and linear understanding of production towards a more systematic, flexible and data-driven structure. Within this framework, the parametric design approach offers the possibility of treating design not as a predefined, fixed outcome, but as a dynamic system shaped through a network of specific variables, relationships and rules (Kolarevic, 2003). Parametric and generative design approaches have formed a significant body of experimental and theoretical work that has paved the way for the emergence of variable typefaces.

A significant turning point in the field of typography occurred with the announcement of the OpenType 1.8 standard in 2016. With this development, variable fonts have redefined typographic production processes by offering a structure capable of containing multiple design parameters (such as weight, width, optical size, etc.) within a single font file. Initially supported by web browsers such as Google Chrome, Safari and Mozilla Firefox, this technology was soon integrated into professional design software such as Adobe Illustrator, Photoshop, InDesign and After Effects, as well as interface design tools like Sketch and Figma. This widespread software support has made it possible to use variable fonts effectively in both digital and print media. The rapid incorporation of variable typefaces into the open-source typography platform Google Fonts, and the fact that a significant portion of the library now consists of these fonts, is one of the key indicators of the global proliferation of variable typography. This development broadens designers' access, paving the way for them to utilise variable typefaces in more experimental and creative ways.

The diversification of new media environments and the proliferation of communication platforms necessitate the redesign of typography for every medium. In this context, variable fonts offer a typographic system adaptable to different contexts thanks to their multi-axis structures. Whilst traditional typographic production requires the creation of separate font files for different usage scenarios, variable fonts significantly reduce this need. Designers can anticipate parameters such as different screen sizes, resolutions and user interactions at the early stages of the design process, and can develop flexible solutions accordingly. This transforms variable typefaces from being merely a typographic tool into an adaptive and data-driven design component (Lupton, 2010).

The scope of variable typefaces spans a wide range, from print publishing to digital interfaces, and from motion graphics to multi-screen experiences. Furthermore, experimental studies conducted in augmented reality (AR) and virtual reality (VR) environments- which are still in their developmental stages- suggest that variable typography could play an effective role in these fields as well. In particular, typographic systems that are responsive to user interaction, context-sensitive and capable of real-time adaptation will occupy a significant place in future design practices.

CORPORATE IDENTITY IN THE CONTEXT OF ALGORITHMIC AND VARIABLE TYPOGRAPHY

With digitalisation, typography has evolved from being merely a tool for legibility into a dynamic and multi-layered communication system. In corporate identity design in particular, typefaces are positioned as one of the fundamental components that visualise a brand's voice and values. In this context, IBM Plex, developed by IBM, goes beyond traditional typographic understanding to offer a variable and systematic design approach.

When we examine the IBM Plex typeface family through the lenses of variable typography, open-source design and corporate identity, it becomes clear that corporate identity is a system that ensures the visual and communicative integrity of the brand. Typography, meanwhile, is one of the most fundamental building blocks of this system. Typefaces can directly reflect the brand's values, such as reliability, innovation and a people-centric approach. Open-source typography facilitates the democratisation of design, offering access to a wider user base. The sharing of IBM Plex as open-source enables corporate design to evolve into a participatory structure. Developed for a brand that embraces diversity on a global scale, Plex is more than just a typeface; it is a defining visual identity element, as significant as the organisation's name and logo. It serves as a representative tool that subtly shapes the tone of the narrative whilst reflecting the organisation's values and design philosophy. It is evident that every decision made during the design process is grounded in a conscious foundation, and that every typographic detail carries a specific function and meaning (Figure 8).

The design philosophy of IBM Plex is intended to represent 'the balance between human and machine'. The typographic form creates a deliberate tension between technical precision and human warmth. This demonstrates that typography is not merely an aesthetic element, but also a vehicle for meaning. One of IBM Plex's most striking features is its extensive family structure, which supports a wide range of type systems. This ensures consistency for global brands and reduces issues of cultural representation, creating a universal language of communication. IBM Plex offers a structure compatible with variable font technology. It can adapt to different screen sizes and offers performance advantages. It creates flexibility in design. In this respect, Plex provides an infrastructure that can be integrated into generative design approaches. The fact that IBM Plex is offered as open source takes typography beyond corporate boundaries, creating a design ecosystem.

Figure 8. IBM Plex typeface in use across IBM Developer brand materials (IBM, 2017)

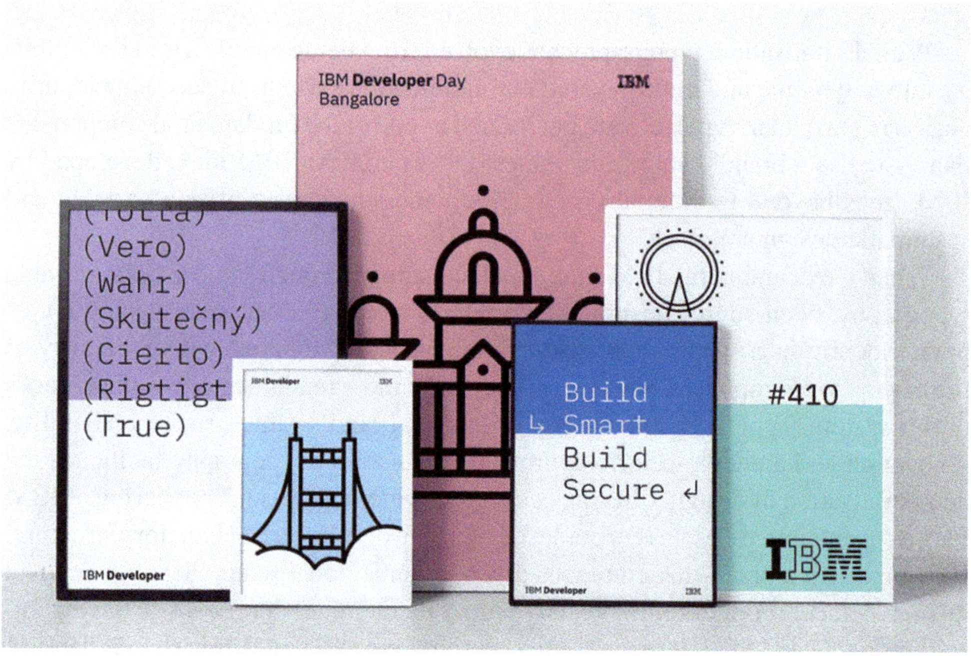

Figure 9. IBM Plex typeface applied in IBM Quantum Composer digital interface (IBM, 2017)

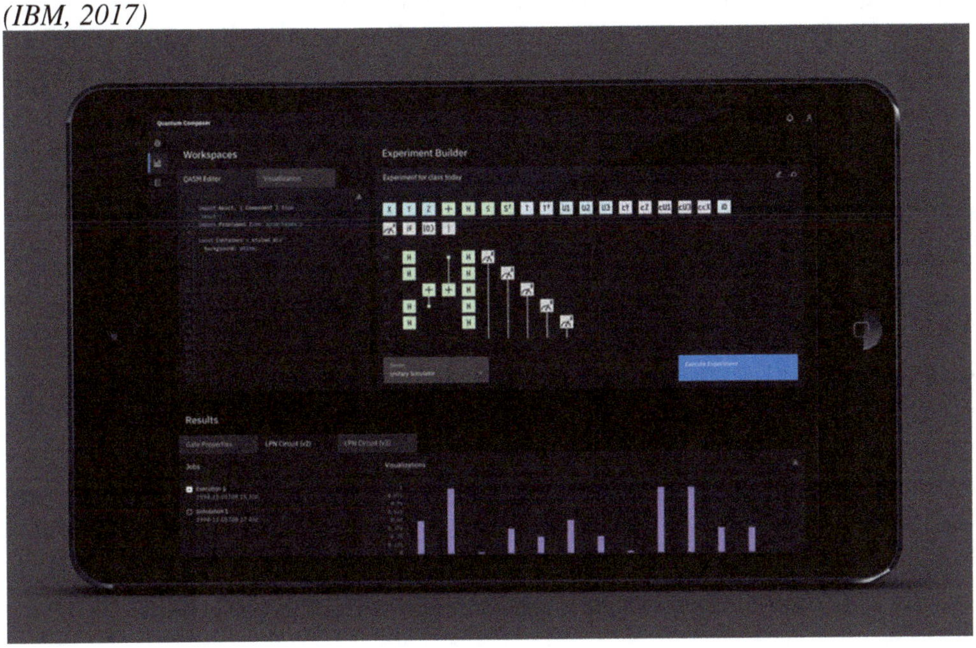

Figure 10. IBM Plex typeface family weight and style specifications across Sans, Mono, Serif, and Condensed variants (IBM, 2017)

Sans	Mono	Serif	Condensed
Thin	Thin	Thin	Thin
Thin Italic	*Thin Italic*	*Thin Italic*	*Thin Italic*
Extralight	Extralight	Extralight	Extralight
Extralight Italic	*Extralight Italic*	*Extralight Italic*	*Extralight Italic*
Light	Light	Light	Light
Light Italic	*Light Italic*	*Light Italic*	*Light Italic*
Regular	Regular	Regular	Regular
Italic	*Italic*	*Italic*	*Italic*
Text	Text	Text	Text
Text Italic	*Text Italic*	*Text Italic*	*Text Italic*
Medium	Medium	Medium	Medium
Medium Italic	*Medium Italic*	*Medium Italic*	*Medium Italic*
Semibold	**Semibold**	**Semibold**	**Semibold**
Semibold Italic	***Semibold Italic***	***Semibold Italic***	***Semibold Italic***
Bold	**Bold**	**Bold**	**Bold**
Bold Italic	***Bold Italic***	***Bold Italic***	***Bold Italic***

This approach encourages collaboration, supports the evolutionary development of design, and paves the way for innovative applications. IBM Plex is a significant example of how typography has transformed in the digital age. This typeface has been designed with a structure that strengthens corporate identity and adapts to variable and adaptive design systems. It offers an expanding structure through an open-source approach. In this context, IBM Plex can be regarded not merely as a font, but as a dynamic and sustainable visual communication system (Figure 9).

The Plex typeface family, developed by IBM, allows the control of the typeface's characteristics- such as weight, width and contrast- through variable parameters. This system offers an adaptive experience to both designers and user interfaces. Typography is no longer a 'fixed form' but a 'programmable structure'. This paradigm shift places the concepts of fiction, system and probability at the centre of the design process. The designer writes the rules that determine the behaviour of the typography; however, the resulting final form is often determined by the system's own internal dynamics. This creates a dialectic of control and surrender in design, both aesthetically and philosophically. The designer is engaged in a relationship of "co-creation" with the system they have produced (Figure 10).

IBM PLEX TYPEFACE UNIT PROCESS ANALYSIS

This section explains the ways in which typography- one of the elements that make up visual design- is used, the characteristics required to produce effective typographic communication, and how these are applied in the IBM Plex typeface. Solutions are proposed to emphasise key points, such as establishing rapid and direct communication with the reader to enhance readability. The text then covers typeface anatomy, the baseline, uppercase and lowercase letters, x-height, letter-specific definitions, the midline, the top line, ascenders, descenders, closed areas, horizontal stroke, curved stroke, serif, eye, absolute measurements, relative measurements, point, pica, em and en spaces, typefaces, quotation marks, classification of typefaces, letter spacing, and word spacing- the fundamental concepts and rules of typography, along with the importance of these rules, are explained.

Quotation marks are an important feature for identifying a typeface and can be used in various forms. It is often said that quotation marks generally improve the readability of a text by helping the eye move from one character to another. Many styles of quotation marks reflect the spirit of their era, with some being more ornate, some bolder, and others more understated or delicate (Ambrose and Harris, 2013).

A set of characters comprising letters, numbers, punctuation marks and other symbols is known as a 'font'. When all the characters of the same font are arranged side by side, they create a visually consistent density and cohesion. The basic elements of a font can be listed as follows: uppercase letters, lowercase letters, numbers, punctuation marks, mathematical symbols, accents and logograms. (Becer, 2007).

Figure 11. IBM Plex typeface design process showing construction grid and eight-weight interpolation of the lowercase 'a' (IBM, 2017)

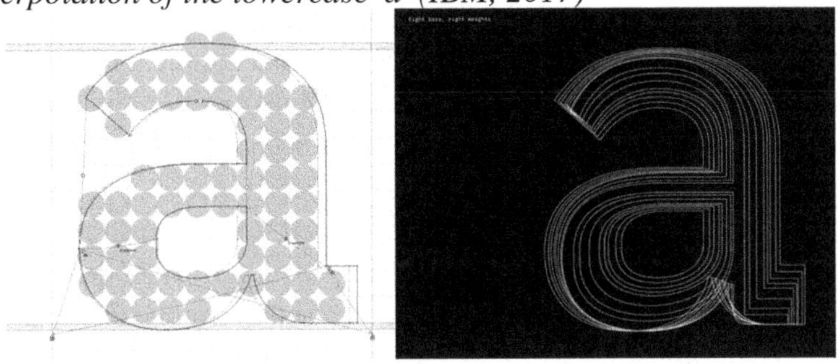

The distance between the horizontal line that determines the x-height of lowercase letters and the baseline is referred to as the 'x-height'. This is the standard height of lowercase letters, and the letter where it can be measured most clearly is the lowercase 'x'. (Becer, 2007) Characters with a larger 'x-height' always ensure better legibility than other characters (Figure 11).

The point size of a character is the distance between a line drawn from the top of its ascender to the bottom of its descender. (İstek, 2005) The x-height varies depending on the typeface. Absolute measurements are easy to understand because they are based on fixed values. For example, a millimetre is a precisely defined increment of a centimetre. Similarly, typographic measurements such as points and picas also have fixed values. All absolute measurements are expressed in quantifiable terms and remain constant. The point is a typographic unit of measurement that is internationally recognised today. 1 point equals 0.37583 millimetres.

A typeface family is created by bringing together all the sizes and styles of a single typeface. For this reason, the point size entered will result in the same letter height (İstek, 2005). Using too many typefaces in a design can cause confusion. Each character evokes a different message and perception. Instead, the use of a rich typeface family ensures a solid, effective, impactful and hierarchical reading experience in the design. The combined use of capital letters takes up more space because the eye scans the same area more frequently, causing eye strain in a long text. Similarly, the use of bold type creates a coarse appearance because the words form rectangles, triangles and circles. Lowercase letters, on the other hand, are perceived more distinctly due to their ascenders, descenders, tails and stems, which enables the characters to move within the eye's field of vision; these are defined as regular (roman), italic, condensed, extended, bold, bold italic, light, light italic, etc.

Letters are design elements with varying amounts of space. These spaces are settings that can be determined by relating them to the font size, the proportions of the typeface's anatomy, and the column width and line spacing in professional graphic design (İstek, 2005). As the text size increases, the spacing must be reduced. For example, whilst the word above appears correctly spaced, the word below requires adjustment of the letter spacing. Letter spacing adjustments should not be applied until the choice of typeface has been finalised. Different typefaces have different structural characteristics, and therefore require specific letter spacing adjustments (Ambrose and Harris, 2013). When words are placed side by side, they form lines. In this case, the spacing between words must be adjusted. It is a fact that word spacing, like letter spacing, is determined by the eye rather than by mechanical measuring instruments. When adjusting word spacing, one must also take into account the punctuation marks used between words (İstek, 2005). Anyone involved in graphic design or visual communication must have a thorough understanding of the rules necessary to create successful typography. The designer must have a good command of the language, be able to analyse it, and establish a successful communication by beginning the design process only after prioritising the information to be conveyed. No matter how successful the design may be, if the message cannot be conveyed accurately and quickly, the layout is considered a failure.

The variety of typefaces used in design should be tailored to the specific requirements. Script fonts, with their handwritten appearance, are appealing but difficult to read. Decorative typefaces, on the other hand, are often quite illegible due to their ornate structures. The desired visual richness can be achieved by using different styles of the same typeface- such as bold, light, and italic- on a single page. Screen fonts such as Geneva, Helvetica, Arial, Times and Courier are more legible. Excessively large font sizes reduce the number of words that can be taken in. If they are too small, the letters are difficult to distinguish and become illegible. For a reading distance of 30–35 cm, the average font size should not be smaller than 9–11 points (12–14 px).

Extra bold text is difficult to read because the inner spaces of the letters are filled in. If the text is too condensed, this causes letters to merge and weakens the inner spaces. If long texts are written in italics, it makes the text appear weak. Aligning text to the left ensures more consistent spacing between words and prevents the formation of white gaps. Centred text can cause tracking issues. If lines are short, the eye's movement is frequently interrupted; if they are long, it becomes difficult for the eye to move to the start of the next line and scan correctly, leading to skipping lines or re-reading the same line.

White space is the space on a web page that displays text and images. In design, white space ensures easy comprehension. Insufficient white space, however, creates confusion and clutter, making comprehension difficult. Image elements placed too close to the text area make it difficult to perceive both the text and the images themselves. There must be at least 4 mm of white space between text and images. It is not at all difficult to turn simplicity into complexity. There are numerous examples of this. The important thing is to simplify complexity. A clean, clear design has a higher chance of being perceived and communicating effectively. The typeface has been analysed within the framework of typographic design criteria.

The unit examples presented in the visuals, meanwhile, demonstrate the integration of these units into the anatomy of the letters and how they are structured within the framework of basic anatomical elements. The fundamental anatomical elements of the character set highlighted in the figure reveal the formal composition implemented in the structural composition of the typeface. The functions performed by these typographic components within the context of the IBM Plex typeface are described below in sequence.

Figure 12. IBM Plex typeface design principles showing the balance between engineering precision and human warmth (IBM, 2017)

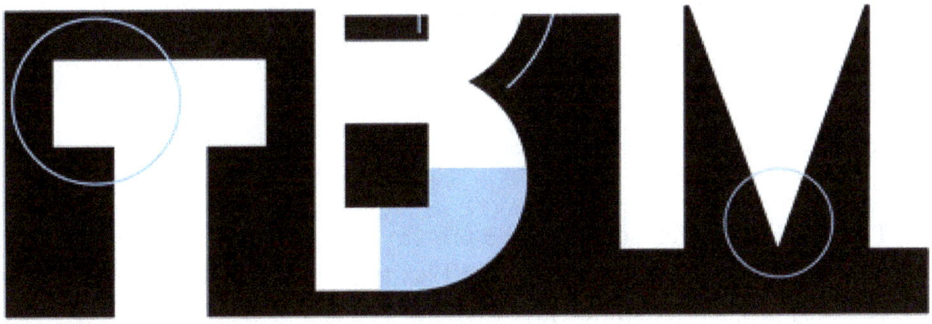

The first prominent feature in this design is the thick, block-like serif structure defined as a slab serif. Furthermore, a distinct contrast is established between the rounded curves of the outer contour and the vertical and angular structure observed in the inner spaces. Additionally, the pointed tip detail at the intersection of the letter 'M' is considered a distinctive feature unique to the typeface (Figure 12).

- This component, which defines the upper limits of the uppercase letters-known as Cap Height-touches the upper horizontal strokes of all uppercase letters in the IBM Plex typeface.

- The x-height value, which indicates the stem height of lowercase letters in the typeface, has been set high in the IBM Plex typeface with the aim of enhancing the legibility and visual clarity of lowercase letters on screen.
- The crossbar component, which defines the middle horizontal strokes of the letters, is positioned in appropriate, letter-specific locations for the letters a, g, R, H and e in the IBM Plex typeface.

Figure 13. Typeface design process

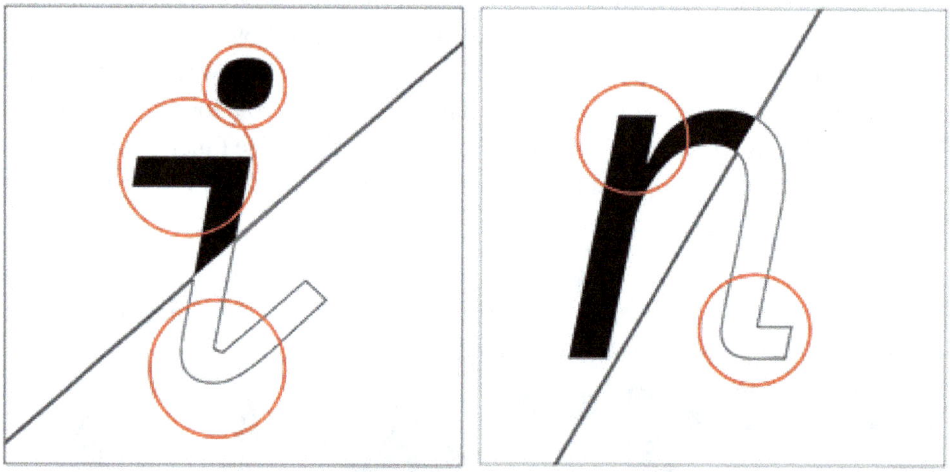

- The baseline, which serves as the primary reference line for aligning letter structures, is positioned in the IBM Plex typeface so that all characters are correctly aligned within the grid system.
- The aperture component, which defines the internal spaces of the letters, has been kept narrow in the IBM Plex typeface so as not to adversely affect legibility.
- The leading component, which determines the spacing between lines, has been arranged in the IBM Plex typeface by leaving proportional distances between line blocks to ensure a comfortable reading rhythm and legibility (Figure 13).
- The stems of both uppercase and lowercase letters are clear. The emphasis on the horizontal stroke of the letters is normal. The curved, emphasised parts of rounded letters are distinctive. (Figure 14)

Figure 14. Design process

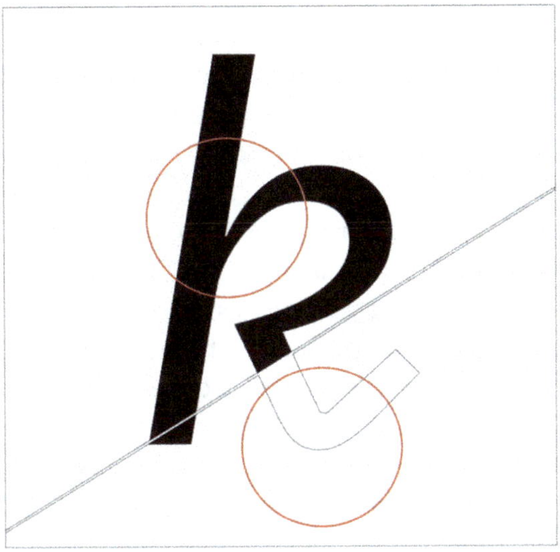

- The stroke, which forms the basic emphasis structure of the letters, has been adapted to a uniform thickness in the IBM Plex typeface; the stroke thickness is consistently and balancedly shaped across all variants.
- The ascender component, which serves as an upper extension in lowercase letters, has been raised to the cap height level in the IBM Plex typeface.
- The stem component, which represents the vertical supporting lines, has been constructed in the IBM Plex typeface using straight modules with a fixed line thickness.
- The descender component, representing the lower extensions of the letters, has been applied with a distinctive level of extension in the IBM Plex typeface.
- The short accent marks at the end of the main stroke have been designed in a distinctive serif style.
- It has been observed that the closed part of the lowercase 'e' is open.

In addition to their structural characteristics, the systematic design of their weight values directly influences the context in which the typeface is used. Comprising three distinct variants- Sans, Mono and Serif- the balance and proportions of the letter spacing have been specifically reworked for each variant. Designed to offer a high level of functionality and flexibility across various digital contexts and design applications, the IBM Plex typeface features the Light variant as the lightest version, the Regular variant representing the typeface's base weight, and the Bold variant providing the most intense visual impact.

Text arranged in accordance with typographic principles retains its functionality in both digital and printed media. Conversely, letter and word structures containing excessive formal emphasis can hinder perception and negatively affect the transmission of the message. Although such typographic deviations are generally not preferred, the level of legibility can vary depending on the context (Willen & Strals, 2009).

Typefaces developed in the PostScript Type 1 format offer a resolution-independent structure, unlike bitmap-based fonts, and can be consistently optimised across different screens and hardware. This feature provides a significant advantage, particularly in improving print quality. The system utilises both outline and bitmap data during the font rendering and output production process; Adobe Type Manager is regarded as a component that supports this process, although it is not mandatory (Strizver, 2014).

In 1985, Zuzana Licko viewed the limitations of digital tools not as a constraint but as an aesthetic opportunity, and reflected this approach in her typeface designs. Whilst many digital fonts of the era remained tied to traditional forms, Licko's work highlighted the visual language specific to digital production processes. Emigre, founded by her and Rudy VanderLans, is recognised as one of the key representatives of this experimental typographic approach (Lupton, 2010).

IBM's visual identity interprets and depicts the power of symbols and technological leadership through a modern typographic approach. The eye and bee visuals symbolising the letters I and B are formed from the famous Eye-Bee-M letters, which are directly associated with the company and its logo (Baird, 2022). These pictograms, which were original for their time and differed from the legibility norms of traditional letter forms, adopt design principles through a grid-based compositional approach.

Within the context of contemporary digital typography, this approach demonstrates that typography can be creatively transformed even in periods when digital tools were limited. In this framework, determining the x-height requires a delicate balance between legibility and character recognisability. Increasing the x-height widens spaces and gaps, but if taken to extremes, it can reduce character distinguishability; conversely, low values can negatively affect the text's readability (Santa Maria, 2014). The web environment has made the challenges faced by designers more complex, as it partially delegates control over the final appearance of typography to the user (Staples, 2000). The early typographic capabilities of HTML significantly limited aesthetic diversity and text layout capacity due to limited font options and simple structures. During this period, content organisation was largely achieved through table-based layouts. The development of CSS, however, has enabled the creation of more flexible, customisable and visually rich layouts.

The typeface design process is a multi-stage structure that begins with the definition of the form and encompasses systematic development, the expansion of the character set, and technical and aesthetic adjustments. The prototype form established in the initial stage serves as the basis for deriving other characters; in the subsequent process, the character set is completed and optimised through refinements such as kerning and hinting. In the final stage, various variants of the typeface are developed (Daniel Wenzel, n.d.).

The IBM Plex family is significant in terms of contemporary typographic research for three reasons. Firstly, it represents the shift in modern corporate typography from neutrality to character; that is, rather than acting as an invisible carrier, it produces brand personality in a controlled manner. Secondly, with its multi-subfamily structure, it demonstrates that typography should no longer be considered monolithic but rather system-based. Thirdly, its open-source structure demonstrates that corporate design can move beyond being a closed proprietary object to engage with broader design ecosystems. The release of IBM Plex under the Open Font License and its distribution via GitHub demonstrates that this approach embodies not only an aesthetic but also a cultural and technological stance. Within this framework, the comparison of IBM Plex Sans / Serif / Mono should not be reduced to a mere formal typographic analysis. The real issue is how different modes of information are typographically represented within the same brand universe. Sans makes public discourse visible, Serif makes corporate thought visible, and Mono makes the technical infrastructure visible. Thus, the IBM Plex family powerfully demonstrates that typography is not merely about legibility, but a strategic design layer that generates meaning, tone, authority and user experience.

IBM PLEX SANS / SERIF / MONO: A COMPARATIVE TYPOGRAPHIC ANALYSIS

The IBM Plex family is not merely a system offering multiple typefaces within contemporary corporate typography; it is also an integrated design infrastructure that adapts a single brand voice to different contexts. In IBM's official typographic approach, Plex is defined as a global, versatile and "distinctively IBM-specific" family. The fact that the typeface family comprises Sans, Serif, Mono and Sans Condensed sub-families; features roman and true italic styles, multiple weights and a scope extending to over 100 languages, makes this system powerful not only aesthetically but also functionally. For this reason, IBM Plex should be regarded not merely as a single font, but as a typographic ecosystem that produces a consistent corporate tone across different communication layers.

Figure 15. Comparative typographic samples of a, g, R, M, e (In order: Sans, Mono, Serif)

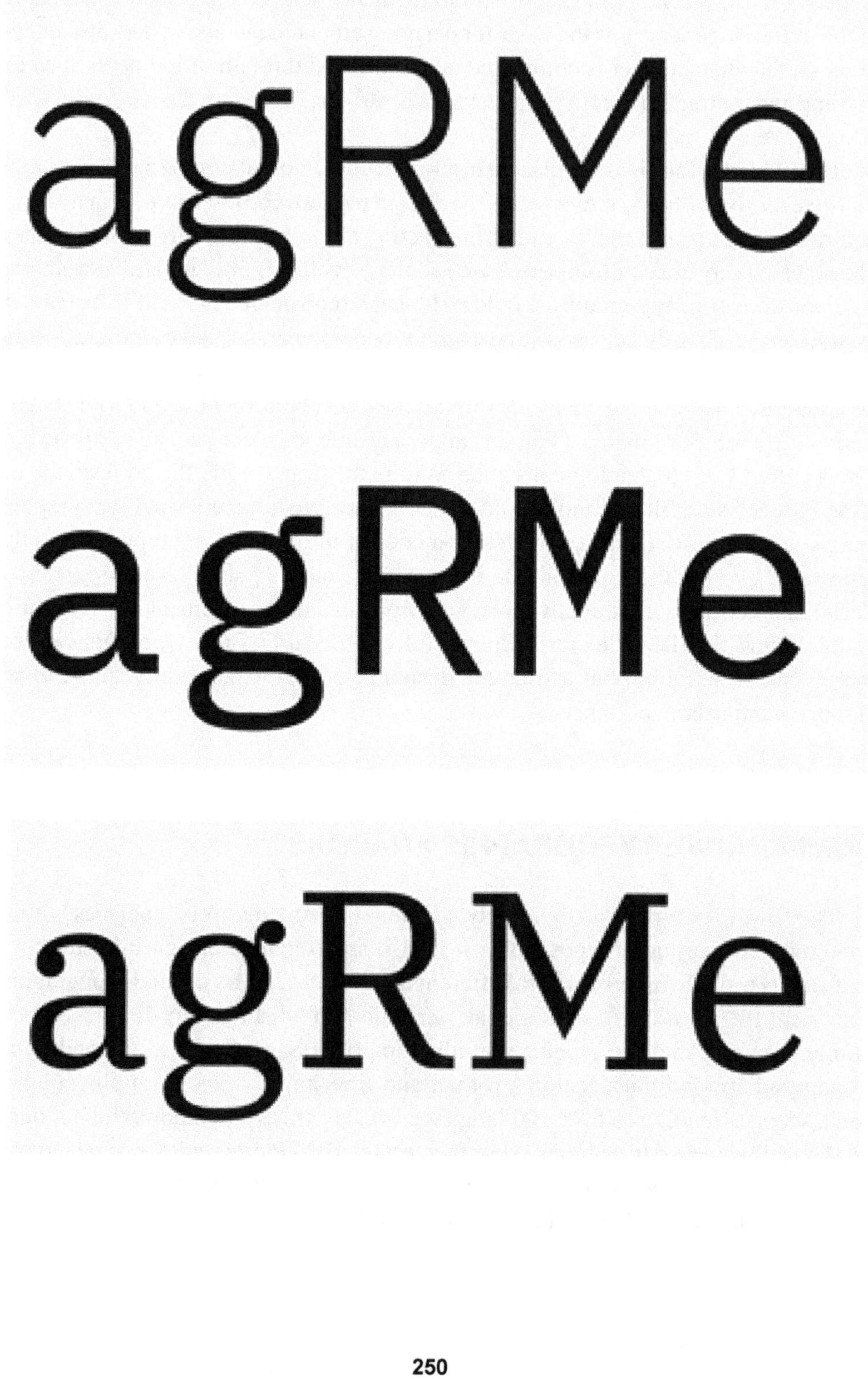

IBM Plex Sans is the most visible and corporate-facing member of the family. According to IBM's design narrative, this typeface was developed by drawing on the grotesque tradition to create an alternative to the modern corporate sans-serif aesthetic exemplified by Helvetica Neue. The defining aim here is to produce a rational yet human voice, rather than a completely anonymous neutrality. Angled terminals, open counterforms and the vertical-angled structure within the inner spaces are balanced by softer curves in the outer contours. This makes Sans a controlled, clear and contemporary option for use in interfaces, corporate communications and headings alike. Sans's primary function is to convey the brand's public and digital identity in the most legible and balanced manner. From a formal perspective, the strength of IBM Plex Sans lies in its ability to remain systematic without becoming overly mechanical. Instead of the horizontal, highly rationalised terminals seen in modernist sans-serif typefaces such as Helvetica, Plex Sans opts for angled terminals that allude to its grotesque roots. Consequently, the typeface maintains its corporate gravitas whilst generating a warmer and more 'conversational' rhythm. In this respect, the sans-serif represents the brand's relationship with technology not merely through technical precision, but through a design language capable of communicating with the user. In other words, Plex Sans is the sub-family that most directly reveals IBM's role as an intermediary between human and machine. (Figure 16)

IBM Plex Serif forms the more textual, cultural and continuity-oriented layer of the same design system. The presence of the Serif sub-family demonstrates that the IBM Plex system is not merely a sans-serif structure focused on digital interfaces; it is designed to function in environments requiring extended reading, editorial layout and a higher level of rhetorical seriousness. Whilst Serif is part of the same design logic as Sans, it offers a more historical tone and a sense of a more established textual tradition. Consequently, Serif plays a more effective role in contexts requiring corporate trust, academic seriousness and editorial depth. The fact that this sub-group is presented within the same system alongside Sans and Mono in IBM's official typeface family ensures that the brand narrative is maintained seamlessly across different media.

The typographic value of Serif lies not in 'softening' the corporate identity, but in assuming a role that supports it with historical legitimacy and textual resilience. Whilst Sans represents a contemporary and functional voice, Serif creates a tone that is more contemplative, more publication-focused and carries a stronger sense of corporate memory. This contrast should be interpreted not as an aesthetic division within the family, but as a distribution of communicative roles. Particularly for long texts, reports, essays or printed corporate publications, the presence of Serif lends the IBM Plex system not only diversity but also discursive flexibility. The fact that a variable font structure has been developed specifically for Serif in the GitHub release notes demonstrates that this sub-family retains its importance in current usage scenarios.

IBM Plex Mono is the most technical member of the family. Its monospaced structure, where each character occupies an equal horizontal space, makes it particularly suitable for coding, data presentation, terminal environments and system-based interfaces. However, Plex Mono is not merely a functional code font; as it adheres to IBM's overall design language, it maintains corporate consistency even in technical contexts. The Google Fonts description notes that the family offers high legibility across print, web and mobile interfaces, whilst specifically highlighting that Mono works well with Serif Regular. This information suggests that Mono is not merely a supporting technical typeface, but a deliberate design element capable of forming an internal family composition. (Figure 17)

Mono's character is based on evoking technical confidence rather than appearing neutral. In contrast to Sans's conversational corporate tone and Serif's textual weight, Mono emphasises a sense of computation, order, infrastructure and precision. Consequently, it plays a meaningful role in user interfaces for code blocks, data tables, in-product technical indicators or developer-focused documentation. The direct integration of Plex's design system into the IBM Carbon system also demonstrates that Mono is not merely a theoretical option, but an actively used component within the product ecosystem.

The fundamental difference between these three sub-families is evident not so much in their form as in their communicative function. Sans operates through high legibility and corporate transparency; Serif conveys textual trust, continuity and editorial seriousness; whilst Mono establishes technical precision, system logic and a sense of digital infrastructure. Nevertheless, these three structures are not disconnected from one another. The strength of IBM Plex lies in its ability to adapt to different contexts without compromising the distinct brand voice of these different sub-families. Thanks to a shared typographic philosophy, sensitivity to proportions, characteristic details and formal harmony within the family, visual kinship is maintained between Sans, Serif and Mono. Consequently, there are not three separate typefaces here, but three different modes of expression for a single corporate identity. (Figure 18)

When viewed comparatively, Sans can be described as the 'primary voice' with the widest range of applications, Serif as the 'secondary depth' focused on intellectual and publishing contexts, and Mono as the 'specialised tone' for technical and structural contexts. This distinction highlights a key strategy in contemporary brand typography: corporate identity is no longer built around a single font, but through font systems that share roles according to different media. The IBM Plex family is successful in this regard; it offers variety without becoming fragmented, and maintains corporate cohesion whilst differentiating itself. (Figure 15)

Figure 16. IBM Plex Sans

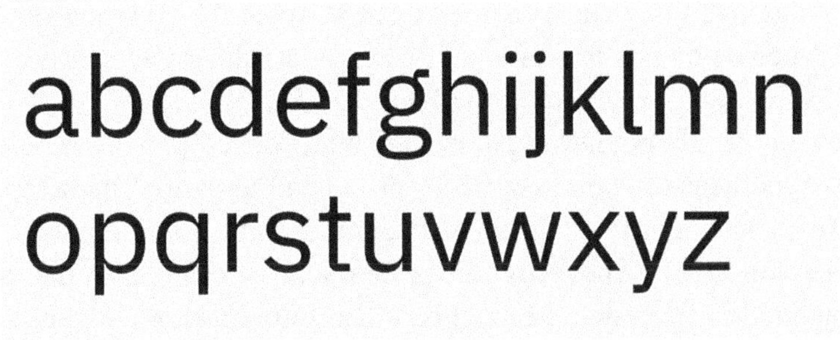

Figure 17. IBM Plex Mono

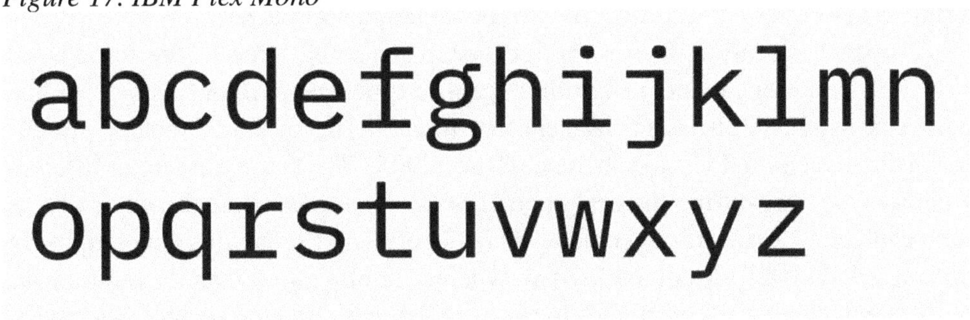

Figure 18. IBM Plex Serif

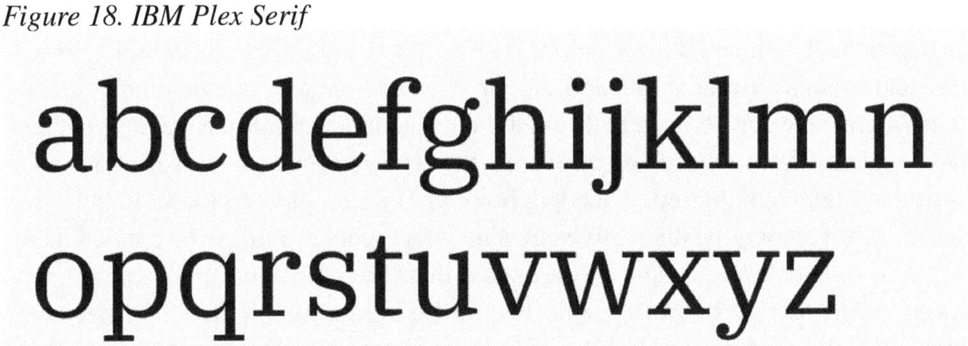

Jan Tschichold, one of the leading designers in the field of typography, outlined and defended many of his new ideas in the field of typography in his 1928 book 'Die Neue Typographie'. 'J. Tschichold recognised the lack of quality in layouts created with distorted typefaces and sought to create a new typography that reflected the spirit, understanding and visual sensibility of the times. The foundation of this new and radical typography lies in a rational design, planned solely to serve communication, whilst avoiding ornamentation (Tschichold, 1995).

Today, a large number of new typefaces are being developed in the field of typography. These typefaces can possess various visual and semantic characteristics, such as rigidity, softness, fragility, traditionalism or modernity. For this reason, during the typeface selection process, not only formal characteristics but also the identity and meaning intended to be conveyed must be taken into account. Advances in digital technology have significantly simplified typeface design processes and contributed to an increase in new typographic productions. However, the widespread adoption of digital design tools has also led to design practices carried out without sufficient knowledge of letter structure and typographic design principles. Traditionally, letterforms are designed according to two fundamental approaches.

A typeface family is formed by the systematic integration of the formal and structural variations associated with a specific typeface. Within this system, the point size used establishes a consistent structure in terms of the characters' proportional dimensions and visual coherence (İstek, 2005). The use of numerous different typefaces together during the design process can lead to perceptual complexity, as each character carries its own unique visual identity and semantic connotations. In this regard, opting for a comprehensive typeface family rather than the random use of different characters contributes to the establishment of a typographic hierarchy, the maintenance of visual balance, and the support of reading flow. The intensive use of uppercase letters can cause the eye to move more across the same visual area, potentially making the reading process more difficult, particularly in long texts. Similarly, the excessive use of bold typefaces can lead to words being perceived as geometric and compact blocks, creating a harsher visual impact. In contrast, lowercase letters enhance readability and support eye movement by creating more distinct distinctions between characters through their ascenders and descenders. Typefaces can adapt to different usage requirements through various stylistic variations such as roman, italic, condensed, extended, bold, bold italic, light and light italic.

Serifs are among the distinctive elements of a typeface and can be applied using different stylistic approaches. It is accepted that these elements enhance the readability of the text by supporting the flow of the eye between letters. Furthermore, serif styles- whether ornate, bold, or simpler and more delicate- reflect the aesthetic sensibilities of their respective eras.

The baseline defines the placement line of the letters, the midline determines the height of lowercase characters, and the top line marks the boundary of uppercase letters. Extensions known as ascenders and descenders refer to the parts of letters that extend above the x-height or below the baseline, whilst the counter defines the empty space within the character. Furthermore, the projections at the serif tips, the main body form; the crossbar and bowl denote the horizontal and curved structural elements, respectively. Details such as the "ear" and "eye" are also considered typographic elements specific to certain letter forms (Sarıkavak, 2004). The x-height is the height between the baseline and the upper limit of lowercase letters (particularly "x, a, e") It has a direct impact on legibility, density and on-screen performance.

Figure 19. IBM Plex Sans, Mono, Serif (x, a, e)

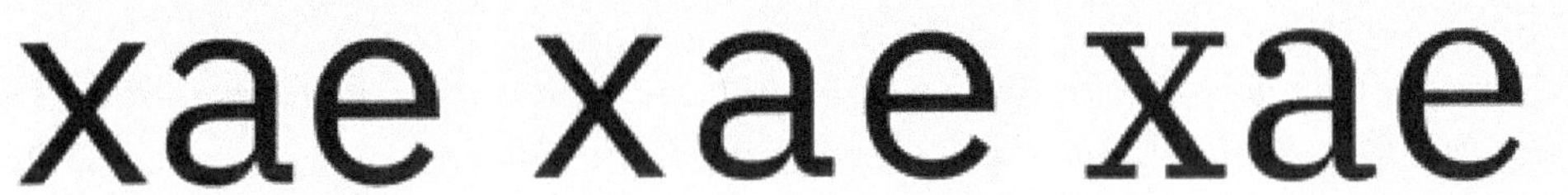

IBM Plex Sans, High X-Height

- The letters "a" and "e" have quite large bodies.
- The x-height is proportionally high relative to the ascenders.
- The counters are open and spacious.
- It is highly legible at small sizes.
- It creates a denser and more compact grey value on the line.
- It is optimised for digital interfaces.

IBM Plex Mono, Controlled / Normalised X-Height

- It is similar to Sans but feels optically more restrained.
- Due to its monospaced structure, the letters appear wider horizontally.
- The 'e' and 'a' are perceived as more mechanical and closed.
- It is optimised for technical readability (code, etc.).
- Even if the x-height is high, the rhythm is different.
- As the letters are of equal width, a 'block effect' is created.

The high x-height enhances the legibility of characters at small sizes, thereby improving accessibility, particularly for screen-based use.

IBM Plex Serif Medium X-Height – Balance and Textual Rhythm

- Ascender/descender areas are more pronounced.
- The serifs enhance vertical movement.
- More classical text proportions are employed.
- It offers a more spacious structure within the line.

- It reduces eye strain in long texts.

The medium x-height, combined with vertical extensions, creates a rhythmic flow within the text, supporting a comfortable reading experience over extended periods. (Figure 19)

Due to the principle of equal width, the perception of x-height is assessed not only in terms of vertical proportions but also in conjunction with horizontal constraints, and this produces a mechanical rhythm within the text texture.

Figure 20. Comparative analysis of x-height and typographic features in the IBM Plex Typeface Family (Sans, Serif, Mono, and Italic Variants)

Feature	Sans	Sans Italic	Serif	Serif Italic	Mono	Mono Italic
x-height	High	High (optically adjusted)	Medium	Medium	Controlled	Controlled
Legibility	Screen-oriented	Supports emphasis	Long-form reading	Enhances reading flow	Technical readability	Technical emphasis
Counter (Aperture)	Wide and open	Slightly narrowed	Balanced	More dynamic	Narrow	Limited
Rhythm	Compact	More dynamic	Balanced	Flowing	Block-like	Semi-block
Structure	Proportional	Slanted	Serif-based	Calligraphic influence	Monospaced	Slanted monospaced

The comparative analysis presented in Figure 20 reveals that the differences within the IBM Plex typeface family are systematically shaped to serve specific functional and communicative purposes. IBM Plex Sans is optimised for digital interfaces requiring clarity at small sizes, featuring a high x-height and open internal spacing. The italic variant, whilst maintaining these fundamental proportions, reinforces emphasis and visual hierarchy through a subtle slant that creates a sense of direction. In contrast, IBM Plex Serif offers a rhythmic structure that supports readability in long texts with a more balanced x-height. The serif italic variant transforms this structure into a more fluid and expressive reading experience through calligraphic effects.

IBM Plex Mono, on the other hand, operates within a constrained system where each character occupies the same horizontal space due to its monospaced structure. This creates a regular, block-like visual texture, making it a preferred choice for technical and code-based applications. Although the Mono italic variant offers limited formal variation due to the fixed-width constraint, it continues to fulfil its function of creating emphasis.

To summarise, the differences between the Sans, Serif and Mono variants and their italic counterparts can be understood through a system where x-height, structural construction and formal variations work in tandem. These variables determine not only the visual quality of the typeface, but also its legibility, rhythm and functionality in different usage contexts.

CONCLUSION

Today, the proliferation of multiple screens and digital platforms is transforming communication forms, necessitating new approaches in design processes. Increasing visual density and an overload of messages limit user attention whilst diminishing the impact of traditional representational forms. Under these conditions, it has become essential for organisations and brands to adopt flexible and distinctive identity systems in order to establish sustainable communication with their target audiences and stand out in a competitive environment. Within this process of transformation, the concepts of typeface and visual identity are also undergoing constant change, adapting to the demands of the modern age.

IBM Plex Sans, Serif and Mono form a typographic structure that is stylistically distinct yet semantically complementary. Sans embodies the contemporary corporate identity; Serif conveys textual authority; whilst Mono represents technical precision and the logic of digital systems. This tripartite structure ensures that the IBM brand not only appears consistent but is also able to communicate with the appropriate tone across different communication channels. For this reason, the IBM Plex family can be regarded as a powerful example worthy of examination in contemporary corporate typography work, in terms of both design strategy and brand language, as well as digital systems.

It is anticipated that this will also lay the groundwork for generative typography, which expands the aesthetic and functional boundaries of algorithmic typographic thinking. Artificial intelligence, machine learning and variable font technologies have ushered in a new era where typography can adapt its form according to time, data and the audience. This transformation points to a communication paradigm in which, in the future, text will be designed not merely to be read, but to interact. Generative typography, which makes visual communication interactive, is able to establish a more solid foundation through the variable structure introduced by algorithmic typography, where form is no longer an end result but, in a sense, a continuous process.

Variable typefaces are an advanced typographic technology that combines different style and weight options within a single font file. Whereas in traditional font structures, each variation such as Light, Regular, Bold or Italic requires separate files, in this system all variants are managed through a single file. This diversity is achieved through 'axes'. The most common axes include weight, width, slant/italic, and optical size, which optimises readability at different dimensions.

Using multiple weights and italic styles in a web interface requires separate files to be loaded for each variation in traditional font systems, which creates an additional performance burden due to multiple HTTP requests. In contrast, variable fonts combine these variations into a single file, reducing data transfer. This approach improves page load times whilst contributing to a smoother and more seamless user experience.

In design processes, variable fonts offer designers a more flexible scope of control by freeing them from fixed typographic constraints. Weight values can be finely adjusted to ensure headings and text achieve the intended visual impact. This adaptable structure provides significant advantages, particularly in interface designs tailored to different screen sizes. For example, to make more efficient use of the limited space on mobile screens, the width of the typeface can be reduced; conversely, the weight can be increased to maintain readability. Whilst such detailed typographic intervention is only possible to a limited extent with traditional static typefaces, variable typefaces provide a higher degree of design flexibility.

By providing precise control over typographic parameters and taking the design process beyond traditional limitations, variable fonts offer significant flexibility, particularly in adapting to different screen sizes; for instance, in mobile interfaces, the width can be reduced to save space whilst the weight is increased to maintain readability. Furthermore, within the scope of micro-interactions, the fluid transformation of typographic properties such as weight rather than merely a colour change, provides the user with stronger and more dynamic feedback, thereby enriching the experience. Such applications point to a level of control that is only achievable to a limited extent with static font structures.

Typefaces also stand out as a typographic solution offering advanced capabilities in terms of accessibility and readability. Thanks to the optical size axis, the typeface can adjust itself to harmonise both functionally and aesthetically across different point sizes. Furthermore, interfaces that allow users to adjust typographic properties such as weight and width according to their individual preferences personalise the reading experience. These qualities demonstrate that variable fonts will continue to offer an effective solution in the future and reduce the need for extensive typeface families.

Variable fonts are regarded as a transformative technology that directly influences key components of UI/UX design, such as performance, flexibility, interaction and accessibility. However, it should not be overlooked that there is a certain learning curve and specific implementation principles to be observed during the usage process. From the user's perspective, the possibilities offered by this technology contribute to the evolution of typographic design towards a more fluid and dynamic structure; it is thought that this goes beyond the static concept of fonts and reshapes the perspective on design. Although support in browsers and design software has advanced significantly, despite the flexibility it offers on older platforms, it also brings certain limitations and may give rise to compatibility issues. Furthermore, the multitude of variation options can make it difficult to maintain consistency in design. For this reason, the pre-definition of specific axis values within design systems is considered an effective approach to managing this complexity.

The original contribution of this study centres on algorithmic typographic analyses using the IBM Plex Sans variable typeface as a case study. It demonstrates how algorithmic design decisions influence the textual experience. This approach overcomes the limitations of traditional analyses in typeface studies which focus solely on letter anatomy and emphasises the need for a systematic evaluation of variable typefaces.

Consequently, the IBM Plex Sans variable typeface represents a holistic typographic design philosophy that is measured, balanced and harmonious with the text. In this respect, the study contributes to typographic literature by re-examining the role of variable typefaces in typeface analysis, highlighting the potential of the IBM Plex Sans typeface family in terms of legibility, readability and perceptibility.

REFERENCES

Ambrose, G., & Harris, P. (2013). *The Fundamentals of Typography* (Turkish ed.). Literatür Publishing.

Baırd, R. (2022). Eye, Bee, M. Logo Histories. Retrieved 29 April 2025. https://www.logohistories.com/p/ibm

Becer, E. (2007). *Modern Art and New Typography*. Dost Kitabevi.

Berlow, D. (2017a). *Amstelvar* [Variable font]. Google Fonts / Font Bureau. https://github.com/googlefonts/amstelvar

Berlow, D. (2017b). *Decovar* [Variable font]. Google Fonts / Font Bureau. https://github.com/googlefonts/decovar

Bohnacker, H., Groß, B., Laub, J., & Lazzeroni, C. (2012). *Generative Design: Visualise, Program, and Create with Processing*. Princeton Architectural Press.

Dinamo Typefaces. (2018). *Font Gauntlet* [Variable font testing tool]. https://fontgauntlet.com Retrieved March 19, 2026.

Galanter, P. (2003). What Is Generative Art? Complexity Theory as a Context for Art Theory. In *Proceedings of the International Conference on Generative Art*. Milan, Italy.

Garnham, P. (2021). The world's first variable font logo for WPP. Monotype. Retrieved 16 April 2025, from Monotype' – world's first variable font logo for WPP.

Hanzer, E. (2018). *Phase* [Variable font]. https://eliashanzer.com

Huot-Marchand, T. (2018). *Minérale* [Variable font]. 205TF. https://www.205.tf/designers/thomas-huot-marchand

IBM. (2017). *IBM Plex: Languages* [Typeface specimen]. IBM. https://www.ibm.com/plex/languages Retrieved March 19, 2026.

IBM (n.d.). IBM Plex specifications. Retrieved 16 April 2025, from IBM Plex Specifications.

İstek, R. (2005). *Typography and Page Layout in Visual Communication*. Pusula Publishing.

Kaplan, E. (2022). Use of Variable Fonts in Corporate Identity Design (Master's thesis). Graduate School of Fine Arts, Department of Graphic Design, Mimar Sinan Fine Arts University, Istanbul, Turkey.

Kolarevic, B. (2003). *Architecture in the Digital Age: Design and Manufacturing*. Spon Press.

Lupton, E. (2010). Thinking with Type: A Critical Guide for Designers, Writers, Editors, and Students (2nd ed.). New York: Princeton Architectural Press.

Mickel, J., & Imas, L. (2018). *Adineue Chop* [Variable font]. MCKL / Adidas.

Monotype. (2019). *The world's first variable font logo* [Web page]. Monotype. https://www.monotype.com/resources/monotype-labs/world%E2%80%99s-first-variable-font-logo Retrieved March 20, 2026.

Penney, L. (2016). *Axis-Praxis* [Variable font playground]. https://www.axis-praxis.org Retrieved March 18, 2026.

Ross, D. J. (2017). *Fit* [Variable font]. DJR. https://djr.com/fit

Santa Maria, J. (2014). *On web typography*. A Book Apart. https://abookapart.com/products/on-web-typography

Sarıkavak, N. K. (2004). *Foundations of contemporary typography*. Seçkin Publishing.

Staples, L. (2000). Typography and the screen: A technical chronology of digital typography, 1984–1997. *Design Issues, 16*(3), 19–34. https://www.jstor.org/stable/1511813. DOI: 10.1162/07479360052053306

Strizver, I. (2014). *Type Rules! The Designer's Guide to Professional Typography* (4th ed.). Wiley.

Tschichold, J. (1995). *The New Typography: A Handbook for Modern Designers* (McLean, R., Trans.). University of California Press. (Original work published 1928)

Van Halem, H. (2017). *Wind* [Variable font]. Typotheque. https://www.typotheque.com/fonts/wind

Wenzel, D. (n.d.). Automation. Daniel Wenzel. Retrieved 16 April 2025, from https://wenzeldaniel.com/w_atd.php

Willen, B., and Strals, N. (2009). Lettering & type: Creating letters and designing typefaces Princeton Architectural Press.

Chapter 10
From Screen to Lifestyle:
Cinematic Branding and the Global Rise of Anime in Visual Communication

Maria Risya Maharani
http://orcid.org/0009-0000-5196-916X
LSPR Institute of Communication and Business, Indonesia

Noprita Herari
http://orcid.org/0009-0009-2497-5340
Universitas Negeri Jakarta, Indonesia

ABSTRACT

This chapter explores the evolution of anime from a niche Japanese subculture into a global visual force that shapes contemporary design and branding practices. Using a qualitative approach that includes literature review, anime analysis, non-participant observation of fandom communities, and interviews with fans and scholars, the study examines how anime has become a strategic site for brand alliances. The findings show that brands increasingly adapt anime's characters, narratives, and symbols to reshape their visual identities, while fan practices such as cosplay, fan art, and digital content creation generate new meanings that circulate across media platforms. Together, these interactions highlight how anime, brands, and fandom co-produce a dynamic cultural-visual ecosystem that influences strategies in communication, cultural branding, and identity design.

DOI: 10.4018/979-8-3373-6680-7.ch010

INTRODUCTION

Over the past two decades, anime has transcended its status as a mere entertainment product to become a complex and globally influential visual art form (Welch, 2024). It synthesizes cinematic aesthetics, distinctive character design, and highly detailed world-building to create an emotionally resonant visual experience. Within this medium, every frame functions not only as a moving narrative but as a canvas saturated with symbols, colors, and affect (Santiago Iglesias, 2021). In the context of visual communication, anime represents a convergence of fine arts, graphic design, and cinematic technology, forging a new paradigm for conveying cultural meanings and values (Deng, 2025).

Central to this medium is character design, the primary element that distinguishes anime from other global animation styles (Kane & Juliau, 2026). Through expressive linework, hyperbolic body proportions, and distinctive facial mimicry, anime design does more than strengthen visual identity; it facilitates a profound emotional bond between the character and the viewer. Anime characters are engineered to live beyond the screen, manifesting in merchandise, memes, and even as symbols of personal identity for fans. Consequently, character design is not merely an aesthetic choice but also a potent form of nonverbal communication that conveys messages about personality, values, and social aspirations (Sagardia, 2017). Every detail (from hair color and costume to combat style) carries specific cultural connotations that are instantly recognizable to a transnational Audience.

Figure 1. Comparative visual mood mapping of Your Name, Demon Slayer, and Attack on Titan

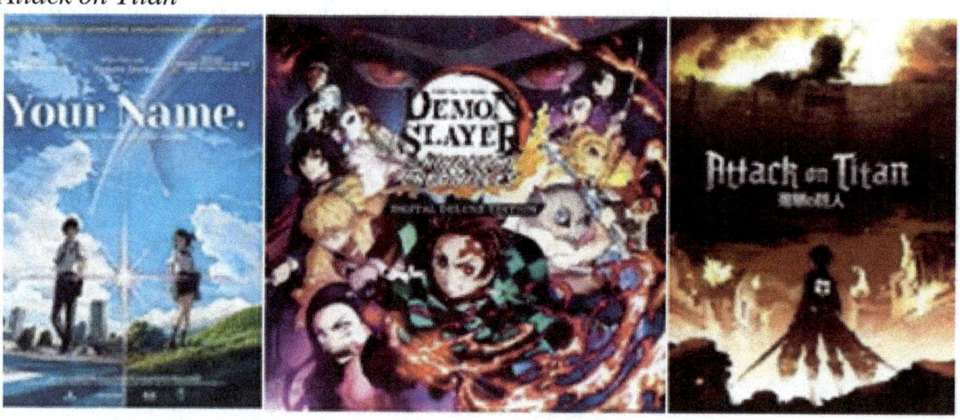

Beyond character design, color plays a crucial role in shaping emotional atmosphere and symbolic meaning in anime. Rather than serving as decoration, it functions as a strategic visual element that guides audience perception. Works such as *Your Name* and *Demon Slayer* use warm tones to evoke hope and nostalgia, while *Attack on Titan* employs darker palettes to convey tension and conflict (See Figure 1). Through these chromatic systems, anime creates emotional experiences that resonate across cultural boundaries. These visual elements form a unified visual grammar that enables anime to communicate meaning efficiently without relying heavily on language. As a result, anime functions as a universal medium of emotional communication, allowing global audiences to interpret narratives intuitively.

METHODOLOGY

This chapter adopts a qualitative exploratory design that combines a focused literature review with semi-structured interviews with anime audiences. The literature review provides the theoretical foundation for examining anime as a form of visual communication, branding as cultural design, and the emergence of cinematic branding as an analytical framework. The interviews were conducted to explore how audiences interpret anime-based collaborations, particularly in relation to authenticity, emotional engagement, cultural legitimacy, and narrative coherence.

As anime has gained greater visibility in popular culture, its aesthetics have increasingly influenced fashion, digital media, and branding. Brands now adopt anime's visual language to convey authenticity, cultural relevance, and emotional appeal, especially among younger audiences. This shift highlights how anime has evolved from a form of entertainment into a cultural resource within contemporary branding. To investigate this transformation, the present study combines conceptual inquiry with audience interpretation, allowing the chapter to connect broader theoretical debates with lived perceptions from anime viewers and fans.

Participants were selected through purposive sampling in order to reflect different modes of engagement with anime culture. The sample included active community participants, casual viewers, and a dedicated merchandise collector, enabling the study to capture a range of perspectives on how anime aesthetics and brand collaborations are understood. Rather than seeking statistical representativeness, the interviews were designed to provide interpretive depth across distinct audience positions. This approach makes it possible to compare how more active fans and more casual audiences assign meaning, value, and legitimacy to anime-based branding practices.

Table 1. Informant's profile

No	Informant Code	Age (y.o)	Informant Category
1.	A	36	Anime enthusiast, active in events and communities
2.	B	25	Anime merchandise collector
3.	C	23	Anime enthusiast, inactive in events and communities
4.	D	24	Anime enthusiast, inactive in events and communities
5.	E	27	Anime enthusiast, active in events and communities
6.	F	23	Anime enthusiast, inactive in events and communities
7.	G	26	Anime enthusiast, active in events and communities

The inclusion of active community members allows the study to capture perspectives from audiences who are deeply embedded in participatory fandom culture, where collaboration, event culture, and symbolic recognition are particularly significant. By contrast, the inclusion of viewers who are less active in communities helps broaden the analysis beyond highly engaged fandom spaces and offers insight into how anime branding is interpreted in more everyday forms of consumption. The merchandise collector provides an additional perspective on anime as material culture, highlighting how products function not only as commodities but also as identity markers and symbolic artifacts within fan communities.

The interviews were semi-structured and focused on participants' perceptions of anime-based collaborations, including authenticity, emotional attachment, narrative fit, lifestyle branding, and ethical concerns. The interview material was interpreted through thematic analysis, with recurring ideas grouped into broader analytical categories such as cultural legitimacy, participatory validation, affective commodification, and narrative integrity. These thematic categories were then linked back to the chapter's three guiding questions:

1. How does anime function as a visual communication system that shapes global consumer perception and emotional engagement?
2. How do brands appropriate anime aesthetics and narratives to construct cultural design strategies in contemporary branding?
3. How has anime × brand collaboration evolved into a form of branding within global pop culture ecosystems?

All participants were informed about the purpose of the study and agreed to participate voluntarily. To protect confidentiality, their identities are anonymized in this chapter through informant codes (A–G). Because the study focuses on non-sensitive perceptions of media and branding practices, the interview material is presented in anonymized form and used solely for academic analysis.

THE ARCHITECTURE OF IMMERSION: WORLD-BUILDING AND SEMIOTICS

One of anime's key strengths lies in its capacity for world-building, where fictional universes function as complex systems of values and social structures rather than mere backdrops (Zahlten, 2010). Through detailed settings such as *Fullmetal Alchemist* or *One Piece*, anime translates philosophical and social ideas into accessible visual narratives, allowing audiences to engage with and internalize these worlds (Minea, 2025). This immersive quality positions anime as a powerful medium of visual communication. Its aesthetics operate as a semiotic system that conveys values such as courage, empathy, and solidarity, while also functioning as a form of cultural diplomacy that introduces Japanese cultural perspectives globally (Alani, 2022). Rather than relying on explicit explanation, anime communicates through affect, inviting audiences to feel and interpret meaning across cultural boundaries (Chiu & Chang, 2018).

From a semiotic perspective, every visual element in anime acts as a signifier of meaning. Composition, lighting, and motion function as communicative tools that allow viewers to interpret and reproduce meaning through engagement and participation (Darmawan et al., 2025; Ahmad et al., 2012). This process extends into digital spaces, where anime aesthetics shape identity expression through avatars, memes, and online interaction, reflecting a shift toward visually driven communication among younger audiences (Maliha & Aziz, 2024; Welch, 2024). Ultimately, anime demonstrates that visual communication is driven not by realism but by emotional resonance and symbolic depth. This integration of aesthetics and meaning not only redefines global visual narratives but also positions anime as a foundation for contemporary branding practices, where visual art and commercial strategy increasingly converge.

Branding as Cultural Design

Over the past two decades, branding has shifted from a commercial function to a form of cultural design, in which brands construct values, symbols, and narratives within society (Cayla & Arnould, 2008; McCracken, 2015). In this context, anime acts as a cultural interface that connects brands with the global pop-culture ecosystem through its distinctive visual aesthetics and symbolic richness (Lamarre, 2009; Napier, 2018; Steinberg, 2012).

Collaborations between brands and anime IPs extend beyond surface-level visuals, involving narrative and aesthetic integration that aligns brand identity with the values of the anime. Through strong iconographic power, anime characters enable the transfer of emotional resonance from fandom to brand, while anime's visual grammar further strengthens this connection (Allison, 2006; Azuma & Abel, 2009; Manovich, 2013).

The Fan Perspective: Utility, Validation, and the "Logic of the Unexpected"

While the concept of branding is a seamless transfer of meaning, the community's reception is often dictated by a blend of utilitarian value and cultural validation. In interviews regarding these collaborations, E (27) expressed a selective engagement strategy:

> *"For me, it depends on whether the brand is something I actually use. If I don't need the product, I might only buy it once out of curiosity or FOMO (Fear of Missing Out). However, if the collaboration involves my favorite food or drink, I'm much more likely to return. Even if the 'merchandise' is just a simple sticker, I'm happy as long as it's a brand I enjoy."*

This highlights that for "Branding as Cultural Design" to succeed, the product must remain functional in the fan's daily life. Yet, even when a collaboration seems conceptually distant (what some might call "narrative dissonance"), fans find value in the societal recognition it brings to their fandom. For instance, reflecting on the surprising partnership between *One Piece* and the NBA, E (27) noted:

> *"I feel happy when my fandom suddenly gets a collaboration because it feels like we are being 'recognized' by the mainstream, even if it doesn't seem to connect at first. Take the One Piece x NBA (basketball) collab, for example. There isn't even any basketball in the anime! It doesn't strictly 'make sense,' but the recognition itself is exciting."*

Convergence and Global Visual Grammar

These industry-crossing collaborations (from *Uniqlo x Jujutsu Kaisen*, where clothing serves as a medium for fandom affiliation (Kawamura, 2016), to Coca-Cola x One Piece, which uses world-building to create immersive digital activations) reflect the logic of convergence culture (Jenkins, 2006). In this environment, brand and pop-culture content mutually reinforce one another's meaning.

In the digital realm, this is most evident on platforms like TikTok, where anime aesthetics have become a global visual grammar. Through filters, audio remixes, and specific editing styles, anime provides an expressive language that transcends borders (Leaver et al., 2020). Ultimately, branding as cultural design positions anime not merely as visual inspiration, but as an active cultural framework that shapes the identity and communication strategies of modern brands.

Fandom and Participatory Aesthetics

Fandom plays a central role in contemporary branding practices. Fans no longer function merely as passive consumers; they are active co-creators who expand, modify, and renegotiate the visual meanings of both brands and anime works. Through practices such as cosplay, fan art, video editing, and community forum discussions, fandoms construct what Jenkins (2006) defines as participatory culture, a creative ecosystem where production and consumption occur simultaneously. This visual activity generates a rich form of participatory communication. Whether through cosplay photography, illustrations, memes, or Anime Music Videos (AMVs), these creations serve as a medium for re-interpreting symbols and characters, strengthening emotional proximity while triggering the circulation of new meanings across digital networks (Lamerichs, 2018).

In this context, fans do not just extend the anime narrative; they construct an aesthetic that demands brands be more responsive and adaptive to community dynamics. To better manage fan-driven content, brands are intentionally creating collaborative spaces and providing official, remixable media to guide fan participation (Reid et al., 2026). However, the community draws a sharp distinction between a collaboration that is "culturally integrated" and one that is merely superficial. A (36) explained during an interview regarding apparel collaborations (such as Uniqlo):

"In my opinion, a culturally successful collaboration includes references from the anime's story itself. When we see a design that follows the plot, we immediately understand the meaning behind it; we get carried away by the emotions of the image, whether it's sadness, excitement, or joy. Furthermore, designs that highlight memorable locations from the story act as a tribute to the fans. It makes you feel like a proud, long-time 'wibu' (otaku) because, usually, it's a 'those who know, know' kind of thing."

This "insider knowledge" creates a sense of belonging and authenticity that resonates deeply within the fandom. Conversely, when a brand fails to integrate into the fast-moving cultural ecology of the fandom, the result is perceived as "shallow branding", or what the community calls *tempel gambar* (merely pasting an image). A (36) also noted the lack of "soul" in such designs:

"The ones that just 'paste' images usually only feature large character faces or the anime's title, so there is no 'soul' when you wear it; it feels ordinary. It becomes very obvious that the brand is just jumping on the bandwagon. For example, when Demon Slayer is out in theaters, suddenly everyone starts selling clothes with that theme."

According to Naeem et al. (2025), adopting an aesthetic style rooted within the community enables a brand to construct a more authentic narrative. By avoiding the "bandwagon" approach and instead engaging the emotional and narrative depth valued by fans, brands can move beyond temporary popularity. This fan response also reflects a broader shift in digital communication, where influence increasingly works through the orchestration of narrative, symbolic identity, and multiplatform visibility rather than through message transmission alone. In this sense, anime-based brand alliances become effective not merely because they display recognizable imagery, but because they mobilize emotional resonance, cultural positioning, and narrative coherence (Riyanto et al., 2026).

EVOLUTION OF ANIME BRAND ALLIANCES (2020-2025)

The globalization of anime as a branding powerhouse resulted from deliberate strategic shifts, evolving alongside digital media trends and the fluid movement of culture across borders. Between 2020 and 2025, anime intellectual properties (IPs) evolved from entertainment assets into symbolic resources that influence consumer identity and lifestyle expression.

The COVID-19 pandemic marked a critical turning point, accelerating digital media consumption and expanding the role of streaming platforms such as Netflix and Crunchyroll. Despite disruptions in the global film industry, anime demonstrated strong resilience and increased global visibility, reinforcing its position within international media markets (MPPA, 2025). This shift enabled anime to reach broader audiences and positioned it as a powerful cultural interface for brands (Denison, 2015; Noh, 2022).

At the same time, the rise of participatory digital culture, driven by algorithmic platforms such as TikTok, Instagram, and YouTube, transformed anime into a transmedia phenomenon embedded in everyday communication (Jenkins, 2006). As platform algorithms increasingly privilege content aligned with user interests, emotional engagement, and patterns of circulation, anime aesthetics have become highly visible and widely shared across digital environments (Herari et al., 2026). This development also reflects broader dynamics within the passion and creator economy, where digital actors sustain visibility not through exposure alone, but through platform literacy, continuous refinement, and the ability to cultivate communities across interconnected media environments (Herari et al., 2025).

In the case of anime, this helps explain why its aesthetics travel so effectively across TikTok, Instagram, YouTube, and merchandise cultures: anime is not merely watched, but continually reformatted, recirculated, and lived through platform-based cultural participation. Within this ecosystem, anime no longer functions only as entertainment, but as a recognizable visual language through which younger audiences communicate moods, identities, and cultural belonging. This expanded visibility has made anime increasingly relevant not only as a cultural form, but also as a strategic resource for contemporary branding.

Industry data further highlights the growing economic significance of anime, with rapid expansion in global markets, licensing, and cross-industry collaborations (AJA, 2025; Dentsu, 2025). As a result, brands across sectors began moving beyond simple merchandise collaborations toward more integrated approaches that combine narrative, experience, and lifestyle branding.

Overall, the 2020–2025 period represents a key transition in which anime shifted from a popular media product to a central element of cultural branding. Within this context, anime–brand collaborations developed increasing strategic complexity, reflecting the convergence of visual culture, digital ecosystems, and consumer engagement. This study, therefore, approaches these collaborations not as isolated campaigns but as part of a broader phenomenon of cinematic branding, where narrative, fandom, and brand identity intersect within global pop culture ecosystems.

Phase I: Digital Acceleration and Mainstream Penetration (2020–2021)

The COVID-19 pandemic accelerated global media consumption toward streaming platforms, transforming anime from a niche subculture into a mainstream phenomenon. The success of *Demon Slayer: Mugen Train* demonstrated the strong global appeal of anime IPs and their ability to compete with dominant film industries (MPPA, 2025; Madaan, 2025).

Despite a decline in overall box office, anime showed remarkable resilience and gained greater visibility, highlighting its growing importance in the global media landscape (Noh, 2024). This shift encouraged brands to recognize anime as a powerful cultural medium capable of reaching broad audiences. In response, brands such as Uniqlo integrated anime into retail strategies through capsule collections aligned with digital releases. These collaborations transformed anime into tangible lifestyle products, allowing audiences to maintain a connection with digital narratives during pandemic conditions (Kiso, 2023).

Phase II: Narrative Integration and High-Street Collaborations (2022–2023)

By 2022, brand alliances began to transcend the rudimentary "logo-slapping" model, pivoting toward a sophisticated paradigm of profound narrative integration. Collaborations involving major cinematic releases, such as *One Piece Film: Red* and *Jujutsu Kaisen*, demonstrated that product design was no longer merely about visual illustration but was instead engineered to reflect a character's intrinsic values and storyline (Yulianti et al., 2025). This period saw the rise of "high-street" and luxury anime collaborations, in which the aesthetics were subtly woven into the garment's DNA rather than displayed as overt branding (See Figure 2).

Figure 2. The evolution of design philosophy: transitioning from superficial graphics to character-driven integrated aesthetics (Dessert Cart, 2026; Dolce & Gabbana, 2022)

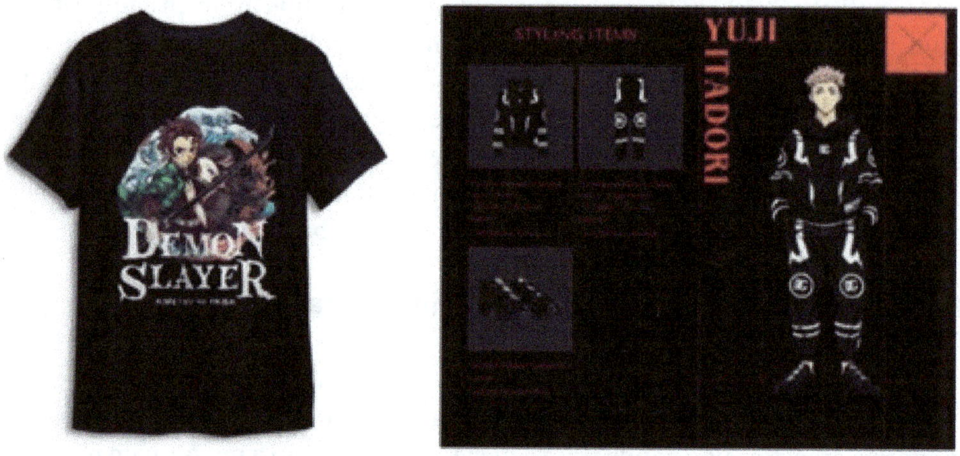

This shift is deeply rooted in the audience's demand for semiotic authenticity. Industry data from Dentsu (2025) supports this, highlighting that approximately 28% of global consumers are willing to pay a premium for products that maintain a deep narrative bond with their favourite Intellectual Properties (IPs). While the data shows a robust positive correlation between fandom loyalty and brand equity, primary interviews conducted for this study reveal the psychological reasoning behind this "premium" value. F (23), though inactive as a member of the anime community, also emphasized that true authenticity lies in "subtle nods" rather than overt imagery:

> *"I always look for the hidden details... it proves that the brand actually understands the lore and the soul of the series... When a brand integrates niche references, it shows they've done their research and actually respect the fan base."*

This insight suggests that a brand's "cultural literacy" (the ability to decode and re-encode anime lore into fashion) has become a prerequisite for market entry. This process involves a strategic "brand acculturation" in which the brand's distinct characteristics are blended with the anime's core content without compromising the original's integrity. When executed correctly, this synergy creates a new sense of "uniqueness" that justifies the collaboration's existence in a crowded market.

However, this psychological shift requires brands to move beyond being external commercial entities. To foster "affective loyalty," they must position themselves as authentic extensions of the anime's fictional universe. Interviews with fans established a rigorous standard for these alliances, as they increasingly reject "lazy" executions that lack a creative *raison d'être*. Insights from the field emphasize that a successful collaboration must transcend surface-level aesthetics, as B (25) said:

> *"It must be more than just placing a logo or a character on a package. It needs to have a narrative, a creative reason to exist, and a level of visual storytelling that respects the source material. Without those elements, it just feels like a hollow product."*

Consequently, in the era of branding, the narrative serves as the primary value driver. By prioritizing storytelling and semiotic depth, brands can successfully transition from mere vendors to meaningful participants in fans' lifestyles, ensuring long-term engagement in an increasingly discerning market.

Phase III: Aesthetic Ubiquity and the Rise of Immersive Lifestyle Ecosystems (2024–2025)

Entering the 2024–2025 period, the landscape of brand alliances has undergone a paradigm shift from passive consumption toward experiential branding. In this phase, alliances are no longer mass-targeted; instead, they are hyper-segmented based on the psychographic profiles of specific fandoms. This strategy represents the pinnacle of *Cinematic Branding*, where the boundaries between physical reality and fictional narratives become increasingly porous.

1. High-Fashion Synergy and the Transformation of Character Symbolism

The integration of anime into high fashion and premium streetwear has evolved beyond aesthetic mimicry, focusing instead on a symbolic synthesis where the narrative of the media aligns with the heritage of the brand. Partnerships such as PUMA x *One Piece* demonstrate how character elements can transfer cultural meaning and identity to consumers, positioning anime as a lifestyle statement rather than mere entertainment (Grand View Research, 2025).

The success of these collaborations depends on cultural literacy, as fans value subtle references and narrative depth over overt imagery. Similarly, collaborations like Dolce & Gabbana x *Jujutsu Kaisen* show how anime aesthetics have been integrated into contemporary luxury, attracting younger audiences who associate luxury with cultural relevance rather than tradition.

2. Domesticity and Family-Centric Alliances: Broadening the Consumer Demographic

Anime has also expanded into everyday consumer sectors through titles such as *Spy x Family*, enabling brands to adopt warmer and more inclusive identities. These collaborations allow anime aesthetics to enter household goods, automotive, and FMCG sectors, positioning anime as an intergenerational cultural bridge (Goswami, 2025). By aligning with narratives of domestic harmony, brands can create emotional connection and relatability, transforming collaborations from decorative branding into meaningful extensions of the story world.

3. Transmedia Ecosystems and AI-Driven Personalization

The rise of transmedia ecosystems further extends anime into digital and technological domains. IPs such as *Solo Leveling* illustrate how anime branding now integrates with gaming hardware and digital environments, creating immersive user experiences (See Figure 3). Through these integrations, anime becomes part of everyday digital interaction, where devices function as extensions of fictional worlds and enhance emotional engagement (Dentsu, 2025).

Figure 3. Anime as digital ecosystem: Hardware integration and transmedia branding (Starforge Systems, 2026)

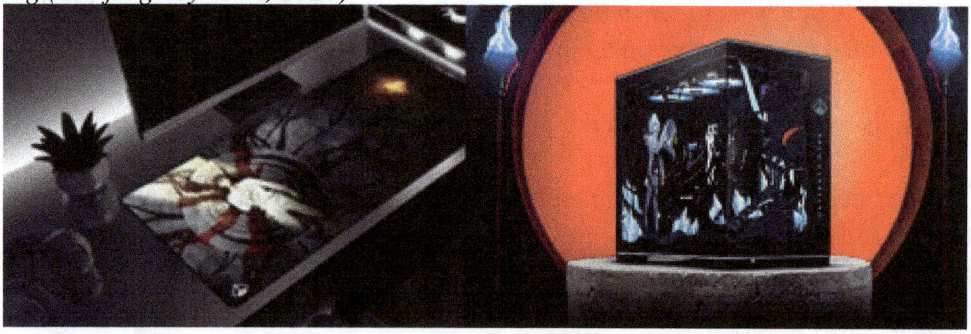

While critics might view this expansion as mere commercialization, members of the community perceive it as a vital evolution of the art form itself. When asked about the "lifestyle-ization" of anime through hardware and consumer goods, A (36) offered a nuanced defense:

> *"I don't think [lifestyle-izing anime] should be seen negatively. While there are people who make a living from it, I don't think it diminishes the artistic meaning. On the contrary, I believe those who turn anime into a lifestyle have enriched*

its artistic significance. Art today has moved past traditional drawing; it has become the way we live and survive. Essentially, instead of diluting the art, these integrations enrich and expand the artistic vision of anime."

This perspective suggests that the integration of anime into physical hardware is not a distraction from the art but a contemporary expansion of it, transforming the "viewing" experience into a "living" experience.

4. The Technological Frontier: AI, AR, and the Risk of Narrative Hollowness

The integration of Artificial Intelligence (AI) and Augmented Reality (AR) represents the next stage of cinematic branding, enabling hyper-personalized interactions between consumers and anime characters as virtual brand ambassadors. Through these technologies, users can engage with characters in real time, creating more immersive and interactive brand experiences.

However, this development also introduces the risk of "narrative hollowness." Without meaningful storytelling, technological integration may be perceived as superficial. To maintain authenticity, AI-driven interactions must preserve the narrative depth and emotional essence of the original work. Ultimately, the effectiveness of these technologies depends on their ability to sustain the "soul" of the anime. Without a clear creative foundation, even advanced innovations risk weakening the emotional resonance that defines the fandom experience.

FROM ADVERTISING TO CINEMATIC BRANDING

Contemporary branding is no longer defined solely by visibility, but by its ability to create meaning, sustain emotional continuity, and foster cultural belonging. This shift is particularly evident in anime-related collaborations, where success depends not on logo exposure but on a brand's ability to integrate into existing symbolic worlds. In this context, branding moves from representation toward immersive cultural participation.

Traditional advertising relied on recognition, repetition, and message clarity, positioning the brand as sender and the consumer as receiver. While this foundational model provides a useful baseline, it fails to capture the complexity of modern pop culture collaborations, where brands function as integrated components within broader narrative frameworks and symbolic ecosystems. Consumers now evaluate not only visual appeal, but also cultural relevance and narrative fit.

Existing frameworks (such as branded storytelling, transmedia branding, experiential branding, fandom-based branding, and cultural branding) each explain aspects of this transformation. However, none fully capture the integration of visual aesthetics, narrative coherence, participatory culture, and cross-platform circulation found in anime-based collaborations. This conceptual gap gives rise to the notion of cinematic branding.

Table 2. Conceptual positioning of related branding terms

Concept	Concise Definition
Branded Storytelling	A branding approach that uses stories to communicate brand values, identity, and emotional meaning in ways that are more memorable and persuasive than factual promotion alone (Quesenberry & Coolsen, 2023).
Transmedia Branding	A branding approach in which brand narratives are distributed across multiple media platforms, with each medium contributing uniquely to a larger, coordinated brand story (Granitz & Forman, 2015).
Experiential Branding	A branding approach that emphasizes sensory, affective, cognitive, and relational experiences, positioning the brand as something consumers live through rather than merely recognize (Schmitt, 2010; Akel, 2022).
Fandom-Based Branding	A branding approach that engages fan communities as active meaning-makers whose participation, interpretation, and symbolic ownership shape the legitimacy and circulation of brand meaning (Guschwan, 2012).
Cultural Branding	A branding approach in which brands gain power by functioning as cultural icons that address collective anxieties, identity tensions, and widely shared social meanings (Holt, 2004).

Rather than displacing established frameworks, the concept of cinematic branding serves as a vital bridge, addressing their theoretical gaps in accounting for the depth of anime–brand collaborations. While branded storytelling addresses narrative, transmedia branding explains cross-platform circulation, experiential branding highlights engagement, and cultural branding captures symbolic meaning, none fully account for the integration of visual aesthetics, narrative coherence, participatory fandom, and ecosystem-based circulation. This conceptual gap gives rise to cinematic branding, a form of cultural communication in which brands move beyond visual identity and advertising exposure to enter symbolic worlds shaped by emotional, aesthetic, and communal meaning. In the context of anime, this shift is particularly significant, as collaborations require brands to engage not only as communicators but as participants within established cultural systems.

Anime intensifies this transformation by offering a dense visual and narrative environment structured by fan interpretation and symbolic attachment. As a result, effective collaborations depend on a brand's ability to move beyond surface representation and become part of a broader experiential and narrative continuum. Cinematic branding can therefore be understood as the convergence of visual art, narrative storytelling, participatory fandom culture, and transmedia ecosystems. These elements redefine the role of branding: visual art ensures aesthetic legitimacy, narrative provides coherence and meaning, fandom introduces participatory validation, and transmedia ecosystems enable continuous circulation across platforms. Moving beyond mere exposure, cinematic branding emphasizes structural integration. In this model, brands are embedded within cultural ecosystems and judged by their capacity to maintain emotional and symbolic resonance across a decentralized network of touchpoints.

To clarify this conceptual transition, the following diagram maps the shift from conventional branding logic to cinematic branding within pop culture ecosystems (See Figure 4).

Figure 4. From visual identity advertising to cinematic branding

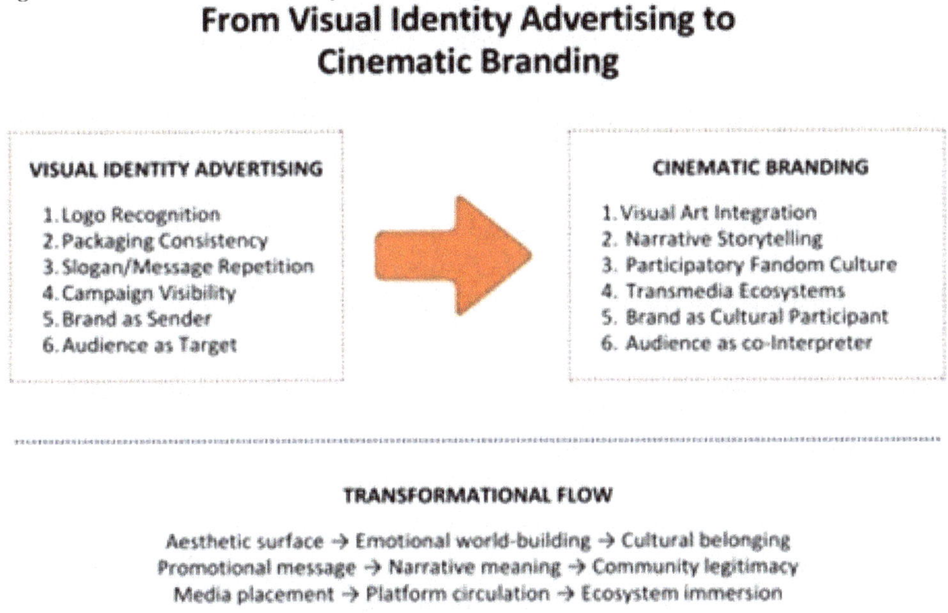

Figure 4 illustrates that the shift toward cinematic branding is structural rather than merely aesthetic. Traditional branding focuses on recognition and exposure, relying on repeated visual cues to maintain visibility. However, in saturated media environments, visibility is no longer the primary challenge, meaning is. Cinematic branding responds to this shift by prioritizing integration over display. Rather than simply being seen, brands must feel culturally embedded within symbolic worlds. This is achieved through the convergence of visual art, narrative coherence, participatory fandom, and transmedia ecosystems, which together create sustained emotional and cultural engagement.

The diagram further highlights a transformation from surface-level aesthetics to emotional world-building, from promotional messaging to narrative meaning, and from isolated media placement to immersive ecosystems. In this model, audiences are not passive observers but active participants who engage with brands as part of a broader cultural experience. In the anime sector, this shift carries unique weight; brands are not entering a vacuum, but rather a space already defined by complex emotional registers and deeply entrenched symbolic hierarchies. Successful collaborations, therefore, depend on alignment with these narrative systems rather than disruption.

In this chapter, cinematic branding is not used as a catch-all synonym for branded storytelling, transmedia branding, or fandom-based marketing. A collaboration is not considered cinematic branding simply because it uses anime imagery, circulates across platforms, or generates fan attention. Rather, the term is reserved for collaborations in which visual aesthetics, narrative coherence, participatory fandom validation, and transmedia circulation work together as an integrated symbolic system. This distinction is important because many anime-related campaigns remain promotional or decorative, while only some achieve the deeper cultural and emotional integration described in this chapter.

Overall, this transition reflects a broader redefinition of branding as a form of cultural design shaped by narrative, participation, and cross-platform continuity. As brands increasingly enter meaningful cultural spaces, this shift also raises important ethical considerations regarding commodification and authenticity.

Navigating the Ethical Tightrope: Affection vs. Commodification

A central tension within cinematic branding is the risk of affective commodification. This occurs when the deep emotional bonds fans share with an IP are treated as a mere resource to be exploited for immediate commercial gain, potentially devaluing the fan experience. Fandoms frequently engage in a "labor of love", an affective labor performed through the voluntary creation of user-generated content. However, a thin ethical line is crossed when brands exploit this community's creativity without fair recognition or compensation, potentially triggering fandom fatigue or collective burnout (Lamerichs, 2018). Dentsu (2025) warns that without a strategy rooted in genuine engagement, Gen Z audiences are likely to resist brands perceived as engaging in "predatory cultural penetration."

The community's perspective on this tension is remarkably nuanced, shifting between skepticism of corporate motives and appreciation for the visibility these collaborations provide. When discussing whether these alliances feel like exploitation or appreciation, B (25) noted:

"It depends on the perspective. On one hand, it can be seen as a form of cultural appreciation because platforms like TikTok allow information to spread so rapidly

within the community. As a fan, the moment a brand announces a collaboration, your first instinct is to investigate: Is it official? Is the design actually good? Where can I buy it?"

This suggests that, for the fan, "commercial exploitation" is often secondary to the product's quality and legitimacy. The aesthetic effort a brand puts into its social media promotion is seen as a performance of "seriousness", a way to convince the target market that the brand is there to pamper the fans rather than just extract value. A (36) further elaborated on this corporate "performance":

"Using anime aesthetics during a campaign feels like an effort by the brand to look serious and convince us they are doing this for the fans, even though we know it's ultimately commercial exploitation. If the brand successfully captures the community's attention on a cultural level, that exploitation is forgiven and viewed as appreciation. Deep down, we know brands might not care who they collaborate with as long as it converts to sales and doesn't hurt their image, but the execution matters."

From "Targeting" to "Facilitating": Building Genuine Engagement

To avoid the perception of being a "predatory" outsider, the community suggests that brands must move beyond selling merchandise and instead strive to become a functional part of the fanbase. Successful cultural integration requires the brand to act as a facilitator of the fan experience. As highlighted by the study participants (Ana, Monica, and Nanda), collaborations like *Demon Slayer x Family Mart* or *5 Centimeters Per Second x Gramedia* succeeded because they extended the experience into the physical and social realms:

"A culturally successful collaboration doesn't just sell items with anime designs; it tries to enter and become part of the fanbase. For example, organizing watch parties or fan meetings creates real engagement. Indirectly, fans feel that the brand is facilitating their desires rather than just treating them as sales targets."

By providing these "third spaces" for community interaction, brands can transition from being perceived as external exploiters to being seen as valuable patrons of the culture. This shift ensures that the "labor of love" provided by fans is met with a reciprocal "labor of service" from the brand, mitigating the risk of fandom fatigue and fostering long-term loyalty.

The Commercialization of Parasocial Relationships and Narrative Distortion

Anime derives much of its cultural power from parasocial relationships between audiences and characters. However, ethical issues arise when brands exploit these emotional bonds by placing characters in contexts that contradict their original narrative identity. Such practices, often referred to as "Out of Character" (OOC) marketing, risk reducing symbolic meaning into mere commercial display and weakening the integrity of the original work (CBR, 2023; Schroeder, 2020).

Narrative Integrity, Market Utility, and the Limits of Interpretation

A key ethical tension in cinematic branding lies between narrative integrity and market utility. When collaborations ignore the internal logic of the story-world, they disrupt the emotional continuity that sustains audience attachment. To remain credible, branding must move beyond surface appropriation toward narrative-consistent integration that respects the original context and preserves symbolic meaning.

Because this study relies on qualitative interpretation, the findings should be viewed as context-dependent rather than universal, acknowledging that fan communities may decode these branding efforts differently depending on their unique perspectives. Nevertheless, it highlights a critical issue: when market priorities override narrative integrity, brands risk undermining both audience trust and the long-term cultural value of the intellectual property.

The Sustainability Contradiction of Cinematic Branding

Cinematic branding also reveals a gap between symbolic value and material production. While anime collaborations generate emotional and cultural meaning, they are often embedded in fast-paced consumption systems characterized by short product cycles and disposability. This creates a contradiction between long-term cultural attachment and short-term consumption practices (Joy et al., 2012). Moreover, sustainability concerns extend beyond environmental impact to issues of labour inequality. While brands capture symbolic and economic value, the creative labour behind anime production often remains undercompensated (Ristola, 2017). This imbalance highlights a broader issue of value distribution within the cultural economy.

Therefore, ethical cinematic branding requires more than authenticity; it demands structural responsibility. This includes transparency, fair labour practices, and sustainable production systems. Without such commitments, cinematic branding risks reinforcing extractive models of capitalism that prioritize short-term gain over long-term cultural and social value (LeBaron et al., 2021).

CONCLUSION: TOWARD A PARADIGM OF CINEMATIC BRANDING

Anime × brand collaborations should no longer be understood merely as promotional tie-ins or visually appealing licensing strategies, but as an evolving mode of strategic cultural communication. Through the concept of cinematic branding, this study demonstrates how visual art, narrative storytelling, participatory fandom culture, and transmedia ecosystems converge to produce new forms of cultural meaning and consumer engagement. The post-pandemic landscape has solidified anime's role as a powerful cultural bridge. Brands no longer use anime for mere reach; instead, they leverage it as an immersive ecosystem to secure the kind of emotional resonance and narrative authenticity that traditional advertising cannot provide.

These findings highlight that anime's strength lies in its capacity to function as a shared symbolic environment, one that audiences do not merely consume but actively inhabit and reinterpret. In this context, branding shifts from external communication toward cultural participation, where success depends on how effectively brands align with existing emotional structures, visual grammar, and narrative logic. Rather than operating as detached commercial entities, brands increasingly act as cultural participants embedded within fan-driven ecosystems.

At the same time, this transformation introduces significant ethical challenges. As brands enter emotionally charged fictional worlds, the risks of affective commodification, narrative distortion, and unsustainable value extraction become more pronounced. When commercial strategies prioritize visibility over narrative coherence, they risk undermining both the symbolic integrity of the intellectual property and the emotional trust that sustains long-term audience engagement. Cinematic branding, therefore, cannot be evaluated solely in terms of market success, but must also be assessed through its cultural and ethical implications.

Furthermore, cinematic branding operates within broader structural tensions, particularly between symbolic value and material production. While anime-based collaborations generate cultural prestige and emotional attachment, they are often embedded within systems of accelerated consumption and unequal value distribution. This underscores the need for a more critical understanding of how creative labour, fandom participation, and commercial profit intersect within the contemporary cultural economy.

Future research should extend this analysis in several directions. First, the concept of cinematic branding should be tested across other cultural industries, including K-pop, gaming, and digital entertainment, to evaluate its broader applicability. Second, more systematic and quantitative studies are needed to examine audience reception across different cultural contexts, age groups, and levels of fandom engagement. Third, further investigation into the political economy of these collaborations is essential, particularly in relation to labour conditions, licensing structures, and sustainability practices.

Ultimately, cinematic branding represents a fundamental shift in how brands operate within contemporary culture, from visibility to meaning, from communication to participation, and from isolated campaigns to immersive ecosystems. Its long-term legitimacy will depend on whether brands can engage with cultural worlds in ways that sustain their symbolic depth and emotional resonance, rather than reducing them to short-term commercial assets. In this sense, the future of branding lies not only in innovation but in the ability to navigate the complex relationship between culture, creativity, and commerce.

REFERENCES

Ahmad, H. A., Koyama, S., & Hibino, H. (2012). Shaping behavior through perception: How do visuals of manga affect its readers? *Bulletin of JSSD*, *59*(1), 83–90. https://www.jstage.jst.go.jp/article/jssdj/59/1/59_1_83/_pdf

AJA. (2025). Anime industry data | . The Association of Japanese Animations. https://aja.gr.jp/english/japan-anime-data

Akel, G. (2022). Handbook of research on interdisciplinary reflections of contemporary experiential marketing practices. IGI Global Scientific Publishing. EISBN13: 9781668443828. DOI: 10.4018/978-1-6684-4380-4

Alani, D. N. (2022). *Diplomacy and anime as soft power and Japanese cultural diplomacy*. https://www.researchgate.net/publication/364341145

Allison, A. (2006). *Millennial monsters: Japanese toys and the global imagination*. University of California Press. ISBN 13: 978-0520245655

Azuma, H., & Abel, J. E. (2009). Otaku: Japan's database animals. University of Minnesota Press. ISBN-13: 978-0816653522.

Cayla, J., & Arnould, E. J. (2008). A cultural approach to branding in the global marketplace. *Journal of International Marketing*, *16*(4), 86–112. DOI: 10.1509/jimk.16.4.86

CBR. (2023, July 15). Top 10 most emotionally manipulative anime series, ranked. *Comic Book Resources*. https://www.cbr.com/emotionally-manipulative-anime-series/

Chiu, Y., & Chang, Y. (2018). Examining the visual styles and visual techniques in animation stories - A case study of the Amazing World of Gumball. 2018 1st IEEE International Conference on knowledge Innovation and Invention (ICKII), 324–326. https://doi.org/DOI: 10.1109/ICKII.2018.8569144

Darmawan, T. N., Linuwih, E. R., & Renfei, X. (2025). Unmasking the persona: A Barthesian semiotic study of Ahmad Dhani's InstagDhani'sf-branding. *New Language Dimensions*, *6*(1), 95–104. DOI: 10.26740/nld.v6n1.p95-104

Deng, J. (2025). The role of anime in cultural dissemination. *Advances in Social Behavior Research*, *16*(8), 73–76. DOI: 10.54254/2753-7102/2025.27941

Denison, R. (2015). Anime fandom and the liminal spaces between fan creativity and industry consumption. *International Journal of Cultural Studies*, *18*(3), 324–341. DOI: 10.1177/1367877913513683

Dentsu. (2025). *Anime: A growing opportunity for brands (2025 global research report)*. Dentsu Consumer Navigator. https://www.dentsu.com/reports/anime_opportunity_2025

Desertcart. (2026). *Desertcart logo*. Desertcart Logo. https://www.desertcart.id/products/537001866-anime-store-demon-slayer-kimetsu-no-yaiba-tanjiro-and-nezuko

Desk, H. T. U. S. (2025, August 21). Top 7 biggest anime movies ranked, demon slayer's new film storms to no 1. Hindustan Times. https://www.hindustantimes.com/entertainment/anime/top-7-biggest-anime-movies-ranked-demon-slayer-s-new-film-storms-to-no-1-101755722700075.html

Dooley, B., & Hida, H. (2021, February 24). Nytimes.com. The New York Times - Breaking News, US News, World News and Videos. https://www.nytimes.com/2021/02/24/business/japan-anime.html

Fashion domain expansion: Jujutsu Kaisen and Dolce & Gabbana collaborate on a special collection vanity teen lifestyle & new faces magazine. (2022, April 20). Vanity Teen Lifestyle & new faces magazine. https://www.vanityteen.com/jujutsu-kaisen-dolce-gabbana-collab/

Fast Retailing. (2021, March 22). UNIQLO appoints Doraemon as global sustainability ambassador. https://www.fastretailing.com/eng/group/news/2103221500.html

Goswami, K. (2025, December 31). 10 top anime brand collaborations in 2025 ranked. Outlook Respawn. https://respawn.outlookindia.com/pop-culture/pop-culture-guides/one-piece-jjk-naruto-the-10-biggest-anime-collabs-of-2025

Grand View Research. (2025). Anime apparel and fashion market size, share, and trends analysis report. https://www.grandviewresearch.com/industry-analysis/anime-apparel-fashion-market-report

Granitz, N., & Forman, H. (2015). Building self-brand connections: Exploring brand stories through a transmedia perspective. *Journal of Brand Management*, *22*(1), 38–59. DOI: 10.1057/bm.2015.1

Guschwan, M. (2012). Fandom, brandom and the limits of participatory culture. *Journal of Consumer Culture*, *12*(1), 19–40. DOI: 10.1177/1469540512438154

Herari, N., Najmi Nuji, M. N., Boer, R. F., & Allifiansyah, S. (2026). Algorithmic Narcissism and the Passion Economy. In Kaygisiz, E. (Ed.), *Digital ideologies in the age of algorithmic culture* (pp. 237–270). IGI Global Scientific Publishing., https://www.igi-global.com/chapter/algorithmic-narcissism-and-the-passion-economy/407330, DOI: 10.4018/979-8-3373-4531-4.ch008

Herari, N., Waluyo, W., & Rubiyanto, R. (2025). Leading Alone, Leading Forward: Solopreneurs and the Quiet Power of the Passion Economy. In Paradiso-Testa, M. (Ed.), *The purpose of passion in leadership* (pp. 333–358). IGI Global Scientific Publishing., https://www.igi-global.com/chapter/leading-alone-leading-forward/385644, DOI: 10.4018/979-8-3373-2404-3.ch012

Holt, D. B. (2004). How brands become icons: The principles of cultural branding. Harvard Business Press. ISBN 13:978-1578517749.

Jenkins, H. (2006). Convergence culture: Where old and new media collide. New York University Press. ISBN 13:978-0814742815.

Joy, A., Sherry, J. F.Jr, Venkatesh, A., Wang, J., & Chan, R. (2012). Fast fashion, sustainability, and the ethical appeal of luxury brands. *Fashion Theory*, *16*(3), 273–295. DOI: 10.2752/175174112X13340749707123

Kane, D., & Juliao, D. (2026). Study.com. study.com. https://study.com/academy/lesson/anime-history-style.html

Kawamura, Y. (2016). *Fashioning Japanese subcultures*. Bloomsbury.

Kiso, V. (2023). Japanese Pop Culture's Response to COVID-19: Embracing Digitalization and Hybridization. ICS Occasional Papers, *105*, 4-21.

Lamarre, T. (2009). *The anime machine: A media theory of animation*. University of Minnesota Press.

Lamerichs, N. (2018). *Productive fandom: Intermediality and affective reception in fan cultures*. Amsterdam University Press.

Leaver, T., Hutchinson, J., & Abidin, C. (2020). *Instagram: Visual social media cultures*. Polity Press.

LeBaron, G., Edwards, R., Hunt, T., Sempéré, C., & Kyritsis, P. (2021). The ineffectiveness of CSR: Understanding garment company commitments to living wages in global supply chains. *New Political Economy*, *27*(1), 99–115. DOI: 10.1080/13563467.2021.1926954

Madaan, J. (2025, September 4). Demon slayer: Infinity castle vs the Mugen train worldwide box office: Akaza's return needs 69% Jump to emerge as #1 anime film! Koimoi. https://www.koimoi.com/box-office/demon-slayer-infinity-castle-vs-the-mugen-train-worldwide-box-office-akazas-return-needs-69-jump-to-emerge-as-1-anime-film/

Maliha, S. R., & Aziz, M. N. (2024). Exploring anime consumers' identity construction in the digital era. *BUFT. Journal of Business Economics*, *5*(1). Advance online publication. DOI: 10.58481/BJBE/2414

Manovich, L. (2013). Software takes command. Bloomsbury. ISBN-13z: 978-1623567453

McCracken, G. (2015). *Culture and consumption II: Markets, meaning, and brand management*. Indiana University Press.

Minea, V. (2025). Where god is becoming: Anime, theosis, and the sacred in process. *Religions*, *16*(8), 1014. DOI: 10.3390/rel16081014

MPPA. (2025). Motion picture producers association of Japan, Inc. . https://www.eiren.org/statistics_e/

Naeem, M., Ozuem, W., Ranfagni, S., & Howell, K. (2025). User generated content and brand engagement: Exploring the role of electronic semiotics and symbolic interactionism on Instagram. *Computers in Human Behavior*, *168*, 108642. DOI: 10.1016/j.chb.2025.108642

Napier, S. J. (2018). Anime from Akira to Howl's Moving Howl's: Experiencing contemporary Japanese animation (Rev. ed.). St. Martin's PressMartin's3:978-1403970527.

Noh, S. (2022). *Global Media Streams: Cosmopolitan Streaming Platforms and the Contemporary Ecosystem of Anime Distribution*. The University of Wisconsin-Madison.

Noh, S. (2024). Global media streams: Netflix and the changing ecosystem of anime production. *Television & New Media*, *25*(3), 234–250. DOI: 10.1177/15274764231206540

Quesenberry, K. A., & Coolsen, M. K. (2023). Brand storytelling: Integrated marketing communications for the digital media landscape. Bloomsbury Publishing PLC. ISBN 13:978-1538176382.

Reid, S. F., Moses, L., & Rylak, D. (2026). "That storrey reminse you to be cefl": A multimodal analysis of a first-grader's blended genre composition. *Journal of Early Childhood Literacy*, *26*(1), 450–481. DOI: 10.1177/14687984251337368

Ristola, J. (2017). Blood, Sweat, Ink, and Tears: Exploitation of Labour in the Japanese Animation Industry. Conference: Global Labour Research Centre Graduate Student Symposium 2016. https://www.researchgate.net/publication/322909809_Blood_Sweat_Ink_and_Tears_Exploitation_of_Labour_in_the_Japanese_Animation_Industry

Riyanto, B., Aulia, G., Akbari, T. T., & Herari, N. (2025). Visionary Voices: When Digital Media Leadership Projects Soft Power. In Paradiso-Testa, M. (Ed.), *The value of vision in leadership* (pp. 217–252). IGI Global Scientific Publishing., https://www.igi-global.com/chapter/visionary-voices/385358, DOI: 10.4018/979-8-3373-2392-3.ch007

Sagardia, S. C. (2017). Dressing the part: Communication of identity in a performative fandom community (Doctoral dissertation).

Santiago Iglesias, J. A. (2021). Not just immobile: Moving drawings and visual synecdoches in Neon Genesis Evangelion. In *Anime studies* (pp. 19–48). Stockholm University Press. DOI: 10.16993/bbp.b

Schmitt, B. (2010). Experiential Marketing. *Journal of Marketing Management, 15*(1-3), 53–67. https://www.tandfonline.com/doi/abs/10.1362/026725799784870496. DOI: 10.1362/026725799784870496

Schroeder, J. E. (2020). *Visual consumption* (2nd ed.). Routledge.

Solo leveling PC bundle. Starforge Systems. (n.d.). https://starforgesystems.com/products/solo-leveling-pc-bundle

Steinberg, M. (2012). Anime's media Anime'sanchising toys and characters in Japan. University of Minnesota Press. Print ISBN: 9780816675494.

Welch, L. C. (2024). Anime: a qualitative study exploring Miyazaki's influence on fans and fan art through the perspective of visual communication within the sociocultural and cybernetic traditions (Doctoral dissertation, Liberty University).

Yulianti, I., Andito, T., & Nugroho, G. S. (2025). Reverting Animal in Post-Anthropocentrism Character Design: A case study of the Papuan bird of paradise (cenderawasih papua). *Environment-Behaviour Proceedings Journal, 10*(SI39), 75–80. DOI: 10.21834/e-bpj.v10iSI39.7675

Zahlten, A. (2010). Meta-, hyper-, inter-, super: Anime, world creation and the role of film festivals. In E. Niskanen (Ed.), *Imaginary Japan*. International Institute for Popular Culture.

Compilation of References

Adanır, O. (2003). *Sinemada anlam ve anlatım* (2nd ed.). Alfa Yayınları.

Affron, C., & Affron, M. J. (1995). *Sets in motion: Art direction and film narrative*. Rutgers University Press. DOI: 10.36019/9781978813199

Agamben, G. (2009). *What is an apparatus? and other essays* (Kishik, D., & Pedatella, S., Trans.). Stanford University Press.

Agresti, A. (2018). *Statistical methods for the social sciences* (5th ed.). Pearson.

Ahmad, H. A., Koyama, S., & Hibino, H. (2012). Shaping behavior through perception: How do visuals of manga affect its readers? *Bulletin of JSSD*, *59*(1), 83–90. https://www.jstage.jst.go.jp/article/jssdj/59/1/59_1_83/_pdf

Ahmed, S. K., Mohammed, R. A., Nashwan, A. J., Ibrahim, R. H., Abdalla, A. Q., Ameen, B. M. M., & Khdhir, R. M. (2025). Using thematic analysis in qualitative research. *Journal of Medicine, Surgery, and Public Health*, *6*, 1–6. DOI: 10.1016/j.glmedi.2025.100198

AJA. (2025). Anime industry data | . The Association of Japanese Animations. https://aja.gr.jp/english/japan-anime-data

Ajzen, I. (1991). The theory of planned behavior. *Organizational Behavior and Human Decision Processes*, *50*(2), 179–211. DOI: 10.1016/0749-5978(91)90020-T

Akel, G. (2022). Handbook of research on interdisciplinary reflections of contemporary experiential marketing practices. IGI Global Scientific Publishing. EISBN13: 9781668443828. DOI: 10.4018/978-1-6684-4380-4

Alani, D. N. (2022). *Diplomacy and anime as soft power and Japanese cultural diplomacy*. https://www.researchgate.net/publication/364341145

Alberge, D. (2004, August 27). Cleaner thought Tate exhibit was a load of rubbish. *The Times*.

Allison, A. (2006). *Millennial monsters: Japanese toys and the global imagination*. University of California Press. ISBN 13: 978-0520245655

Allwood, J. M., Laursen, S. E., Rodriguez, C. M., & Bocken, N. M. P. (2006). *Well dressed? The present and future sustainability of clothing and textiles in the United Kingdom*. University of Cambridge Institute for Manufacturing.

Ambrose, G., & Harris, P. (2013). *The Fundamentals of Typography* (Turkish ed.). Literatür Publishing.

AMPAS. (2020). *ACES overview*. Academy of Motion Picture Arts and Sciences. https://www.oscars.org/science-technology/aces

Anderson, P. T. (Director) (2007). *There Will Be Blood* [Film]. Paramount Vantage.

Anderson, J. D. (1996). *The reality of illusion: An ecological approach to cognitive film theory*. Southern Illinois University Press.

An, K., & Cerasi, J. (2020). *Who's afraid of contemporary art?: An A to Z guide to the art world*. Thames & Hudson.

Antoine, J.-P. (2013). The historicity of the contemporary is now! In Dumbadze, A., & Hudson, S. (Eds.), *Contemporary art: 1989 to the present* (pp. 28–36). John Wiley & Sons.

Aristotle, . (1984a). Metaphysics. In Barnes, J. (Ed.), *The complete works of Aristotle: The revised Oxford translation* (Vol. 2; Ross, W. D., Trans.). Princeton University Press.

Arnold, R. (2009). *Fashion: A Very Short Introduction*. Oxford University Press.

ARRI. (2022). *LED wall shooting guide: On-set virtual production*. ARRI.

Austin, T. (2020). *Narrative environments and experience design: Space as a medium of communication*. Routledge. DOI: 10.4324/9780367138073

Azuma, H., & Abel, J. E. (2009). Otaku: Japan's database animals. University of Minnesota Press. ISBN-13: 978-0816653522.

Bachelard, G. (1994). *The poetics of space* (Jolas, M., Trans.). Beacon Press.

Bada, E. (2005). *Performance and Greek Roma identity: A visual anthropological study* [Doctoral dissertation, Napier University].

Baird, R. (2022). Eye, Bee, M. Logo Histories. Retrieved 29 April 2025. https://www.logohistories.com/p/ibm

Bardecki, M. J. (2019). Multi-disciplinarity. In Leal Filho, W. (Ed.), *Encyclopedia of sustainability in higher education* (pp. 1179–1184). Springer., DOI: 10.1007/978-3-030-11352-0_90

Barker, T. (2012). *Time and the digital: Connecting technology, aesthetics, and a process philosophy of time*. Dartmouth College Press.

Barnard, M. (1998). *Art, Design and Visual Culture: An Introduction*. Macmillan. DOI: 10.1007/978-1-349-26917-4

Barnard, M. (2002). *Fashion as communication* (2nd ed.). Routledge.

Barnwell, J. (2004). *Production design: Architects of the screen*. Wallflower Press.

Barthes, R. (1967). *The Fashion System*. Hill and Wang.

Baudrillard, J. (1994). *Simulacra and simulation* (S. F. Glaser, Çev.). The University of Michigan Press.

Baudrillard, J. (2005). *Le complot de l'art: Entrevues* [The Conspiracy of Art: Interviews]. Lotringer, S., Ed.). Galilée.

Bazin, A. (1967). *What is cinema?* (Vol. 1). University of California Press.

BBC News. (2014, February 20). Cleaner throws out "rubbish" Sala Murat artwork.

BBC News. (2015, October 25). Art binned by cleaner in Italy "restored".

Becer, E. (2007). *Modern Art and New Typography*. Dost Kitabevi.

Benitah, C. (2011). Photos-Souvenirs [Embroidered photographs]. Retrieved May 22, 2026, from https://www.carolebenitah.com

Benjamin, W. (1977). *The origin of German tragic drama* (Osborne, J., Trans.). Verso. (Original work published 1928)

Bense, M. (1971). The projects of generative aesthetics. In J. Reichardt (Ed.), *Cybernetics, art and ideas* (pp. 57–60). Studio Vista. (Original German text published 1965)

Berger, R. (2015). Now I see it, now I don't: Researcher's position and reflexivity in qualitative research. *Qualitative Research, 15*(2), 219–234. DOI: 10.1177/1468794112468475

Berlow, D. (2017a). *Amstelvar* [Variable font]. Google Fonts / Font Bureau. https://github.com/googlefonts/amstelvar

Berlow, D. (2017b). *Decovar* [Variable font]. Google Fonts / Font Bureau. https://github.com/googlefonts/decovar

Betancourt, M. (2013). Ideologies of the real in title sequences, motion graphics, and cinema. In Betancourt, M. (Ed.), *The history of motion graphics: From avant-garde to industry in the United States*. Wildside Press.

Bick, R., Halsey, E., & Ekenga, C. C. (2018). The global environmental injustice of fast fashion. *Environmental Health : A Global Access Science Source*, *17*(1), 92. DOI: 10.1186/s12940-018-0433-7 PMID: 30591057

Billard, J. (2017, November 16). 8 times Ruben Östlund's *The Square* accurately portrayed the art world and embarrassed us all. *Artspace*.

Block, B. (2008). *The visual story: Creating the visual structure of film, TV and digital media* (2nd ed.). Focal Press.

Bode, L. (2017). *Making believe: Screen performance and special effects in popular cinema*. Rutgers University Press.

Boden, M. A., & Edmonds, E. A. (2009). What is generative art? *Digital Creativity (Exeter)*, *20*(1–2), 21–46. DOI: 10.1080/14626260902867915

Bodini, A., Manohar, A., Colecchia, F., Harrison, D., & Garaj, V. (2024). Envisioning the future of virtual production in filmmaking: A remote co-design study. *Multimedia Tools and Applications*, *83*(7), 19015–19039. DOI: 10.1007/s11042-023-16308-7

Bogost, I. (2007). *Persuasive games: The expressive power of videogames*. MIT Press. DOI: 10.7551/mitpress/5334.001.0001

Bohnacker, H., Groß, B., Laub, J., & Lazzeroni, C. (2012). *Generative Design: Visualise, Program, and Create with Processing*. Princeton Architectural Press.

Bommasani, R., Hudson, D. A., Adeli, E., Altman, R., Arora, S., von Arx, S., Bernstein, M., Bohg, J., Bosselut, A., Brunskill, E., Brynjolfsson, E., Buch, S., Card, D., Castellon, R., Chatterji, N., Chen, A., Creel, K., Davis, J., Demszky, D., . . . Liang, P. (2021). On the opportunities and risks of foundation models. *arXiv preprint arXiv:2108.07258*. https://arxiv.org/abs/2108.07258

Bonner, J. (2017). *Islamic geometric patterns: Their historical development and traditional methods of construction*. Springer. DOI: 10.1007/978-1-4419-0217-7

Bordwell, D. (1989). Historical Poetics of Cinema. In Palmer, R. B. (Ed.), *The cinematic text: methods and approaches*. Georgia State Literary Studies.

Bordwell, D. (2005). *Figures traced in light: On cinematic staging*. University of California Press. DOI: 10.1525/9780520938007

Bordwell, D. (2008). *Poetics of cinema*. Routledge.

Bordwell, D., & Thompson, K. (2019). *Film art: An introduction* (12th ed.). McGraw-Hill.

Bott, E. (2010). Favourites and others: Reflexivity and the shaping of subjectivities and data in qualitative research. *Qualitative Research, 10*(2), 159–173. DOI: 10.1177/1468794109356736

Boutellier, A., & Raptis, P. (2023). Teaching virtual production: The challenges of developing a formal curriculum. *Film Education Journal, 6*(2), 69–81. DOI: 10.14324/FEJ.06.2.01

Bowman, D. A., Kruijff, E., LaViola, J. J., & Poupyrev, I. (2004). *3D user interfaces: Theory and practice*. Addison-Wesley.

Brady, R. H. (1987). Form and cause in Goethe's morphology. In Amrine, R., Zucker, F. J., & Wheeler, H. (Eds.), *Goethe and the sciences: A reappraisal* (pp. 257–300). D. Reidel. DOI: 10.1007/978-94-009-3761-1_14

Braun, V., & Clarke, V. (2006). Using thematic analysis in psychology. *Qualitative Research in Psychology, 3*(2), 77–101. DOI: 10.1191/1478088706qp063oa

Braun, V., & Clarke, V. (2013). *Successful qualitative research: A practical guide for beginners*. SAGE Publications.

Braun, V., & Clarke, V. (2019). Reflecting on reflexive thematic analysis. *Qualitative Research in Sport, Exercise and Health, 11*(4), 589–597. DOI: 10.1080/2159676X.2019.1628806

Braun, V., & Clarke, V. (2021). One size fits all? What counts as quality practice in (reflexive) thematic analysis? *Qualitative Research in Psychology, 18*(3), 328–352. DOI: 10.1080/14780887.2020.1769238

Braun, V., & Clarke, V. (2023). Is thematic analysis used well in health psychology? A critical review of published research, with recommendations for quality practice and reporting. *Health Psychology Review, 17*(4), 695–718. DOI: 10.1080/17437199.2022.2161594 PMID: 36656762

Braun, V., & Clarke, V. (2024). A critical review of the reporting of reflexive thematic analysis in Health Promotion International. *Health Promotion International, 39*(3), 1–12. DOI: 10.1093/heapro/daae049 PMID: 38805676

Braun, V., Clarke, V., & Hayfield, N. (2022). 'A starting point for your journey, not a map': Nikki Hayfield in conversation with Virginia Braun and Victoria Clarke about thematic analysis. *Qualitative Research in Psychology, 19*(2), 424–445. DOI: 10.1080/14780887.2019.1670765

Braun, V., Clarke, V., Hayfield, N., & Terry, G. (2019). Thematic analysis. In Liamputtong, P. (Ed.), *Handbook of research methods in health social sciences* (pp. 843–860). Springer. DOI: 10.1007/978-981-10-5251-4_103

Bright, D., McKay, A., & Firth, K. (2024). How to be reflexive: Foucault, ethics and writing qualitative research as a technology of the self. *International Journal of Research & Method in Education, 47*(4), 408–420. DOI: 10.1080/1743727X.2023.2290185

Bright, S. (Ed.). (2013). *Home truths: Photography and motherhood.* Art/Books.

Brown, B. (2016). *Cinematography: Theory and practice* (3rd ed.). Focal Press. DOI: 10.4324/9781315667829

Brown, E. H., & Phu, T. (Eds.). (2014). *Feeling photography.* Duke University Press.

Brown, S., & Vacca, F. (2022). Cultural sustainability in fashion: Reflections on craft and sustainable development models. *Sustainability : Science, Practice, & Policy, 18*(1), 590–600. DOI: 10.1080/15487733.2022.2100102

Buchanan, R. (1992). Wicked problems in design thinking. *Design Issues, 8*(2), 5–21. DOI: 10.2307/1511637

Bucher, J. (2018). *Storytelling for virtual reality: Methods and principles for crafting immersive narratives.* Routledge.

Burch, N. (1973). *Theory of film practice.* Princeton University Press.

Burnham, J. (1968). Systems esthetics. *Artforum, 7*(1), 30–35.

Burrell, J. (2016). How the machine 'thinks': Understanding opacity in machine learning algorithms. *Big Data & Society, 3*(1), 1–12. DOI: 10.1177/2053951715622512

Buskirk, M. (2003). *The contingent object of contemporary art.* MIT Press. DOI: 10.7551/mitpress/2139.001.0001

Butler, J. (1990). *Gender trouble: Feminism and the subversion of identity.* Routledge.

Butler, J. (1993). *Bodies that matter: On the discursive limits of 'sex.* Routledge.

Byrne, D. (2022). A worked example of Braun and Clarke's approach to reflexive thematic analysis. *Quality & Quantity, 56*(3), 1391–1412. DOI: 10.1007/s11135-021-01182-y

Caldwell, J. T. (2008). *Production culture: Industrial reflexivity and critical practice in film and television.* Duke University Press.

Calleja, G. (2019). *In-game: From immersion to incorporation.* MIT Press.

Cameron, J. (Director). (2009). *Avatar* [Film]. 20th Century Fox.

Campbell, B. (2011a). *The Dad Project* [Personal essay]. Briony Campbell Photography & Film. https://www.brionycampbell.com/wp-content/uploads/2013/03/The_Dad_Project_Briony_Campbell.pdf

Campbell, B. (2011b). The Dad Project [Photograph]. Retrieved May 22, 2026, from https://www.brionycampbell.com

Cardwell, M. E. (2025). Through the looking glass: A step-by-step guide to arts-based reflexivity. *Qualitative Research*, *26*(1), 208–227. DOI: 10.1177/14687941251398971

Carew, A. (2018). Art attack: Social responsibility and discomfort in the square. *Screen Education*, (91), 50–57.

Carrington, M. J., Neville, B. A., & Whitwell, G. J. (2010). Why ethical consumers don't walk their talk: Towards a framework for understanding the gap between ethical purchase intentions and actual buying behaviour of ethically minded consumers. *Journal of Business Ethics*, *97*(1), 139–158. DOI: 10.1007/s10551-010-0501-6

Cayla, J., & Arnould, E. J. (2008). A cultural approach to branding in the global marketplace. *Journal of International Marketing*, *16*(4), 86–112. DOI: 10.1509/jimk.16.4.86

CBR. (2023, July 15). Top 10 most emotionally manipulative anime series, ranked. *Comic Book Resources*. https://www.cbr.com/emotionally-manipulative-anime-series/

Chadwick, H. (1986). The Oval Court [Photographic installation]. © The Estate of Helen Chadwick.

Chadwick, H. (n.d.). Art, like crying, is an act of self-repair [Artist's notes]. As cited in Warner, M. (2022). *Helen Chadwick: The Oval Court*. Afterall Books/MIT Press.

Chang, H.-Y., Chang, Y.-J., & Tsai, M.-J. (2024). Strategies and difficulties during students' construction of data visualizations. *International Journal of STEM Education*, *11*(1), 11. DOI: 10.1186/s40594-024-00463-w

Chen, M. (2024). The impact of virtual technology on film and television performance: A paradigm shift in performance from green screen to virtual production. *Economic Society and Humanities*, *1*(6), 56–62. DOI: 10.62381/E244609

Chen, X., Memon, H. A., Wang, Y., Marriam, I., & Tebyetekerwa, M. (2021). Circular economy and sustainability of the clothing and textile industry. *Materials Circular Economy*, *3*(1), 12. DOI: 10.1007/s42824-021-00026-2

Chiu, Y., & Chang, Y. (2018). Examining the visual styles and visual techniques in animation stories - A case study of the Amazing World of Gumball. 2018 1st IEEE International Conference on knowledge Innovation and Invention (ICKII), 324–326. https://doi.org/DOI: 10.1109/ICKII.2018.8569144

Chung, H. J. (2018). *Media heterotopias: Digital effects and material labor in global film production.* Duke University Press. DOI: 10.1215/9780822372158

Cixous, H. (1976). The laugh of the medusa (K. Cohen & P. Cohen, Trans.). *Signs: Journal of Women in Culture and Society, 1*(4), 875–893. (Original work published 1975)

Cixous, H. (1998). *Stigmata, escaping texts.* Routledge.

Clark, H. (2008). Slow + fashion—An oxymoron—or a promise for the future? *Fashion Theory, 12*(4), 427–446. DOI: 10.2752/175174108X346922

Coen, J., & Coen, E. (Directors). (2007). *No Country for Old Men* [Film]. Miramax Films.

Compton, K. (2016, February 10). *So you want to build a generator* [Blog post]. Tumblr. https://galaxykate0.tumblr.com/post/139774965871

Çoruh, L. (2025). Immersive digital creation environments in design education. *International Journal of Technology and Design Education, 35*(5), 1841–1870. DOI: 10.1007/s10798-025-09961-6

Creswell, J. W. (2014). *Research design: Qualitative, quantitative, and mixed methods approaches* (4th ed.). Sage Publications.

Cronbach, L. J. (1951). Coefficient alpha and the internal structure of tests. *Psychometrika, 16*(3), 297–334. DOI: 10.1007/BF02310555

Cross, N. (2006). *Designerly ways of knowing.* Springer.

Cuarón, A. (Director). (2013). *Gravity* [Film]. Warner Bros. Pictures.

Curtin, M., & Sanson, K. (Eds.). (2016). Precarious creativity: Global media, local labor. In M. Curtin & K. Sanson (Eds.), *Precarious creativity: global media, local labor.* University of California Press.

D'Cruz, H., Gillingham, P., & Melendez, S. (2007). Reflexivity, its meanings and relevance for social work: A critical review of the literature. *British Journal of Social Work, 37*(1), 73–90. DOI: 10.1093/bjsw/bcl001

Darmawan, T. N., Linuwih, E. R., & Renfei, X. (2025). Unmasking the persona: A Barthesian semiotic study of Ahmad Dhani's InstagDhani'sf-branding. *New Language Dimensions*, *6*(1), 95–104. DOI: 10.26740/nld.v6n1.p95-104

Davis, F. D. (1989). Perceived usefulness, perceived ease of use, and user acceptance of information technology. *Management Information Systems Quarterly*, *13*(3), 319–340. DOI: 10.2307/249008

de Saussure, F. (2011). *Course in general linguistics* (W. Baskin, Trans.). Columbia University Press. (Original work published 1916)

Debevec, P., & LeGendre, C. (2022). HDR lighting dilation for dynamic range reduction on virtual production stages. *arXiv*. https://doi.org//arXiv.2205.07873DOI: 10.1145/3532719.3543243

Della Rocca, M. (2008). *Spinoza*. Routledge. DOI: 10.4324/9780203894583

Deng, J. (2025). The role of anime in cultural dissemination. *Advances in Social Behavior Research*, *16*(8), 73–76. DOI: 10.54254/2753-7102/2025.27941

Denison, R. (2015). Anime fandom and the liminal spaces between fan creativity and industry consumption. *International Journal of Cultural Studies*, *18*(3), 324–341. DOI: 10.1177/1367877913513683

Dentsu. (2025). *Anime: A growing opportunity for brands (2025 global research report)*. Dentsu Consumer Navigator. https://www.dentsu.com/reports/anime_opportunity_2025

Desertcart. (2026). *Desertcart logo*. Desertcart Logo. https://www.desertcart.id/products/537001866-anime-store-demon-slayer-kimetsu-no-yaiba-tanjiro-and-nezuko

Desk, H. T. U. S. (2025, August 21). Top 7 biggest anime movies ranked, demon slayer's new film storms to no 1. Hindustan Times. https://www.hindustantimes.com/entertainment/anime/top-7-biggest-anime-movies-ranked-demon-slayer-s-new-film-storms-to-no-1-101755722700075.html

Dinamo Typefaces. (2018). *Font Gauntlet* [Variable font testing tool]. https://fontgauntlet.com Retrieved March 19, 2026.

Dinur, E. (2017). *The filmmaker's guide to visual effects: The art and techniques of VFX for directors, producers, editors and cinematographers*. Routledge.

Donaldson, M. (2025, November 10). Museum volunteer ruins artwork by "cleaning" display with toilet paper. *GB News*.

Dooley, B., & Hida, H. (2021, February 24). Nytimes.com. The New York Times - Breaking News, US News, World News and Videos. https://www.nytimes.com/2021/02/24/business/japan-anime.html

Dorin, A., McCabe, J., McCormack, J., Monro, G., & Whitelaw, M. (2012). A framework for understanding generative art. *Digital Creativity (Exeter)*, *23*(3–4), 239–259. DOI: 10.1080/14626268.2012.709940

Drakou, A., Papachristou, E., Tarnanidis, T., & Bilalis, N. (2024). Transforming fashion education: The impact of AI-driven 3D design on learning, creativity, and sustainability. In *Proceedings of the 13th Hellenic Conference on Artificial Intelligence (SETN 2024)* (pp. 1–6). ACM. https://doi.org/DOI: 10.1145/3688671.3688794

Duncan, C. (1995). *Civilizing rituals: Inside public art museums*. Routledge.

Dunne, A., & Raby, F. (2013). *Speculative everything: Design, fiction, and social dreaming*. MIT Press.

Dwivedi, Y. K., Hughes, L., Ismagilova, E., Aarts, G., Coombs, C., Crick, T., Duan, Y., Dwivedi, R., Edwards, J., Eirug, A., Galanos, V., Ilavarasan, P. V., Janssen, M., Jones, P., Kar, A. K., Kizgin, H., Kronemann, B., Lal, B., Lucini, B., & Williams, M. D. (2021). Artificial intelligence (AI): Multidisciplinary perspectives on emerging challenges, opportunities, and agenda for research, practice and policy. *International Journal of Information Management*, *57*, 101994. DOI: 10.1016/j.ijinfomgt.2019.08.002

Eglash, R. (1999). *African fractals: Modern computing and indigenous design*. Rutgers University Press.

Elhefnawy, H., Saada, M., Abdelkareem, S., Elemam, Y., Subaih, R., & Hassabo, A. (2026). Color Theory and Semiotics: Exploring the Relationship Between Visual Semiotics and Color. *Journal of Textiles. Coloration and Polymer Science*, *23*, 9–15. DOI: 10.21608/jtcps.2024.259782.1322

Ellen MacArthur Foundation. (2017). *A new textiles economy: Redesigning fashion's future*. Retrieved January 22, 2025, from https://www.ellenmacarthurfoundation.org/assets/downloads/publications/A-New-Textiles-Economy_Full-Report.pdf

Elsaesser, T., & Hagener, M. (2015). *Film theory: An introduction through the senses* (2nd ed.). Routledge. DOI: 10.4324/9781315740768

Entwistle, J. (2015). *The fashioned body: Fashion, dress and modern social theory* (2nd ed.). Polity Press.

Enwezor, O. (2007). Artforum. *Artforum*, *46*(1), 382–386.

Epic Games. (2019). *Unreal Engine for virtual production*. Epic Games. https://www.unrealengine.com/en-US/uses/film-television

Eraş, E., & Türker, S. H. (2025). Türkiye'de tekstil ve hazır giyim üretim sürecinde artırılmış ve sanal gerçeklik uygulamaları: Sürdürülebilir tasarım üzerine etkileri. *Asya Studies*, *9*(33), 289–310. DOI: 10.31455/asya.1676374

Esanu, O. (2012). What was contemporary art? *Art Margins*, *1*(1), 5–28. DOI: 10.1162/ARTM_a_00003

Etherington, K. (2004). *Becoming a reflective researcher: Using our selves in research*. Jessica Kingsley Publishers.

Ettedgui, P. (1999). *Production design & art direction screencraft*. RotoVision.

Fashion domain expansion: Jujutsu Kaisen and Dolce & Gabbana collaborate on a special collection vanity teen lifestyle & new faces magazine. (2022, April 20). Vanity Teen Lifestyle & new faces magazine. https://www.vanityteen.com/jujutsu-kaisen-dolce-gabbana-collab/

Fast Retailing. (2021, March 22). UNIQLO appoints Doraemon as global sustainability ambassador. https://www.fastretailing.com/eng/group/news/2103221500.html

Favreau, J. (Creator). (2019-). *The Mandalorian* [TV series]. Disney+.

Fazi, M. B. (2018). *Contingent computation: Abstraction, experience, and indeterminacy in computational aesthetics*. Rowman & Littlefield International. DOI: 10.5040/9798881812027

Fernández Jiménez, M., Martinicorena Zaratiegui, S., & Paris Arranz, I. (2020). Políticas europeas de la "hostipitalidad" en el cine de Ruben Östlund: el caso de *The Square* (2017) [European Policies of "Hostipitality" in the Cinema of Ruben Östlund: The Case of *The Square* (2017)]. *Fotocinema. Revista Científica De Cine Y Fotografía*, (21), 221-245. https://doi.org/DOI: 10.24310/Fotocinema.2020.v21i.10041

Ferreira, D. (2015). The meaning potential of procedurality. In *Proceedings of the 14th Brazilian Symposium on Computer Games and Digital Entertainment (SBGames 2015)*. SBC.

Field, A. (2013). *Discovering statistics using IBM SPSS statistics* (4th ed.). Sage Publications.

Findeli, A., & Bousbaci, R. (2005). L'éclipse de l'objet dans les théories du projet en design. *The Design Journal*, *8*(3), 35–49. DOI: 10.2752/146069205789331574

Fletcher, K. (2014). *Sustainable fashion and textiles: Design journeys* (2nd ed.). Routledge., https://ualresearchonline.arts.ac.uk/id/eprint/7537

Flick, U. (2018). *An introduction to qualitative research* (6th ed.). SAGE.

Forsythe, A., Nadal, M., Sheehy, N., Cela-Conde, C. J., & Sawey, M. (2011). Predicting beauty: Fractal dimension and visual complexity in art. *British Journal of Psychology, 102*(1), 49–70. DOI: 10.1348/000712610X498958 PMID: 21241285

Fox, A. (2000). My Mother's Cupboards & My Father's Words [Artist's book/Photographs]. Retrieved May 22, 2026, from https://www.annafox.co.uk

Friedlander, J. (2020). Repeating the square: From satisfaction to jouissance. *Crisis and Critique*, *7*(2), 91–103.

Frueh, J., Raven, A., & Langer, C. L. (Eds.). (1988). *Feminist art criticism: An anthology*. Routledge.

Galanter, P. (2003). What is generative art? Complexity theory as a context for art theory. In *Proceedings of the International Conference on Generative Art (GA2003).* Politecnico di Milano.

Galanter, P. (2003). What Is Generative Art? Complexity Theory as a Context for Art Theory. In *Proceedings of the International Conference on Generative Art.* Milan, Italy.

Garnham, P. (2021). The world's first variable font logo for WPP. Monotype. Retrieved 16 April 2025, from Monotype' – world's first variable font logo for WPP.

Garrett, D. (2018). *Nature and necessity in Spinoza's philosophy*. Oxford University Press.

Gasouka, M. (2026, March 7). Gynaikeia grafi ston androkentriko kosmo tis logotechnias [Female writing in the male centered world of literature]. *I Efimerida ton Syntakton*. https://www.efsyn.gr/nisides/503284_gynaikeia-grafi-ston-androkentriko-kosmo-tis-logotehnias

Gebauer, G., & Wulf, C. (1995). *Mimesis: Culture, art, society* (Reneau, D., Trans.). University of California Press.

Geczy, A., & Karaminas, V. (2012). *Fashion and art*. Berg.

Geissdoerfer, M., Savaget, P., Bocken, N. M. P., & Hultink, E. J. (2017). The circular economy – A new sustainability paradigm? *Journal of Cleaner Production, 143*, 757–768. DOI: 10.1016/j.jclepro.2016.12.048

Gerwig, G. (Director). (2023). *Barbie* [Film]. Warner Bros. Pictures.

Gibbs, J. (2002). *Mise-en-scène: film style and ınterpretation*. Wallflower Book.

Gibson, J. J. (1979). *The ecological approach to visual perception*. Houghton Mifflin.

Glogar, M., Petrak, S., & Mahnić Naglić, M. (2025). Digital technologies in the sustainable design and development of textiles and clothing: A literature review. *Sustainability (Basel)*, *17*(4), 1371. DOI: 10.3390/su17041371

Goethe, J. W. von. (1952). Versuch die Metamorphose der Pflanzen zu erklären. E. Trunz (Ed.) Hamburger Ausgabe, Vol. 13). C. H. Beck. (Original work published 1790)

Goethe, J. W. von. (1962). Italienische Reise. E. Trunz (Ed.) Hamburger Ausgabe, Vol. 11). C. H. Beck. (Original work published 1816)

Goldstein, E. B. (2014). *Sensation and perception* (9th ed.). Cengage Learning.

Goswami, K. (2025, December 31). 10 top anime brand collaborations in 2025 ranked. Outlook Respawn. https://respawn.outlookindia.com/pop-culture/pop-culture-guides/one-piece-jjk-naruto-the-10-biggest-anime-collabs-of-2025

Granata, F. (2017). *Experimental fashion: Performance art, carnival, and the grotesque body*. I.B. Tauris. DOI: 10.5040/9781350986312

Grand View Research. (2025). Anime apparel and fashion market size, share, and trends analysis report. https://www.grandviewresearch.com/industry-analysis/anime-apparel-fashion-market-report

Granitz, N., & Forman, H. (2015). Building self-brand connections: Exploring brand stories through a transmedia perspective. *Journal of Brand Management*, *22*(1), 38–59. DOI: 10.1057/bm.2015.1

Grønstad, A. (2020). Conditional vulnerability in the films of Ruben Östlund. In Dancus, A. M., Hyvönen, M., & Karlsson, M. (Eds.), *Vulnerability in Scandinavian art and culture* (pp. 19–31). DOI: 10.1007/978-3-030-37382-5_2

Guan, X., & Wang, K. (2022). Visual communication design using machine vision and digital media communication technology. *Wireless Communications and Mobile Computing*, *2022*(1), 6235913. Advance online publication. DOI: 10.1155/2022/6235913

Guillemin, M. (2004). Understanding illness: Using drawings as a research method. *Qualitative Health Research*, *14*(2), 272–289. DOI: 10.1177/1049732303260445 PMID: 14768462

Guillemin, M., & Gillam, L. (2004). Ethics, reflexivity, and 'ethically important moments' in research. *Qualitative Inquiry*, *10*(2), 261–280. DOI: 10.1177/1077800403262360

Gullette, C. M. (2018). *Challenging Swedishness: Intersections of neoliberalism, race, and queerness in the works of Jonas Hassen Khemiri and Ruben Östlund* [Unpublished doctoral dissertation, University of California, Berkeley]. UC Berkeley Electronic Theses and Dissertations.

Gürer, E., & Küçükersen, F. (2021). Performing a new agenda for a first-year interior architecture studio: Theatre space. In Garip, E., & Garip, S. B. (Eds.), *Handbook of research on methodologies for design and production practices in interior architecture* (pp. 218–256). IGI Global Scientific Publishing. DOI: 10.4018/978-1-7998-7254-2.ch011

Guschwan, M. (2012). Fandom, brandom and the limits of participatory culture. *Journal of Consumer Culture*, *12*(1), 19–40. DOI: 10.1177/1469540512438154

Guyas, A. S. (2007). Re-constructing self within the family: Re-building the family album. *Visual Culture & Gender*, *2*, 14–23.

Gwilt, A. (2020). *A practical guide to sustainable fashion*. Bloomsbury Visual Arts., DOI: 10.5040/9781350067059

Halliwell, S. (2002). *The aesthetics of mimesis: Ancient texts and modern problems*. Princeton University Press.

Hanzer, E. (2018). *Phase* [Variable font]. https://eliashanzer.com

Harrison, S. (2003). *Pop art and the origins of post-modernism*. Cambridge University Press.

Hello Games. (2016). *No Man's Sky* [Video game]. Hello Games.

Henninger, C. E., Alevizou, P. J., & Oates, C. J. (2016). What is sustainable fashion? *Journal of Fashion Marketing and Management*, *20*(4), 400–416. DOI: 10.1108/JFMM-07-2015-0052

Herari, N., Najmi Nuji, M. N., Boer, R. F., & Allifiansyah, S. (2026). Algorithmic Narcissism and the Passion Economy. In Kaygisiz, E. (Ed.), *Digital ideologies in the age of algorithmic culture* (pp. 237–270). IGI Global Scientific Publishing., https://www.igi-global.com/chapter/algorithmic-narcissism-and-the-passion-economy/407330, DOI: 10.4018/979-8-3373-4531-4.ch008

Herari, N., Waluyo, W., & Rubiyanto, R. (2025). Leading Alone, Leading Forward: Solopreneurs and the Quiet Power of the Passion Economy. In Paradiso-Testa, M. (Ed.), *The purpose of passion in leadership* (pp. 333–358). IGI Global Scientific Publishing., https://www.igi-global.com/chapter/leading-alone-leading-forward/385644, DOI: 10.4018/979-8-3373-2404-3.ch012

Hirsch, M. (2002). *Familial frames: Photography, narrative and post memory.* Harvard University Press.

Holt, D. B. (2004). How brands become icons: The principles of cultural branding. Harvard Business Press. ISBN 13:978-1578517749.

hooks, b. (1994). *Teaching to transgress: Education as the practice of freedom.* Routledge.

Human Development Report (2025). Human Development Report 2025, May 6, 2025 https://hdr.undp.org/content/human-development-report-2025

Huot-Marchand, T. (2018). *Minérale* [Variable font]. 205TF. https://www.205.tf/designers/thomas-huot-marchand

Hvass, K. K. (2014). Post-retail responsibility of garments: A fashion industry perspective. *Journal of Fashion Marketing and Management, 18*(4), 413–430. DOI: 10.1108/JFMM-01-2013-0005

IBM (n.d.). IBM Plex specifications. Retrieved 16 April 2025, from IBM Plex Specifications.

IBM. (2017). *IBM Plex: Languages* [Typeface specimen]. IBM. https://www.ibm.com/plex/languages Retrieved March 19, 2026.

İnceoğlu, S. (2022). Mimarlık ve sinema arakesitinde bir yönetmenin analizi: Wes Anderson. Master's thesis, Mimar Sinan Güzel Sanatlar University, Türkiye.

İstek, R. (2005). *Typography and Page Layout in Visual Communication.* Pusula Publishing.

James, O., Achard, R., Bird, J., & Cooper, S. (2021). *Color-managed LED walls for virtual production.* SIGGRAPH: International Conference on Computer Graphics and Interactive Techniques, New York.

Jameson, F. (1983). Postmodernism and consumer society. In Foster, H. (Ed.), *The anti-aesthetic: Essays on postmodern culture* (pp. 111–125). Bay Press.

Jameson, F. (1991). *Postmodernism, or, the cultural logic of late capitalism.* Duke University Press.

Jamieson, M. K., Govaart, G. H., & Pownall, M. (2023). Reflexivity in quantitative research: A rationale and beginner's guide. *Social and Personality Psychology Compass, 17*(4), 1–15. DOI: 10.1111/spc3.12735

Jencks, C. (1992). The post-modern agenda. In Jencks, C. (Ed.), *The post-modern reader*. Academy Editions.

Jenkins, H. (2006). Convergence culture: Where old and new media collide. New York University Press. ISBN 13:978-0814742815.

Jenkins, H. (2004). Game design as narrative architecture. In Wardrip-Fruin, N., & Harrigan, P. (Eds.), *First person: New media as story, performance, and game* (pp. 118–130). MIT Press.

Jipson, J. A., & Paley, N. (Eds.). (1997). *Daredevil research: Re-creating analytic practice*. P. Lang.

Joy, A., Sherry, J. F.Jr, Venkatesh, A., Wang, J., & Chan, R. (2012). Fast fashion, sustainability, and the ethical appeal of luxury brands. *Fashion Theory, 16*(3), 273–295. DOI: 10.2752/175174112X13340749707123

Kääpä, P. (2018). *Environmental management of the media: Policy, industry, practice*. Routledge., DOI: 10.4324/9781315625690

Kadem, F. D., & Özdemir, Ş. (2024). An overview of digital textile printing technologies. *Osmaniye Korkut Ata University Journal of The Institute of Science and Technology*, *7*(2), 889–901.

Kane, D., & Juliao, D. (2026). Study.com. study.com. https://study.com/academy/lesson/anime-history-style.html

Kant, I. (2000). Critique of the power of judgment. (P. Guyer, Ed. & Trans., E. Matthews, Trans). Cambridge University Press. (Original work published 1790) DOI: 10.1017/CBO9780511804656

Kaplan, E. (2022). Use of Variable Fonts in Corporate Identity Design (Master's thesis). Graduate School of Fine Arts, Department of Graphic Design, Mimar Sinan Fine Arts University, Istanbul, Turkey.

Kaplan, C. S. (2005). Islamic star patterns from polygons in contact. *Proceedings. Graphics Interface (Conference), 2005*, 177–185.

Karth, I., & Compton, K. (2023). Conceptual art made real: Why procedural content generation is impossible. In *Proceedings of the Foundations of Digital Games 2023 (FDG '23)*. ACM. DOI: 10.1145/3582437.3582470

Kavakli, M., & Cremona, C. (2022). The virtual production studio concept: Analysing the impact of LED volume technology on film and television production. In *2022 IEEE Conference on Virtual Reality and 3D User Interfaces (VR)* (pp. 29-37). IEEE. https://doi.org/DOI: 10.1109/VR51125.2022.00020

Kawamura, Y. (2005). *Fashion-ology: An introduction to fashion studies.* Berg. DOI: 10.2752/9781847888730

Kawamura, Y. (2016). *Fashioning Japanese subcultures.* Bloomsbury.

Kelly, S. (2018, March 1). Artist Terry Notary explains that uncomfortable dinner scene in Oscar contender *The Square. Los Angeles Times.*

Kelly, C. J. (2008). Personal is political. In O'Brien, J. (Ed.), *Encyclopedia of gender and society* (pp. 643–644). SAGE Publications.

Kidman, G., & Tan, H. (2025). Interdisciplinary thinking in STEA+M: Cognitive integration, makerspaces, and knowledge creation. In *Knowledge generation in STEM and STEAM education* (pp. 89–121). Springer., https://link.springer.com/chapter/10.1007/978-3-032-03247-8_4 DOI: 10.1007/978-3-032-03247-8_4

Kirchherr, J., Reike, D., & Hekkert, M. (2017). Conceptualizing the circular economy: An analysis of 114 definitions. *Resources, Conservation and Recycling, 127,* 221–232. DOI: 10.1016/j.resconrec.2017.09.005

Kiso, V. (2023). Japanese Pop Culture's Response to COVID-19: Embracing Digitalization and Hybridization. ICS Occasional Papers, *105*, 4-21.

Kolarevic, B. (2003). *Architecture in the Digital Age: Design and Manufacturing.* Spon Press.

Kolb, D. A. (2015). *Experiential learning: Experience as the source of learning and development.* Pearson Education, Inc. (Original work published 1984)

Kosinski, J. (Director). (2022). *Top Gun: Maverick* [Film]. Paramount Pictures.

Koszewska, M. (2018). Circular economy—Challenges for the textile and clothing industry. *AUTEX Research Journal, 18*(4), 337–347. DOI: 10.1515/aut-2018-0023

Krasner, J. (2013). *Motion graphic design: Applied history and aesthetics* (2nd ed.). Focal Press. DOI: 10.4324/9780240824703

Küçükersen, F. (2026). A design learning cycle: Transforming experience into foundational design learning through reflection. (Doctoral dissertation). Istanbul Technical University, Graduate School, Istanbul.

Küçükersen, F., & Özemir, P. (2025). Dialogic interactions in foundation design studio: An unsolicited diary research. *International Journal of Art & Design Education, 44*(3), 728–742. DOI: 10.1111/jade.12599

Küçükersen, F., Özemir, P., Dinçer, D., & Demirbilek, O. (2026). Beyond Kolb: Constructing a design learning cycle for the foundation studio. *Journal of Experiential Education, 49*(1), 158–191. DOI: 10.1177/10538259251362141

Kuzmichev, V. (2025). Clothing design in the era of artificial intelligence. *Journal of Computer and Communications, 13*(5), 121–136. DOI: 10.4236/jcc.2025.135008

Kwon, M. (2002). *One place after another: Site-specific art and locational identity*. MIT Press. DOI: 10.7551/mitpress/5138.001.0001

Lageira, J. (2025). Imaginary Subject. In Chateau, D. (Ed.), *Subjectivity: filmic representation and the spectator's experience* (pp. 161–184). Routledge., DOI: 10.4324/9781003704515-13

Lamarre, T. (2009). *The anime machine: A media theory of animation*. University of Minnesota Press.

Lamerichs, N. (2018). *Productive fandom: Intermediality and affective reception in fan cultures*. Amsterdam University Press.

Lazard, L., & McAvoy, J. (2020). Doing reflexivity in psychological research: What's the point? What's the practice? *Qualitative Research in Psychology, 17*(2), 159–177. DOI: 10.1080/14780887.2017.1400144

Leaver, T., Hutchinson, J., & Abidin, C. (2020). *Instagram: Visual social media cultures*. Polity Press.

LeBaron, G., Edwards, R., Hunt, T., Sempéré, C., & Kyritsis, P. (2021). The ineffectiveness of CSR: Understanding garment company commitments to living wages in global supply chains. *New Political Economy, 27*(1), 99–115. DOI: 10.1080/13563467.2021.1926954

LeGendre, C., Lepicovsky, L., & Debevec, P. (2022). Jointly optimizing color rendition and ın-camera backgrounds in an rgb virtual production stage. *arXiv*(July), 1-12. https://doi.org//arXiv.2205.12403DOI: 10.1145/3543664.3543681

Leitch, D. (Director). (2022). *Bullet Train* [Film]. Columbia Pictures.

LeWitt, S. (1967). Paragraphs on conceptual art. *Artforum, 5*(10), 79–83.

LeWitt, S. (1969). Sentences on conceptual art. *Art-Language, 1*(1), 11–13.

Likert, R. (1932). A technique for the measurement of attitudes. *Archives of Psychology, 22*(140), 1–55.

LoBrutto, V. (2002). *The filmmaker's guide to production design*. Allworth Press.

Long, D., Bogart, R., Stephens, S., Kennel, G., & Fazakerley, A. (2025). Color management principles for LED panels in on-set virtual production. *SMPTE Motion Imaging Journal, 134*(2), 43–52. DOI: 10.5594/JMI.2025/XEJK1138

Lu, P. J., & Steinhardt, P. J. (2007). Decagonal and quasi-crystalline tilings in medieval Islamic architecture. *Science, 315*(5815), 1106–1110. DOI: 10.1126/science.1135491 PMID: 17322056

Lupton, E. (2010). Thinking with Type: A Critical Guide for Designers, Writers, Editors, and Students (2nd ed.). New York: Princeton Architectural Press.

Lupton, E., & Phillips, J. C. (2015). *Graphic design: The new basics* (2nd ed.). Princeton Architectural Press.

Lynch, J. (2020). "Please leave a message": The media ecology of Ruben Östlund's *Play, Force Majeure*, and *The Square. Journal of Scandinavian Cinema, 10*(2), 145–160.

Lynton, N. (1980). *The story of modern art*. Phaidon.

Lyotard, J.-F. (1979). *La condition postmoderne: Rapport sur le savoir* [The Postmodern Condition: A Report on Knowledge]. Éditions de Minuit.

Lyu, H. (2025). A study of the role of color in visual communication in the digital perspective. *Mediterranean Archaeology & Archaeometry. International Journal, 25*(1), 352–357.

Macbeth, D. (2001). On 'reflexivity' in qualitative research: Two readings, and a third. *Qualitative Inquiry, 7*(1), 35–68. DOI: 10.1177/107780040100700103

Madaan, J. (2025, September 4). Demon slayer: Infinity castle vs the Mugen train worldwide box office: Akaza's return needs 69% Jump to emerge as #1 anime film! Koimoi. https://www.koimoi.com/box-office/demon-slayer-infinity-castle-vs-the-mugen-train-worldwide-box-office-akazas-return-needs-69-jump-to-emerge-as-1-anime-film/

Malevich, K. (1959). *The non-objective world*. Paul Theobald.

Maliha, S. R., & Aziz, M. N. (2024). Exploring anime consumers' identity construction in the digital era. *BUFT. Journal of Business Economics, 5*(1). Advance online publication. DOI: 10.58481/BJBE/2414

Manovich, L. (2013). Software takes command. Bloomsbury. ISBN-13z: 978-1623567453

Manovich, L. (2013). *Software takes command.* Bloomsbury Academic. DOI: 10.5040/9781472544988

Manovich, L. (2024). Separate and reassemble: Generative AI through the lens of art and media histories. *MATRIZes, 18*(2), 7–18. DOI: 10.11606/issn.1982-8160.v18i2p7-18

Manzini, E. (2015). *Design, when everybody designs: An introduction to design for social innovation.* MIT Press. DOI: 10.7551/mitpress/9873.001.0001

Margolin, V. (2002). *The politics of the artificial: Essays on design and design studies.* University of Chicago Press. DOI: 10.7208/chicago/9780226518374.001.0001

Mateas, M. (2005). Procedural literacy: Educating the new media practitioner. *On the Horizon, 13*(2), 101–111. DOI: 10.1108/10748120510608133

McCloud, S. (1993). *Understanding comics: The invisible art.* HarperCollins.

McCormack, J., & Dorin, A. (2001). Art, emergence and the computational sublime. *Proceedings of Second Iteration: A Conference on Generative Systems in the Electronic Arts* (pp. 67–81). CEMA.

McCracken, G. (2015). *Culture and consumption II: Markets, meaning, and brand management.* Indiana University Press.

McIntyre, P., & Delaney, K. (2020). Reimagining STEM education: Critical, transdisciplinary, and embodied approaches. In *STEM Education: New Directions in Theory and Practice* (pp. 1–18). Springer. https://link.springer.com/chapter/10.1007/978-3-030-29489-2_1

McKinsey & Company. (2023). The state of fashion 2023: Holding onto growth as global clouds gather. https://www.mckinsey.com/industries/retail/our-insights/state-of-fashion

McNeill, L., & Moore, R. (2015). Sustainable fashion consumption and the fast fashion conundrum: Fashionable consumers and attitudes to sustainability in clothing choice. *International Journal of Consumer Studies, 39*(3), 212–222. DOI: 10.1111/ijcs.12169

Medina, C. (2010, January). Contemp(t)ory: Eleven theses. *e-flux*, (12). https://www.e-flux.com/journal/12/61335

Mezirow, J. (2000). *Learning as transformation: Critical perspectives on a theory in progress*. Jossey-Bass.

Mickel, J., & Imas, L. (2018). *Adineue Chop* [Variable font]. MCKL / Adidas.

Milgram, P., & Kishino, F. (1994). A taxonomy of mixed reality visual displays. *IEICE Transactions on Information and Systems*, *77*(12), 1321–1329.

Miller, G. (Director). (2015). *Mad Max: Fury Road* [Film]. Warner Bros. Pictures.

Minea, V. (2025). Where god is becoming: Anime, theosis, and the sacred in process. *Religions*, *16*(8), 1014. DOI: 10.3390/rel16081014

Mirzoeff, N. (2009). *An Introduction to Visual Culture* (2nd ed.). Routledge.

Monaco, J. (2009). *How to read a film: Movies, media, and beyond* (4th ed.). Oxford University Press.

Monotype. (2019). *The world's first variable font logo* [Web page]. Monotype. https://www.monotype.com/resources/monotype-labs/world%E2%80%99s-first-variable-font-logo Retrieved March 20, 2026.

Morgner, C. (2014). The evolution of the art fair. *Historical Social Research (Köln)*, *39*(3), 318–336. DOI: 10.12759/hsr.39.2014.3.318-336

Moser, S. (2008). Personality: A new positionality? *Area*, *40*(3), 383–392. DOI: 10.1111/j.1475-4762.2008.00815.x

MPPA. (2025). Motion picture producers association of Japan, Inc. . https://www.eiren.org/statistics_e/

Mukherjee, K., Yin, B., Sherman, B. E., Lessard, L., & Schloss, K. B. (2021). Context matters: A theory of semantic discriminability for perceptual encoding systems. *arXiv*. https://arxiv.org/abs/2108.03685

Mulvey, L. (1975). Visual pleasure and narrative cinema. *Screen*, *16*(3), 6–18. DOI: 10.1093/screen/16.3.6

Muratbekova, P., & Shamoi, A. (2023). Color-Emotion Associations in Art: Fuzzy Approach. *arXiv preprint*. arXiv

Murray, J. H. (2017). *Hamlet on the holodeck: The future of narrative in cyberspace* (Updated ed.). MIT Press.

Murray, J. H. (1997). *Hamlet on the holodeck: The future of narrative in cyberspace*. Free Press.

Mykhalovskiy, E. (1996). Reconsidering table talk: Critical thoughts on the relationship between sociology, autobiography and self-indulgence. *Qualitative Sociology, 19*(1), 131–151. DOI: 10.1007/BF02393251

Naeem, M., Ozuem, W., Ranfagni, S., & Howell, K. (2025). User generated content and brand engagement: Exploring the role of electronic semiotics and symbolic interactionism on Instagram. *Computers in Human Behavior, 168*, 108642. DOI: 10.1016/j.chb.2025.108642

Nancy, J.-L. (2010). Art today (C. Mandel, Trans.). *Journal of Visual Culture, 9*(1), 91–99. DOI: 10.1177/1470412909354265

Napier, S. J. (2018). Anime from Akira to Howl's Moving Howl's: Experiencing contemporary Japanese animation (Rev. ed.). St. Martin's PressMartin's3:978-1403970527.

Nazarbaeva, N. (2018). *Thinking inside and outside of The Square: Barriers, audience engagement, and contemporary art in Ruben Östlund's film The Square* [Unpublished master's thesis]. Lund University.

Negri, A. (2008). Contemporaneity between modernity and postmodernity. In Smith, T., Enwezor, O., & Condee, N. (Eds.), *Modernity, postmodernity, contemporaneity* (pp. 23–29). Duke University Press.

Netflix. (2023). *What is Virtual Production?* Netflix Technology Blog. https://partnerhelp.netflixstudios.com/hc/en-us/articles/1500002552642-What-is-Virtual-Production

Neuendorf, K. A. (2017). *The content analysis guidebook* (2nd ed.). SAGE.

Nietzsche, F. (1874). *Unzeitgemässe Betrachtungen* [Untimely meditations]. Verlag von E. W. Fritzsch.

Niinimäki, K. (2013). Tenets of sustainable fashion. In Niinimäki, K. (Ed.), *Sustainable fashion: New approaches* (pp. 12–29). Aalto University.

Niinimäki, K., & Hassi, L. (2011). Emerging design strategies in sustainable production and consumption of textiles and clothing. *Journal of Cleaner Production, 19*(16), 1876–1883. DOI: 10.1016/j.jclepro.2011.04.020

Niinimäki, K., Peters, G., Dahlbo, H., Perry, P., Rissanen, T., & Gwilt, A. (2020). The environmental price of fast fashion. *Nature Reviews. Earth & Environment, 1*(4), 189–200. DOI: 10.1038/s43017-020-0039-9

Noh, S. (2022). *Global Media Streams: Cosmopolitan Streaming Platforms and the Contemporary Ecosystem of Anime Distribution*. The University of Wisconsin-Madison.

Noh, S. (2024). Global media streams: Netflix and the changing ecosystem of anime production. *Television & New Media*, *25*(3), 234–250. DOI: 10.1177/15274764231206540

Nolan, C. (Director). (2008). *The Dark Knight* [Film]. Warner Bros. Pictures.

O'Doherty, B. (1976). *Inside the white cube: The ideology of the gallery space*. Lapis Press.

Okun, J. A., Zwerman, S., & Thurmond O'Neal, S. (2025). *The ves handbook of visual effects: ındustry standard vfx practices and procedures* (4th ed.). Routledge., DOI: 10.4324/9781003534259

Östlund, R. (Director). (2017). *The Square* [Film]. Plattform Produktion

Ovid. (1916). *Metamorphoses* (F. J. Miller, Trans.). Harvard University Press. (Original work written c. 8 CE)

Ozuem, W., Willis, M., Ranfagni, S., & Omeish, F. (2025). Thematic analysis in an artificial intelligence-driven context: A stage-by-stage process. *International Journal of Qualitative Methods*, *24*, 1–15. DOI: 10.1177/16094069251362982

Pallant, J. (2020). *SPSS survival manual: A step-by-step guide to data analysis using IBM SPSS* (7th ed.). McGraw-Hill Education.

Pallasmaa, J. (2001). *The architecture of image: Existential space in cinema*. Rakennustieto Publishing.

Pal, R., & Gander, J. (2018). Modelling environmental value: An examination of sustainable business models within the fashion industry. *Journal of Cleaner Production*, *184*, 251–263. DOI: 10.1016/j.jclepro.2018.02.001

Panourgia, N. (1995). *Fragments of death, fables of identity: An Athenian anthropography*. University of Wisconsin Press.

Papadimitriou, M. (1998). T.A.M.A. (Temporary Autonomous Museum for All) [Photography/Installation]. Retrieved May 22, 2026, from https://www.mariapapadimitriou.com

Papanek, V. (1985). *Design for the real world: Human ecology and social change* (2nd ed.). Thames & Hudson.

Patton, M. Q. (2015). *Qualitative research & evaluation methods* (4th ed.). SAGE.

Penney, L. (2016). *Axis-Praxis* [Variable font playground]. https://www.axis-praxis.org Retrieved March 18, 2026.

Perlin, K. (1985). An image synthesizer. *Computer Graphics*, *19*(3), 287–296. DOI: 10.1145/325165.325247

Petteni, O. (2022). The contemporary legacy of Goethean morphology: From *Anschauende Urteilskraft* to algorithmic pattern recognition, generation, and exploration. *Goethe Yearbook*, *29*(1), 43–72. DOI: 10.1353/gyr.2022.0002

Piedra, L. M. (2023). Positionality-An analytical building block. *Qualitative Social Work: Research and Practice*, *22*(4), 611–618. DOI: 10.1177/14733250231183294

Piedra, L. M. (2025). Paradigms, positionality, and the responsibilities of inquiry. *Qualitative Social Work: Research and Practice*, *24*(6), 641–649. DOI: 10.1177/14733250251384424

Prince, S. (2012). *Digital visual effects in cinema: The seduction of reality*. Rutgers University Press., https://www.jstor.org/stable/j.ctt5hj5pv

Probst, B., & Berenson, L. (2014). The double arrow: How qualitative social work researchers use reflexivity. *Qualitative Social Work: Research and Practice*, *13*(6), 813–827. DOI: 10.1177/1473325013506248

Prusinkiewicz, P., & Lindenmayer, A. (1990). *The algorithmic beauty of plants*. Springer-Verlag. DOI: 10.1007/978-1-4613-8476-2

Queloz, M. (2021). *The practical origins of ideas: Genealogy as conceptual reverse-engineering*. Oxford University Press. DOI: 10.1093/oso/9780198868705.001.0001

Quesenberry, K. A., & Coolsen, M. K. (2023). Brand storytelling: Integrated marketing communications for the digital media landscape. Bloomsbury Publishing PLC. ISBN 13:978-1538176382.

Rahman, M. M. (2020). Applications of digital technologies in textile and fashion industry. *Technium*, *3*(1), 114–127. DOI: 10.47577/technium.v3i1.1140

Reed-Danahay, D. E. (1997). *Auto/ethnography: Rewriting the self and the social*. Berg.

Reeves, M. (Director). (2022). *The Batman* [Film]. Warner Bros. Pictures.

Reid, S. F., Moses, L., & Rylak, D. (2026). "That storrey reminse you to be cefl": A multimodal analysis of a first-grader's blended genre composition. *Journal of Early Childhood Literacy*, *26*(1), 450–481. DOI: 10.1177/14687984251337368

Riis, J. (2024). Symbolic purposes of style: Ruben Östlund's *The Square. Journal of Scandinavian Cinema, 13*(3), 283–297. DOI: 10.1386/jsca_00100_1

Rinchen, K., Banham, V., & Pelden, S. (2025). Reflexive researcher: Navigating positionality while interviewing participants in a close-knit community for a deeper exploration of their lived experiences. *International Journal of Qualitative Methods, 24*, 1–12. DOI: 10.1177/16094069251371471

Ríos, C. D. L., & Patel, L. (2023). Positions, positionality, and relationality in educational research. *International Journal of Qualitative Studies in Education : QSE, 36*, 1–12. DOI: 10.1080/09518398.2023.2268036

Ristola, J. (2017). Blood, Sweat, Ink, and Tears: Exploitation of Labour in the Japanese Animation Industry. Conference: Global Labour Research Centre Graduate Student Symposium 2016. https://www.researchgate.net/publication/322909809_Blood_Sweat_Ink_and_Tears_Exploitation_of_Labour_in_the_Japanese_Animation_Industry

Riyanto, B., Aulia, G., Akbari, T. T., & Herari, N. (2025). Visionary Voices: When Digital Media Leadership Projects Soft Power. In Paradiso-Testa, M. (Ed.), *The value of vision in leadership* (pp. 217–252). IGI Global Scientific Publishing., https://www.igi-global.com/chapter/visionary-voices/385358, DOI: 10.4018/979-8-3373-2392-3.ch007

Rodriguez, R., & Miller, F. (Directors). (2005). *Sin City* [Film]. Dimension Films.

Roe-Dale, A., & Pfaff, C. (2019). Vera Molnar's machine imaginaire. *Journal of Mathematics and the Arts, 13*(3), 221–245.

Rose, G. (2016). *Visual methodologies: An introduction to researching with visual materials* (4th ed.). SAGE Publications.

Ross, D. J. (2017). *Fit* [Variable font]. DJR. https://djr.com/fit

Ryan, M.-L. (2015). *Narrative as virtual reality 2: Revisiting immersion and interactivity in literature and electronic media*. Johns Hopkins University Press. DOI: 10.1353/book.72246

Saehrendt, C., & Kittl, S. T. (2007). *Das kann ich auch!: Gebrauchsanweisung für moderne Kunst* [I can do that too!: A user manual for modern art]. DuMont Buchverlag.

Sagardia, S. C. (2017). Dressing the part: Communication of identity in a performative fandom community (Doctoral dissertation).

Sanders, E. B.-N., & Stappers, P. J. (2008). Co-creation and the new landscapes of design. *CoDesign*, *4*(1), 5–18. DOI: 10.1080/15710880701875068

Santa Maria, J. (2014). *On web typography*. A Book Apart. https://abookapart.com/products/on-web-typography

Santiago Iglesias, J. A. (2021). Not just immobile: Moving drawings and visual synecdoches in Neon Genesis Evangelion. In *Anime studies* (pp. 19–48). Stockholm University Press. DOI: 10.16993/bbp.b

Sarıkavak, N. K. (2004). *Foundations of contemporary typography*. Seçkin Publishing.

Schloss, K. (2024). Color semantics in human cognition. Current Directions in Psychological Science, 33(1), 58–67. https://doi.org/, C. L. (2025). Postdigital visual literacy: Visual entanglements and dynamic learning processes in art education. *American Journal of STEM Education, 14*, 49–58. https://doi.org/DOI: 10.1177/09637214231208189Schwarz

Schmitt, B. (2010). Experiential Marketing. *Journal of Marketing Management*, *15*(1-3), 53–67. https://www.tandfonline.com/doi/abs/10.1362/026725799784870496. DOI: 10.1362/026725799784870496

Schroeder, J. E. (2020). *Visual consumption* (2nd ed.). Routledge.

Scott-Hoy, K. (2002). The visitor: Juggling life in the grip of the text. In Bochner, A. P., & Ellis, C. (Eds.), *Ethnographically speaking: Autoethnography, literature and aesthetics* (pp. 274–294). Altamira Press.

Sengupta, R. (2020). Things I Can't Say Out Loud [Photographs]. Retrieved May 22, 2026, from https://www.ritisengupta.com

Sharma, D. (2024). Skeptimentality: The Square And The Aesthetics of Complicity. *The Nordic Journal of Aesthetics*, *2024*(68), 10–32. DOI: 10.7146/nja.v33i68.152362

Shaw, A., & Colette, J. (2023). *Motion design toolkit: Principles, practice, and techniques*. Routledge.

Shiner, L. (2001). *The Invention of Art: A Cultural History*. University of Chicago Press. DOI: 10.7208/chicago/9780226753416.001.0001

Silva Jasaui, D., Martí-Testón, A., Muñoz, A., Moriniello, F., Solanes, J. E., & Gracia, L. (2024). Virtual Production: Real-Time Rendering Pipelines for Indie Studios and the Potential in Different Scenarios. *Applied Sciences (Basel, Switzerland)*, *14*(6), 2530. DOI: 10.3390/app14062530

Skukauskaite, A., Yilmazli Trout, I., & Robinson, K. A. (2022). Deepening reflexivity through art in learning qualitative research. *Qualitative Research, 22*(3), 403–420. DOI: 10.1177/1468794120985676

Slater, M. (2009). Place illusion and plausibility can lead to realistic behaviour in immersive virtual environments. *Philosophical Transactions of the Royal Society of London. Series B, Biological Sciences, 364*(1535), 3549–3557. DOI: 10.1098/rstb.2009.0138 PMID: 19884149

Slater, M., & Wilbur, S. (1997). A framework for immersive virtual environments (FIVE): Speculations on the role of presence in virtual environments. *Presence (Cambridge, Mass.), 6*(6), 603–616. DOI: 10.1162/pres.1997.6.6.603

Smith, M. (2021). *Degrees of artificiality in the works of: Roy Andersson, Aki Kaurismäki, Ruben Östlund, Thomas Vinterberg, and Lukas Moodysson* [Unpublished master's thesis]. Queen's University.

Smith, G., & Whitehead, J. (2010). Analyzing the expressive range of a level generator. *Proceedings of the 2010 Workshop on Procedural Content Generation in Games (PCGames '10).* ACM. DOI: 10.1145/1814256.1814260

Smith, T. (2009). *What is contemporary art?* University of Chicago Press. DOI: 10.7208/chicago/9780226131672.001.0001

Smith, T. (2011). Currents of world-making in contemporary art. *World Art, 1*(2), 171–188. DOI: 10.1080/21500894.2011.602712

Smith, T. J. (2012). The attentional theory of cinematic continuity. *Projections (New York, N.Y.), 6*(1), 1–27. DOI: 10.3167/proj.2012.060102

SMPTE. (2023). *The On-Set Virtual Production initiative will be the first RIS from SMPTE.* Society of Motion Picture and Television Engineers. https://www.smpte.org/

Snyder, Z. (Director). (2006). *300* [Film]. Warner Bros. Pictures.

Solo leveling PC bundle. Starforge Systems. (n.d.). https://starforgesystems.com/products/solo-leveling-pc-bundle

Souriau, E. (1953). *L'univers filmique*. Flammarion.

Spinoza, B. (1985). *The collected works of Spinoza* (Vol. 1; Curley, E., Trans.). Princeton University Press. (Original work published 1677)

Stallabrass, J. (2004). *Contemporary art: A very short introduction.* Oxford University Press.

Staples, L. (2000). Typography and the screen: A technical chronology of digital typography, 1984–1997. *Design Issues*, *16*(3), 19–34. https://www.jstor.org/stable/1511813. DOI: 10.1162/07479360052053306

Steinberg, M. (2012). Anime's media Anime'sanchising toys and characters in Japan. University of Minnesota Press. Print ISBN: 9780816675494.

Stiny, G., & Gips, J. (1975). *Shape grammars and their uses: Artificial perception, shape generation and computer aesthetics*. Birkhauser.

Strizver, I. (2014). *Type Rules! The Designer's Guide to Professional Typography* (4th ed.). Wiley.

Stump, D. (2021). *Digital cinematography: Fundamentals, tools, techniques, and workflows* (2nd ed.). Routledge. DOI: 10.4324/9780429468858

Sun, Q., & Zhu, Y. (2022). Teaching analysis for visual communication design with the perspective of digital technology. *Journal of Educational Multimedia and Hypermedia*, *31*(2), 145–160. PMID: 35903440

Sweller, J., Ayres, P., & Kalyuga, S. (2011). *Cognitive load theory*. Springer. DOI: 10.1007/978-1-4419-8126-4

Swords, J., & Willment, N. (2024). The emergence of virtual production: A research agenda. *Convergence (London)*, *30*(5), 1557–1574. DOI: 10.1177/13548565241253903

Symeonidis, V., & Impedovo, M. A. (2023). Where internationalisation and digitalisation intersect: Designing a virtual exchange to enhance student teachers' professional awareness as European teachers. *European Journal of Teacher Education*, *46*(5), 821–839. DOI: 10.1080/02619768.2023.2243644

Tarkovsky, A. (1986). *Sculpting in time: Reflections on the cinema* (Hunter-Blair, K., Trans.). University of Texas Press.

Taylor, B. (2005). *Contemporary art: Art since 1970*. Pearson Prentice Hall.

Taylor, R. P., Newell, B. R., Spehar, B., & Clifford, C. W. G. (2001). Fractals: A resonance between art and nature? *Symmetry: Art and Science*, *1–2*, 194–197.

Thomas, K. (2020). Cultures of sustainability in the fashion industry. *Fashion Theory*, *24*(5), 715–742. DOI: 10.1080/1362704X.2018.1532737

Thompson, D. (2008). *The $12 million stuffed shark: The curious economics of contemporary art*. Palgrave Macmillan.

Thompson, D. W. (1942). *On growth and form* (2nd ed.). Cambridge University Press. (Original work published 1917)

Trainor, L. R., & Bundon, A. (2021). Developing the craft: Reflexive accounts of doing reflexive thematic analysis. *Qualitative Research in Sport, Exercise and Health, 13*(5), 705–726. DOI: 10.1080/2159676X.2020.1840423

Trujillo, P. (2018). Desbordando los cuadrados: *La forma del agua* de Guillermo Del Toro y *The Square* de Ruben Östlund [Overflowing the Squares: *The Shape of Water* by Guillermo del Toro and *The Square* by Ruben Östlund]. *Orillas: Rivista d'ispanistica*, (7), 505–508.

Tschichold, J. (1995). *The New Typography: A Handbook for Modern Designers* (McLean, R., Trans.). University of California Press. (Original work published 1928)

Van Halem, H. (2017). *Wind* [Variable font]. Typotheque. https://www.typotheque.com/fonts/wind

Villeneuve, D. (Director). (2021). *Dune: Part One* [Film]. Warner Bros. Pictures.

Villeneuve, D. (Director). (2024). *Dune: Part Two* [Film]. Warner Bros. Pictures.

Vlasopoulos, M. (2016). Spinoza's God in Goethe's leaf: Morphology as a theory of the attributes. *Goethe Yearbook, 23*, 117–140.

Waititi, T. (Director). (2022). *Thor: Love and Thunder* [Film]. Marvel Studios.

Walkerdine, V. (1997). *Daddy's girl.* MacMillan Press.

Ware, C. (2013). *Information visualization: Perception for design* (3rd ed.). Morgan Kaufmann.

Warner, M. (2026, March). Things I can't say out loud [Essay on Riti Sengupta]. In LensCulture Editors (Eds.), *Women shaping photography today — 19 artists to discover.* LensCulture. Retrieved May 22, 2026, from https://www.lensculture.com/articles/lensculture-editors-women-shaping-photography-today-19-artists-to-discover

Warner, M. (2022). *Helen Chadwick: The Oval Court.* Afterall Books/MIT Press.

Weaver, G. C., McDonald, P. L., Louie, G. S., & Woodman, T. C. (2024). Future potentials for international virtual exchange in higher education post COVID-19: A scoping review. *Education Sciences, 14*(3), 232. DOI: 10.3390/educsci14030232

Weijers, O. (1978). Contribution a l'histoire des termes 'natura naturans' et 'natura naturata' jusqu'a Spinoza. *Vivarium, 16*(1), 70–80. DOI: 10.1163/156853478X00049

Welch, L. C. (2024). Anime: a qualitative study exploring Miyazaki's influence on fans and fan art through the perspective of visual communication within the sociocultural and cybernetic traditions (Doctoral dissertation, Liberty University).

Wenzel, D. (n.d.). Automation. Daniel Wenzel. Retrieved 16 April 2025, from https://wenzeldaniel.com/w_atd.php

Whitehead, A. N. (1978). *Process and reality: An essay in cosmology* (D. R. Griffin & D. W. Sherburne, Eds., Corrected ed.). Free Press. (Original work published 1929)

Whitehead, J. (2017). *Creating interior atmosphere: Mise-en-scène and interior design*. Bloomsbury Visual Arts.

Whitelaw, M. (2004). *Metacreation: Art and artificial life*. MIT Press.

Willen, B., and Strals, N. (2009). Lettering & type: Creating letters and designing typefaces Princeton Architectural Press.

Witt, C. (2003). *Ways of being: Potentiality and actuality in Aristotle's Metaphysics*. Cornell University Press.

Wong, W. (1993). *Principles of form and design*. John Wiley & Sons.

Wright, G. (2024, October 8). Dutch museum finds beer can artwork in bin. *BBC News*.

Wright, S. (2024). *Digital compositing for film and video: Production workflows and visual effects* (5th ed.). Routledge. DOI: 10.4324/9781032418070

Yin, R. K. (2018). *Case study research and applications: design and methods* (6th ed.). SAGE.

Yip, S. Y. (2024). Positionality and reflexivity: Negotiating insider-outsider positions within and across cultures. *International Journal of Research & Method in Education, 47*(3), 222–232. DOI: 10.1080/1743727X.2023.2266375

Yulianti, I., Andito, T., & Nugroho, G. S. (2025). Reverting Animal in Post-Anthropocentrism Character Design: A case study of the Papuan bird of paradise (cenderawasih papua). *Environment-Behaviour Proceedings Journal, 10*(SI39), 75–80. DOI: 10.21834/e-bpj.v10iSI39.7675

Zahlten, A. (2010). Meta-, hyper-, inter-, super: Anime, world creation and the role of film festivals. In E. Niskanen (Ed.), *Imaginary Japan*. International Institute for Popular Culture.

Zembylas, M. (2025). Rethinking positionality statements in research: From looking back to building solidarity. *International Journal of Research & Method in Education, 48*(5), 1–13. DOI: 10.1080/1743727X.2025.2475762

Zhang, T. (2024). *From digital visual effects to emerging in-camera visual effects: investigating the change of workflow, occupational roles and common challenges in Southeast Asian and East Asian countries*. Master's thesis, Nanyang Technological University, Singapore. https://hdl.handle.net/10356/174920

About the Contributors

And Algül, born in 1973, graduated from Bilkent University, took his master's degree from Marmara University, and completed his PhD at Yeditepe University. He is working at Üsküdar University, Faculty of Communication, Department of Visual Communication Design Studies, conducts studies about Virtual Reality, Informatics Society, Surveillance Society, Technological Determinism, Social Media, New Media, Interaction, Culture, Society, Design, Digital Games and Communication Tools.

***

Amir Ahmadoghlu is a transdisciplinary designer, educator, and visual storyteller specializing in motion design, animation, and transmedia narratives. He holds a Ph.D. in Graphic Design from Dokuz Eylul University, Izmir. His work has been exhibited internationally in cities including Berlin, New York, Beijing, Venice, and Istanbul, and has been recognized by institutions such as Taiwan Design Week and the Toyama Museum of Modern Art. With professional experience in art direction and co-founding a new media studio in Istanbul, he bridges creative industry practice with academic research. He is currently a Lecturer in the Department of Media and Visual Arts at Koç University, where he teaches motion design, animation, and interdisciplinary approaches to art and design, while conducting research on immersive media and cultural heritage.

Dide Akdağ Satır is an Associate Professor in the Department of Graphic Design at Yıldız Technical University (YTÜ), Istanbul, Turkey. Her research interests focus on graphic design and typography, exploring the theoretical and applied dimensions of visual communication. She has contributed to academic scholarship through publications and projects at the intersection of design practice and design theory. She is actively involved in interdisciplinary research initiatives and has collaborated on edited academic volumes addressing emerging approaches in design, art, and visual communications.

Gamze Çoban currently serves in the Department of Interior Architecture and Environmental Design at Afyon Kocatepe University, Turkey. She holds advanced degrees in Architecture from Yaşar University and Gazi University (Turkey). Dr. Çoban has contributed to the academic discourse through various written works that explore conservation practices within architectural and interior architectural contexts.

İhsan Eken received his B.A. in Visual Communication Design from İstanbul Commerce University (2009) and his M.A. in Advertising and Brand Communication Management from Bahçeşehir University (2011). He earned his Ph.D. in Media and Communication Studies from İstanbul Commerce University. His doctoral dissertation, "Accessible Communication for All: Mobile Accessibility for Visually Impaired Users—An Analysis of Mobile Applications through a Usability Approach," critically examines mobile accessibility through a usability-centered analytical framework. Eken began his academic career as a lecturer at İstanbul Commerce University. Since 2018, he has been affiliated with İstanbul Medipol University, where he currently serves as an Associate Professor (since 2021). His research adopts an interdisciplinary perspective to interrogate the transformative implications of digitalization across communication, visual culture, and socio-technical systems. In particular, his work engages with user behavior in digital media environments, AI-driven content production, and the epistemological challenges of information reliability in the post-truth era. His areas of specialization encompass usability studies, interface and user experience (UX/UI) design, digital media design, 3D modeling, animation, and artificial intelligence applications. His recent scholarship foregrounds AI-generated content, deepfake technologies, algorithmic culture, and digital visuality, with a critical emphasis on how these technologies reconfigure aesthetic production processes as well as the construction of perception, representation, and social reality. Eken has an extensive record of publications in national and international peer-reviewed journals, alongside book chapters and conference proceedings. In addition to his research and teaching at both undergraduate and graduate levels, he actively contributes to the academic field through the supervision of master's and doctoral theses, fostering scholarly inquiry and advancing knowledge production within interdisciplinary media and communication studies.

Tolga Gürocak graduated from Anadolu University, Department of Cinema and Television. He completed his master's degree at Anadolu University and his doctorate in video art at Ege University. He worked as a producer, director, and cameraman at TVA for three years, shooting various programs. He has short films and documentaries. He participated in over fifty exhibitions featuring his photography, film, and video works. Since 2010, he has been working for Afyon Kocatepe University, Türkiye. He has articles indexed by ESCI and Scopus, as well as book chapters and symposium proceedings on cinema, documentary, TV dramas, and video art.

Magna Anissa Aming Hayudini is currently working as faculty at the College of Health Sciences in Mindanao State University-Sulu. Her academic rank is full professor 6. At present, she is designated as director for internationalization

Noprita Herari, M.I.Kom is a lecturer and researcher in Communication Studies at Universitas Negeri Jakarta (UNJ), Indonesia. Her academic and professional interests lie at the intersection of communication, creative media, and digital culture, with a particular focus on the passion economy, visual communication, and media-based cultural strategies. She has extensive experience in teaching and developing curricula in digital marketing strategy, organizational communication, and media convergence, while also serving as a contributor to international book chapters and journal publications indexed by Scopus and Web of Science.

Christo Kaftandjiev is a Professor, Ph.D., and Doctor Habilis of marketing semiotics, and digital and AI marketing communications Faculty of Journalism, Sofia University, Bulgaria. Professor Kaftandjiev conducts seminars in many European and Asian universities and at more than 150 business conferences, advertising festivals, trade expos, and other events across Europe and Asia. Christo is the author of numerous SCOPUS and World of Science articles and 10 books on these topics, including: "The Language of Advertising. Graphics and Text"; "Visual Communications", "The Texts of Print Advertising"; "Harmony in Advertising Communication", "The Images of Women in Advertising", "Absolut Semiotics in an Absolut World", "Heroes and Beauties in Advertising", "Mythological Archetypes in Advertising", "Integrated Marketing Communications", "Marketing communications during the Black Plague (Coronovirus 19)". Kaftandjiev is the Editor-in-Chief of the American Journal of Linguistics.

Evangelia Katsaiti is a visual artist, curator, and lecturer in Photography and Gender Narratives at the University of West Attica. She holds a BA (Hons) in Photographic Arts from the University of Derby, an MA in Fine Art Photography from the University of Sydney, and a Postgraduate Degree in Research Practice from Nottingham Trent University. She has taught photography at universities across Greece, Australia, Finland, and Norway. Her research focuses on gender identity, memory, displacement, and photographic narrative as acts of resistance and empowerment. She is a recipient of the Agfa UK Award and her photographs have been exhibited at the Smithsonian Institution.

Fırat Küçükersen (Ph.D.) is a Research Assistant at the Faculty of Architecture, Istanbul Technical University. He was a Visiting Researcher at the University of New South Wales School of Built Environment from 2024 to 2025. His research interests include experiential learning and reflective practice.

Maria Risya Maharani, S.Hub.Int is a researcher at LSPR Institute of Communication and Business, specializing in branding, digital media, and popular culture. Her work focuses on how visual communication, fandom, and cultural industries intersect within contemporary media ecosystems. She has conducted research on brand alliances, anime culture, and digital marketing strategies. Currently, she is involved in projects examining participatory aesthetics and identity design in online communities.

Beyza Buzol Mülayim, born in 1979 in Kırklareli, graduated from Uludağ University with a degree in Textile Engineering in 2002. She completed both her master's degree and PhD in Textile Engineering at Tekirdağ Namık Kemal University, receiving her doctorate in 2019. She has been working at Kırklareli University, Vocational School since 2008 and currently serves as the Head of the Design Department.

Nicole Simon is a Professor in the STEM disciplines at SUNY Nassau Community College, where her work centers on strengthening academic momentum for students—particularly during the critical first year and at key transition points along their academic pathways. With more than two decades of experience in academic advising, curricular planning, assessment, and first-year programming, she develops scalable, evidence-based course and program designs that support student persistence, progression, and completion. Nicole holds a doctorate in Educational Technology Management and Instructional Design and is a Certified Instructional Designer. She served as SUNY EmTech Director and is the recipient of the SUNY Chancellor's Award for Creative and Scholarship. She is a certified OSCQR Trainer and Creative Commons Certified professional, and she has been engaged in Collaborative Online International Learning (COIL) for over a decade, serving as a COIL Trainer supporting globally networked learning initiatives. She teaches a Sustainability course aligned with the United Nations Sustainable Development Goals (SDGs), integrating COIL projects to foster global collaboration and applied problem-solving. Nicole has authored several works on Generative AI, cybersecurity, academic assessment, and equity-focused learning, and has participated in numerous grant-funded initiatives advancing innovation in teaching and learning.

Işıl Tombul is graduated from Ege University Communication Faculty Radio Television and Cinema Department. She got her master and PhD degree at Ege University Social Sciences Institute Radio Television Cinema Department. Her research areas are cinema, mythology, media studies. She is an associate professor of media studies.

Halim Yentür is an academic in the Department of Cartoon and Animation at Anadolu University, Türkiye. His work examines procedural thinking, node-based generative systems, and the philosophical foundations of computational form generation. Drawing on long-standing practice in animation and visual effects, he approaches procedurality not only as a technical method but also as an aesthetic and epistemic orientation. Alongside his scholarly work, his directorial work in animation has been selected for the Annecy International Animation Film Festival. His current research explores how generative processes reframe questions of authorship, form, and creation in digital art.

Index

www.ingramcontent.com/pod-product-compliance
Lightning Source LLC
LaVergne TN
LVHW080900300926
849162LV00003B/498
* 9 7 9 8 3 3 7 3 6 6 8 0 7 *